FINITE AND INFINITE

Philosophical works by the same Author

THE FREEDOM OF THE WILL
(Gifford Lectures)

THE GLASS OF VISION
(Bampton Lectures)

Also, in Biblical Theology

ST MATTHEW AND ST MARK

A STUDY IN ST MARK

A REBIRTH OF IMAGES
The Making of St John's Apocalypse

And for devotional use

THE CROWN OF THE YEAR
Weekly Paragraphs for
the Holy Sacrament

DACRE PRESS : A. AND C. BLACK

FINITE AND INFINITE

A Philosophical Essay

BY

AUSTIN FARRER

DOCTOR OF DIVINITY AND FELLOW OF TRINITY COLLEGE, OXFORD

dacre press
westminster

FIRST EDITION 1943
SECOND EDITION 1959
REPRINTED 1964

A. AND C. BLACK LTD: DACRE PRESS
4, 5 AND 6 SOHO SQUARE, LONDON, W.1

PRINTED IN GREAT BRITAIN
BY JOHN DICKENS & CO. LTD., NORTHAMPTON

PARENTI OPTIMO
VT DIERVM SIC STVDIORVM ORIGINI
FAVTORI INDEFESSO
A.J.D.F.

REVISED PREFACE TO THE SECOND EDITION

ANYONE who wishes to introduce the name of God into a philosophical treatise is confronted with the awkward choice between speculation and ecclesiasticism. As to the former, surely no one desires a further addition to the private theologies of individual philosophers, who, having discovered that God is the last emergent struggling into existence or something else not previously remarked, turn to the belief of all these centuries with the apostolic words, 'Whom ye ignorantly worship, Him declare I unto you.' Yet if on the other hand we recognise that theologies are not made by philosophers but by men with a different gift, we seem condemned to a servile ecclesiasticism (to accept the term which philosophers like using in this connexion). Our conclusions will all be given before we start, and we shall be simply finding exterior reasons for religious faith.

The dilemma is an awkward one. But we may hope to avoid the worst faults on either side if we take up the traditional theology without having decided either what area of its extent is capable of direct philosophical support, or what degree of strength and demonstration that support can attain. It is generally recognised that there are some metaphysical questions which must be settled if we are to vindicate the significance of any theological statements whatever of the traditional type. And we can approach these questions without committing ourselves to the discussion of issues that never could be philosophical, because of their dependence upon contingent facts of the historical order; and, again, without committing ourselves to the perfect demonstration of even one basic theological proposition. We may find that we can only show its possibility or probability. We have, then, to be ready to draw the ancient line between rational and revealed theology, though not necessarily in the ancient place, nor with the ancient optimism about the strength of demonstration in the rational branch.

Still, it is rational theology that we have on the one side of the line; that is, it is a philosophical enquiry and not something else, and one can, with due humility, hope that philosophers will interest themselves in it, and find nothing to be shocked at in its procedure. This does not mean that we shall use no philosophical principles but those which are now most in fashion. Philosophical doctrines are in some degree the function of the philosophers' preoccupations; and philosophy has been for half a century looking so hard in another direction that it would be naive indeed to attempt now the nineteenth-century trick of leading philosophers into explicit theology up the garden path of their own presuppositions. Perhaps they were never much inclined to tread it, or if they did, perhaps the theology it led to was little like the genuine thing. But now we know very well, and the philosophers best of all, that the presuppositions are not there. We shall have, then, to see on what additional principles rational

vii

theology rests, and to hope it may be possible to commend these. It should be, since they happen, we believe, to be true.

Recent philosophy has not so much rejected metaphysics, as wearied of previous metaphysicians. We like now to do our metaphysicizing for ourselves; we look for philosophically unprocessed data, for pieces of live discourse, having a use outside speculative debate, and a form unbedevilled by metaphysical construction. If theology is in question, we take those of her articles which most directly bear on the business of living. It may be that the Creed begins with an assertion of the Creator; but the practical bearing of that article seems at best indirect. God's creatorship establishes Him in a position of absolute control, from which He can be seen to exert in all things a sovereign will. This will it is that touches us; we aim to co-operate with it, and we hope to be saved by it. Unless, therefore, a general and sovereign Providence makes sense, the link is cut between life and creationist belief, and the investigation of that belief appears superfluous.

Our philosophers turn, then, to the doctrine of a general Providence. What does it mean? That things fall out as though a benevolent and all-powerful mind were directing them? That the supposition of such a directive mind enables us to anticipate our destiny? Alas, as has been sufficiently shewn, this line of approach is a blind alley. Providential control makes little sense, if we regard it as simply a hypothesis called for by empirical fact, or even as a hypothesis capable of organising empirical fact. But what follows from the admission of this negative? We shall let ourselves off too lightly if we dismiss the pretensions of belief without more ado. For it may be that the doctrine of Providence is not offered in interpretation of empirical facts alone, but of such facts taken in conjunction with a prior belief; a belief in that very article we so rashly set aside, the creation of heaven and earth. If all things have indeed a creative Cause, He must surely be allowed such a mastery of events as to permit of His effecting His creations. We see on empirical evidence that the forms of creatures are not brought to perfection without the concurrence of innumerable circumstances. In such a world as ours, a Creator who lacked providential control of circumstance could create nothing that might seem worth the creating. There can be no creation here without a supporting Providence.

If, then, the assertion of a general Providence rests on a prior conviction of creation, we are driven to scrutinize creation after all, and on its own evidence. Apart from any seeming purposefulness of the universe, can we see a meaning in the assertion that things were created, rather than not? Why, yes, it has been traditionally answered, for they are of themselves plainly insufficient to exist. If they were not created, they would not be.

But how can we know, or even meaningfully suggest, that things are insufficient of themselves to exist? Some things, of course, are ephemeral, but they arise out of the totality of process; and what can be meant by the suggestion that this totality is insufficient of itself to proceed? It just does;

and what more can we say? Much, the old metaphysicians replied. We can make an analysis of finite being, or finite process, as such, which will reveal its existential insufficiency.

Of all the philosophies which have attempted such an analysis Thomism may strike us as the most searching and the least superficial. How, then, does the Thomist go about it? He brings to bear a battery of categories, potency and act, matter, form, essence and existence : categories which have their home in an abstract account of our descriptive speech. And it seems nowadays to call for a philosophical naivety which can no longer be recovered, if an admittedly neat formula for setting out the general structure of our descriptive language is to be accepted as revealing the structural character of every describable thing.

Eighteen to sixteen years ago I sat down and wrote this book, because I was possessed by the Thomist vision, and could not think it false. The core of the doctrine must somehow be sound, only it must be freed from the period trash in which it was embedded ; it must be rescued from dependence on the breath-taking naivety of old linguistic realism. I told myself that I had to reconstruct the doctrine of substance ; by which I meant, that I could not be content to derive the structure of being from the grammar of description ; I must unearth it where it could be genuinely apprehended. And where was that? Initially, anyhow, in myself, self-disclosed as the subject of my acts.

My starting-point was correct, and my procedure materially sound ; but my methodology was ill-considered. I talked of a genuine apprehension, where the structure of one's own existence was concerned. Yet if it was an apprehension, it was nothing like certain standard examples, say the appreciation of a sensible quality or a visible shape. I could point to no act of apprehending which was anything other than the act of approving a description. What was I doing, in fact, but finding a certain abstract, artificial and diagrammatic account of my active being applicable or luminous? What right had I to claim that any such account was *the* account? Might not alternative accounts, or rival diagrams, be found equally useful, equally illuminating? And if my account was not, after all, *the* account, how could it bear the metaphysical weight I laid upon it? How support the stupendous hypothesis which inverts the world, and moves the centre of things clean out of our universe? The fatal gap between language and reality yawns again, and unless we can close it nothing like a metaphysical argument in the traditional manner can be attempted.

Never mind, for the gap can be closed, and at the place where I proposed to close it. For language is otherwise related to our acts, than it is to anything else. Speech is the very form of our linguistic activity, and linguistic activity is but a specialised type of intentional action in general ; which, as it were, attains to explicitness in the spoken mode. A grammar of being is not a chimerical project, where the being in question is our own. Every grammar is a grammar of speech, but speech is human being, and uniquely revelatory of the rest of it. And as I trust I was able to show in this book, we both do and must think of the being of all things through an extension of our self-/ understanding.

The paragraph I have just written would require a treatise to expound. No such exposition can be attempted in the revised preface to an old book, but if my readers think it worth while to open a new one, they may find some suggestions towards a development of it. I refer them to my *Freedom of the Will* and especially to chapters VII, IX and X. Meanwhile, if the adumbrated correction to my talk about 'apprehension' be borne in mind, I venture to hope that the analyses and discussions which my old book contains may still be found of use.

Is this a book about the Philosophy of Religion? But what is the Philosophy of Religion? In its more general sense, it is a range of topics which seminary teachers have not the time to expound separately. Towards the middle of this soft amalgam the student encounters a harder core, centred on the traditional arguments for the existence of God. It is with this core that we are here concerned, but equally with the general topics of metaphysics which are its necessary support. More properly, 'Philosophy of Religion' is the banner of a sect; for it describes its subject of study according to a Kantian or post-Kantian conception of philosophical enquiry. According to this conception, certain types of human experience and human activity are accepted as occurring, and the philosopher's business is to extract from these the *a priori* principles or universal forms presumed to be embedded in them. As, then, we may have a philosophy of science, of morality, or of art, so we may have of religion, if religion is to be reckoned a genuine and distinct type among the operations of the human spirit.

Now if to accept the description 'Philosophy of Religion' is to accept this account of method, then we do not accept it, for this centring of metaphysics in the act of thought is vicious. Acts of understanding are specified by their objects and not *vice-versa*; religion is whatever man does about the unique object, God. God is not usefully defined as whatever man concerns himself with in an activity of a certain type, called religion; for the definition is circular. The 'type' of religion is concern about God, neither more nor less. Of course there are imperfect and depraved types of religion, but we do not use them for a definition, any more than we define man from the embryo or the idiot.

Religion, then, is concern with God, and includes many sorts of acts; among them acts of believing, understanding, reasoning. These are cognitive, in so far as they are determined by their object. If we wish to philosophise about God, we shall not escape an examination of these acts; for the object we are principally concerned with will be the object which these acts attain. If our study is rational theology, it will involve us in the study of theological reason. In so far as reason differs in one sphere and another, it is because of the difference of its objects here and there; and in this sense theological reason differs from reason in other fields. If the war cry 'Rational Theology' as opposed to 'Philosophy of Religion' is taken to mean that to reason about God is the same as to reason about finite beings, or that it is a simple extension by inference from such reasoning, then this label is as misleading as the other. But if we allow our activity to be specified by its object, then 'rational theology' is an excellent description, for it speaks of a reflective cognitive activity appropriated to the knowledge of God from universal grounds.

CONTENTS IN OUTLINE

PART I

ANALYSIS OF RATIONAL THEOLOGY

PART II

EXAMINATION OF FINITE SUBSTANCE

PART III

DIALECTIC OF RATIONAL THEOLOGY

CONTENTS IN DETAIL

PART II C

EXAMINATION OF FINITE SUBSTANCE: GENERALISATION OF THE SUBSTANCE-FORMULA

PART III

DIALECTIC OF RATIONAL THEOLOGY

ANALYSIS OF RATIONAL THEOLOGY

I

INTRODUCTION

(i) *That Rational Theology is possible*

THE possibility of a certain type of study follows excellently from the fact of its successful prosecution, and hardly from any other argument. The way to prove the possibility of rational theology is to write it in such a way as to convince the reader that one is writing about something and not about nothing. Still, it may be much to ask anyone to read three hundred pages in the hope of finding out whether they are about nothing or something, and there are strong dogmatic prejudices to be met which deny the possibility of the science; so an introductory note in plea for a fair hearing may have its use.

Liberals believe in a diffused, and Calvinists in a particular, spiritual revelation, and some of us are hardy enough to believe in both. But on these grounds it may be argued: If supernatural revelation or spiritual illumination is required to make God known to man, what place is left for a science which claims to demonstrate him from general considerations of reason? In reply to this we have three things to say:

(*a*) The conclusions of rational theology are severely limited; there is plenty left for revelation to do. We refer the reader to the last pages of this book for large admissions on this head.

(*b*) The principles of rational theology are supposed by the theologian to be evident in themselves, but he knows they are not evident to every mind. If the revelationist likes to say that only a light reflected from revelation sufficiently purifies the intellect for it to perceive these principles, he may. But to the rational theologian as such this consideration is perfectly irrelevant. It is his business to make these principles as evident as he can to reason, and by processes proper to reason. He is not concerned with the conditions necessary for the presence of the appropriate faculty in his readers, any more than a writer of aesthetic philosophy is concerned with the causes why some persons are colour-blind and tone-deaf, others not. If the revelationists say that he is wasting his time in any case because he will only convince those who are already convinced by illumination, he may reply first, that even granting this, it is an absorbing enquiry to discover what the rational principles are which are the real ground for the convincingness of what convinces the convinced; and second, that the objection does not really follow from the revelationist principle. Illumination, whether direct or by reflection from historical revelation, may be a *sine qua non* of conviction; but without the presentation of some intelligible object, it cannot be the total and sufficient cause. A man may be under the influence of the illumination and yet require to hear reason for the object to be made intelligible and the illumination to take effect in convincing him; and since it is never possible for anyone to know certainly that no illumination direct or reflected is falling upon himself or any other man, we can proceed cheerfully with our rational theology, for we never need despair of its convincing anyone.

(*c*) Those who accept a revealed theology place among its articles the Creator of heaven and earth; this is the foundation upon which the rest is built. To know God as the absolute origin of all things is to know Him as God simply; the further revealed truths are concerned with what God, being such, has in particular done and said and, by these actions and words, shown or declared Himself to be. But these further revelations presuppose the first; nor is it easy to see how it itself can be a revelation in quite the same sense. What another man does and says may be his revelation of himself to me, and if he had not moved and spoken, it is very possible that I should not have noticed that he was there or have mistaken him for a waxwork. But should I have recognised his persona self-revelation, without some knowledge of the rudiments of human personality derived from some other source, since I do not seem to introspect the other man's mind? And unless I had some mental machinery for thinking the bare notion of God, could I recognise His revelatory action as that of God? That machinery might never have worked before. Let us suppose it works now for the first time, when the revelation occurs. Still it does work now, and it is possible to study it and see how it works and what is the notion it produces. As we shall learn, to study this notion of God, of a supreme and original being, is to study what the mind can only see in and through the general nature of finite and dependent being. And this is to study rational theology.

There is a superstition among revelationists, that by declaring themselves independent of any proof of God by analogy from the finite world, they have escaped the necessity of considering the analogy or relation of the finite to the infinite altogether. They are completely mistaken; for all their statements about God must be expressed and plainly are expressed in language drawn from the finite world. No revelationist supposes these statements to be perfectly literal; God is not a man and human language requires to be read with some tacit qualification before it applies to Him. What is this qualification? It is the relation of 'eminence' which exalts God above man and all the finite sphere, and unless we can say, or at least implicitly know, something about this relation, our statements about God are just so much noise; as though we should say that an electron is kind, in whatever sense the word 'kind' applies to an electron, but we do not know what sense that is. This problem of analogy is in principle prior to every particular revelation. For the revelation has to be thought about to be received, and can be thought about only by the aid of words or finite images; and these cannot signify of God unless the appropriate 'mode of signification' functions in our minds.

We shall see, and will not here pause to demonstrate, that the problem of analogy and the problem of the knowledge of original being through created being are the same; and this two-sided problem is the subject matter of rational theology.

(ii) *What Rational Examination Theism allows*

The reader who faces so exacting a topic as rational theology may be ready to be wearied, but not to be deceived. Honesty is the author's first duty, and this covers not only the substance of his theme, but the manner of its presentation. So let us begin by abandoning all pretence to novelty, to demonstration, and to dramatic order.

As to novelty, it is indeed absurd to propose new grounds for belief in the existence of God. The belief has stood more than 2000 years, if we are to speak of the essentials of transcendental theism. If belief has been reasonable, it has had a reason, and our only business must be to draw this out and re-state it. If we are the first to have found true reasons, we must condemn our predecessors in faith as simply superstitious. It would be as though Copernicus had been preceded by certain devout Sun-Worshippers, who had concluded that luminary to be the centre of our system because it is so useful and so beautiful. In that case his subsequent demonstration would hold a merely accidental relation to their previous opinion.

But it may be objected that the comparison is not fair. Why should there not be several reasons for believing in the existence of something, each independent of the others? A party of three explorers may believe that there is a mountain-lake behind a high ridge in front of them; one on the evidence of the water that spills out, another on that of rising mists, another on the apparent configuration of surrounding heights. After two have found probable reasons, the third may come forward with his own independent and quite convincing reason; independent, because it rests on a distinct chain of connexion between lake and observer.

This analogy fails in two respects. First, because those who have believed in God have believed in Him as bearing to all finite things a single necessary relation—necessary to the finites, that is, and to all in the same way; as performing for all of them a single function which they could not do without. If then (to apply the comparison) God is for us behind the clouds and has to be proved, the proof will lie in following back the single sort of connexion which binds to Him every part of the world, exemplified in indefinitely many instances, but still the same connexion. Of this connexion former believers were either aware, or they were not. If they were, it can hardly be a useful ambition to look for a new awareness; if they were not, they held a random supposition, and our seeking valid grounds for it would be a random experiment, like fitting out an expedition to find mermaids.

Again, the invisible lake though now invisible is an instance of a thing already seen elsewhere, so that the description we give ourselves of it can be independent of all the three grounds for which we propose to believe in it, and this can be so, even while its existence continues to be hypothetical. We can agree as to what we are believing in though we dispute one another's reasons for belief. But God is not an instance of a type of being already elsewhere directly experienced. The description we give ourselves of Him cannot (with any justification) be independent of the ground on which we propose to believe in Him, viz., the function He performs for all the finites. He must be understood as the Agent of this very effect. If our predecessors have not grasped this function they have not known God at all.

It is indeed sometimes suggested that they did grasp it, and really believe because of it, but that their apprehension remained implicit; when they came to give a rational expression of their grounds for believing, they were misled by irrelevant fashions and prevailing philosophies, and made up some other argument. Neglecting the true Jacob's-ladder of living religion, because it looked creaky and unsafe to a metaphysical eye, they built Babel-towers of spurious demonstration, for joining the earth to a God whose real connexion therewith they had confusedly felt, but not intellectually clarified.

There is of course some truth in this contention; such Babel-building is not without instances. It is obvious that the connexions between the world and God established by some philosophers are quite off the line of what concerns religion. No one, for example, ever thought of praying to God *qua* guarantor of the correspondence between sensation and its object. But on the other hand, the conception of God as Pure Being, the Necessary Ground of all contingent existences, has entered deeply into the devotion of Catholic Christendom; and this is essentially the conception on which the traditional arguments are based. Now the grateful re-appropriation by religion of the philosophical arguments, not as a means of proof only, but as an illumination of the Object, is the best evidence we can have that those arguments in their essentials were a true clarification of the relation with God which religion had always confusedly known.

But if it is absurd to suppose that we can find new grounds for belief, it is equally absurd to say that we can make the old grounds cogent. An 'inescapable demonstration' *must* be a fallacy. For if a proof of this kind could be produced it would have been produced. Anselm thought he had produced it, so perhaps did St. Thomas; but Gaunilo and Kant and Russell are not convinced, and they are as good men to follow an argument as any others.

And from the side of belief itself objections arise. The matters we are dealing with are mysteries, and it is impious of the philosopher to suppose he can handle them with demonstration, as plainly as he might chalk and cheese. No doubt it is fair to reply that mysteries must have some intelligible sense even for us, and we must find out what this is, and at which point our intellectual grasp fails, and for what reason; that it must be in virtue of their intelligible, not their unintelligible aspects that they are to be believed. But it will remain that the presence of the unintelligible aspects excludes perfect demonstration.

Let us make a brave attempt to satisfy the sceptics, the mystics, and the theistic rationalists all at once. We will say, here is at any rate some bundle of ideas, exhibiting some appearance of structure. The whole may be, as a unity, not properly thinkable, even less demonstrable. But it certainly contains elements of meaning, whencesoever derived; they offer the appearance of a system, the appearance of a rational connexion with our world. Let us try, then, to analyse, treating the system with respect, but without favour. We might then hope to discover *on what assumptions* the system would become credible. It will then become possible for believers and unbelievers to agree about the structures of ideas which give to theism whatever form it has, and about the flaws and breaks as well. The believers can then put up with the flaws, on the ground that it is reasonable to assume that such obscurities will occur in our view of a transcendent reality, and accept on the positive grounds. The unbelievers can stand out for flawless intelligibility and reject the whole. This would be a very edifying result if we could obtain it, for we should have stated the rational grounds for belief without committing the absurdity of making the difference between the believing and unbelieving philosopher lie in the greater logical competence of the former, or in his superior judgment of empirical evidence (in any ordinary sense).

We do not, then, expect to convince the sceptical philosopher, but we think he might be interested in following such an analysis as the present. For if he wants to arrive at an impartial morphology of our error, he may think it useful to read the exposition of the deluded alongside that of the enlightened. For the enlightened is as likely to be betrayed by impatience into superficiality, as is the deluded to fall through favour into advocacy. Even though he accepts the psycho-analytical reduction of religious belief, he need not wholly despise us. He may continue to think it evident that the motive of belief is non-rational wish-fulfilment. But whatever the motive, a belief must have some structure and some sense, and it is legitimate to examine what these are. The psychoanalytical explanation cannot indeed be complete until this has been done, for the fact that a belief satisfies cravings is no evidence against its truth: e.g. belief in the existence of police-protection.

The analytical part of philosophy ought to be a matter of agreement. If we refrain from judging systems of thought on preconceived grounds, and examine them from within, we ought to be able to agree where the system works and where it breaks down, as we may, for example, in the case of Spinozism, since this is a matter of logic. It is at the next stage where agreement ceases; when, assuming that all systems have flaws, we ask which, taken as a whole, is least unsatisfactory as an account of what is, or when one of us refuses to philosophise at all outside the area where he thinks exact demonstration to be possible, whereas another is prepared to extend a crepuscular and imperfect reasoning into a crepuscular fringe of our experience and belief. Our purpose, then, will be to separate the analysis of logic from the exercise of judgment, so that we may have agreement in proceeding with the former. In so far as our exposition involves assumptions and breaks, we will not disguise them. And we will try not to mix up that dialectic reasoning which persuades us we cannot but make assumptions, with the analytical reasoning which examines the order of a system.

Something has been said about novelty and demonstration. We promised also to renounce dramatic order. By this is meant an order which produces the rabbit of theistic proof from the hat of impartial cosmology. It is indeed traditional to use several hats indifferently, in order, one must suppose, to underline the fact that between hat and rabbit there is no connexion whatever; so sometimes it is impartial cosmology, sometimes impartial ethics, sometimes epistemology, or even aesthetics that plays the part; no doubt one could think of others. We work up an insoluble antithesis, we fence round a lacuna of explanation, bang goes the pistol, and therefore, we say, God!

There is nothing essentially wrong with the constructive method of demonstration, and there would be no other way of proceeding, if we were trying to lead a philosophical but wholly uninstructed mind to understand why and what we believe. It would be possible to follow this line without cheating, but it would be difficult to persuade one's philosophical contemporaries to read it without invincible suspicion, because so much cheating has in fact been done; in the best of good faith, no doubt. And so it seems wiser to let the rabbit out of the hat from the very start—to begin with an examination of theistic belief, and to proceed to the exploration of its prior assumptions. This will increase for readers the opportunity of finding out quickly what the thesis is. It will, on the other hand, ruin dramatic pleasure; but that is a satisfaction which it is possible to purchase too dear.

(iii) *Analysis and Dialectic*

The renunciation of dramatic order can be more narrowly described as a beginning with analysis and not with dialectic. It is more natural to proceed the other way about; for it is the dialectic argument which leads to belief, and it seems proper first to get belief, and then to analyse what it is we are believing. But, on the other hand, dialectic involves apparent frauds, and it is only after the analysis that we can see why the frauds are not really fraudulent. If, then, we begin with the dialectic, the reader will refute every argument as he proceeds, and gather such a weight of prejudice by the time he reaches the analysis, that if ever he reads it at all (which would be much) he is unlikely to give it a fair hearing.

In order to perplex the reader no longer with ambiguous terms, we proceed to an exposition of the distinction between analysis and dialectic in rational theology, asking him by way of preface not to assume that we are using the words in a Kantian, Aristotelian or any other special sense, until he has seen how we do use them. And it will be more illuminating to proceed by way of deduction than by way of definition, even though deduction necessarily involves assuming what will have to be shown later. The assumption which, for the present, we postulate is this: If God exists, He is unique, and if other beings are related to Him, that relation is also unique. By the 'unique' in this argument we do not mean simply that which alone exemplifies certain special characteristics; we mean that which shares no identical characteristic with anything else, and so cannot be placed in a proper class with others. Now if this is so, by what sort of reasoning could the existence of God possibly be proved? Neither He nor the world's relation to Him can be made the instance of a rule, as has been shown *ad nauseam* by those who criticise the Causal Argument; and this criticism does not depend on a nominalist view of (physical) causality, although the critic usually makes the job easier for himself by assuming such a view. For whatever view we take of causality, the difficulty remains: The demand for a First Cause is a demand for an instance of the genus 'cause', and the activity of God being unique is at best an analogy to that genus, but not an instance of it. It is easy of course to cheat, by beginning with a definition of 'cause' which includes both divine causality and causality as known within the finite sphere. But this is to cheat indeed, for (*a*) it involves assuming the validity of a notion we are setting out to demonstrate—viz. divine causality; and (*b*) it assumes that the difference of divine causality from natural causality is not precisely such as to unfit it for the part of first term to the series of natural causes. But this assumption can only be justified if we have independent knowledge of what divine causality is.

Well then, neither under the head of causality nor under any other head can God or His activity be made the case of a rule, or the instance of a class, and therefore He cannot be demonstrated in the ordinary sense; for no principle can be found for a proof. It is not merely that (as St. Thomas says) He cannot be demonstrated *a priori*, i.e. from what is prior to Him in existence—since *ex hypothesi* nothing is so. He cannot be demonstrated *a posteriori* either, i.e. from His effects, because we must first know that they are effects, and effects of a perfectly unique activity. But to know that they are effects in the relevant sense is to know the nature of the activity; for the character of being an effect is conferred on a thing merely by its relation to the activity of which it is the effect. And again, to know the activity is, in this case, to know the Agent, for (as will be shown later) we know God simply as the Agent of activities, so far as is necessary for the apprehension of those activities. So then, to argue from effects is to begin by positing the divine activity and the divine Agent, and begs the question.

If the *a posteriori* demonstration will not do, how can the existence of God possibly be shown? It seems we shall be driven back on the first Cartesian position—that we do in fact have the idea of God and of His activity in the finite, and that there are reasons for supposing this to be an apprehension rather than a misapprehension. Now this position has two parts: (*a*) There is a certain classical system of theistic ideas, which makes a certain sort of appeal to the mind. (*b*) There are reasons for supposing that these ideas are (as they pretend to be) representative of what is. (We must be allowed for the moment to use the ambiguous and probably vicious Cartesian terms 'idea' and 'representation'.)

Descartes himself thought that he could get (*b*) out of (*a*). If we examine the ideas, he thought, we find them to be so clear and distinct, so rich in ' objective reality', that we cannot but believe them to be true. Now this argument is in itself a respectable argument, were its factual basis sound; respectable in itself, that is, whether or not it makes a good fit with the rest of the Cartesian system. The argument, in effect, is as follows:

(*a*) The human mind is incapable of absolute creation. Our 'ideas' all 'represent' actualities or abstractions from actualities, or combinations of these.[1]

—— (*b*) The idea of God expresses an unique object evidently not reducible to an abstraction from any other object (e.g. myself) or to a combination of abstractions.

(*c*) Therefore the idea of God is derived (by whatever mysterious channels) from a really corresponding object; otherwise stated, therefore God exists.

In this argument there is a great deal to be said in favour of (*a*), and nothing to be said against the logic of (*c*), but the fact alleged in (*b*) cannot be made good. It is not evident that the idea of God is irreducible. We are therefore faced with two tasks: to make of that idea an analysis sufficient to show that though synthetic it is not absurd, and to find reasons why so ambiguous a notion should be taken as veridical.

Descartes is on the right line when he suggests that what we have to do is to show that in and through and with His effects our minds grasp God—since we have seen that God cannot be inferred, and it remains that He should be apprehended. Analysis of the 'idea' must show whether the hypothesis that He is apprehended through this idea is even worth considering. But it cannot establish the probability of that hypothesis. How can we do this?

It used to be conventional at this point to invoke 'coherence' and 'rationality'. Let us see, it was said, whether a theocentric or a godless universe makes a better intellectual pattern. This criterion might be valuable if any precise sense could be attached to it. But unhappily it cannot, as may be seen from two quite opposite senses that have been and are attached to the terms ' rationalist' and 'rationalism':

1. A rationalist is one who demands the highest degree of quasi-purposive significance, or of a quasi-aesthetic design, in the account of the universe which he accepts.

2. A rationalist is one who limits his account of the universe to what is clear and distinct in itself and can be constructed into a system containing no mysteries, ambiguities, metaphorical terms, or logical flaws of any kind.

[1] Descartes did no good to his plea by treating this axiom as a case of the Causal Axiom, and as thence deriving its validity. It is in fact more evident than the Causal Axiom, and stands best on its own feet.

The former of these two men is probably a Catholic or an Idealist, the second a Logical Positivist, or anyhow an atheist of one brand or another. The former will admit a hierarchy of being and of value, the latter will plane everything down to an uninspiring simplicity. And why will they take these opposite courses? Because they start with completely different views of what constitutes 'coherence' and 'rationality', of what 'satisfies the mind'. The first man is looking for the sort of order in the universe which, on a theistic or at least pantheistic assumption, one would expect to find, and so, when he argues that he has to postulate God to get such an order, his argument is circular. The other man takes an aspect or sphere of being which we can construe with a certain degree of clarity and order, makes this his standard, and automatically rules out the hypothesis that there is anything of a higher and to us more obscure sort for us to be aware of.

The question, then, must not be 'What view is more rational, more coherent?' but 'What sort of coherence or order is in the things, and what sort of things are there?' If we must use the word 'rational', i.e. 'worthy of a reasonable mind', let us recall the Aristotelian doctrine that mind is in a manner all things; the nature of mind is simply to be the characters of its objects in the state of understood-ness. What is 'rational', what is felt to 'satisfy the mind' must, in the long run, be a correct account of what is there for the mind. Unless 'rational' means this, it must mean simply 'that which is in accordance with the formal procedure of the discursive reason'. But this in turn either reduces to the absolute formality of pure logic—the principles which must be exemplified in every system of terms with which we are able to think at all—or else means 'that which is consistent with the principles of one assumed system'. But what system should we assume? That is the question.

Theism, needless to say, is not just one of several alternative ways of construing the same phenomena; it also recognises and finds a place for an alleged phenomenon (or noümenon) which other systems exclude. This extra term, God, implies a certain system in the rest, which are 'ordered towards Him' as the garden at Hampton Court is ordered towards the central window of the palace. Therefore the theist will remain unmoved by the pragmatist contention that any scheme will do with which the phenomena can be construed; for he will say that none but a theistic scheme enables him to include and construe one highly significant unique reality, God. A pragmatist and a theist will naturally not agree as to what is datum and what is construction, but that is another story.

For the theist, the reality of that unique object and the validity of the construction by which all things are ordered towards Him are, of course, inseparable. To think theistically is both to recognise the being of God and to construe things in this order. And therefore the theist's first argument is a statement; he exhibits his account of God active in the world and the world existing in God, that others may recognise it to be the account of what they themselves apprehend—or, if you like, that others may find it to be an instrument through which they apprehend, for perhaps apprehension here is not separable from interpretation.

But such apprehension is not necessarily forthcoming at once, for it is evident that deity is, like other things, e.g. the unity and freedom of the self, obscure to our vision, and may need some straining of the eyes before it is brought into focus. So two men may dispute as to the outlines of something faintly descried in the distance, and none the less arrive at a convincing interpretation in the end, when the steadying of vision and the fixing of interpretation are arrived at together and by means of one another. But meanwhile one of us may maintain that there is nothing there, or nothing but a discoloured patch in the obscuring vapour; or perhaps we have not succeeded in directing the eyes to the right spot. Similarly it seems often plain to the believer that the man to whom he is talking has not the least apprehension of what he is talking about, even though he knows the ordinary senses of the terms that are being used.

Now on the theistic assumption, God's activity is there for the mind, and there is hope of bringing it into view. But if so, it is unlikely that it has remained wholly latent hitherto; if the world is in God, it is likely that those who habitually look at it have some crypto-theism in some parts of their interpretation of it, some sub-awareness of certain aspects of the divine activity. If we wish to enlarge the vision of these persons, we shall do ill to throw a formulated theology at their heads, set out according to the *ordo essendi*; we had much better start from their scraps of crypto-theism and show how these can only be upheld in a full theistic position, and how the denial of such a position removes them wholly. Such a proceeding is what one finds in almost every proof of God known to history, and we call it dialectic reasoning. For example, the premise of St. Thomas's *Via Prima* is not 'constat quaedam moveri in hoc mundo' but is the habit men have of reading into the system of events an absolute agency which can find its ultimate agent in God alone. If we start by assuming Causality with so very large a C, it can be shown that finite causes can be no more than the instruments or prolongations of it. We are free, then, after appreciating his demonstration, to accept the whole scheme, or to reject it, including our original scrap of crypto-theism. If we accept it, it will not be simply for the sake of maintaining with logical justification our previous habit but because from that as starting-point our vision has (so we imagine at least) been enlarged.

Dialectic, then, exhibits the necessity of proceeding from fragmentary to total theism, from crypto-theism to the explicit doctrine, from half-way positions (pantheism, finite or impersonal God, etc.) to the full position. If we can insist that those who do not accept theism should refrain from all use of dishonest substitutes, if we can present the naked difference between rejection and acceptance, that is all we can do, and for the rest must trust to apprehension and to judgment.

It is almost unnecessary to say that the man who continues in disbelief will regard such dialectic as an argument which sets out to make men through and through as bad as their worst inherited prejudices. He might enjoy the following parallel: A young nationalist has been brought up to construe and evaluate political and other events by relation to his belief in a metaphysical super-personal entity called the Race. This belief has involved the assigning to all relevant things and happenings of relative predicates—predicates expressing the relation of each to the great chimaera. He would never indeed have taken up with the chimaera, unless the consequent relative predicates appeared to enlighten, dignify or dramatise the real world; there would be small temptation to keep a chimaera *bombinans in vacuo*. As this way of construing events becomes second nature, the relative predicates lose their conscious relatedness, and the chimaera drops more and more out of sight. As we grow older we become less speculative, but not necessarily any more rational; a Public School master who has long debated whether he believed in God or not, may compromise in middle life, and opt for a system of Absolute Values.

One day our youth comes across seditious philosophisings against the chimaera, and begins to doubt its existence. But a logical friend saves his faith by appealing to the relative predicates. The doubter cannot, by this time, think these any longer out of his world; and he can be led to see that they involve that to which they are related. So one may cast supersubstantial bread on experiential waters, and have it crammed down one's throat after many days.

This parallel, as well as giving pleasure, as we hope, to the sceptical reader, may serve to show what a difficult game the dialectic is; for we shall have not only to make our appeal to crypto-theism, we shall need also to show that the theistic vision arises out of a pure metaphysical interest in Being, in contrast to various idolatries whose impure motive can be seen. Indeed dialectic, to be complete, would have to do battle with every rival; and if every system were of equal importance, and if nature were not strong and the soul *naturaliter deicola*, we should certainly never produce conviction.

Before we leave for the present this topic of theological dialectic, it may be useful to contrast its procedure with what Kant thought himself able to do, not in the part of the *Critique* called Dialectic, but in the Transcendental Deduction of the Categories, and in the Principles. He was faced, as the theologian is faced, with the necessity of justifying a certain way of construing phenomena, of which the principles must be simply *a priori* and cannot be induced.[1] And this he thought he could do, by showing that without the application of these principles of construction, we could not have any distinct experience at all. What form could such an argument take? It must take the form (*a*) of exhibiting an account of our experience, showing the part played in it by the categories, and calling upon us to recognise that this account is true, (*b*) of asking us to recognise that the removal of these categories would leave a lacuna which could neither be filled by anything else nor managed with, if empty: i.e. a *reductio ad absurdum* of the alternative 'No Categories'.

---

[1] Here the parallel is not exact. The sense in which God's activity is or is not an object of experience and induction needs careful definition, but in no case can we allow that theology is *a priori* in Kant's exact sense.

If we compare the task of theology, it is not so tidy nor so demonstrative. We cannot pretend that theology is necessary if we are going to be able to have any conscious experience whatever, or even if we are going to be able to give some coherent account of it. We can indeed make our exposition, parallel to (*a*) above; but when we come to (*b*) we must be more modest. We can go no further than to challenge men to recognise that, with theology and its consequences rigorously excluded, we must exclude from our account of the world things which in our thoughts and actions we cannot but assume to be there.

After this account of the nature and scope of dialectic, the reader may congratulate himself that he is not about to be launched upon such an ocean of discourse. But before we pass to our chosen task of analysis, it will be fitting to adjust the distinction between analysis and dialectic to the traditional proofs of God, upon which we said we had no intention to innovate. The distinction enables us, indeed, to explain the unity and the multiplicity of these proofs. For however many bases dialectic may appear to take, its principle must always be the cosmological idea which analysis is to analyse: the idea of God as effecting the world and the world as the effect of God. In this sense all the proofs can be reduced to the cosmological, including even the Moral Argument—a piece of dialectic which has gained more notoriety than it deserves, on account of the decay of metaphysics—and, if one can call it an argument, the Argument from Religious Experience, which baldly states that men do, in fact, sometimes indulge theistic thinking and believe themselves in experience to apprehend the divine activity.

The only exception seems to be the heretical argument of Anselm. It is not surprising to find this to be an exception, since it is not an argument. It claims that we have a self-authenticating apprehension of God in and by Himself. Were this an appeal to a mystical Ineffable, it might convince those who are privileged to enjoy it; but as it attempts to prove its case from a description or definition of God which can be stated, it fails immediately because the description is in terms of the creation and manifestly defines God through a function which He exercises relatively thereto.[1] To make the proof good we must scrutinise this function, and so we fall into an analysis of the cosmological idea after all. If we like to give the name 'Ontological Argument' to the consideration that in the long run the cosmological perception (God in the world and the world in God) must be self-authenticating, there is nothing to prevent our doing so, but it is not likely to help in the clear understanding of philosophical history. It is indeed odd that while everyone rejects Anselm's argument, so

[1] *Quo maius cogitari nequit* involves the assumptions (*a*) that degrees of reality ('greatness') are thinkable; (*b*) that a supreme degree of it is thinkable: while the proof demands further (*c*) that what is thinkable is founded in what is. Now Anselm does not claim that we apprehend the idea of God *qua* in Himself as *fundatum in re*. What we apprehend as so founded is the supreme term in a scale of being. This scale must itself then be *fundatum in re*. The idea of God as the otherwise undefined notion of supreme term must derive its significance from the terms and structure of the series which it heads. These terms and this structure are known to us from the finite world if known at all. And so the conclusion stated above follows.

many feel it a duty to defend the name as a label for something different; as though we were obliged by discipline verbally to profess 'Credo in unam demonstrationem ontologicam' but free to attach to the formula any sense we could. But if discipline can be said ever to have been on either side, it is against belief in this demonstration.

To return to analysis: we shall not, in this, be concerned so much with the explicit demonstrations of tradition, since these are usually dialectical, but with the constructive accounts given by the philosophers of the relation of the world to God, and of the manner in which God is apprehended through and in His activity in the world; and of the sense in which He can be described and thought about.

II

THE FINITE-INFINITE RELATION

(i) *The Elements of Rational Theology*

DESCARTES, *Med.* iii

1. I ought not to suppose that I conceive the infinite by no genuine idea, but by the mere negation of the finite, as I understand rest and darkness by the negation of movement and light. For on the contrary . . . the idea I have in me of the infinite is in a manner prior to that I have of the finite, the idea of God to the idea of myself. For how would it be possible for me to know that I doubt and that I desire, viz. that I lack something and am not all perfect, unless I had in me some idea of a being more perfect than mine, by the standard of which I recognised the defects of my nature?

2. Now were I independent of every other and myself the author of my being, I should doubt of nothing, should conceive no desires, should (in short) lack no perfection, for I should have given myself all those of which I have in myself an idea; and so I should be God.

3. The idea (of God must have been) born and produced with me from the moment of my creation, as was the idea of myself. And indeed it should not be thought strange that God in creating me should have placed in me this idea to be as it were the mark of the workman imprinted on his work. Nor is it necessary that this mark should be anything different from the work itself; but from the mere fact that God created me, it is perfectly credible that he has somehow produced me in his image and likeness, and that I know this likeness in which the idea of God is contained, by the same faculty by which I know myself.

4. That is to say that when I reflect upon myself, not only do I recognise that I am a thing imperfect, incomplete and dependent upon another, which tend and aspire continually towards something better and greater than I; but also I recognise at the same time that He upon whom I depend possesses in Himself all the great things to which I aspire and of which I find the idea in myself.

IF we neglect the epistemological heresy in which these sentences are embedded, and treat them as simply descriptive of certain notions which their author in fact entertains, we can find here a pleasant and naive expression of the elements of theistic thinking. The naivety will be left behind soon enough. It has its advantages at the outset, because it enables the matter to be included within a narrow compass, before it gets so divided and sophisticated that it is less easy to hold in one vision. We find, then, in these sentences of Descartes the following positions:

1. The notion of finitude is a relative notion. When men argue from the finite to the infinite they are really arguing in a circle. We call things finite in the

only sense relevant for theology, in so far only as we contrast them with infinity. Infinity is also, of course, a relative term, describing the nature of God in so far as it excludes finitude. That which is finite and that which is infinite get called by these names through being compared. We can, then, speak of things as being finite in this sense only if we already think we know what we mean by the notion of a being such as to contrast with these things in the way expressed by the terms finite and infinite. If we are convinced that in recognising the (metaphysical) finitude of things we are recognising a real character, then we must equally be convinced that we have some intelligible notion of a being that is not finite.

Descartes himself, it may be, falls into the easy trap of confusing any particular limitation with absolute or metaphysical finitude. If I find myself complaining of my limitations, e.g. my inability to jump over the moon or understand higher Algebra, I need not be contrasting myself with God, but simply with one who was able to perform these two feats. Limitation in this vulgar sense has plainly to be admitted, because I can always imagine a being able to pass any particular barrier against which I find myself fretting. But this is irrelevant to the proof of God, unless I am conscious of the privation of not being the Absolute Being.

2. 'Now were I independent' . . . etc. This unusually naive sentence contains the idea, which for theism is axiomatic: the existence of perfection requires no explanation, the existence of limited being requires explanation. It is the case, says Descartes, that I conceive reality to admit of degrees of perfection, and that I conceive also a supreme degree beyond which it would be impossible to go. The existence of no being would be a simple fact, the existence of the fullness of being equally a simple fact, and of simple facts no explanations can be asked. ('But who made God?' was the question of someone who had not yet emerged from the nursery.) But the existence of one or more limited beings is not a simple fact. Why this limitation rather than that, or why any at all? A ground cannot be sought in the existence of nothing, so it has to be sought in the existence of the fullness of being, i.e. of God.

This piece of thinking is not an argument but an exposition. It does not prove theism but explains what it is to think theistically. The definition of 'simplicity' is relative to this way of thinking, i.e. to a dynamism in the mind which in fact 'aspires' (to use Descartes's word) and sees the finite as the limited expression of the infinite.

3. This paragraph describes the relation between 'creation' and 'likeness'. Since the very notion of creation is that the Absolute Being contracts being into limited and reduced forms in actualising it alongside Himself, the connexion between creation and likeness is readily seen. This connexion is not dependent upon the general axiom 'Nihil dat quod non habet' or any interpretation of causality in general as the communication of characteristics by what has them to another that is capable of them. 'The reduction of being from the Absolute to the finite' is the specifying differentia of creation, just as 'sequence

according to a rule' is the specifying differentia of physical causality phenomenalistically considered, and as the action of human free will has some other specifying differentia of its own.

To know one's self is to know God, says Descartes; for the complete
view of myself includes my character as effect of God. This effect gets recognised as an effect by presenting along with itself some notion of the Absolute
who has uttered myself as a reduced expression of Himself; and my clue to the
nature of that Absolute Being is, that He is the Absolute of which I am a
reduced expression, or is the positive characters of my being raised to the mode
of absoluteness. It follows that the total fact of my existence provides all the
material for my knowledge of God's existence.

4. This paragraph explains that if there is a double object presented by my
existence, viz. God and myself, this is not an anomaly. It corresponds to the
structure of my existence. I am not, in fact, a simple monad, but my God-
relatedness enters into my very being, giving rise to the polarity of aspiration.
My existence cannot be identified simply with its own limitation; this limitation
is its starting-point, by which its whole course is determined and confined; but
it is itself more than this limitation, it is an act of aspiration towards the Infinite
and Absolute.

The philosophical reader may smile at these venerable phrases. It takes
many more words to speak correctly, and before we begin the attempt it was
worth while to get a compact account of the subject in time-honoured figures,
so that we might know what it is that we are trying to disentangle.

(ii) *The Relation: Finite—Infinite*

We are to analyse the 'cosmological idea'—the scheme of God and the
creature in relation. Let us start with the formula aRx, where a is a constant,
the supposed transcendent entity (God), x a variable, whose values are the
various finite entities with which we get acquainted, and R a relation obtaining
between a and any value of x.

Let us attend first to R. We have already seen reasons for not attempting
to treat R as an instance of a known relation called 'Causality'. Let us try the
plan of going to the opposite extreme and giving R the value of 'is implied by';
since this is the highest degree of formal abstraction. a is implied by x; not
x-without-a; no finite without the infinite.

But implication is a merely logical relation, it expresses a rule of speech,
that x is not to be asserted and a denied; that I am proposing to fix the meaning
of x in such a way, that it must always be accompanied by a; as for example, I
fix the sense of 'explosive' in such a way that I will never assert it and deny
detonation-when-in-contact-with-flame, I will never assert it of that which is
in contact with flame and does not detonate. If we give to x the sense 'creature',
then we can of course say 'No creature without Creator'. But it will remain a
question whether anything which exists deserves the name of 'creature'.

If we asked this question about the term 'explosive', we should not find it difficult to give some kind of an answer. Does anything deserve the name 'explosive'? Well, objects can be found with certain perceptible qualities in conjunction, and such objects have been observed constantly to explode under certain perceptible conditions; and we confidently believe that such objects will do so in the future where those conditions are realised.

No answer of this sort can be supplied in the case of 'creature'; no answer in terms of observed sequence or concomitance. It is plainly not good enough to say: 'I have never observed an entity but that, by attending, I have also been able to observe the activity of God present with it.' We have confessed (it is true) that the theist will have to claim some sort of apprehension of God along with apprehension of the creatures. But this apprehension is not a sensation—what it is, remains to be seen—and the pretence of induction in the formula just given is spurious. For induction is (a) concerned with differences, and (b) never perfectly verified by any number of instances, and (c) is concerned with a relation expressible by AND; and none of these qualities belongs to the believer's (alleged) awareness of God's activity.

(a) Explosiveness is concerned with the character of some objects in distinction from others; but creatureliness belongs to everything not qua this or that, and to everything equally.

(b) One instance is enough; it would be as silly to establish creation by enumerating instances as to establish number or logic by such a method. If we are rightly thinking about the fact that there is anything capable of appearing to us at all, we have the evidence of theism, but the induction of many instances will not help us to decide whether we are thinking rightly or not.

(c) Although the formula: 'That creature exists AND Creator exists may be asserted: that creature exists AND NO Creator exists may not' is acceptable as far as it goes, it is a logical abstraction from the real relation we are dealing with, and the abstraction cannot be made concrete by throwing in time- and space-connexions, as with phenomenal uniformities.

Theism cannot be anything but nonsense, if we are not allowed any sort of connexion but either the accidental concomitance established by induction, or the formal implications between the terms of a language qua language. We must be able to claim to see a mutual belonging together of entities in their actual existence so that one cannot be itself without the other; and since we are setting out to find the presuppositions of theism, let us make it clear from the outset that this is presupposed. We must allow the propriety of Hegel's fundamental question, 'What can we think as existing?' i.e. what structure of elements is required to make up anything that can be thought of as an existent in its own right? We can think what we like of Hegel's answer, or of the whole procedure he adopted in looking for one; but we cannot refuse his question. If the question turns out after all to be nonsensical, there is an end of theism.

It is the question implicit in the most naive distinction between substance, attribute and accident. The latter two can only be constituents, never complete existences; and for the constitution of a substance, a certain mutual connexion of attributes is necessary. Once again, we are free to think what we like of this demoded substance-doctrine. But we can reject it only as a wrong answer, not as the answer to a nonsensical question. For the theist must give 'Divine Activity' as part of the answer to the question, 'What is a sufficient complex of factors for any (finite) thing to exist?'

Who will deny the *prima facie* plausibility of an account which divides the genus 'connexion' into the two species accidental (inductive) and essential (language implication), and treats Hegel's question as arising through a confusion between the two, a confusion which has a famous and appealing name— 'projection'? What more likely than that unhealthily reflective minds should project the mental into the physical? There are so many other indubitable examples of the process.

Against this plausible contention our case is not much fortified by an apologetic which exhorts us to distinguish between the *logic* of terms and the *reason* in the things which, through the terms, we symbolise. Why 'reason' and not just 'order' or 'structure'? To say 'reason' is simply to ask for trouble. For, whatever blessed ambiguity may have attached to the words *logos*, *ratio*, the associations of 'reason' are strongly subjective. Could one ask for a more naive projection than 'The *reason* that is in the *things*'? Piety towards the memory of Plato is hardly worth the price. Nor is it safe simply to discount the word, and suppose that our theologians do not intend the subjective association. For there are pages to be found in this literature where it is represented as a special providence that things should be intelligible. Intelligibility is a character additional to existence, with which 'things' have been decorated by a benevolent deity, in order that mind might be able to understand them. It is with a delighted surprise that the theologian stumbles across so much intelligibility in the universe; in whatever direction he pushes his studies, the angels have been before him, reducing the chaos of being to the order of reason, so that an excellent affinity (*syngenia*, Plato again) is found to exist between mind and world, evidently by a pre-established harmony; and a pre-established harmony is well known to be the happiest argument for theism—it would have been so unlikely to have been an accident.

This doctrine is not Platonism, but a benighted traveller that invokes the spirit of Plato for comfort, when it has got stuck half way back from Kant to common-sense. Kant assigned (as is notorious) all order to the mind, and only crude material to the other factor in experience, and was, by consequence, what he himself called a 'transcendental idealist'. Now this doctrine feels bound to admit that there is *a lot in* the Kantian position; but then surely Kant *went too far*. The order we construct, we construct indeed on the principles of human mentality, principles emanating from within; but it is found to be *applicable*, because such an order is (what luck!) also in the things.

Against this sort of talk we must oppose the question: 'Has the mind, or has it not, the power of *apprehending* the order that is there?' If it has not, we must return to the Kantian position or some more modish variant; if it has, then why should the 'innate tendency' to think e.g. in terms of real causality, be anything else than a custom evolved by a mind actually faced since its origin with a causally-ordered world? If there are universal orders in the world, and actually apprehensible by us, it would be odd if our minds had not developed habits agreeable thereto. If causality is the law of the mind, it may be so because it is the law of existence, and the mind knows existence. If the nature of mind as such is to be an apprehension of what is (*mens est quodammodo omnia*) then 'to be intelligible' is not a character of things, but a relation between them and some mind whose particular finitude does not act as a filter straining out the things in question.

What we have to establish, then, is an order in the world, an order other than that of accidental concomitance, and quite other than that of logical implication. To find this order is to find the starting-point of metaphysics. We cannot here undertake the whole question; we are simply establishing the presuppositions of theism, and this is one of them.

(iii) *There are Other Metaphysical Relations*

If there is such a thing as this metaphysical order, this real connexion, it would be possible to suppose that there is but one instance of it, and that, the relation of finites to God. If we take this view, we shall have an extremely simple form of pantheism. In the finite sphere, there will be no real difference between attributes and substances, qualities and things; we may accept all that phenomenalists and positivists have to say about the 'conventional' and 'constructed' nature of our thing-language, and even our person- and self-language. In the finite sphere there is simply a manifold of neutral stuff, neither physical nor mental, but occurring in certain bundles and patterns, as disciples of Hume have suggested. But this manifold is, by metaphysical connexion, directly and solely dependent on God, who is a real and inner necessity for the existence of every element in it; while no element is (in this sense) necessary to the existence of any other. This, of course, is Berkeley's view, with the additional simplification, that the finite minds have been got rid of by Hume's methods of reduction; or it might be what Spinoza would have said, if Spinoza had been an Englishman, and lived in the century after his own.

Such a view is not logically impossible, but there could never be good reasons for holding it. For

(i) the metaphysical connexion of elements in a finite self (myself, for example) is more evident, or if you take the other view, more specious, than the connexion of finites with God, or in God; as is shown by the general opinion of mankind. If we are prepared to accept Hume's reduction of the finite self, we shall hardly boggle at accepting a reduction of the cosmological idea. We do not need to look far for such a reduction; there is a good choice of them, they are sold in every market. As to Spinoza, he did not arrive at his position by considering what orders of metaphysical connexion are presented to us, but by *a priori* reasonings which are manifestly fallacious.

(ii) The motive-force and spring of the cosmological scheme is found, not in the nature of simple elements as such—atomic, momentary qualities, or a flux of these—but in the nature of finite substances or agents, e.g. selves. A simple and instantaneous flash of quality does not present the notion of a reality that could have degree, so that we ask ourselves, 'Why just *this* degree?' Two tastes of mustard differ in degree, but it is not a degree of reality, of actuality, and it does not suggest an absolute degree. It is from 'creatures' not *qualia*, that the ascent of the mind to God takes its spring.

From this point of view, pantheism looks like nothing but an immense hyperbole; when, having in fact risen to the knowledge of God through that of ourselves, we see that the divine completeness excludes the existence of other substances that are substances in the same sense; and so we use the denial of our own substantiality as an expression of the omnicompetence of the divine substance, not noticing that this means the pretence of sawing away the branch on which we really sit. But there is a baser pantheism which springs directly from the outraged ghost of selfhood. When a mistaken belief in continuous deterministic order (as with Spinoza) has prevented us from assigning selfhood, or finite substance, any habitation here or there in the universe, we cannot lay the ghost, and that which we cannot place anywhere appears to be everywhere, and that which we cannot delimit appears to be one.

(iii) When anyone, pantheist or not, comes to give an account of God and of the relation which phenomena bear to God, he is obliged either to abandon the attempt, and content himself with negations; or else to apply to God, by analogy, terms whose first and proper application is to finite substance, or selfhood. God cannot, in fact, be described in proper terms, nor yet by the analogy of phenomena *qua* phenomena. Therefore the pantheist would either have not to speak, or to hold that the possibility of speaking about God depends upon the *illusion* of finite substance; that the possibility of our speaking truth depends upon our being the victims of error. This position would be odd, to say the least of it; and it would seem natural to take the step of allowing that the illusion of finite substance is not pure illusion, that although 'they reckon ill who leave Him out' and attribute absolute independence to finite substance, yet this last does represent a genuine metaphysical order and grouping in the things.

The three reasons just given are not reasons against everything that could be called pantheism or theistic monism, but only against the suggestion that the relation of finites to God might be the only example of metaphysical order or connexion.

(iv) *Table of Metaphysical Relations*

If there are in fact a number of metaphysical relations, it may help to give the following fourfold division, in which the first member is not really an instance of metaphysical order in the sense we have given to it, but is useful by way of analogy:

(i) Phenomenal Abstraction. Berkeley, as we know, pointed out that we habitually select for attention aspects of phenomena which could not be even imagined as appearing without the concomitance of other aspects. Colour cannot be imagined without spatial extension, nor spatial extension without one or more from a list of alternative quality-fillings. What is complete enough to be imagined (e.g. a mouth) we will call phenomenally concrete, what is not (e.g. a smile) we will call phenomenally abstract, although we should not have Berkeley's goodwill for so using the term.

Phenomenal abstracts have hardly a sufficient independence for us to talk of their being united by metaphysical connexion ('a mutual belonging together of entities in their existence, so that one cannot be itself without the other'). They undoubtedly belong together in their existence, and cannot be themselves without each other. Their defect is in the opposite direction: their distinction from one another is not sufficient to allow of their relations being real; it appears to be a mere 'distinction of reason'. Still, we can ask about any phenomenal abstract what is necessary to it in order that it may be phenomenally concrete, and this affords an analogy to the genuinely metaphysical questions which arise in connexion with the true metaphysical relations.

(ii) Finite substantiality: (*a*) Substance and constituent. We have seen that finite substance has to be vindicated if theism is to be upheld; we defer the endeavour and content ourselves here with noting three metaphysical connexions belonging to it; and first of these, the relation of constituent to substance.

What is sufficiently concrete for appearance is not sufficiently so for existence. For *ESSE* is not *PERCIPI*, *ESSE* is *OPERARI*, and an *operatio*, ἐνέργεια, has a plurality of elements entering into it. It is a real concentration[1] in which they are drawn together in a certain pattern, so that they could not exist nor be conceived to exist without it, nor it without them. Operation with its characterising pattern has a certain continuity. Such a continuity of operation, with its necessary constituents, is a finite substance.

(iii) Finite substantiality: (*b*) Agency and interior effect. Operation as such is immanent; it effects the modification of itself and of its own constituents. Thus it really gives rise to its own next phase. This phase does not follow upon it simply by rule of sequence, it follows upon it by the operation, it is what the operation does or becomes, it is created thereby, though never with more than limited freedom. We can speak, then, of a relation of agency to interior effect, which is other than that of substance to constituent.

[1] For this word see ch. xvii, below

(iv) Finite substantiality: (c) Operation and external affection. The operation of one substance affects those of others. This is so in any case—we cannot move without trampling the daisies: but where teleology enters, the affection of the other may be its aim, as when we choose to cultivate our flowers. External affection is perhaps no more than the setting of conditions in view of which the operations of others must determine themselves, and therefore it lacks the immediacy and creativity of interior effect.

So much for the three connexions belonging to finite substance. We must apologise for opaque phrases and undefined terms, referring the reader to the sections on finite substance, and hoping meanwhile that the distinction between these three connexions will be granted as at least specious at a certain level of thinking which the reader may for the present regard as heavily mythological if he chooses.

(v) Infinite substance and finite substance. This is the relation of creativity proper. When it is said to obtain between infinite and finite substance, the latter is understood to mean the whole system of finite substance, or rather substances, so that the three relations which we have just specified become interior to finite substance. Or, to take the well-known metaphor of spatial dimensions: these three relations connect, as it were, the several parts of a surface; the new relation gives the backing in depth which this surface, as a surface, must have.

This fifth type of connexion is itself, and is none of the others. Everything that is not reducible to other things must be apprehended itself for what it is. Thus there can be no question of defining such a relation. Divine creativity is a real connexion accounting for the existence of that system of finite substance which operates in its own finite manner. Such a statement cannot define the connexion; it declares simply what difference it makes (existence/non-existence) and to what it makes it (the finite inclusively considered); and even this statement is hopelessly incorrect, since to be or not to be is not a difference which can be applied to a subject capable of either, for then the subject would have (ex hypothesi) to be already in some manner. Whereas creation is a relation which simply posits one of its terms. The standard type of relation is one which arises between two already existing terms and affects both; creation effects the existence of one, and leaves the other unaffected; as follows from its being a reduction from the absolute to the finite.

It is impossible to over-stress the importance of realising that creation is an unique relation. No theology can survive the assumption that it is reducible to some other, for manifest absurdities result. But if it is unique it must have its specifying marks. And yet we are always meeting the person who finds it a scandal that these cannot be reduced. 'Show me anywhere else', cries one, 'an instance of an agent which is unaffected by its activity and I will believe.' To which we can only reply: 'Show us such an instance, and we will cease to believe, for if deity is reducible to some other genus, it cannot be deity.'

(v) *Analogy of Inter-Finite Relations to Finite-Infinite Relation*

About that which is simply unique there can be no discourse; we can only repeat its name, and say that it is itself and not any of the others. Where, however, analogy exists, it is possible to make significant comparisons which bring out for us and fix our appreciation of that with which these analogies are drawn. The notion of an analogy which reposes upon no generic identity will be discussed and defended later. We are here making applications of the doctrine, and proceed to compare the relation of Creator and creature with the three relations which we catalogued as belonging to finite substance.

First (ii), the relation of constituent to substance. This analogy has the merit of stressing the absolute dependence of the creature. For the constituent, though in a manner *something*, is not sufficient to exist by itself; the substance is required for its existence, which it supports in a non-temporal manner, or to speak more exactly, in a manner which makes abstraction from temporal succession. For though the existence of both constituent and substance is in temporal succession, the relation of constituent to substance is not one of temporal succession, but of *esse*.

But if there is analogy in these respects, the difference must not be ignored. For (a) the relation of a finite substance to anything else cannot be the same as the relation of its constituent to it, for then the substance would not be a substance, and if we press this analogy we deny finite substance in effect. (b) A substance is not independent of its constituents but, at the most, of *this* constituent in the sense that some other is substitutable for it. (c) A substance is not really prior to its constituents and therefore cannot be the cause of their existence.

The result of equating (v) and (ii) is pantheism of the type to which we have referred above. We happened there to be approaching it from the other end, and asking what happens if we treat the divine activity as being simply related to the constituents of substance without the mediation of finite substance. This was in effect to make it perform the rôle of finite substance (or of finite operation). But now we ask what happens if we regard it as a case of the relation between (finite) substance and its constituents, and conclude that it must usurp the place of finite substance and become directly related to the constituents.

Next we take (iii), the relation of agency to interior effect. This offers an analogy of singular value, in supplying the notion of creation. The operation of a substance actually gives rise to its own next phases. And it should be noted that what we call intellectual and aesthetic 'creations' are interior effects. The painter does, of course, in painting, exteriorly affect the operations and the mutual relations of the substances which compose brush, pigments and canvas. But the picture which is the 'creation' is not a state of any or each of these substances nor of them as a whole. It is a phase of the artist's sight—a sight which has ordered itself by the use of instruments, by exercising control over the things that determine it. It is essentially as immanent as is imagination.

But this analogy also has shocking defects. For the operation that was, gives rise to its next phase by ceasing to be or by becoming other. If we evade. this consequence by defining the operation as the identity and continuity of the process, then the phase must be reduced to a mere modality, which falls into a constituent relationship to it, and we are no better off.

Is there a theological heresy which corresponds to the abuse of this analogy? One must not expect to find the pure type; but we may see a strong influence from it in the Bergsonism of *L'Évolution Créatrice*, while the evasion just noted would give us the historicist aspect of Hegelianism, as developed by the Italian Idealists.

Last we have (iv), operation and external affection. This analogy also has its decisive advantages; for it comes nearest to securing the independence of God, and the substantiality of the creatures. It is employed in the classic figure of God as Demiurge, working upon materials; as in the biblical account of the creation of Adam, or in the Paleyan comparison of the watchmaker. There is no statement of theism which can dispense with this analogy; yet there is no more vulgar or trivial statement of theism than one which relies upon it principally.

For its defects are evident. It fails to express the one-sided dependence of the creature in its very existence, it makes divine action as external to the creature as any action can be, and it reduces God to the level of His creatures, a substance affecting other substances and differing from them only in degree of quality and power.

It is not difficult to identify the theological heresy which results. It is deism or, if pushed to an extreme, downright paganism (a finite deity entering as a member into the system of substantial beings). It is what pantheists suppose Christians to believe.

Let us summarise the results of this threefold comparison. The first analogy expresses the necessity of God to the creatures; the second, His creativity; the third, His distinctness (independence). The first expresses the character of the creature as dependent, the second, as effect, the third, as substance.—But it would be absurd to suppose that the notion of the cosmological relation is simply a bouquet culled from these three trees. For it exceeds each of them in the kind proper to each. None of them and no combination of them can suggest the absolute unconditionedness of the divine activity; which characteristic serves us indeed for a criterion in selecting certain aspects from the three analogies and rejecting others. So that those who wish to make out that the notion of divine creation is an artificial construction must include this fourth element of absoluteness (whatever else they exclude). We shall see that they will have to include several more besides.

The notion of unconditionedness, however, is not on the same footing with the three analogies. They are contributions towards a quasi-description of the relation;[1] 'unconditionedness' does nothing towards describing its nature

---

[1] viz. an analogical description

but simply indicates a problem. The idea of unconditionedness is, as a formal notion, intelligible. We apply it to the notion of metaphysical connexion, or rather to the groundedness of such a connexion in an infinite term. This simply creates the problem: what kind of connexion would satisfy the description 'unconditioned', if any will? As though we were to apply the notion of 'being the fastest of its kind' to the notion of 'being a mammal'. This would simply create the problem: what *sort of* a mammal satisfies the description? None might do so, e.g. if it belonged to the nature of mammals to be capable of a fixed velocity. But if there is a fastest mammal, the description 'fastest mammal' does not advance an inch in the direction of specifying it.

Let us get a little clearer the place occupied in the argument by the three analogies. Are they as important as they pretend to be? Is there not a host of possible analogies which would cast light on the nature of the relation? To this we reply that there are a great number, but they reduce to these as instances. This is true, so far as we adhere strictly to the notion of relation in our original formula aRx, and ask always and only: 'What is the nature of the real dependence of x on a?' It is a different matter if we take our stand within a, and consider the activity of God in creating, as an activity; if we ask with the Rabbi: 'The Holy One (Blessed be He) when He is creating the world, whereunto is *He* like?' It will then be very proper, no doubt, to decide that God's action is spiritual and intentional, and that His own nature serves Him in a manner for exemplary and final cause, etc., etc.

Or again, if we took our stand within the creature, we might ask in how many ways in its own activity it orientates itself towards God and His activity. But we are not asking these things, but rather by what sort of a joint the divine activity passes over into the existence of the finite activity. And it is difficult to see how, for this purpose, any analogy can be closely relevant except an analogy with metaphysical connexions having to do with finite substance. There may be other such beside these three, and if so, they may be relevant. Generation, the production of one substance by others, might seem to be such a further connexion, and a peculiarly appropriate one. And yet, for reasons which we hope will appear in our treatment of finite substance, generation is a relation which we must suppose to be metaphysically real, *ut cum homo generat hominem*, yet into whose nature we can have no insight. Phenomenally we observe it, but metaphysically we can only wonder at it, and it is in respect of its obscurity that it puts us in mind of creation. If generation contributes any light, and not merely 'darkness visible' to the argument, it is in respect of the comparison between the natures of the terms—the begetter and the begotten—not in respect of the relation itself.

And here we will leave the analogical description of the active relation between infinite and finite.

III

THE FINITE AND INFINITE TERMS

(i) *Comparison of the Terms*

WE have just been drawing a distinction between the nature of the actual relation and any mere comparison between the natures of the terms that it relates. And indeed to talk about the proportion of the finite to the infinite is not to talk about the way in which the infinite gives rise to the finite. The distinction is good; but, as with the case of 'phenomenal abstraction',[1] its validity does not mean that either of the things distinguished makes sense by itself. You cannot think of particular colour-tones without understanding spatial extension, even though understanding means 'leaving to be understood'. And you cannot think of the relation in the cosmological idea without at least 'leaving to be understood' infinite and finite being; you cannot think of it as a relation which might obtain between some other pair of terms, or just 'terms' in general.

And conversely, as St. Thomas shows in the second syllogism of the *Via Quarta*,[2] you cannot think of the comparison between infinite and finite without at least leaving to be understood the active relation between them. The lack of independence enters too deeply into the nature of finitude for that; and it is only through, in, and as creative activity that the infinite can be grasped by the finite.

We have already had an example of the former half of this convertible connexion in our use of 'unconditionality' to specify the cosmological relation. For that which is properly 'unconditional' is God's existence, that is, His activity, and this determines the way in which we are obliged to think that this activity gives rise to the existence of the finite. That is an instance of the essential connexion of the nature of the relation with the nature of one of its terms. It is not less essentially related to the comparison between the two terms, as we implied when, in the process of picking Descartes's brains, we remarked that 'the reduction of being from infinite to finite is the specifying differentia of creation, just as sequence according to a rule is the specifying differentia of phenomenal causality'.

'Specifying differentia' might seem highly exceptionable, since what is external to the relation (comparison of the terms) cannot be the specifying differentia of the relation's nature. But, since the relation is *ex hypothesi* unique,

---

[1] *vide supra*, p. 21

[2] In the first half of this argument St. Thomas simply states (*a*) that we recognise different degrees of reality in several finite things, (*b*) that this is to recognise them as approximations to an absolute reality. In the second half he proceeds to show by analogy that we cannot consider side by side the absolute and that which is in degree, without admitting the former to be the *cause* of the latter.

nothing else can be this, either. No proper differentia can be stated. We have the choice of analogical description on the one hand; we have said something about that. Or on the other, we have the statement of the relation's context. This dilemma should be pretty familiar in philosophy, which largely deals with irreducible notions. If I wish you to recognise the meaning of 'subject' in epistemology, I can either give you analogies, or define its context in terms of object and act of apprehension, etc., delimiting, as it were, the exact area of the lacuna which needs to be filled, by specifying the items which surround it. It is then to be hoped that you, with your eyes on the reality which is assumed to be open to us all, see what does fill the lacuna and so become acquainted with the meaning of my term. It follows, then, to consider the comparison of the terms, infinite and finite being; not only because they help us to look in the right direction for recognising the cosmological relation, but also because they are constituent parts of the cosmological idea (or scheme) itself.

What we are eager to know is by what dynamism and on what evidence the mind passes from the one term to the other, from the finite substance to God. But we must resolutely put this aside for the present, in order to see with what elements or tools the mind works when it supposes itself to do so. If the mind is able at all to pass from the notion of the finite to that of the infinite, it is plainly required that the two terms shall be comparable, and in particular that the finite should afford analogy to the infinite.

We have seen that if we are to know God at all, it is necessary to suppose some apprehension of Him, as opposed to any mere inference. But this apprehension will be of something unique; and if we are going to do anything more than name it, if we are going to have any discourse about it, we must do so by bringing other matters into the argument. We might indicate its context, by saying it is that to which finite being is related by the cosmological relation. But if we wish to comment on its *nature*, we can do so only by comparison or analogy with finite being.

But further, if the remarks we made upon Descartes's doctrine of aspiration can be justified, it will follow that comparison with the finite is more necessary to our knowledge of the infinite than *vice versa*. For though we then said that it would be impossible to identify our existence with its own limitations or finitude, though I must claim that I am an act which aspires from this finitude in the direction of the infinite, yet I am plainly more identified with my limitation than my goal, with the datum than with the task of cognition. Leaving then, for the present, the question of how we know the infinite, we will concentrate on the analogy of the finite to it, being assured that it is anyhow important for knowledge of the infinite itself.

What we have to deal with is of course the kind of substantial being which, when compared with the infinite, comes to deserve the description of 'finite'. We are not dealing with the notion of finitude as such, which is simply relative, as was seen. We ask what is the comparison of the substance of which our own is an instance, with the being of God.

(ii) *God as Absolute Existent*

Esse est operari—the substance is a unit of activity, and we think of God also as unit of activity, when we think of Him as the perfection of which we are the limitation. Someone may here object—and it might be Descartes himself—that we conceive God as the perfection, not of activity simply, but of spiritual or personal activity. That may well be; yet whenever we try to apply to God these fuller and more concrete descriptions, the problem arises, how far and in what sense they apply. We remember a wearisome topic canvassed in our youth, whether God should be called Personal, Impersonal, or Superpersonal? It was not a very helpful division, but it did mask a real difficulty. We find ourselves withheld from thinking of God as 'a Person' *simpliciter*; we have to think of Him as a somewhat in a certain not exactly defined relation to personality. Of course we may if we like say 'God is a Superperson *simpliciter*'; but that is merely to cover the mental hiatus with verbal plaster.

Now, however many descriptions we may withhold from God in their plain sense—however zealous we are not to place Him *in genere*—we cannot dispense with one: we must have a subject to whom these descriptions are thus oddly related; God must be agreed to be somewhat, to be an *existent*.

It is here that we run against as hard a stone wall as prejudice has ever built across the line of advance. Here is the old Phocian rampart, the Thermopylae secure in its Laconic defence: 'Existence is no predicate'. The historical parallel may disincline us from a frontal attack, but inspire hope that the position may be turned.

It may be tactful to begin by saying what we do *not* mean, and admitting several senses in which 'existence is no predicate'. It is commonly asserted (*a*) that the fact of existing is not a predicate of any subject, (*b*) that the character of being an existent is not a predicate of any subject.

(*a*) The mere fact of existence, i.e. of actuality as opposed to possibility, adds nothing to the character of anything whose existence is asserted. A possible something is a possible existent; if we remove the qualification 'possible', we do not add to our notion, rather we simplify it. We can of course predicate actuality of something, but this is only to assert that it is given; not to say anything about *what* is given. The fact of 'givenness' is perfectly simple and the same for all instances. The illusion which leads us to regard givenness or actuality as an addition of character may well arise from the habit of regarding the possible as an abstract, the actual as a concrete. The concrete is, of course, richer in character than the abstract; but there is nothing in the mere notion of possibility that makes it abstract, however hard it may be for us to deck out the possible with all the detail of flesh-and-blood actuality. And even admitting that the possible is by its very notion abstract, we must still point out that the additional character in the concrete consists of additional characteristics, and not in a supposed quality of existence.

(*b*) The description 'existent' may be taken in abstraction from the distinc tion of actual and possible (for the possible is a possible existent) and regarded as the *summum genus* of all characters whatsoever. Whatever we think about is an actual, possible or fantastic existent, i.e. constituent in fact. But in that case the class of existents is the class of all characters and therefore has itself no character; to predicate it of anything cannot conceivably add to the notion of that thing, but only suggest it for comparison with other things whatsoever, according to any principle of comparison whatsoever.

(c) We will add another sense in which it is to be conceded that 'existence is no predicate'. Even taking that metaphysical sense of 'existence' which we are about to define, we must say that *in the order of reality* existence is not a predicate or rather, not an attribute. Existence is that which has attributes, which expresses itself in all modes. None the less, the term *connotes character* in a way that we shall indicate, and that is the point at issue; for then we shall be able to say that God is the supreme instance of this character.

Now to the definition. To exist means to be an expression of that which is something *in itself*. Existence then (not further defined) connotes a relation to something which is in itself, such that it is in the being of this thing-in-itself that the existent is. Aristotle in his categories wished to show in how many ways that which terms connote may be related to being-in-itself: i.e. the various modes of existence. In so far as the connotation of a term can be a wilful and conscious abstraction, the doctrine of the categories may look merely logical— as pointing us to the fact that the abstraction finds its real home in that from which it is abstracted; and this seems to be merely a doctrine of the relation of words to that about which they speak. But there is a second element in the doctrine; for phenomena, complete in themselves *qua* phenomena, are referred to substance (which does not simply appear, but is in itself) as the subject in which they inhere.

Every phenomenon for sense, or real character grasped by the understanding, presents itself as *existent*, i.e. as belonging in some bundle which has a completeness sufficient for, and actually constituting, self-being. The mode in which it is to be referred to self-being may be still indeterminate; but the reference is demanded, and we may very often begin by hypostatising our existent, i.e. attributing to it by itself the self-being which it only partakes by being a constituent in something else. We may then proceed to correct our hypostatisation.

It follows that 'existence' may be considered as a composite notion, involving the notion of that which is in itself, and of relation thereto. (The relation may, of course, be one of identity; that which is in itself certainly exists most properly, most underivatively.) So it may seem that existence is secondary to substance, for it is either substance, or that which is in substance. And this is so, in the final view; but in the order of coming to know, existence as a confused and implicit notion may be prior to substance. The distinction of substance and constituent clears it up.

'That which is in itself' may be considered in two aspects. Regarded in its intrinsic quality or nature, it is activity, operation; as has been already asserted. To be is to function, or to belong to a functioning. Regarded in its scope or extension, it is substance; a substance is a unit of operation which is sufficient for a certain sort of independence.

Thus existent, operant and substance may often coincide in their denotation; certainly the supreme existent would be the supreme operation or activity. We might hesitate to say 'and supreme substance', since this term is often defined in a manner which connotes finitude.

To conclude: Existence, if the notion is made explicit, connotes activity or operation, and that structure which is necessary for the functioning of any activity whatsoever; the existent either is the activity which has (or fills) the structure, or else it is an element finding its place in that structure or in that activity. So existence is not merely givenness; it connotes a character, viz. of operating independently. If there is a higher sort of operation and operational independence than that of finite substance, then all existence will have reference to that, as well as to finite substance.

Now, if we say that God is, we mean that He is, in Himself, operation, for otherwise we should not even have rejected the suggestion that He is a quality of ourselves, or of sunsets and skylarks, as some appear to suppose. And if we say that He is an x such as to stand in some highly problematical relation to personality and other descriptions, we may expel these descriptions from the residual x, but the character of being an existent we cannot expel, or we should be saying nothing. If we say 'an x' we can never mean 'the simply indeterminate', unless we are talking about logical terms qua terms, and even then we mean 'a term'. But if we are supposed to be talking of realities, 'an x' cannot mean 'an undetermined', but always 'a so-and-so, but undetermined in certain respects'. In the case of deity, the last 'so-and-so' that we can take is the high abstraction of being an existent, undetermined as to the mode of His existence.

The statement that we can never mean by 'an x' the simply indeterminate, when we are speaking of realities, may appear to conflict with a famous formula for analysing propositions. 'This building is the Bodleian' is said to stand for: 'Here is an x which satisfies the functions of (a) being a building, and (b) being, and alone being, the Bodleian.' The purpose of such a formula is to expel from the subject of the sentence all determinations, in order that nothing may be taken for granted about the nature of the subject (e.g. that it is a building). All such determinations are to be explicitly predicated. Yet is it not plain that the x is not absolutely indeterminate, and that if it were, the proposition would be nonsense? The x means here, most likely, 'an object of visual and tactual awareness', with the shadow of the idea of metaphysical existence accompanying its phenomenality. And about objects of sense much is habitually predicated a $priori$, as Kant and others have claimed; and about metaphysical existents also, as we shall claim.

If this be granted, the next step we must take is the attachment of God's perfection, or absoluteness, to His existence. In discussing the Cartesian text, we saw that by God we mean the absolute or perfect mode of something which in the creature is qualified and imperfect. But of what is He the absolute mode? We have seen that if we say that He is the absolute mode of spirit we get into difficulties, because we can but think spirit in the manner in which we are it, and we cannot assert that an absolute expression of spirit in this form would be more than perfection within a given kind—as we might suppose a perfect circle. And so we must describe Deity as a perfection standing in a certain relation of analogy to what we can but mean by spirit.

Thus the predication of perfection is prior to, and more unqualified than, the predication of spirit, or any other genuine predicate. But perfection must be the perfect expression or degree of some character; otherwise it is meaningless. It follows by elimination that what is said to be in perfection is the *character of being an existent*. To say that God is simply Absolute is to say that He is the *perfect existent*.

(iii) *How an Absolute Degree of Existence is Thinkable*

It is necessary to indicate next what it would mean to suppose:

(*a*) that there can be degrees of *esse* = *operari*,
(*b*) that there can be an absolute degree of it.

(*a*) To 'place' metaphysically the reality referred to by any term which has reality-reference, is to identify it as a constituent of activity, or a mode of activity. If it is a constituent, it is incomplete, metaphysically abstract, and so not a character *additional* to activity but a distinction within it. If it is a mode of activity it is *an* activity and so again not a character additional to it. If all that is, is activity, if every character is a manner of being active, then to the character of activity no character other than itself can be added. Activity has modes, but neither attributes nor accidents.

Activity, then, certainly has variety of mode, for all differences which can be expressed as between one being and another are modes of it. But also it has degree. For when we compare the humblest active unit with a rising scale of substances up to man, the ascent is ascent in mode of activity. We normally think of some modes as roughly equivalent in degree, others as decidedly unequal, and it is conceivable that when we so think we are right. For let it be remembered that we are not here attempting any demonstration, but only an analysis of the cosmological idea, together with an indication of the assumptions on which it rests. The verification of these is to be dealt with later.

If, in speaking of the several modes and degrees of activity, we reject the scheme of genus and species, we must have some similar scheme to distinguish activity *as such* from this or that mode and degree of it. We reject the genus-species relation, because that suggests distinction between (1) a wider class characterised by some common characteristic, (2) several smaller classes each characterised in addition by some other characteristic peculiar to it. Whereas in this case the special characteristics turn out to be instances of the generic characteristic.

A better way of putting this matter is by appeal to the impossibility of abstracting the character of the supposed genus (activity as such). If we wish to state mammality as a generic character of the several mammalian species, we must be able to explain or at least point to the common characteristics which justify the common description. With 'activity as such' this is manifestly impossible. No form can be picked out as common to the instances. If we take the most elementary form that we think we can describe, it does not simply remain in the higher instances; the higher instances are higher not by adding to, but by modifying the form of the lower.

If, on the other hand, we found some element of structure common to all degrees and modes—e.g. multiplicity-and-unity, pattern or 'form'—this would not be a description of the common notion 'activity' but of a *constituent* in all activities. Activity is the description of the complete process: to be an activity is to be some mode and degree of activity; that is evident. It is irrelevant to point out that to be a mammal is also to be some species of mammal, for 'mammal' is not the description of the complete thing *qua* complete, though it *refers* to the complete thing. The idea of a mammal is of 'an x such as to be a mammal', an x satisfying the function 'being a mammal'. But we cannot apply this scheme to our instance. For if we say 'an x, such as to be an activity' we have used the same term twice, for x here, as in the case of God[1], must stand for 'activity'.

But from the inapplicability of the genus-species scheme we cannot conclude that no common notion is expressed by the word 'activity', for we have seen that this inapplicability follows from the profound generality of the notion, and not from any obscurity or failure to clarify what conceivably could be clarified. Nor is it easy to see what has given genus and species the right to strut about arm-in-arm proclaiming: 'We are what is, and what is not we, is not.'

Activity-as-such, then, stands for a certain comparability and potential continuity of character between the several types of it. We can scale these in degree—Degree of what? Of activity—and we can see that some pairs of modes are more like than others, without their likeness being likeness of anything but activity. If I wish to think of activity-as-such, and to give proper explicitness to my thought, I must present to myself at least two instances of activity and consider what it is to compare the two. For I cannot abstract and fix its character, as I can with the character 'dog'. It may be that in order to abstract dogginess from all specialities of 'mongrel, puppy, whelp and hound, and cur of low degree', I must have originally had a plurality in view. But once I have done so, I can get on with a single instance, so long as I affix labels, presumably verbal, to certain intellectually abstractible (not separately imaginable) aspects. If for example I have that bundle of labels which is an adequate defini-

[1] *vide supra*, p. 30

tion, and apply this to the single instance, not including more than the labels mark out, I shall know where I stand.

But in the case of activity-as-such, I cannot do this; I cannot take an instance, and, guided by verbal labels, pick out what belongs to the character of being activity-as-such. Activity-as-such is inseparable from the scale in which activities are related, and apart from it is perfectly senseless.

Activity-as-such is sometimes described as the barest and most abstract of notions, that 'cui omnia adduntur'. If by this it is meant that it is the most general and least determinate way of referring to anything, we may agree. But in another sense it is not abstract for it cannot be abstracted, but falls back into full flesh-and-blood concreteness before we know where we are: a relapse which we can only prevent by setting several instances disputing one another's right to the title of activity-as-such.

We have now seen in some manner what it is to assert degree of activity. It is to assert a distinction between activity-as-such and its modes. We have still to consider (b) what it is to assert an absolute degree of it. We may here recur with better equipment to our remarks on Descartes, where we glossed 'absoluteness' by 'the elimination of the arbitrary', or rather, 'that state on which arbitrary limitations have never been imposed'. This conception plainly depends on the distinction between activity-as-such, and given modes of activity. A true genus can be identical and characteristic of itself in all its species. But activity-as-such has no common distinguishable characteristic; it has, as it were, to realise itself differently in every modification. Where, then, does it realise *itself*? Surely it can somewhere just 'be itself'. This would be its absolute mode. And since its modifications do not arise by addition of characters to it, its absolute mode cannot be its lowest, but must be its highest possible, from which all others arise by limitation or reduction.

Such a 'proof' is, of course, pure dialectic, and obtains its force from the application of concealed analogies, which have been chosen for the very reason that they lead in this direction—or, to put it less scandalously, for the reason that they serve to bring out the nature of that relation which we claim obscurely to apprehend. Before we proceed to the discovery and statement of these analogies, we may note the completion of a threefold scheme which in itself is proper and not expressed through analogy. We had already distinguished activity-as-such from its modes. We must now add the conception of the mode in which activity is simply itself, and which, being indistinguishable from the full expression of activity, ought not to be called a mode. This, then, is the division:

> Activity as such
> Any mode of activity
> Activity absolute.

The famous philosophumenon: 'God's essence is identical with His existence; in all others there is a real distinction between existence and essence' is simply an expression of this scheme. Existence is activity, essence is mode; in God alone mode is the simple and necessary expression of activity, there alone the form activity has is the form that belongs to it when not interfered with.

(iv) *Analogies to Absolute Existence*

We proceed to detail the analogies by which the notion of Absolute Activity is made describable.

(i) The relation of Absolute to finite mode is like that of a higher mode to a lower. As amoeba to frog and frog to man, so man to God—except that the distance is not finite but infinite, and God not only higher but highest.

The disadvantages of this scheme are so painful, they leap to the eye. If we simply ascend up the hierarchy and extrapolate, there is no reason why we should ever reach a highest possible term. Indeed we are placed in a dilemma: either we say there is such a term, in which case the difference between it and any finite must be measurable; or else, in order to maintain an infinite—which can only mean 'indefinite' in this scheme—difference, we must say that the way to God is a *progressus ad indefinitum* and that the first term is never reached.

But it has its advantage none the less. It conveys the idea that God is a kind of being as different from us as one can be from another—more different than we are from the amoeba.

(ii) The relation of Absolute to finite mode is like that of the perfect expression of a species to the indefinite variety of incomplete, maimed and perverted examples. 'They are one way good, and evil every way'; normality is humanity in and as itself, while eccentricity, stupidity, mania, deficiency, idiocy are various privations of its proper character. And yet they belong to the species, or at least to no other: whether an idiot is to be called a man or not is an unprofitable question; he is a man so spoilt or diminished that one may hesitate to apply the name. Where normality is not achieved we say that the specific character has been tampered with or inhibited.

The advantages and disadvantages of this analogy are the direct opposites of those attaching to the previous one. For it gives a satisfactory notion of the absolute degree, but fails to suggest at all that the several diminished forms are different kinds from the highest form and from one another. A man is not simply a diminished God, he is a *man*, and *therefore* a diminution from the divine image.

These two analogies, then, must be always used to supplement one another's deficiencies. That does not mean that they can be combined in one picture. We alternate between the two, like a circus-rider between two horses.

(iii) The relation of Absolute to finite is like that of the metaphysically complete to the metaphysically incomplete, of (finite) substance to constituent. For in order that God should be sufficient to exist, no outside factor is needed.

But in order that a finite mode should suffice for existence a further factor is needed, viz. the activity of God. And so the finite is incomplete or abstract in itself and obtains concreteness only by 'composition' with God's creative activity, which serves it in the place of the missing constituent.

This analogy has the merit of stressing the metaphysical inferiority of the finite. But the analogy of 'composition' is very forced, and if pressed, gives pantheism and denies the substantiality of the creature, i.e. that it is a mode of activity in its own right at all. The scheme will be recognised as an old friend by students of Spinoza, who uses (in effect) against Descartes the dilemma: 'Substance is metaphysical completeness. Then if the creatures and God are dependently related, the creatures are not substantial, or if the creatures are substantial, they stand on the same footing with God.' Such a conclusion results from taking this analogy as not an analogy but as a proper statement.

There are perhaps other analogies, but these three will yield without much trouble the mysterious major premises of the dialectical syllogisms connected with St. Thomas's *Via Quarta* (*vide supra*, p. 26).

In the threefold division 'activity as such: any mode of activity: activity absolute' the third item is directly related to the first, i.e. that of which activity absolute is the absolute expression, is activity as such, and not any particular mode. It is no doubt proper to say that 'to Absolute Being all the riches of existence belong', so that nothing can appear in any mode which is not a reduced and splintered version of something in God; to the creature only the reduction and the splintering can be peculiar. But as we do not yet know *how* the particularity of this and that mode is archetypally expressed in God, this does not seem to give us any very precise or valuable information. And therefore the notion of Absolute Being is a very outline description indeed; it is the notion of the absolute degree of activity-as-such, and therefore activity of the character (whatever it may be) which fits that position in the scale. 'Supra-personal rather than infra-personal.'—Oh, undoubtedly; supra-personal, superessential, supersubstantial, super-everything; but what does that amount to in real information?

Thus the mere notion of the Absolute Being is the name of a problem. It stands for 'An existent (or activity) having that character which fits it to occupy a certain place (viz. the highest) in the scale of existents; or to perform a certain function in the system of existents'. The notion specifies the nature of the 'place' and the 'function', but the 'character' it cannot of itself specify; it merely dictates 'some character', and leaves the determination of this indeterminate to some other consideration.

The attempt at determining it constitutes a well-marked division in rational theology, and it is here that the science really begins to be difficult. The mere notion of Absolute Being is the formal description of theistic doctrine as such, and it is no superhuman task to define the notion and to lay bare the intellectual mechanism by the aid of which we think it. To explain how we *characterise* absolute existence, and what relations we must suppose our characterisations bear to the reality if any, is a very different matter. It is possible for several doctrines to arise at this point, equally theist and with something like an equal degree of plausibility. Profiting by the division of the philosophic forces, Revelationists attempt to seize this territory for their own. We shall dispute it with them, however, and see what a reasonable analysis can do in this field.

IV

THE LADDER OF ASCENT

(i) *The Necessity of Analogy*

WE may regard our present task as the endeavour to fill an empty form with content. Such language need not lead us into the absurdity of supposing that there is in God an actual distinction of form and material filling. In the reality the filling is the form—to have the 'essence' or nature which God has, is to be the Absolute Existent. The distinction is a distinction for our minds only. We know God piecemeal and with the aid of diagrams. It would be odd to conclude that He is either a diagram or a collection of pieces.

We have, therefore, to find the content for the form. And first we are met with the attractive suggestion that we have got all the time what we are looking for, that the demand for a search arises only because we insist on looking away from its goal. The cosmological idea consists of the elements—absolute activity (or being), finite activity (or being), and the relation between these. Very well then: is it not probable that the problem of characterising the absolute, of giving content to it, arises from the initial fault of vicious abstraction? We elevate the absolute activity into a thing-in-itself, and then are at a loss to tell what sort of thing it is. But the difficulty vanishes if we cancel the abstraction, redintegrate the cosmological idea, and let the absolute activity find its content in giving rise to the finite activities. The answer to the question, 'What is God?' is therefore 'Our Creator—*caeli et terrae effector*'; and this answer gives not merely a description by external relation, but an essential *definition*.

This solution makes a specious appeal to the practical interests of religion; for, it is said, what business can we have with speculating upon aspects of the divine being which do not enter into our own existence? Surely religion knows God as He is for us, it can have no concern in demonstrating a transcendent deity. And, from the side of philosophy, we are referred to an exact parallel—a parallel so exact, indeed, that it is more than a parallel, it is the model on which this argument is constructed. It is the notion of the finite subject. If we take the subjectivity of the ego, and abstracting it, make it transcendent over its activities, as though independent of them, and free to indulge in them when it chooses by a sort of condescension,—then we are utterly at a loss how to conceive this mysterious being. The *formal* character of subjectivity it retains, but to give it content exceeds our wit. But the problem is a false problem. The subject is the subject *of* its activities, it is the focal and subjective point in them, it cannot be conceived in itself. Withdraw the false abstraction, and the problem evaporates.

We shall have cause to illustrate hereafter the general correctness of this treatment of the finite subject. How could it help being correct? For it happens that we *are* ourselves, the materials for making up the picture lie embedded in our own existence, which we do but take to pieces in order that we may piece it together again. What we find to be abstract will be so because we have abstracted it, and what we have abstracted we can redintegrate with its context. There is no place in this sphere for any blanks which we must confess ourselves unable to fill, any formal insights which carry with them no specification of their content, so that we should have to set about trying to supply one through some kind of analogising. Hence the Hegelian method of rejecting whatever is found to be abstract and looking always for the intelligible concrete synthesis, is here at home and justified, however perversely it may have been worked.

But this, as we see, rests on special *a priori* grounds (viz. on the significant tautology that we are ourselves). It is not equally evident that we are the Absolute Being, even in our highest philosophic flights, and therefore the extension of the method into theology begs every question. If we may refer again to our initial lessons from Descartes, the activity of aspiration, though it does not identify us absolutely with the finite pole of the bipolar movement, does place us at it; from it we aspire and 'know' God as him whom our aspiration seeks by knowledge to embrace, and therefore as one of whom we have an outline and an indication, a knowledge that is yet no knowledge.

But the case against this solution of our problem does not rest simply on these *a priori* grounds, but on its inability to formulate itself intelligibly after all. The method of concrete synthesis when applied to the notion of Absolute Being fails to apply, and the content thereby offered to the form does not fit it but removes it. The thesis is: Creation of the finite is the content of absolute existence. But if so, we must choose between alternatives. Either the creative activity is distinct *qua* activity from the finite activities with which it wholly concerns itself, or it is not distinct. And whichever alternative we choose we get into trouble.

To begin with the former: it is distinct. On this hypothesis, finite activities furnish the absolute activity with all its materials or objects; but it has, so to speak, its own subjectivity, a real focus from which, regarded as objects of creation, they radiate, in which, regarded as constituents or modes of activity, they concentrate, and at which, if they may be regarded as objects of knowledge, they are enjoyed. We must, in fact, with whatever caution, apply the analogy of the self. The self may be wholly concerned with natural objects, and God with the world. But the self is not simply reducible to the external objects of its concern, though it may be to its concern with them; and if the 'life' of God is to 'live' the world, He is reducible not to the world but to His living of it. But if so, to understand God is not to understand the range of His objects, but the mode of their subjective concentration—or, if this language is unfair, let us simply say, the mode in which these objects either emanate from or enter into the divine activity.

But towards the understanding of this, our hypothesis advances us not an inch. We had hoped that we could make a real distinction of formal and material which would completely divide the field; the material was to be the finites, the formal was to be absolute-activity-as-issuing-in-them. We now discover that the division is incomplete; a mediating term is required, viz. the structural character of such an activity. But this is what traditional theism tries to determine by analogy. Presumably our immanentist does not want to declare either that this has an identical structure with our own activity, or that the two are 'simply diverse' and so God's purely ineffable.

If it is a matter of expressing some difference between the Absolute Activity and ours, it may fairly be claimed that the immanentist is in a position of disadvantage; for he can assign none but unconditionedness, i.e. this quasi-self with its materials must be *in vacuo*; whereas we can assign actual completeness or ideal perfection to the Absolute Activity as it is in itself, and to its creativity, the act of reduction from that infinity to various finitude. Without this specification of creativity, it is hard to see what will keep the creative act from ousting the finite activities from their place, or how one unconditioned activity and several conditioned activities are to 'live' the universe at the same time. And in fact, this sort of immanentism is not averse from confusing them, and telling us that creation consists in the absolute activity's becoming variously the several finites—a Proteus with no shape of his own, and as truly fire, oak, fish and lion, as he is the old man of the sea. This, taken seriously, is a mystification and mythologising beyond what transcendentalist theology has ever proposed. But it is better not to take it seriously, but as simply a hyperbolical expression of the second hypothesis.

The second alternative: the creative activity is not distinct from the finite activities. On this hypothesis, the creative activity has no focus or activity-structure, no mode of unity that is its own. It is multifocal, and its foci are the finite activities. But it then reduces to a set of propositions about the many activities, and ceases to be an activity at all. What are these propositions? (1) That the finite activities abstracted from the context which all supply to each are unthinkable as real; (2) that the system of finites is (on the contrary) complete and equivalent to *that which is*; (3) that the system is actualised, however, in the finite centres or concentrations, and is not a simple extension of parts externally related.

But these propositions are simply a description of the system of finites, and a good description, except that we should like to add to (2) the words: 'on the finite level'. They take no account of the alleged metaphysical necessities which theology envisages; they are not a substitute for, but an ignoring of, theology. The former rôle they can only affect to play by producing the ghost of the alternative hypothesis, and supposing that the many activities somehow express a unity which is wholly immanent in them. But 'wholly immanent' is a nonsense-expression; the unity must be distinct from the plurality, and must be a mode of actuality, i.e. activity, and if so we must be able to state its differentia, either in straight or in analogical terms.

In fact, the only plan for the immanentist, and one which he really follows, is to oscillate with continuous rapidity between the two hypotheses. Now we

ourselves have pleaded guilty to oscillation [1] and shall have to plead guilty to
it again. But then we are admittedly finding analogies for that which transcends
our power to describe, and the only way of delivering ourselves from slavery
to one analogy is to oppose to it another; and the impossibility of synthetising
the two is the measure of the transcendence of our object. But such a procedure
is hardly open to the immanentist. Either we can perform the concrete synthesis, or we cannot. But if not, what has become of his method?

These grave-side tributes may seem gratuitous, when the immanentist
school has taken so macabre a pleasure in elaborating the funeral oration of its
own intelligibility. But it seemed worth while just to point the moral, for the
benefit of those who allow that immanentism is 'nonsense' but assume that
transcendentalism, as being 'more metaphysical', must be greater nonsense
still. This does not follow, for the nonsensicality might arise from the mixed
and impure form of a metaphysic which has not the courage of its convictions;
or if otherwise, still the nature of nonsense can be perhaps more usefully studied
in the pure case, to which therefore we will return.

We have, then, to determine the mode of the absolute activity, we have to
assign it a content, and as that content is not to be found in the finites, it must
presumably be found in some analogy with them. Now in the course of the last
paragraphs it has become clear that what we require is not 'content' in the sense
of material detail; it is a logical content for the description 'absolute activity',
i.e. a further determination of that determinable, through some description of
the type of activity which is the absolute one. There is a certain silliness about
concern with the actual 'detail' of the divine existence. No doubt we do not
intend to reduce the content of the divine life to an abstract simplicity, as perhaps Aristotle meant with his 'intellection of intellection' (the object of the
divine contemplation a pure and abstract form). No doubt it is right to regard
the unity of God as a positive unity which perfectly unifies a content infinitely
rich. But to speculate as to what enters this content is absurd, for how shall we
set about to exhaust infinity by enumeration? Where all is present, what have
we gained by specifying some? The notion of God as *Ens Realissimum*, if that
means a pool of all possible predicates somehow synthetised into one being, is
the most abjectly vulgar of theological ideas. We do not know how these predicates are contained in the mode of perfection which is somehow their archetype,
and to enumerate them is to give an inventory of the world from which we have
drawn them, not of the God to whom we know not how we should assign them.
We must begin the other way about, and having determined as best we may the
nature of the divine activity, assign to it *exempli gratia* such a detail as our
imagination can integrate with it. If we can allow the idea of a self-sufficient
activity, we shall have far less difficulty in believing that it is capable of determining its own detail; we shall hardly find a Christian philosopher whose faith
depends on the possibility of particularising the riches of existence shared by the
Persons of the Blessed Trinity.

[1] *vide supra*, p. 34

(ii) *The Scale of Nature*

We turn therefore to the ascent of the mind towards God, the attempt to approach Him by climbing the scale of creatures, in order that we may somehow advance from the modes that we know to the mode we do not. It has been customary indeed to talk of *the* scale of nature or of creatures as though we could with confidence plot all finite modes on a single line of ascent, so that an anthropoid ape, for example, should lie in the direct line from a baboon to a man, as one note must lie on a single line of ascent or descent when compared with others in the musical scale. Given p and r, is q above, between or below them? The alternatives are exhaustive.

However unplausible the single-track theory may appear, let us pretend it for the moment, and continue to construct the most convenient *scala naturae* imaginable for climbing heaven. By returning presently to the realities, we shall be able to see the full difficulties of our task. That the single-track ladder would be convenient, is indisputable. For then, if we have confidence in our power to arrange the creatures in roughly the right order, we have only to extrapolate upwards, and we shall be sure of going in the right direction; we need not be afflicted with any fears that what we are treating as a universal tendency of being as it ascends, is really the limitation and idiosyncrasy of a certain line of ascent, to which other lines run parallel, each with some other specifying limitation.

We are going to pretend, then, that the track is a single one, and we will add a supposition which will be equally convenient. It is that we are able to observe throughout the rising scale the progressive emergence of a single group of structural characteristics in virtue of which it is that we reckon the order of the creatures. It will then be reasonable to assume that the attainment of absolute expression for this group of characteristics will be the attainment also of absolute Being. To consider the inconvenience of the contrary hypothesis: Suppose that we are able to recognise the order of the creatures as we do the visible colours of the spectrum. Each kind is simply different from others, and though there is a gradual passage between those contiguous, this involves no intelligible serial order over any considerable number of degrees. Characters emerge, attain an acme, and fade out again as we proceed, like the red or the green in the spectrum; and though (unlike the spectrum) the scale reveals progressive elevation, we should be irrational to suppose that the character dominant at the point where the ascent escapes our vision will continue to dominate behind the clouds. On this hypothesis, then, we should be unable to draw from the scale of creatures any inference about the probable character of the divine activity. We could only say that it would be highest, and that we know what relation 'to be higher' is. But this we were supposed to have known already.

If we compare the two convenient hypotheses, it is not difficult to decide which it would be more inconvenient to dispense with. It is the second. Without this we can do nothing at all; whereas even if we lack assurance that the track we are able to follow is the only track, yet if there is continual ascent on that track, we are at least advancing in the right direction—towards, it may be, the determination of one only among the 'infinite attributes' of Spinoza's deity; but that is not nothing. The difference may be illustrated by the following diagrams:

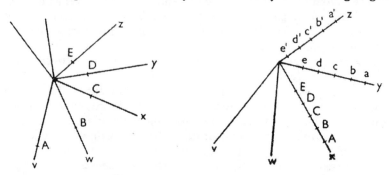

The former diagram represents the first 'convenient hypothesis' without the second; the latter, the second without the first. In the former, we have a series of continuous approximation towards the centre, and yet each term is on a line receding from the centre in a different direction, i.e. represents a different aspect of the divine nature. It is not because E is in the Z line of representation that it is nearer than A, which happens to be on the V line; and the series A-E gives us no power to conjecture what F-N will be like. But in the other diagram, advance from A to E is an ascent in Xness, which is an approximation towards the centre anyhow from one direction, and this is unaffected by the existence of series a-e, a'-e' on other lines.

With these distinctions in mind, let us look at the classical form of the *scala-naturae* doctrine, the doctrine, that is, of the medieval schools. This is not committed to the simple-minded version of the one-track ascent, the baboon-hypothesis mentioned above. But neither does it fall into either of the positions indicated by our two diagrams. There is one ladder of ascent, going in one direction, but it is very wide, so that there is room for an indefinite number of species on any given rung, the baboon and the gorilla may be accommodated side by side. For there are certain structural characteristics which run horizontally right through the order of creatures, so that there is room for difference of mode, i.e. of species, without difference of the structural characteristic. Those that have the same structural characteristic are on the same rung of the ladder, and nothing can help being on one rung or another. And the structural characteristics form a series, such that a certain principle of structure is exemplified with progressive completeness in them as we ascend.

This principle of structure is the principle of the dominant form. In the lower strata of being, form is heavily and confusedly embedded in its matter. To follow the scale upwards is to see its progressive emancipation. The absolute state of form is the absolute state of being. We may here neglect the Thomist subtlety about the angels which are free from material composition and yet not absolute, for it is irrelevant to our point.

But, it will be said, what conclusion does this allow, even if the premises are granted? If we can say that in God form is absolute, how much better off are we for that piece of knowledge? Ah, but it is here that we come to the decisive step. It is claimed for an evident truth that the higher ranges of form possess consciousness. As form is liberated from the darkness of material confusion, it becomes, so to speak, luminous by its own light. The more absolute the form, the more absolute the luminosity. Mind is the development of form, and the development of form is mind. Absolute being is absolute spirituality, whatever more it may be besides.

How, then, is it written: 'We know of God not how He is, but rather how He is not'? It is necessary to emphasise the limited scope of this negation. It refers, ultimately, to the mode in which spirituality exists in God. With this mode we are not and cannot be acquainted. All we can do is (a) barely to assert that His spirituality is absolute, i.e. such as is proportionate to absolute being, (b) to strike out those aspects of our own spirituality which plainly belong to its lowly degree, and so will have no counterpart in God—e.g. dependence on a body. To make these negations is not to know what the absolute counterpart is like; the spirit that we know, divorced from its body, has suffered a privation, and even if we can make the abstraction, we are thereby provided with no idea of such spirit as, by its very nature, excludes dependence on a body. We shall have more to say later about the significance and possibility of these negations.

As (a) is not a description, and (b) contains only negations, we can uphold the proposition that as to the *mode* of God's being (*quomodo Deus est*) we know —or at any rate can state—only what it is not. It is difficult to see how any theology can say otherwise, without gross absurdity. If we wish to state the differentia of the divine mode, we must say that there is in it the counterpart to some only of the aspects of ours, or that it is such an archetype of ours as to exclude its corresponding to aspects of our existence which connote limitations. We conclude, therefore, that this famous proposition in no way prevents medieval doctrine from profiting to the full by its highly convenient scale of creatures, or arriving at the most positive possible account of the Infinite Being.

Such is the mediaeval scheme, and attempts have been made in our time to re-state it from a more or less evolutionary point of view, by Fr. Lionel Thornton, for example. If, in historical fact, higher forms of existence have been imposed upon the lower, and the lower developed to afford the material of the higher, it may seem reasonable to suppose a continuity of order, a progressive perfection of the same principle of activity at the several levels, and the mysterious data of physical, biological and psychological science may permit of such a construction. No one can complain that the attempts should be made; and yet there are two considerations which make us hesitate to assign to it decisive importance in rational theology.

One of these is the position from which we began, and to which we have several times recurred—that rational theology ought to make explicit, and to define, nothing else but what is and what has been implicit in genuine theistic belief. Now it does not seem plausible that the way to God goes round by such a by-pass as is the construction of the *scala naturae*. It would, on the other hand, seem plausible (*a*) that men should be aware of a relation between their own existence and God, and (*b*) should feel bound to interpret this as the instance of a relation between finite existence as such, and God, and so universalise the analogy, recognising God wherever they recognised existence. It is this scheme, anyhow, that we shall concern ourselves with, and not the *scala naturae* in the medieval sense.

The other consideration is, that the claim to be able to construct the *scala* awakens agnostic doubts. The construction appears a good deal less evident than the theology it is supposed to support. The reasons for such agnosticism we will hope to provide when we come to deal with finite substance. We must content ourselves here with a dogmatic summary. That of which we are thus sceptical is the possibility of having sufficient insight into the mode of activity exercised by the other creatures, to construct the scale. That some creatures have an activity 'nobler' than that of others, we can reasonably believe, and that is what was required for the analogy we found it necessary to use above.[1] It is another matter so far to determine the natures of all the creatures' activities, that we can lay out the scale.

For we have direct insight into our own activity alone; of other things not without the analogy of our own, guided by the phenomena of the things. We know indeed by a direct noesis that there is activity in the things—*ESSE est OPERARI*—but it is another matter to determine the mode of that activity. Our ability to specify the activity of other things will be in proportion to their approximation to ourselves. Any scale that we can construct may therefore be condemned beforehand to be a scale in degrees of anthropomorphy. As such, it may have a high proportion of correctness, but it is hardly thereby qualified to determine a scale of real activities, since 'non-anthropomorphic' is not a real character. In proportion as things recede from our own type, a more and more sketchy abstraction from our activity must be applied to them; but this need not mean that their existence is sketchier and sketchier, but only that we are more and more leaving out the real character that it has.

Now it may be that man is truly the measure of all things, but it seems more likely that he is not so in a metaphysical sense, but, in an epistemological, simply has to 'put up with being measure' as Protagoras said to Socrates, ἀνέχειν μέτρῳ ὄντι.[2] Is it not rather naive, then, to accept 'progressive anthropomorphy' as the formula for the scale of creatures, and to conclude that the extrapolation of this line must conduct us in the direction of the absolute mode of being?

[1] p. 34   [2] *Theaetetus*

(iii) *The Interior Scale*

What are we to do, then, and with what scale are we to work? With a scale of briefer compass, but upon which our information (let us hope) is more reliable—a scale within ourselves. Here again we must irritate the reader by referring him forward for a fuller treatment of the subject, and for the present dogmatise, unless we wish the thread of the argument to be lost. We state, then, that our own voluntary conscious acts form a continuous scale of ascent and descent. They are not all voluntary, conscious, or even acts in the same degree or sense. Nor can one draw the line at a certain level, and say that these characters are found above but not below it. Downwards they sink towards a vanishing-point; upwards it is difficult to assign a limit to the possible enhancement of rationality and freedom.

Now this scale has, compared with the other alleged scale of creatures, one decisive advantage: it slides, or, if you like, our existence slides up and down it. By contrast, I cannot slide up and down between what it is to be an amoeba, and what it is to be a man; still less can the amoeba. So that the scale of modes within our own activity is likely to be the indispensable clue to any scale of activity whatever. If in ourselves the continuous activity, by sliding, produces several modes, this will have something to do with our tendency, above noted, to recognise several species of creatures as modes of a fundamental something which we called activity-as-such. We would recommend the sceptic to pronounce this tendency to be an instance of projection, but we for our part will experiment with the hypothesis that it is legitimate interpretation by the clue of a just analogy.

Within our own life, then, there is a scale, and the ascent through this scale is not only logical or metaphorical, as is the ascent up the scale of creatures; it is an actual movement, a movement which, in running through degrees, increasingly realises the forms of apprehension (objective grasp of realities), rationality (appropriate response to them) and will (freedom).

But suppose that these facts are granted: this scale may be real, but how can anything of so slight a compass be used as evidence for the tendency of all being, and the system of the universe? This question requires a double answer:

(I) We long ago agreed that there is no question of demonstrating God from the creatures by a pure inference. God, being an unique existent, must be apprehended if He is to be known at all. But it appeared that He must be apprehended in the cosmological relation and not in abstraction from it, and that if we were to be able to have any discourse about His nature, we must be able to set it in analogy with some aspect of the finite. We are still engaged in the attempt to express that nature. We must not then forget that we have set aside dialectic and all argument designed to commend the cosmological idea; we are simply examining its structure. We have made the hypothesis that God is apprehended, and are asking how this happens. And at the present stage of our search we have seen the necessity for some positive character which it must be

supposed that we carry up from finite modes to God. We hoped that the religious mind is not so unreasonable as arbitrarily to select a phase of finitude
and predicate it of the infinite; and so we looked for what we lacked in some
characteristic that appears to increase and progressively to realise itself through
some scale of being. We considered the claims of a scale of all creatures to be this
scale, but rejected it on two grounds: (a) that it is a sophisticated construction,
which hardly can have been implicit in the faith of the simple; (b) that it is probably an artificial construction, drawing all its positive elements from elsewhere,
so that it cannot really contribute anything even to those who are not simple.

All that we need, then, is a scale which is (a) relevant to men's theological
thinking in general, (b) genuine; and these qualifications seem to belong to the
internal scale which we are sponsoring. As to (a), how can that fail to be relevant with which the act of aspiration is directly connected? Is it not when we
have ascended to the height of our powers of apprehension, rationality and will
that we 'aspire' beyond them to the ideal of them? But for the interior scale,
would this aspiration be possible? Had we but one determined level of activity,
is it conceivable that we should be led to distinguish what belongs to our
limited essence *qua* men from the line of ascent through it towards its infinite
source? Aspiration is inseparable from the internal scale.

As to the place occupied by the scale in the order of being, it may be of
use to refer back to our two diagrams.[1] In the former of these, we have represented the hypothesis that there is indeed a rising scale of creatures, but that
each represents the divine nature in a different aspect, so that an approximation
towards God *in that aspect* would trace a separate line from each creature towards Him. Suppose we assume that the creation is such—there cannot be two
sorts of creatures on one line, but only the same sort in a more and a less perfect
exemplification. Were this so, then the only possible scale of ascent which
would reveal a continuous line would be the ascent of a given creature, for
example, of E a series E_1, E_2, E_3. And if the only God who presents Himself to
our apprehension presents Himself through such a scale, then our reason for
believing that the upward direction of the scale gives an indication of His
nature is as good as our reason for believing in God at all.

Descartes, then, was nearly right when he rejected the scale of nature and
found in the self a sufficient divine 'image'—that is, sufficient (finite) material
for arriving at the notion of God through it. Only nearly right, because in spite
of his language about aspiration and upward tendency he so emphasised the
simplicity and pure rationality of the self as to miss the vital importance of the
interior scale; and because we do apply the analogy of several distinct creatures
of various level, in order to understand that God is not human spirit to the
Nth, but a different being.[2]

In short, then, the first of the two answers promised above is that the
internal scale, being real and being the actual indicator through which aspiration
descries God, is sufficient. This may seem to raise problems about the relation

[1] p. 42   [2] *vide supra*, p. 34

of other creatures to God. These we will deal with presently, but must give next attention to our second answer.

(II) In the present stage of our analysis, we have taken the bare notion of absolute being, or activity, as already established, and are proceeding to characterise such being, so far as we can. But we must remember that such order is logical only, not real in any way. It is not a real possibility that anyone should come to apprehend the bare notion of 'that degree of activity which is supreme' without giving to it any character. We may use the illustration, so far as it applies, of Kant's *a priori*. His *a priori* forms were, as he knew, detached by us only through abstraction. In spite of their transcendental priority, they make themselves known to us originally as applied to the manifold of experience and filled with it. Apart from such complete experience, there would be no possibility of knowing them.

Similarly for us: if God presents Himself to some sort of apprehension, what we apprehend of Him first will not be a high abstraction difficult to hold pure in the mind even when we have made it. This abstract form, though logically prior, will be found *applied*. What is meant by this logical priority and this application? We made a sketch of it when we showed that God's absoluteness attaches primarily to His activity or existence.[1] God, the absolute form of existence, is apprehended in the instance 'my existence'.[2] But for all that, it is *qua* absolute form of existence *in general* that God is the cause of my existence, for the notion of creaturely dependence has been seen to be bound up with God's being simply absolute, not absolute in some genus; and but for the presence of this form to our aspiration, that aspiration would be simply towards a being capable of performing the spiritual operations of which we feel ourselves to come short. God, then, is grasped as 'the absolute Being, archetype of human spirit'—neither of these without the other.

But will not this mean that all the character we can give to our notion of God belongs to Him only in so far as He is the archetype of ourselves, and of other things in so far only as they resemble us? That only the bare form of absolute existence or activity describes the God of the universe, while the characters of spirituality describe our God alone? The suggestion is that expressed in the figure:

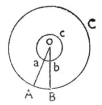

[1] p. 31

[2] It says nothing to this, that we may not be impressed first by *our* createdness. Where the existence of something impresses us, we apprehend God, for we interpret that existence by the clue of our own. That we should explicitly recognise in 'projection' what we have not yet so recognised in its original, is sufficiently instanced and no difficulty.

Let AB represent the place occupied in creation by such activity as ours, and ACB that occupied by other sorts. Then our knowledge of God as spiritual will represent *abo* of His nature, while *acbo* remains unaccounted for. But if so, how can we venture to pronounce that God *is* spirit or person? To this fallacious suggestion of quantitative comparison we must reply, that spirituality of its very nature characterises the complete form of an unitary being and cannot be a detail in some other synthesis, or an element of material for some other form. God, therefore, is through and through spiritual, and unimpededly so; whatever other aspects His activity may have cannot dilute this. And since spirituality is of general scope, all things are related to God as spirit in so far as He wills, loves and knows them, though it may not be His spirituality that they represent in the inferior mode.

It may not be, but then again, it may. With regard to the possible 'infinite attributes' of God, we must show a pious agnosticism more complete than Spinoza's. We eschewed the *scala-naturae* argument as lacking evidence, but the opposite view equally lacks evidence and must do so, from the very nature of our understandings. We can but think as we can think, and what is outside our scope is not capable of discussion.

V

THE WAY OF NEGATION

(i) *The Scale and the Idea*

THE previous chapter consisted of general considerations about the function of our own existence as *imago Dei*, and argued that such a function may reasonably be attached to it. We have still to show in more detail how it functions and what knowledge about God we can hope to attain through the use of it. Such an exposition requires two stages. First we have to see how we ascend, as it were, within ourselves to the top of ourselves in the act of fulfilling our own nature; what it is that ascends, and what sort of top it attains. Then second, we have to take this summit of the human spirit, and discover in what way it can be further elevated to stand as an indication of the divine nature.

In these two stages of the argument we shall be pursuing the same aim. What we have to do is to purge human nature of those aspects which are inapplicable to deity; but to this end we propose to employ two instruments in turn. First we see how far the ascent of man within his own scale can show us what is capable of further ascent and what must be left behind as transcended. Secondly we ask what modifications to the height of human ascent are imposed by the application thereto of the idea of a Supreme Being.

Omnis determinatio est negatio. In any creature there must be a distinction, evident at least to the divine mind, between that reality by which it represents an aspect of God, and the limitation which makes it other than God. To call the limitation purely negative may not be right, if we consider that there is some positive purpose served by the existence of the creatures in distinctness from God, and that the limitation is a condition of their distinct existence. Reality must, as it were, be translated into a medium of finitude to be anything distinct from God. So that limitation is positive for the fact of the existence of the creatures, but negative for their representation of the divine nature.

Now we cannot purge out the limitation so as to have the reality pure, for reality can exist pure only as the divine reality; yet we may hope to make within the finite a purely notional distinction between aspects of limitation and aspects of positivity. While leaving these to complement one another as before, we remember that some are positively the representation of God, and others the medium which makes the representation other than Him and so a representation.

The model which suggests itself for such a distinction is phenomenal abstraction,[1] e.g. the abstraction of colour from spatial extension, and *vice versa*. It is unlikely, however, that anything so exact can be hoped for here. In order to be the mode we know it for, reality requires the limiting finitude it has. The formula for phenomenal abstraction seems to be substitutibility; it is

---

[1] *vide supra*, p. 21

49

because we can substitute other phenomenal fillings of extension for a coloured filling, that we can abstract extension. But does the form of voluntary freedom, for example, have such substitutible limitations that we can abstract it? No doubt freedom can, in a sense, have substitutible limitations, e.g. chains or a prison, a habit of smoking or a habit of alcoholism. But each member of these pairs belongs to the same mode of limitation as its opposite member, and it is from the modes of limitation themselves that we are trying to abstract. It belongs intrinsically to the free activity which we know, to have physical limits and to be limited by habit. These sorts of limit are not substitutible but complementary, and we cannot abstract from them. A man whose physical conditions are convenient and whose habits are disciplined is not limited so painfully, but he still is limited by the habitual and the physical, for these things belong to the pattern of existence as known to us. How, then, can we abstract from them?

There is no question of the substitution of one limitation for another, but there is possible an increasing satisfactoriness in the relation of our activity to its limitations, and the fact that we are aware of this shows that we can and do distinguish between that which is positive and that which limits it. In the case of phenomenal abstraction, we are looking at the external and simply given; coloured extension is given as one for us, and we have no dynamic empowering us to divide it but such as arises in us from comparison of it with an extension which is not coloured. But in the case of voluntary activity and its limitations, we are not spectators of the externally given, into the inner drama of whose existence (if any) we have no insight. We are contemplating that which we are, and therefore we do not need several instances with substitutible 'shapes' or 'fillings' in order that comparison may supply the dynamic for distinction. The dynamic is in our existence; we *are* the act of will asserting itself as well as it may against its limitation, and therefore we are very well capable of a notional distinction between freedom and what contains it. That does not mean that we are capable of a pure abstraction of freedom, of conceiving it as abstracted from the field of limitation proper to the existence of men 'in their earthly pilgrimage' and as supplied with a substitute-field. On the contrary, if freedom and its limitation are felt as opposites, it is a case of 'dialectical interdependence of opposites'. Freedom is felt as distinct because it actively copes with such a field of limitation, but we cannot actually conceive it as doing otherwise.

The notion of 'coping with its limitation' involves that of the interior scale. If freedom can cope with limitation, it does so by realising a higher degree or mode of activity which places it in a more satisfactory relation to its own limitation; and this is to rise in the interior scale.

The unique position of the mind in face of its own activity results immediately in the formation of an unique sort of abstraction to represent its positive aspects. Phenomenal abstraction naturally yields a description containing a blank with a limited number of alternative fillings, e.g. phenomenal extension (coloured? touch-felt? etc.). With equal propriety, this other abstraction yields an '*idea*', a perfectly unique mental type, the notion of e.g. the endeavour and positive direction of freedom as such—more simply, of freedom itself. Its structure corresponds to its nature; it is not distinguished from its conditions by a blank that can be diversely filled but by that dynamic distinction we have referred to, and therefore the dynamism of real action must continue to tingle in the image by which we know it. But so long as the distinction is there, it is sufficient for the purpose we have in hand. It is possible for the mind to mark this as having a counterpart in the divine being, its limitedness as having none; though it will remain (as we predicted) unable to construct or imagine that counterpart in any way, being unable to assign to freedom a different field from that which it has in us.

But however applicable to theology once it has been obtained, the 'idea' arises quite independently of any theology through the consideration of human activity as such. To think it fully, we need only the thought of its limitations and its scale, and an aspiration involving the bare notion of an indefinite upward extrapolation of the scale. We do, perhaps, in merely thinking the idea think of the goal of its perfect realisation, as that towards which it aspires; the extrapolation is vaguely thought to be carried to a point at which freedom obtains complete mastery of its tools. But we can perfectly well think of freedom while accepting a merely problematic definition of this point; it is just such a point of elevation (whatever that point would be) as allows freedom complete mastery. The believer may say, if he chooses, that any attempt at a more positive definition of this point must turn out to be a description of the Absolute Being: a contention which will be considered in the last section of this book. If he likes, he can even describe this state of affairs by saying that the awareness of freedom is the confused or implicit knowledge of God; but only in the sense that the knowledge of a problem is the implicit knowledge of its solution.

A further step and a different form of argument is necessary if we are to pass from the problematic to the defined knowledge of God; and this necessity is foreshadowed in the form of orthodox belief itself. Knowledge of God would be contained in the fact of human aspiration simply, if the natural goal of that aspiration were to become God. But it was the Devil and not the unperverted conscience that said 'Eritis sicuti dii'. The human will, in aiming to realise the freedom of which it is capable, 'implicitly' aims (says orthodoxy) at a cooperative dependence upon the divine will; and so does not 'implicitly contain' the form of God as the continuous development of its own being. In so far, then, as the will is an implicit theologian, its awareness is not of the problem 'What do I naturally aspire to be, in myself?' but of the problem, 'What is the object that will satisfy me?' And this second problem is to be answered not by raising the question about my will in isolation, but by raising the question about the Supreme Being and therefore the question of the cosmological idea

As it is with the will, so it is with the intellect. It is plain to us that our awareness of other realities (things in themselves) is mediated and filtered through sense-signs and terminological interpretations. With and in these there is some grasp of the noümenon, and Kant was wrong to reserve all noesis for a purely 'intuitive understanding', of which we can have no real notion. But noesis is related to its clumsy instruments as freedom to its limitations. There is no question of getting rid of them, or of conceiving a noesis independent of them—there Kant was right. But whence, on Kant's view, the ideal even of the 'intuitive understanding', or the notion of the thing-in-itself? Is it not that noesis, like freedom, is dynamically distinct from its conditions, which it struggles to use to its own best advantage, so generating a scale of ascending noesis, characterised by a progressively more satisfactory relation between noesis and its instruments, though there is no question of its dispensing with those instruments or so much as conceiving itself without them?

The parallel of noesis and freedom need not be further drawn out; what has already been said of the latter in its function of *imago Dei* will apply equally to the former, and it is time that we proceeded to the second part of our task— the application to the 'ideas' of the notion of an Absolute Being. Or should we first make a list of the 'ideas'? But are there any, beyond the two that we have mentioned—the perfections of intellect and of will (creativity)? The further aspects of spirit are contained in these: *delight* in their fulfilment, *goodness* in their realisation of their own principles, *love* in their pure interest in and foster- ing of their objects, and enjoyment of *beauty* in the contemplation and creation of the forms of things. All these appear to us to be aspects of the idea, and ends of aspiration, and predicable—so far as we can yet determine—of God.

(ii) *Proportionality*

Such then is the material offered by the human self. As we seek further to purify it, we fall naturally into the four-term formula: As our spirituality is appropriate to our level of finite being, so will God's spirituality be to God's infinite being. This is the traditional formula of *proportionality* in contradis- tinction from *proportion*. Proportion is the relation of any two terms which are related in degree; the description must be accepted in a wide sense, so as to include under 'degree' the relation of absolute and finite, as well as that of several finites. So then all finite activities are in proportion to God, however shocking that may sound according to the common use of the word. Where we think of God as 'the absolute activity' we are using a scheme of simple propor- tion, though of course in a highly abstract manner.

Proportionality, on the other hand, is a relation of four terms (it might be three, but that does not concern us). Its traditionally 'most perfect' form com- pares two creaturely terms in mutual relation with two divine terms in mutual relation. For example, as creaturely intelligence to creaturely existence, so divine intelligence to divine existence. This formula presupposes three terms determinate and one indeterminate and sets out to determine this indeterminate (viz. the modality of divine intelligence) by means of the comparison. It pre- supposes that intelligence can be attributed to God, and declares how it is to be understood when it is attributed to Him and not to the creature, viz. as differing from its creaturely mode with a difference analogous to that by which the divine existence differs from the creaturely. And so it presupposes also the 'proportion' between the two 'existences'.

This proportionality claims to hold between four terms, and not two relations. We are not saying: 'The way in which the divine intelligence is related to the divine existence resembles the way in which the creaturely intelligence is related to the creaturely existence', for that is exactly what we have to deny. The way in which the several aspects of the divine being (e.g. intelligence) have their synthesis into one, itself differs from the way in which the several aspects of the creaturely being have their synthesis into one, *as* the divine being itself differs from the creaturely. What we are saying is completely different, viz. 'Divine intelligence is appropriate to divine existence as creaturely to creaturely.' We do also use in theology an apparently four-termed comparison which is really the simple comparison of two relations, as when we say that the relation of the creature to God is like the relation of accident to substance, etc., but that is another matter.

Proportion logically underlies proportionality, but this need not mean that we originally entertain the notion of the proportion 'divine existence/creaturely existence' except as the foundation for a proportionality; the two are distinguished by philosophical analysis only. This would harmonise with the conclusions of the last chapter. The natural use of the proportion is inseparable from that of the proportionality, as the apprehension of the very fact of the divine being is inseparable from some apprehension of its mode.

The scheme of proportionality looks as uninformative as it is unexceptionable. Whatever mode of activity is referred to God (e.g. intelligence) must be referred through this scheme; but we cannot do the sum which the formula appears to propose to us. As 5 to 13, so X to 117. Then $X = 45$. And the theological proportionality would be equally handy if the notion of absolute existence were a notion of what the absolute mode of existence is. In that case, we could, so to speak, write down its number, and work the sum. But *ex hypothesi* we do not know what the absolute mode of existence is; it is precisely this that the proportionalities are called in to begin determining. And so the scheme of proportionality has something fraudulent about it, when it is given this mathematical appearance. Only God could use it; and He does not need it.

Yet proportionality is not indefensible, and we shall defend it under two heads:

(I) If proportionality describes an operation which we are unable to perform, and declares that exact knowledge of God would be obtained by performing it, does it therefore give us no information? Does it not at least sketch out an area or a direction in which the truth lies? And may not this be, in fact, the best information that we can get? In order to obtain the abstraction of 'absoluteness', I must let all modalities slip through my fingers, and attach that notion to the bare idea of existence-(=activity-)-as-such. In order to recover modality, I must let go of absoluteness; and yet I know that God is where these meet. I can see no intrinsic absurdity in the notion of their meeting; on the contrary, the naturalness of theism is the naturalness of supposing that they do. And I can see why I, as a finite mind, should in the nature of the case be unable to reach the meeting-place.

Further there is the general consideration that this puzzle arises only in the (finite) terms with which we are bound to express the unique Divinity if we are to have any discourse about Him at all. That which originally comes to bear on the mind is not the scheme of proportionality, but God as active in us, a reality which drives the mind to such straits as these in the effort to comment upon it. Comment is an ill-chosen word if it suggests something optional and extrinsic. This comment is internal, and necessary to any distinct apprehension. We shall deal at length with this. It was necessary to have just mentioned it here.

(II) Although proportionality does not offer us, in the notion of absolute being, the 'number by which the sum can be worked', it does offer in that notion certain factors which can be applied to the finite analogue to fit it the better for its analogic function, and so does not disappoint us entirely. This brings us back to our self-appointed task of purifying or elevating the ideas of human spirit. We were to discover whether the mere idea of absolute being would afford us criteria for this purpose. It will do so, but these are necessarily negative. Since the mere notion of an absolute being is not a notion of what sort that being is (it is this we are trying to add by the aid of our human 'ideas'), it cannot make any positive contribution. But we can take several aspects of the 'ideas' and ask ourselves whether the attribution of them to an infinite being can be entertained. And so we may hope to carry further the process of 'notional distinction' by which, in the concrete fact of human activity, we mark certain aspects as unworthy of God, without being able actually to abstract them and leave the remainder.

The most convenient way to conduct this experiment is to begin by deducing certain aspects of the notion of absolute being as already known to us. It may be easier to apply them to the ideas than so to apply the notion as a whole. What we seek to learn from the ideas is something about the general form of the divine being, for spirituality is a general form of activity, able to cope with an indefinite 'matter' of experienced and enacted detail. Let us therefore suppose such a form as exemplified in an absolute being, and see whether we can state anything about it *a priori*. For this purpose we may consider it in three relations: (*a*) its relation to its own 'matter', (*b*) its relation to anything outside it, (*c*) its relation to possible matters, i.e. its scope.

(*a*) Its relation to its own matter or constituents is one of perfect unity or *simplicity*. It belongs to the notion of the absolute being to exclude 'accident', mere side-by-sideness, compositeness; for this, by contrast with what is organically one, is seen to be the very type of the arbitrary or non-self-explanatory.

(*b*) Its relation to beings other than itself is one of complete independence or *self-sufficiency*. For the absolute being is fully what it is in and by itself; other things are its mere effects without reciprocal action upon their effector.

(*c*) Its relation to all possible matters must be that of *universality*; its scope, *qua* form of activity, must intrinsically be such as not to be restricted to this or that, but to concern itself with being *qua* being. If there are any possibilities that the divine being does not apprehend and actualise within itself, it will be not because of any positive characteristics which fall outside the scope of the divine activity, but because they add nothing to what is already actualised there, but merely dilute it with negations.

We will now apply these three criteria to the 'ideas'.

(iii) *The Negative Criteria*

(*a*) *Simplicity*. The acceptance of this criterion does not mean that we are committed to a 'classicist' or formalist view of the divine nature. In so far as there is no collocation of form with detail, formal limitation evaporates as truly as material does, it ceases to be a distinction within the divine nature. It is absurd to think of God as a finite being that has impoverished itself by endeavouring as far as possible to regiment under 'form' all the material of its life: a human pedant, for example. The notion of God is the notion of richness without accident. Accident belongs to the finite, and to eliminate it would be to impoverish the finite, were such elimination in fact possible. But though we are obliged to remember that the richness, inseparable for the finite from accident and collocation, has its archetype in God, yet if we are endeavouring to conceive the mode of the divine existence, no form of collocation is an analogue.

If we try to apply this criterion in an absolute form to the finite activity which is offered as *imago Dei*, we shall of course simply strike it out. Even the unity of the finite is a head of division, it distinguishes itself against a plurality which it fails to organise. Nevertheless, finite substances hold together and are themselves more by reason of their unitary structure than their manifoldness; indeed in virtue of that structure they are something, and the aspect of formal unity in the structure can be distinguished by a notional distinction and held to represent the mode of the divine being in a way that its (always actually implied) material plurality does not. There is not much mystery about this, and we need go through no logical agonies to conceive how the unity of formal structure comes to be abstracted, since it happens to be the typical instance of abstraction. That there is real formal structure in the finite substance, and not merely artificial schemes by which we construe our objects, will be shown when we are treating of finite substance.

The image of the divine unity, then, must be the structural aspect of the self, the pattern or system of the spiritual ideas (or rather, of their objects). But the proper use of this criterion is in the purification of these ideas. Thus the mere distinction which we made between the idea and its limitations we made on dynamic grounds; limitations are as they are felt to limit. But the criterion of unity requires us to strip away whatever falls under the formal objection that it involves sheer collocation—for example, spatial extension and temporal sequence.

At this point a cry is often raised: Deity is being made inconceivable. But whoever said that Deity was conceivable? When God is exempted from the form of time it is not meant that His existence is like certain objects sometimes supposed by us to be indifferent to the time with which they are correlative, e.g. a geometrical axiom (*sicut aeterna veritas*). It means that His existence is like what full-blooded activity would be, could it be expressed (which by us it plainly cannot) in a most full-blooded and consequently non-temporal mode. If we wish to conceive the divine activity, we must undoubtedly conceive it as temporal and have full licence to do so. We are merely warned that in our conceived image it is the activity not the temporality that represents God.

It is the habit of some theologians to say that there are certain experiences or states in which we are on the way to escaping duration and so at a halfway house to God's eternity. This manoeuvre is of no value except to comfort the hearts of those who find the rigours of the *via negativa* excessive. Philosophically it is pernicious in that it blurs the lines of rational theology and sets us on an impossible quest which is bound to disappoint us—the *Schwärmerei* which hopes to reduce analogies to true images. The type of instance selected is a man listening to music who is so absorbed as to lose awareness of durational flux. But what of it? This is nothing but an extreme case of abstraction. He so attends to the form of the tune as to abstract from the plain fact that this form (not to mention his reception of it) is by its very nature displayed in durational succession. The selective attention which we call abstraction is the glory and the misery of the human mind; we can only suppose that, though it is necessary to take things thus to pieces in order to understand them, it is equally necessary to put them together again in order to know them. If to abstract from duration is to approximate to eternity, the imitation of God would not be anything very impressive; drug-addicts and maniacs might have a privileged approach to Deity.

The only even partial image of eternity is an activity which can span time and hold it together (so to speak) and not be simply at its mercy, and of this the musician may be an instance; but not in virtue of his abstraction from the durational character of the reality.

True mysticism does not come into this argument. In religious contemplation, the believer must suppose, there is through and with all images some noesis of the supreme noümenon, God Himself. In so far as mysticism is a privileged heightening of the noesis, it is a fuller grasp of Him who is eternal. But that has nothing to do with finite analogies, or with terms of discourse. It may be that this musician who is so insistently proposed to us is a mystic *per accidens*, and wittingly or unwittingly contemplates God through the figure of the music. In that case he also has the ineffable noesis, but not *qua* musician.

The three criteria can be employed each in three ways: distinctionally, synthetically and comparatively. Of these the first is the most important, and we have already illustrated it. Wherever it is possible to mark off a single aspect, e.g. the form of temporal succession, as condemned by the criterion, we make this distinction, and there is the distinctional use of the criterion. But sometimes there falls under that condemnation a form of plurality or composition which it is not so easy to name by a name, or to distinguish from the unity which it divides. For example, intellect and will are in us paradoxically separate though mutually conditioned. Now if we like we can give the name 'spirit' or some other name to the activity which finds expression in this curiously double form, and the name 'intellect-will division' to the form of disunity or compositeness which thus divides it. We may then make our notional distinction between 'spirit' and 'intellect-will division', asserting the former of God and denying the latter. But this is a doubly unnatural way of proceeding; for intellect-will division is not a form which we ever think of as a form—as we do of temporality or corporeity—it is simply a function of intellect and will as we know them. And on the other side we have no full idea of a something unitary which is expressed in this divided way and labelled 'spirit'. On the contrary, we start naturally from the two things divided, intellect and will; and the effect of the criterion is synthetic, for we see that this mutual externality of the two faculties will violate the divine simplicity. But though in appearance synthetic, this application of the criterion remains really negative. In the whole pattern of finite intellect and will it negates a certain externality of the one to the other. It does not supply any actual mode of synthesis.

When the distinctional method has been over-drastically employed, the synthetic may appear to act as a corrective; but this is accidental, and shows merely that the use of the first method has been incorrect. For example: we may by the distinctional method set aside sensation from the divine way of cognition because it involves passivity and so (to anticipate) offends against the second criterion. But if this leaves us supposing that God's knowledge is abstract, it is time we resorted to the synthetic method and reminded ourselves that the positive moment of concreteness and immediacy belonging to sensation, and that of activity and penetration belonging to thought, are united in the one divine act. But we ought never to have supposed, to start with, that the rejection of sensation meant that of immediate and concrete apprehension but only of corporeal passivity.

Thirdly, the negative criteria can be applied comparatively. For example, we know that activity with time struck out is not possible for us to conceive, and so, while remembering that God is in fact non-temporal, we seek an image for Him in that activity which is most advantageously related to its temporal medium, contrasting it with another that is less so. We then say that God is more like the first than the second, and that all of Him is like our best. This was that 'only even partial image of eternity' mentioned above. It hardly needs showing that this use of the criterion is essentially as negative as the other two; for it is completely secondary to them and does no more than apply them to the finite scale to extract an image less exact but more easily conceivable.

(b) *Self-sufficiency*. The distinctional application sets aside the whole aspect of our activity which makes it dependent on previously existing objects and conditions. God wills and knows all He is, and is all He wills and knows. He is in real relation to nothing in the sense that nothing outside Him conditions His activity.

Everything else is in real relation to God but for whom it would not be. But in so far as Creation is an act which produces an expression of the Absolute in the inferior mode, it excludes any dependence of the Absolute on what is created or on the activity of creating. Neither can there be any conditionedness of an agent by what exists simply because he acts, and otherwise does not exist. Those who wish to make theology easier for the imagination by receding from this position, have removed every metaphysical reason for believing in God at all. There may be other reasons, and if there are men who have had particular experience of an eminent archangel, let them come forward and depose their testimony. God may condescend to the creature and make His activity wait on ours; that is another matter. He who condescends must be free and absolute in himself. The condescension of God does not belong to rational theology. Revealed theology is about little else.

The apparent bleakness of these negations is relieved by the aid of the synthetic method. Solipsistic mania cannot be the image of God; the reality of disinterested love and objective knowledge must be brought within the divine being, and only the form of externality denied of these things as we know them. We must remind ourselves that the 'selfishness' of self-love is its irrational partiality; the ideal of love is to be a steady care for all being in so far as it is, or can by us be helped to be. But God loves Himself not for the accidental reason that it is Himself, but for the essential reason that it is the fullness of being, the height of perfection. This statement seems to be sufficient; and so we cannot on grounds of reason alone assert what reason none the less does not exclude, that the organic unity of the divine being may include the analogue of human society without mutual externality or accidental collocation of persons, just as it includes the analogue of intellect and will, without that mutual externality of the two 'faculties' which we find in ourselves. The former concept is of course much more difficult than the latter, because while the tendency of the will and intellect towards unity is a fact even in us, the tendency of friends towards numerical identity of being is not (in spite of all that theologians have unwisely urged) anything better than a bad metaphor. And so the doctrine of the plurality (let alone trinity) of divine Persons is not more than an even probability apart from particular revelation.

Comparatively applied, the criterion of self-sufficiency tells us that the activities in which the human spirit (through greater dominance over its matter, but not through any cramping abstraction) is more self-sufficient are more like God than others. Such an application demands very great discretion. For we are social beings, and in a thousand other ways dependent on what is outside us for the data of our proper and indeed our highest activity. There is certainly nothing godlike in the timidity which is afraid to contract strong personal ties for fear that destiny may sever them, or in the self-contained meanness that is incapable of desiring them. But we may judge unfavourably the man whose affections and interests are tied by the mere particularity of habit, and incapable of reorientation when the objects on which they happen to have fastened are removed. Inconsolable bereavement which finds no further good in anything earns our pity but not our approbation; like the tradesman or the hobbyist who, denied the tools of his particular craft, can find himself in no other. And in general, those activities or experiences in which we leave it to environment to amuse, satisfy and direct us are less deiform than those in which, with whatever dependence on materials, we achieve our own good.

(c) *Universality.* The distinctional application reminds us that the ideas are of universal scope only in their highest abstraction. It is the innate tendency of knowledge, will, love, delight to concern themselves with being as being; but in us this is merely the tendency of powers working outwards from a limited area of interest and identified with the range and destiny of a mortal body. The very principle of our activity is selection; as a box must be emptied of one content to receive another, so in us concern with one thing excludes concern with another. But in God there is not preoccupation; He is concerned with everything in so far as it exists, or rather, it exists in so far as He is concerned with it. It is not even proper to say that He is concerned with one thing more than another, except in the sense that there is more in one thing than another for Him to be concerned with. His concern for each is complete, and adequate to its existence; on each omnipotence is brought to bear. God's concern with several things cannot conflict in Him; but only in the finite sphere where in virtue of their own finitude they run against one another. If God wills the survival of the boy rather than of the sparrows when the boy shoots the sparrows for food, then only does His concern with one take precedence of His concern with the other. But in the concerns that make up the divine life as it is in itself apart from all creatures, not even such a conflict can arise.

The synthetic application of this criterion is perhaps merely corrective. For us, universality is obtained by practical detachment and theoretic abstraction; we can only attend to many things, by attending to them as a class of *such* things, and neglecting their individuality as this, that and the other. But the universality of the divine mind and will combines the reality of our particular, with the breadth of our generalising, acts.

Comparatively, the application of this criterion follows very closely that of the last, and requires the same caution in its use.

(iv) *Conclusion*

The purpose of this chapter has been to show how the reason proceeds in arriving at the familiar characteristics of Deity as Spirit, knowledge, will, goodness, love, joy; as simple, impassible, eternal, infinite, self-sufficient, omnipotent, and so forth. It has not been our object to say all that can be said about these attributes; that would involve a needless repetition of traditional conclusions, or else a pious meditation upon them. But we have wished to show the following facts about them:

(i) The attributes do not all stand on a level. Some are aspects of the function of being the supreme existent simply; some are elements of our spirituality referred to God; some are negations attached to these to fit them for that reference.

(ii) The accusation levelled against the traditional negative theology, that it makes the doctrine of God cold, abstract and dead, and belongs to a shadowy metaphysic irreconcilable with living faith, is unjust. Faith is just as concerned as is speculation with the eternity and omnipotence of God, and speculation is no more inclined than faith to understand these attributes in a sense exclusive of a fully personal life. The negative theology does not assert negations of God; it merely denies limitations of Him.

(iii) A more pointed accusation is that which complains that God is made simply inconceivable. Yet this is not the fault of the negative theology. God is (in the sense implied) inconceivable, and it is necessary to face this fact; any doctrine that says otherwise must fall into limitless absurdities. And it is important to have realised this, even if at first the experience is dismaying. But the real purpose of the negative theology is to provide a rule for thinking about God without confusion, in the limited sense in which we are able to think about Him at all. God is more perfectly one than any real being, and yet we are condemned to think of Him piecemeal, by attributing to Him some analogy with several aspects of finitude, aspects which we are unable to synthesise in the divine unity. The negative theology explains to us the necessity and the structure of this piecemeal thinking, and why its apparent paradoxes are not contradictions. So far from limiting the conception of God, it emboldens us to positive conceiving; for it enables us to see (for example) that the timelessness of God does not preclude us from using as the image of His being acts which in us have a temporal form.

It remains that the act of thinking the divine perfection strains to the uttermost the powers of the human mind. How could it be otherwise, if God is God? In this act there is no rest; to think of the divine perfection is always to have taken our start from various and impure finitude and to be in the process of purifying and simplifying it in the direction of the absolute and the one. But we have never arrived; as we seem on the point to do so, our thought evaporates in the emptiness of mathematical unity, or, as happens to some, passes into an ecstasy and ceases to be thinking. If we wish to think on, we must return humbly to the bottom of the ladder, and climb again.

In this act there is no rest—no rest for our faculties, for the discoursing mind. And yet there is rest for the spirit, which through the act of discourse maintains contact with that which alters not, and acquiesces in it. Either we accept our theology, or we do not. If we accept it, we shall do so because in the act of discourse we think we exercise an act of noesis which through the discourse apprehends the object. The discourse is concerned with the manipulation of terms. Only thus is God known, but to know Him is not to know the terms. Yet what we know in knowing Him cannot be further stated. Written philosophy is of the terms.

We have now given some account of the cosmological idea, under the three divisions—(1) Nature of the relation: (2) Comparison of the terms, subdivided into (a) comparison in respect of the mere aspects referred to by the words 'infinite and finite being', (b) comparison in respect of nature. Under the two heads of comparison we have considered explicitly the absolute term; but it has been evident throughout that to do so is to compare, and to determine the deficiency of the finite in determining the eminence of the absolute.

Is it still necessary to explain the statement that we know God as the agent of His activities in the creature, and not otherwise? Perhaps it might be useful, if only for restoring the balance, since our recent preoccupation with the comparison of the terms may have let the actual relation slide into the background. And emphasis on 'aspiration' may have tended to suggest that there is an ascent of the mind to God independent of the act by which God causes the mind to descend from Himself, that is, to exist as distinct from Him.

But aspiration is, and knows itself to be, a tracing over in inverse direction of the real creative relation, and this becomes evident when we examine what it is that the aspiring mind is able to say about its divine object. It must use itself as the *imago Dei*, and can add to this no fresh content; it can simply apply to it the notion of creator as such. But how, if so, do we arrive at the thought of God as absolute in Himself prior to all creative action? Because creation—the notion of the cosmological relation—posits the absoluteness of its first term, apart from the relation. Hence the paradox commented on above [1] that if we give 'Creator of all things', as a *definition* of God, making His activity coterminous with His creativity, we remove the idea of creation itself, since that is essentially relative to what is absolute apart from it.

Here, also, is the answer to the type of criticism used by Kant very rightly against the 'physico-theological proof', though he knew better than to use it against the cosmological. 'How', he asked, 'can one argue from a finite effect to an infinite cause? A cause need only be adequate to its effect.' But the cosmological relation involves the absoluteness of the 'causal' term, if we have to use that word. All our rational knowledge of God reduces, therefore, to the knowledge of such a being as is the creative agent of effects. This cannot mean, as we have seen, that our knowledge is simply mediate; we must have direct awareness of the activity, as well as of the effects, and of the agent so far as implicit in the activity.

Must, if the idea is to be veridical; for let us conclude this examination of the cosmological idea by remembering our bargain with the sceptical reader. We have found it convenient to omit repeated qualifications and to write on the

[1] pp. 37 *ff*

hypothesis that the theology is true, and have examined how, in that case, it gets constructed and how it refers to its object. We do not, however, imagine ourselves to have demonstrated anything. How could an analysis demonstrate? We have only wished to show that theology ought to go like this, if there is to be any, and that its procedure is not wholly unintelligible.

It is here, then, that we leave our sketch of the cosmological idea, i.e. of the direct content of rational theology, and turn to that investigation of substance in which the validity of its assumptions is to be examined.

EXAMINATION OF FINITE SUBSTANCE:
LOGICAL PROLEGOMENA

VI

SUBSTANCE AND LOGICAL CATEGORIES

(i) *Logic and Substance*

IT is as much as one can expect, if the reader has advanced enough credit to float the huge structure of hypothesis we have hitherto put forward. We must make no more drafts on his readiness to suppose things; and now that we are turning from the analysis of theism to the examination of its principal presuppositions, it is only reasonable to try to pay our way as we go, and to begin from some point where we may hope to claim agreement or at least understanding. And, in view of the bias of contemporary philosophy towards logic, it is most tactful to begin there. In some ways the logical problem, 'How are significant propositions about substantial being possible?' is best treated after the examples have been given; for the possibility of a certain type of significant statement follows, like other possibilities, from the actual occurrence of the thing in question. All we can do is to describe it clearly and define its relations to other types of statement or—should we say?—statements about other types of things.

And yet, if we do not begin from the logical end, we are in danger of being counted out all along for talking nonsense, and so we will begin from logic, though this will in fact involve a description of the metaphysical facts from a certain angle, and with a certain type of interest: a description which will require the fuller account of finite substance to support it; and this shall duly follow.

As soon as the word 'substance' is mentioned, a spring is touched off in the philosopher's mind, and that spring closes a door. Substance is not admitted. The notion produced metaphysical grotesques in the seventeenth century, and, after those last convulsions, has been dying quietly enough. To-day it is not only buried, but its very ghost is laid. We no longer feel any need to place the awkward notion. The philosophy of the past seems to have been one huge blindfold game of hanging the donkey's tail on the donkey; we no longer fumble for the right hook; the tail has evaporated between our hands into the thin smoke of a verbal confusion.

The Aristotelian logic, by a momentous advance in empirical realism, declared that all language, in its real reference, either directly or indirectly designates substances, whether as being what they are, or as possessing a characteristic, or as being in a state, etc., etc. Language might indeed depart from its

63

true norm by verbally hypostatising adjectives, but reflection would find this out; and language reduced to proper expression was the true declaration of thought. Thought, then, has a proper form, under which it has a constant real (or existential) reference to substances, whether directly or indirectly; and our acquaintance with substances is, either directly or indirectly, by the senses. In order, then, that language and thought may be correct, it is necessary justly to appreciate what bundles of sense-presented stuff constitute or indicate true substantial units.

The fate of philosophy ever since has largely been bound up with the question: What sort of entity does thought (=corrected language), by its logical form, designate? If not the Aristotelian substance, then what? Spinoza, Leibniz and Bradley give different answers.

The signal merit of modern logic has been to go behind the apparent thing-reference of language—which might be no more than a particular and accidental habit of the human race hitherto—and to enquire into the very structure of any thought-language as such (i.e. of any with which we seem to be able to think). The conclusion reached and, in our opinion, established is that the form of language as such is neutral with regard to the units designated by it as real in existential statements. The form of language as such is that of terms related to one another by a few simple types of relation, out of which complicated types of relation can be built up; and then, for any such structure of terms-in-relation, a single term can be substituted to stand for it; and this can enter into further complexes. A *correct* language, is, therefore, not one in which all terms and complexes of terms are stated in such a way as to make plain their reference to substances, or to monads, or to the whole, or to anything else. A correct language is one which accurately represents the structure of terms related in complexes, and then in super-complexes of these, in such a way as to avoid confusion between terms and relations, or between the simpler and the more complex.

If we ask, then, what kind of world a correct language can represent, the answer is a general, and metaphysically a neutral, one, viz. 'Any world which can be represented by a system of terms related in complexes of terms.' The dialectic of the whole and its parts has, on this strictly logical ground, no sense. We cannot say that the reality-unit is what corresponds to the simple term; nor that it is what corresponds to the complex of terms. Neither is the whole more real than the parts, nor the parts than the whole. From the merely logical point of view, thought is related to the field of experience as geometry is related to the field of space. Geometry can divide space as it wills; it is the science of the relations which arise between any such possible divisions when made; and the making of all of them is arbitrary. We no longer use the science of geometry to prove that Extended Reality is one thing, or that it is infinitely many things. And so it is with thought: we are not to use the form of 'Judgment' to prove that reality is essentially substances, or one organic Whole, or monads, or atomic sense-qualities, or atomic facts, or anything else.

It follows that if we are to make good our thesis that there are substances, we will not do it by an appeal to the form of logic. But that is not to say that no case for the thesis can be made. And though Aristotle was wrong in stating that language as such has substance-reference, he had undoubtedly hit upon a characteristic of our ordinary language, which *is* about 'things'. This may be a convention due to convenience, a convenience, even, which with changing modes of thought has ceased to be convenient; or it may represent an awareness of the structure of reality based not on logic but on acquaintance with reality itself. That is what has to be looked into.

(ii) *Where to Look for Substance*

If the form of thought is quite neutral as to the complexes which we recognise as significant wholes, then that recognition must rest on something else. In theory, our experienced world might be represented by as many terms as it contains distinguishable elements; the limit to the multiplication of terms would be the limit of our power to distinguish. Again, these terms might be grouped in as many ways as we are able to see similarities of any kind between them, or any other sort of relation of which the mind can become aware. There would be, then, n ways of construing a given experiential field. A very mild example would be the various ways in which we construe the shapes in the fire. And in any one of these n constructions we could pay chief attention to subcomplexes of an A, B, or C grade of complexity or to the primary terms, treating whichever of these we chose as the units of our further thinking, as our 'things'.

What is it, then, which induces us to construe experience in one of the n ways, and to treat certain complexes within our construction as especially significant? The answer given by positivists is certainly right so far as it goes. We use a certain construction, and note certain complexes, because we can thereby represent to ourselves elements in our experience-field which constantly recur together and recur according to a rule of sequence upon other complexes. What we mean by a 'thing' is a complex of elements which in our experience holds together and 'behaves' as a whole. The single book, just as much as the row of books, may be analysed into its perceived and perceivable sense-qualities; but the single book falls off the shelf as one lump, and the row does not; so the book is a thing and the row is things.

This is an over-simplification; for we come to think of the 'thing' as not equivalent to the sense-qualities, but as standing behind them, and yet this makes no material difference to the present argument.

For the positivist proceeds: if it is nothing but empirical coherence of experience-bundles which leads us to treat them as 'things', then their thing-hood ought to mean just neither more nor less than their empirical coherence. No inference can be drawn from it. We cannot say, 'It (the experienced world) is things', unless we mean simply that structures in it have been observed to, and are further expected to, cohere according to certain rules—and also break

c

up according to certain rules. Further, the positivist challenges us to tell him what we can so much as mean by attributing to thinghood any further sense.

This sounds like solipsism: all that is, is my experience-stuff. No, for that would be already 'metaphysics', i.e. the assigning of a privileged status to a certain grouping of what appears. The 'subjective order' is just one way in which the stuff gets counted or construed, and overlaps with other orders, having each their own relevance to several types of question. We cannot say that the stuff is there *qua* 'mine'; the last word is, that it is there. And this 'thereness' is not only indifferent to the distinction between several groupings; it is equally indifferent to the distinction between groupings and detail. Any marking-off of elements within the experience-field is purely relative; what is just 'there' is not there *qua* simple, nor *qua* complex of a certain structure, nor *qua* anything rather than anything else. The 'thereness' has no unit; it is no more whole than part, nor part than whole, no more one than many, nor many than one; it is no more 'it' than 'they', nor 'they' than 'it'; it/*they* is/*are* that/*those* in which all such distinctions equally lie.

This sort of language about the object sounds semi-mystical, and not at all in the spirit of positivism; and indeed it would not occur to a positivist to use it, except to signify his rejection of various metaphysical assertions about the object, as being all equally meaningless. He would say that the error which leads us into the necessity of using such mystical terms is the error of talking about '*the* object' or '*the* experience-field' at all. Those are just variables, whose values are particular objects and experiences. What the language means, when it has been translated into more proper terms, is this: Everything which is grasped and expressed as being experienced, is so grasped and expressed as being *there*, however simple or complex, however large or small in area. But we know that, if we were to shift our grip and take hold of a different area which overlapped this, if we were to break up this complex and re-assemble all or some of the elements in a different complex, if we were to embody this complex into a large one or resolve it into its elements, then the fresh unit which the mind took would be just as much *there* as the old one. 'Thereness' is only experienced as the 'thereness' of some area taken—'some unit' perhaps we may say, since the mind is perhaps incapable of holding a content before it without taking some standard unit, whether the whole or the part. But no such unit is privileged.

On this view, then, the notion of substance might seem to arise from a vicious mental habit. We become so used to treating certain (convenient) areas of the experienced as constant units, that we begin to think that what is there is there *qua* assembled in the units. Hence the lazy simplification of Aristotle and common-sense, telling us that language is only 'proper' when it designates these units, and rejecting as artificial and secondary any analysis which cuts across them and which, if taken at its face value, would disturb our mental habit and force us to reflect. So the conviction of substance is found to rest on the vested interest of habit, as the middle-aged man's conviction of moral or political principle may rest on the same thing; and so psycho-analytic doctrine comes in to the aid of positivist analysis.

Even this cannot be the whole of the story, because the notion of thing-hood or substance not only inclines us to recognise certain bundles as privileged; we do not merely think it would be odd if phenomena failed to belong to such complexes. We also assign to them a certain mysterious 'self-being' which is other than their givenness to sense. It would be weary work to go over Berkeley's arguments and their rejoinders. Suffice it to say that if his position be re-stated as intelligent modern phenomenalism re-states it, and common opinion still declares that something has been left out in the account of the object, then it will be this omission of which we are speaking when we speak of 'self-being'.

Now the more positivistic we are, the more are we bound to give a genuine analysis of all phenomena, and one of the phenomena is the working of people's minds in this supposed recognition of objectivity, whether they then work logically and justifiably or superstitiously and absurdly. Suppose, then, we suggest the following analysis of it, and of its genesis:

1. We have more or less implicit expectations of future experience-data that may follow upon the present according to sequence-rules—not only those that will follow in the determinate situation, but others that would, if other conditions were given.

2. We make a vague summation of these, and treat them as a predicate, or predicates, of the present complex of data, through treating its relation to them as a quality of it.

3. We project some vague analogy from our experience of interior psychic connexion, by way of added glue to the compound.

4. We react to it with some emotional reaction, which likewise we project as a quality in the 'thing'.

There is no need to enlarge on this account, since it is in principle that of Hume, whom we have all read. We would like, however, to underline (3) as by far the most significant element: the comparison of the 'thing' with the 'self'. I treat the thing as an 'other' over against 'me', and though I do not call myself a 'thing' or the 'thing' a 'self', I do erect a pseudo-genus of which 'thing' and 'self' are species. This habit of mind may fairly be traced to a biological root. We grow up in a field where individual lives are in mutual relation, each functioning in a way that will maintain it in face of the others or at their expense, unless the laugh happens to be with the others. Our conscious experiences find themselves framed from the start by this system; the organism or quasi-organism is from the start the natural unit of our thought, and not those sense-elements with which a sophisticated analysis first makes us acquainted. The competition of organisms is the most useful formula for the earlier history of man's existence, and into these terms everything is forced, whether it has a right to be considered an organism or not.

There is nothing in this account which either favours or undermines positivism. The utility of the formula would account for its prevalence, but has nothing to say this way or that as to its metaphysical importance. We still have to ask whether the notion of the thing-self genus, or of either of its species, cannot be resolved by positivist analysis into a grouping of phenomena that just is so grouped. But we can draw a different and previous conclusion. It is on this ground that the question of substance must be tried, for this is its only natural place. We have to consider the self, and a 'thing' which is sufficiently self-like to be over against the self.

This accounts for the connexion between the two notions, 'privileged bundle' and 'self-being' (real existence), which meet us in the notion of thinghood. That which confronts us in the thing is something finite-organism-like enough to be considered as the self's opposite number. Hence the monstrous unnaturalness of Cartesianism, which confronted many selves with one extended substance, thereby overthrowing the nature of the substance it asserted.

(iii) *Positivist Reduction of Substance*

Even if we make the question of the substance that of the self, and of things in some way self-like (and may we beg for a generous construction to be put upon the last phrase, until it has transpired what the self-likeness of things has to be?) we have still to face the positivistic analysis of selfhood. As to the result of this, we know beforehand. For the positivist analysis is Morton's Fork. It will be bound to pronounce that the unity of the self is just one grouping that may be taken among the phenomena; which in themselves are no more many than one, no more one than many, etc. The application of positivist analysis is not a demonstration, but a foregone conclusion. The only demonstration required or given by it is the demonstration that some phenomenalist sense can be given to the term under discussion, thus explaining how we can have been using it significantly. In the case of 'self' that is not difficult. We often do make a merely naturalistic (empirical) use of it, or uses rather (for there are many such); regarded as a symbol for use in naturalistic description, 'self' is only too rich; it has a whole bundle of associated meanings.

We will now, just for the sake of keeping the thing in mind, give a simplified version of the positivist principle which makes the removal of metaphysical allegations so painless a procedure. It is, of course, the 'verification-principle' and states that all propositions are significant of that subject-matter which is given to the mind, only in so far as they make or imply the assertion of an experienceable difference. If they do not, then either they are senseless or they express linguistic conventions merely, as for example when we define a term of discourse by other terms.

The principle, which would more usefully be called that of 'experienceable difference' than that of 'verification', can be most simply stated as a rule for testing the real reference[1] of propositions. Take any proposition, and state its

---

[1] i.e. their reference to what common-sense calls 'things', 'reality', 'the world', as opposed to what is logical or linguistic.

contradictory. Then ask: Is the quarrel between these two a quarrel which any imaginable experience could settle one way or the other? We take an easy example:

(1) The Lord thundered out of Heaven.
   The Lord did not thunder out of Heaven.

Experienceable difference, thunder-phenomena or no thunder-phenomena. Yes, but how much of the form of statement is relevant to any experience-reference? So let us try:

(2) It is the Lord that thunders.
   It is not the Lord that thunders.

Experienceable difference (perhaps), the providential or non-providential occurrence of thunder; if this occurred on the occasion in question, or on many past occasions, very conveniently, as for example when Samuel has asked for an omen, or when a storm in the faces of the Philistine hosts is of military value to Israel. But now we have to try:

(3) The quasi-providential occurrence of thunder is due to a personal will.
   The quasi-providential occurrence of thunder is not due to a personal will.

The game appears to be up. Perhaps an experienceable difference might here also be found, but we should only be putting off the evil day. Either we have got to consent to the identification of 'The Lord' with the name of a sequence-law which experience is found to exemplify (or could be imagined to exemplify), or else we must abandon the term as senseless. This is the Morton's Fork of which we spoke.

But, you may protest, the principle cannot apply to the instance; for how can one have an 'experienceable difference' concerning that which is absolutely universal? *Ex hypothesi* the activity of the Lord is everywhere if it is anywhere. Just so. It is exactly such alleged universal features in 'reality' or 'experience' that the principle excludes. If, for example, we assert that freedom, or activity, is to some measure present in all consciousness as such, this becomes a non-differing factor and we cannot imagine experiences such as to 'verify' (*a*) its presence, (*b*) its absence. If we point to the different degrees of it at different times as capable of such verification, the principle will deny us the right to call them different degrees *of it*, and will allow us only a class of substitutable qualities.[1] If we claim that these qualities play a privileged part in experience and are relevant to the occurrence or non-occurrence of actions in some way other than that of preceding or accompanying those actions according to a uniformity-

---

[1] i.e. there is always present one of these and never more than one and the relational context in which they occur has constant aspects; the stock instance is the several shades of colour in their relation to the visual field.

rule, we shall be challenged to explain how this statement could possibly be verified by any experience. And we shall not be able to meet this challenge.

The 'metaphysical proposition' is defined by positivists as one that is condemned under this test. 'Metaphysics' is a class of absurdity. And, oddly enough, this way of talking has made its fortune, so that it is accepted even by those who do not profess the positivist doctrine. We have remarked earlier on the curious convention of professing belief in the value of the Ontological Proof among philosophers of an older school; you could mean very much what you liked by it, but it was not good form quite to deny it. So now, but the other way about. You must profess disbelief in metaphysics, and grant that the positivists have given it its death-blow. *Abrenuntio Satanae*; but just what is Satan? We are sure we are renouncing *something*; but surely the positivists have *gone too far*. Now what is it we are sure they have exploded?   Is it the question about substance? Or is it the making of assertions with real reference, but which can be checked by no appeal to 'experienceable difference'? But if the latter, it is difficult to see wherein they have gone too far, for grant them this, and it seems you must grant them all. If, on the other hand, you do not grant them this, there is nothing left of their case against the substance-question, and your rejection of it will have nothing to do with theirs.

It looks as though we were sure that there is *something in* the principle of experienceable difference, but suspect that it has been stated too narrowly. We may suspect, for example, that it makes an 'experienceable difference' in some sense we could attach to the phrase, whether one asserts free will or denies it, and that a definition of 'experienceable difference' which results in the discounting of this question as 'metaphysical' cannot be correctly stated.[1]

We observe that polemic against positivism commonly throws down one of these two challenges:

(*a*) Prove your own first principles.

(*b*) State your system in a way which neither uses nor implies propositions offending against your own canon of the proposition.

These exemplify two universal formulae of academic debate, available for making a case against anything. They are what Aristotle called 'positions' and discussed in his *Topics*—positions, that is, that could usefully be taken up by a man who has decided to attack something, and hopes he will soon think of some reasons for doing so.

About (*a*) it may be said that no first principles can ever be proved except dialectically [2] and if the admission of this impossibility makes special difficulties for positivism, this may only be due to indiscreet statement of the positivist position, and may be capable of remedy. And in fact the principles commend

---

[1] More shocking still is the discounting of the question, whether 'persons' other than one's self have a subjective aspect or merely yield phenomena which occur *as though* this were so: cf. the third position in our theological example above. But it may be possible to re-state positivism so as to avoid this particular conclusion, so we forbear to use it.

[2] *vide supra*, pp. 6 *ff*

themselves as evident; no one can go through such exercises as the simple one we gave above without a strong suspicion that he is asking the right kind of question for getting at the distinction between what is significant and what is not. Further, the principles are capable of dialectical proof, in so far as we are able to give a plausible reduction of all other alleged types of significance to our own.

About (b) we can object that (I) it is inconclusive, and (II) it could only be effective if a more fundamental objection is also effective. (I) It is inconclusive, because it may after all be no more than a challenge to linguistic dexterity. Even if there is no positivist clever enough to state positivism throughout in positivist terms,[1] such a prodigy may yet arise. (II) If it is effective, it is so because the positivist in stating positivism must recognise facts which cannot be positivistically stated. But the important consideration here, from the point of view of the holy angels, is not that the positivist in stating positivism must recognise such facts, but that such facts are so, and therefore ought to be recognised. But if so, these may not be the only facts of which positivism fails to give an account. The solid objection to the system will not be that it does not quite succeed in taking a one-eyed view of what is, but that the view it nearly succeeds in taking is a one-eyed view; and even if it succeeded completely, the objection would still stand.

The would-be philosophical theologian cannot feel a call to mingle in the fray that rages round heads (a) and (b) above; he least of all men. He would be very unlikely to distinguish himself, not being equipped with the appropriate types of skill; and he cannot feel a very lively interest in these *ad hominem* arguments. It is his business to call attention to certain highly important and commonly neglected aspects of reality, and to show that they can be talked about sensibly. It is the importance of what positivism excludes that is for him the appropriate argument; and it also happens to be the argument against the value of positivism to men in general. It is better not to wear permanently spectacles that prevent one's seeing most of what is there, even if they sharpen one's eye for certain distinctions of detail.

From this somewhat desultory discussion we may collect a conclusion as to our task. It is, to give an account of thinking which both preserves what happens to be sound in the verification (experienceable difference) principle and also explains how we can make statements about those aspects of reality which positivism forbids us to talk of.

[1] A phrase which must include propositions *rejecting* various non-positivist formulations. The importance of these in giving an account of the true doctrine will emerge later.

VII

SUBSTANCE-PROPOSITIONS AND THE FUNCTION OF LANGUAGE

(i) *The Practical Setting of Language*

LANGUAGE arises from a response of a conscious organism to its environment. The ultimate elements that we have to recognise are two: the presence of the environmental facts to the creature through its senses, and a varying reaction of the creature to those facts, according to their variation from time to time. To recognise a fact is not the same as to react to it, and yet there is no recognition without reaction. The datum which we call 'a stink' is not our reaction to it in expressions of disgust, in aversion of the nose and checking of the breath. But it is only in making some such reaction that we attend to this sort of object, and only by repeating it that we remark that sort as a *class* of sense-object.

The response of creatures having any degree of consciousness we may conjecture never to be immediate as physical effects are supposed immediate. There are always tentative responses which do not run through into action until they have approved themselves against tentative checks and other tentative responses. All of this may take place with great swiftness and at a subconscious level. However that may be, a stage is some time reached where the tentative or non-committal character of the first response is so emphasised, that there is required an artificial or conventional piece of behaviour to be its vehicle, and give it an existence separate from the effective and truly active response. The conventionalisation of a response is the suspension of a decision. If I see a bull and am incapable of conventional response, I must mark my awareness of it, and my associated expectations of its behaviour, by doing something appropriate, e.g. approaching and hitting it with a stick, or barking at it. But by the time I have done this I am committed, and it is too late to consider the probable consequences. If on the other hand I can say, 'Ah, bull', by way of first response, I am in a happier position. Language is indeed a developed type of conventional response, which also has other uses, e.g. to stimulate in others responses to the same facts, and to direct our own imagination, as when by the use of such symbols we set ourselves to conceive what several consequences are likely to follow from several treatments of the same bull-situation.

If we take the first of these uses of language, we can see two possible attitudes to the symbol, both of which embody the form of delayed response. Our hesitation may concern the application of the term; we may be quite clear what is to be done about it if the term does apply. If it is a bull, one runs; but is it a bull? So we say, 'Bull?' and the response, 'Bull it is' is all we need, or can indeed be made by running without repetition of the symbol. But our hesitation may not concern the appropriateness of the symbol, but what is to be done about it. 'Bull; h'm!' is the expression of this. In that case, 'Run!' or 'Pretend not to see it' is the second stage required, which again might take the form of action.

In the former case, we first question, and then judge, that it is a bull; in the latter case we take for granted at both stages that it is a bull, being occupied in judging something else on the basis of that assumption. Both judgment and assumption may be described as involving, or being cases of, belief. Now the significance of symbol-groups as expressing real [1] *propositions* seems to depend on their fitness to fill a belief-context. The significance, then, of 'Here's a bull' depends on the possibility of our conceiving a situation which would provoke us to use these words. And since a reaction to environment must be a genuine alternative to some other, or it cannot be called a reaction, we must also be able to conceive a situation which would provoke us to reject them. And when we say 'provoke', the word must not be taken in an emotive sense; the provocation is to use the symbols in a context not of exclamation, but of belief, i.e. of either judgment or assumption.

So, from a biological starting-point, we come round again to our principle of experienceable difference very quickly. It would not have been so quickly if we had given a less sketchy account; but the sketchiness will not affect the argument and is sufficient to show how it is that the principle commends itself as plausible. For it squares with what looks like being the fundamental function of language; and if language has become vastly sophisticated, there seems an *a priori* probability that the sophistications will be variations on this basic theme, and not a jump into another kind.[2] It seems a very disquieting suggestion that there could be two or more quite distinct sorts of objective significance capable of attaching to symbolic groups. No doubt words may be used for other purposes than to express propositions about real facts, e.g. to ventilate emotion or to stir it. That causes no scandal. But the burden of proof lies heavy on the man who would maintain that 'significance' can mean more things than one when it is propositions about facts that our symbols express; or who wishes to hold that while significance remains the same, it may have lost all touch with the type of context to which it was originally relative.

That its connexion with that context can become loosened, who will deny? A proposition may express a very high generalisation, so that no single experience-situation could verify it, but only a wide field of these; and so that it could not be verified directly by these situations, but only through the mediation of other propositions. Or again, our use of symbols may become more and more like the manipulation of a calculating machine: we pass from proposition to proposition by purely conventional links, by the manipulation of our word-system itself, and the implicit reference to imaginable experience sinks further and further into the background or ceases altogether to be felt. And yet, unless

[1] Sense of 'real' as above, p. 68*n*

[2] e.g. in the case mentioned above, when we use words to carry or direct constructive imagination, their use as proper responses to the imagined experience is plainly presupposed.

the propositions are themselves to express relations of symbols in the calculating machine as such, the possibility of recovering mediately or immediately
the verifying experienceable difference seems the evident condition of recovering significance, of returning from words to 'things', from calculation as calculation to anything that we are calculating about.

(ii) *Positivism and Practical Relevance*

To attempt an exhaustive treatment of the modalities of propositional
form, and their reducibility to the primitive type, would be to write a textbook
of logic; and since we are not taking up the gauntlet on this ground, it would
be a waste of time to proceed further, even if we had the skill. It is our business
to consider wherein the plausibility of the positivist principles lies. And we see
it to lie in the relation of the word-using faculty to behaviour as a whole. We
may tabulate the following propositions, as representing the position:

(*a*) Word-using serves behaviour.

(*b*) Behaviour reacts to, copes with and exploits only what can be experienced, i.e. experienceable differences.

(*c*) Therefore the significance of word-uses will lie in their relation to
experienceable differences (in so far as word-uses refer to the given
and not to our reactions, etc.).

(*d*) Any alleged articulation of 'things as they are themselves' (as distinguished from their appearance to and affecting of us) is irrelevant
for any reaction to, coping with, or exploitation of the things.

(*e*) Therefore no such articulation is referred to by word-use, and metaphysics (= the substance-question) is an absurdity.

Of these propositions (*c*) and (*e*) are conclusions, against the logic of
which we have no complaint. We allow (*a*) and (*b*), though we suspect the
phrase 'experienceable differences', because it might be given a sense narrower
than belongs to it in the inherently plausible form of the proposition. We
therefore offer the gloss: 'differences such that they can be appreciated by us,
and such that there is appropriate to them a scale of behaviour-reactions *other*
than linguistic (conventional) reactions.' It is not plausible that we should
be able to talk about types of things, about which we can do nothing but
talk.

In this sentence the words 'types' and 'do' both require attention. 'Types',
because we can obviously talk about single things about which nothing else
but talking can be done, e.g. the back of the moon. But this belongs to a *type*
of object about which much can often be done, for the description is simply
given in terms of physical reality and spatial relations; and so we are able to
imagine what could be done about the back of the moon, e.g. if we could fly
there. 'Do', because doing may include not only what we usually call action
about an object, but such behaviour as leads to a continued apprehension of the

object, as for example, when we pause in our walk, dilate our nostrils and draw in our breath that we may continue to enjoy a country smell that pleases us.

There remains proposition (*d*). If we accept this as it stands, we are plainly sunk. But need we? Its plausibility is certainly strong at first sight. The philosopher, thought Plato, divides, like the good cook, where the joints are; and though Plato was speaking of what we should call logical analysis, he thought that this should represent an order in reality. It was possible to make the 'order and connexion of ideas the same as the order and connexion of things', as Spinoza says it is in the divine mind. But the belief that there can be an articulation of things 'as they are themselves' and that we can grasp it, seems part and parcel of a belief in pure reason, a disinterested intellectual penetration of reality having no bearings on any behaviour but word-behaviour. And not only is this belief itself unplausible on the grounds of the general nature of language; it seems easy also to explain its illusory origin. Take the case of Plato just mentioned. He was doing verbal analysis, that is, he was conforming his account to a real articulation prior to it, but that articulation was itself an articulation of correct word-usages. Does not the idea of pure reason arise from the simple but absurd confusion, that there must be in 'reality' an articulation to which a verbal system may correspond, in the way in which an account of a verbal system may correspond to that system? Is not Platonism, for example, the most naïve possible development of this confusion? And are not all doctrines of a pure reason sophistications upon the same theme?

We have seen that it is expected of us to pronounce the formula: 'I disbelieve in metaphysics.' Let us seize the present opportunity to make this orthodox renunciation and secure our standing in the philosophic fold. Let metaphysics mean the deliverances of a pure reason or pure intellection having no bearings on any but word-behaviour, and we renounce it with all our heart. It is not here that the dispute lies; if we contest proposition (*d*), we contest the direct form of its statement, viz. that any articulation of things as they are in themselves is irrelevant for any reaction to them.

This proposition is not evident at all, and would, for example, have been hotly denied by Plato, in spite of his unwisely cherished ideal of a pure reason. For, he would have said, does not rationality in its active aspect mean just this, that we behave towards several entities as the very natures of them demand? That we can react, or respond, to what they are in themselves, and not only exploit the effects they have on us? Proposition (*d*) in fact becomes plausible only if a particular and narrow limitation is placed on the notion of possible reactions. If to react means to cope with or to exploit, to shun what happens to hurt or displease us, and to seek what happens to help or delight us, then an interest in things as they are in themselves can have no relation to behaviour. But if the ultimate selector of goals and *bêtes noires*, of *fugienda* and *petenda*, is not always brute emotion or automatic habit or prudential calculation, but sometimes an appreciation of the nature of things as they are in themselves, then proposition (*d*) is not plausible at all.

But Heaven help us, what is this? Are we to violate the sacred autonomies of Ethics and Epistemology? To attempt the joining of what University Syllabuses have put asunder? There seems to be a grave risk that we shall; and perhaps after all it is not excessive for a theologian to profess belief in some validity of the moral consciousness. But if so, he may also ask the question: Are duties ever owed to things or persons as they are in themselves, or simply as they happen to affect us? Can ethics be reduced to (*a*) mere emotion, (*b*) intelligent manipulation? Of course the reduction has often been, and still is, attempted, but there is a very common opinion that to accept it is to deny morality as such.

We may be told that the immediate concern of ethics is with acts, or pieces of voluntary behaviour, not with persons or things. So be it; but an act is no act unless it is the execution of a more or less consciously entertained project. Now would the project continue to qualify as the project of an act relevant for ethics, if it expressed no (intended) reaction to any thing or person as they are in themselves, but only to exploitable data? This question cannot be answered with a light-hearted affirmative.

But, if we are asserting some connexion of metaphysics and ethics, let us not be accused of reducing them to one another. We declined to reduce our apprehension of a stink to the appropriate behaviour-reaction, although we maintained their mutual connexion; and similarly there is no question of reducing our apprehension of what a good man is in himself to our dutiful attempts to foster his purposes. The evidence for awareness of what things are in themselves, is just as much that we are conscious of this awareness, as that we are conscious of reactions that presuppose it.

(iii) *Types of Practical Relevance*

Here is a table of the relevance of factual propositions to behaviour. We describe them as relevant to the answering of several questions. It must be understood that these are behaviour-questions, and not fact-questions. There is only one fact-question, viz. 'What is, was, will be, the case?'

(*a*) Data relevant to the answering of 'What?' questions. What objects is it $\begin{Bmatrix} \text{right} \\ \text{worth while} \end{Bmatrix}$ to attend to, and what is it $\begin{Bmatrix} \text{right} \\ \text{worth while} \end{Bmatrix}$[1] to do about them?

(*b*) Data relevant to the answering of 'How?' questions. Let it be assumed that the 'What?' question is answered or taken for granted: that we have a table of *fugienda* and *petenda*, or are confident in some judgment or instinct that will settle that question as it arises. We want now to know how to get, shun, manipulate, cope with and exploit.

(*c*) Data relevant to the answering of the 'Who?' question. If, having

---

[1] As a term covering these two varieties, we might suggest 'claim', if it were not so metaphorical. 'What objects *claim* our attention, and what do they *claim* that we should do about them?'

answered the question (*a*) and (*b*) I wish to know whether it is any good endeavouring to carry out the suggested course, I may need evidence about myself as an endeavourer.

The 'Why' question is not a separate question, but according to several varieties of it, it coincides with the others. If I want to know why I should bother to act at all and not just drift, (*a*) and (*c*) are relevant. Who am I? and what range of objects is presented to me by environment? If I want to know why I should pursue an aim that I find myself pursuing, I return to (*a*) and ask myself whether it is chosen on good grounds. If, assuming an aim, I ask myself why I should continue to adopt the course I have chosen for securing it, I must review the reasons for adopting that course, which will mean a return to (*b*) questions. 'Why?', then, is not a question requiring data of a special kind to answer it, but arises from a secondary or reflective attitude to the other questions.

It is obvious that any one of these questions may be completely neglected, while attention is focussed on another of them. The answer to (*c*) may be taken for granted for a lifetime, and never brought into clear consciousness. The answer to (*a*) may also be taken for granted, if we are content always to allow it to be given by subconscious processes, and such appears to be the habit of Logical Positivists. The answer to (*b*) may be taken for granted, as by a girl who is wondering whether to say yes or no to a proposal of marriage, if she is simply considering the worth-whileness of the match, having at some previous time thought out to her own satisfaction how it is likely to develop.

What sorts of data will be relevant to these three questions?

(*α*) Propositions about what things are in themselves, or propositions about how they affect our interest.

(*β*) Empirical propositions of every sort, including those that guide us to explore fields where we anticipate the occurrence of *petenda* we have not yet begun to have appetite for, but anticipate on some analogy that we shall.

(*γ*) Propositions about what I am, not as a field of data open to empirical (naturalistic) introspection, i.e. Kant's 'phenomenal self'; for these belong to (*β*): but about what I am as an agent. What this means will be seen later.

Now the Logical Positivist's principle is the principle of a man who asserts that either only the (*b*) question can be asked, or if the (*a*) question can also be asked, then only the second mentioned class of (*α*) propositions is available for answering it. He denies that we need faith in our moral freedom (*γ*), or that we use intellect in the selection of ends (*α*1). These denials have nothing new in them, and they have no connexion with the principle which we claim to underlie the plausibility of the verification-principle, viz. that of the relation of real propositions to practical responses.

It must be confessed that no positivist would be likely to feel much interest in the treatment here accorded to these questions. He would express detachment and perhaps some amusement at our 'biological deduction' of his principle; he would certainly not wish to take any responsibility for it. If his principle falls into line with some biological facts, so much the better. But he will say: 'As to the alleged propositions of the (α1) and (γ) types, I am perfectly prepared to hear about them if you can succeed in causing me to become aware of the experienceables to which they refer. Otherwise I shall not know the difference between asserting and denying them. I note with pleasure your renunciation of a pure reason, and of the absurd opinion that a knowledge of "how things are in themselves" can be arrived at by inference from the sense-data. Since I would not be so uncharitable as to attribute to you a belief in innate ideas or principles, I conclude that you believe yourself to experience certain characters which I for my part have never taken account of. Far be it from me to dogmatise about the range of your experience or the propriety of your private language-habits, and if you tell me you experience characters other than the sense-objects we all recognise, I congratulate you. But if you want me, or the rest of mankind, to agree with you in a more active manner, you must by the use of words already common to us or by some other means direct our attention to these at present unobserved experienceables.'

We are grateful for such a statement of the problem, and are willing to undertake the task as it has been defined for us. To have weakened a little the *a priori* plausibility of the positivist's principle of exclusion is not to have established the reality of the objects which we complain he has excluded; and this is our proper business, as we confessed above. And the proper performance of it can be nothing else but the description of substance in its most evident instance, to which we shall pass presently.

VIII

PROBLEMS OF SPEECH ABOUT SUBSTANCE

(i) *How Substance-Language can refer to Practical Differences*

IF it be assumed that propositions about substantial being may have the practical relevance necessary for real significance, there still remain certain puzzles about the way in which they signify. We may consider first the difficulty that whereas practical relevance involves reference to practically important differences—it is so, it might have been conceived to be otherwise, its being so and not otherwise is important to us—'substance' and 'activity' appear to be universal terms, which do not signify differences; for the metaphysician will have to allege that everything which is, is substance and act.

Yes, but the differences are found in the several ways in which the 'manifold' is tied up in substantial bundles, and the several bundles in which it is tied up; nor is it true that *everything is activity* in the sense that all experienceable characters are activities, but only that such characters exist always in a bundle of which activity is the unifying principle, and that bundle is substance.

'Substance', then, may be said to describe a class of substitutibles, just as 'colour' does. Whatever fills visual extension is a shade of colour, but it may be any shade; whatever holds simple characters in a 'bundle' capable of existence, is substantial connexion; but several arrangements of such connexional patterns are possible, and the place in its bundle of the detail we are concerned with varies from instance to instance.

A class of substitutibles is relevant to a type of context. For example, 'visual extension' is not simply a way of saying 'colour', or even a way of indicating the quantitative aspect of colour-phenomena. It expresses also a relation to our eyes, and to the behaviour which we call opening them, and to other behaviour which is turning them in several directions. The context of 'substance' is even more general, it is provided by all sense-objects as such; yet this is no scandal since e.g. spatiality has a context equally general.

There is, in fact, nothing peculiar in the assertion of a class of substitutibles having so general a scope. The true difficulty is still Hume's difficulty, viz. that of grasping the 'real relation' which binds the substantial bundles together. For the several members of the class of substitutibles which is substance are not just several qualities, as the shades of colour are; they are several patterns of connexion. But what now is this connexion? For it still seems plausible, as it seemed to Hume, that the class 'relation', so far as it has to do with what is given, is exhausted by (*a*) phenomenal order, (*b*) recurrences of phenomenal order, with the addition, perhaps, of (*c*) the relation of the phenomenally abstract to its complementary abstraction (*vide supra*, p. 21).

It will be our business to show that this enumeration is not exhaustive, but that a sort of relation exists beside, such as to be the bond of substance. That will be, again, our descriptive task, but we will mention here a logical puzzle to which it seems to give rise.

(ii) *How can the Unique be Described?*

It is commonly agreed that the simply unique cannot be described in a proper sense. If we are to attempt to call another's attention to it, we must assume that it is before him and that the problem is merely (*a*) to bring his attention to bear on it, (*b*) to isolate or distinguish it. For these purposes we may point, we may describe the context and then explain that it is *not* any of the other elements in that context; if it can be placed in a class of substitutibles, we shall mention that class, as that it is a 'colour', etc. Now the difficulty that besets us is this. If we wish to bring substance to light, everything turns on exhibiting the relation which unifies it. But for the exhibition of this relation these usual aids are difficult to apply. We can place it in no class of substitutibles except the class 'relation'; and if we indicate its context, i.e. the complex of terms that it unites, we fail to differentiate it, since these terms are also admittedly united by those other phenomenal relations to which positivists wish to reduce this relation of ours. So 'the relation obtaining between *a, b* and *c*,' is a description which gets us nowhere.

What remains then? We might try the negative method, we might, having specified the context, remove all other relations one by one, hoping that those to whom we speak will realise that our negations leave something unaccounted for, and identify this with the object of search. But it does not seem at all likely that this will succeed. These persons have always up to the present confused their apprehension of this relation with their apprehensions of the other relations, so as to suppose it to be exhausted in them: and if we remove these one by one, our hearers will continue to make the same confusion, and the object of search will then be found to have vanished with these; as blind Polyphemus tried to isolate the Greeks by driving out the sheep, but failed because he was unable to distinguish the sheep from the Greeks who clung under their bellies.

Then some use of analogy appears to be the only remaining hope. This mysterious relation has analogy to some other, and indeed to several in several respects. But since those to whom we are talking are not looking at the mysterious X, they will hardly get their minds on to it by being told that it has some analogy with things from which none the less it is, as a kind, diverse. Let us start at least in the context where X is lurking and select the element with which we may suppose our hearer has confused X: let us take the ram under which we suppose Ulysses hangs.

(1) Let this be A. 'You may think', we tell them, 'that A gives us all we want; but allow us to tell you that there is an X which, however analogous to A, cannot be squared with the following aspects of A.' We proceed to draw out

certain properties of or consequences from A which cannot be attributed to X, and describe X as an A-like thing whose character excludes, however, the A-properties or A-contexts mentioned. We hope that as we do this our hearers will jump to the recognition and isolation of the X which, though somehow A-like, makes these exclusions.

(2) But in doing this, we shall hardly limit ourselves to mere negation; we shall introduce a *second* analogy, declaring these A-aspects to fall foul, or short, of X in virtue of certain B-like properties that X, we allege, possesses. B will probably come into the argument because it forms with A some fairly obvious opposition or disjunction. Again, we may hope that the jump to recognition will take place. What is this which excludes A-aspects in virtue of certain B-aspects?

From this point on we can develop our dialectic in several ways. For the understanding of its nature, we must remember that the term 'an X' fails to give our hearer any help. It is not as with theology, where 'an *ENS*' already means something.[1] We are here on the search for *ENS*; we have not reached it. No, 'an A-like X' gives no character even of the most general kind other than that of A. It merely tells us that X is not simply an A, but bears to it the relation of likeness—we can help ourselves out by the analogy of any two terms whatsoever that stand in a likeness-relation to one another. But as to the character of X, we have simply to think of it as 'an A—with a caution'. And this state of affairs persists until X is identified. From being just 'an A, with a caution' it becomes 'an A—but with characters excluding Ap, Aq, Ar'. Then: 'an (A) B, a NOT Ap, Aq, Ar'. But as soon as B appears, several formulations and several paths of dialectic become possible.

(3) It has become plain by now that X cannot be an A simply; we may, then, try the experiment of treating it as a B. From this two possibilities open. We shall show the impossibility of treating it as simply a B, but this may be done *either* by holding on to and re-asserting its A-like aspects as excluding certain B-aspects:

(4) *Or* (on the assumption that A is discredited) we may experiment with C, D, E and so on until the range of apparently significant analogies is exhausted. Supposing that A and B had been a complete disjunction, there would be no C to take in the same genus; but in that case we should reject the whole A-B disjunction as having been after all the wrong one, and try a parallel disjunction, let it be the disjunction C-D-E.

Whether we sway the scales between A and B, or run out along a line of successive experiment ABCDE . . . the result must be the same at last. We shall declare that no analogy satisfies, and that several express something, and we shall try to balance and combine them.

(5) Now the natural model for such a procedure is classification. X is in the class A, but not to be confused with the whole extension of that class, e.g. with its other members V and W, because it is also in the class B, which

[1] *vide supra*, p. 30

excludes these; while its membership in A excludes it from the other members of B, such as Y and Z.

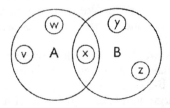

But in the case of analogy, which we are considering, this cannot apply; X is not a special instance of genera A and B, and A and B cannot really overlap. All we can know is that while A and B exclude one another, X by mere likeness 'overlaps' them both, so that it cannot be identified with either.

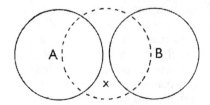

We are supposed to have as yet no independent knowledge of X; it is only its B-ness that makes it Not-A, and *vice versa*.

This seems highly unsatisfactory, and it is natural to pretend a synthesis, and the simplest form of this is boldly to assert the former figure above: X is an A that is also a B.

(6) But this is quickly seen to be impossible, for A and B exclude one another: an AB is a square circle. So we try the eclectic method, and tear from A certain aspects, hoping that these will combine with certain that have been similarly wrenched out of B. For are not these the aspects in virtue of which we compare A and B with X? And if these are the X aspects of A and of B, they must combine with one another.

Vain hope, for A and B are merely analogous to X; in these respects, maybe, but only analogous all the same: and so these elements of A and B are found to clamour for the restitution of the A and B contexts to which they respectively belong. But need we acquiesce in this?

(7) May there not be some neutral context or medium in which they will unite? Let us seek for it: let it appear to be provided by C, or certain aspects of C. Needless to say, we fail, and for the same reasons, to get anything intelligible as a combined structure.

No doubt there are further dialectical positions, but these will do. Throughout the process, the hidden spring of movement is the character of X, which drives us from one position to another—this is the positive spring; a *negative* motive of instability is the mutual incompatibilities of the analogues. And the purpose of the whole is that the listener may grasp the underlying dynamism and jump to the apprehension of X itself.

This scheme of analogical dialectic is no great mystery; there seems to be something cheap and puerile about it: and yet it must hold a central place in any account of metaphysical procedure, or epistemological, for that matter; since it is certain that in these studies we shall find ourselves trying to describe unique terms, and so analogising. Yet it would be false to conclude that these sciences are nothing but a tissue of dialectical paralogisms, since analogy may be used simply to bring to light a real structure, thus eliminating itself. No doubt the danger is great that we shall mistake dialectic for proper inference, and suppose that arguments based on analogues are firmly grounded in the natures of their analogates; but it is equally possible that we shall avoid this absurdity.

The presence of analogical propositions and reasonings in all metaphysics offers the easiest target to critical arrows, and a handle to attack the whole science as nonsensical. The argument of Kant's Dialectic is a case in point. The metaphysicians, he sees, are driven to place their 'transcendent' objects under the scheme of disjunctions provided by the 'empirical' employment of the Categories. From this all sorts of contradiction are seen to result: these objects cannot be described straight with the (schematised) categories, nor described at all without them. What does Kant conclude from this? His radical followers would like him to have declared that the metaphysicians are talking about *nothing*. But this he cannot bring himself to say. They are talking about something, but something which it is not possible to talk about, or to think, or to know. This agnosticism, it is commonly agreed, he fails to state consistently, and falls an easy prey to positivist attack.

But cannot his mystery be cleared up by an understanding of the nature and function of analogical dialectic? May it not be that the metaphysicians' objects are indescribable in proper terms not because they are 'transcendent' but because, though 'immanent' in our existence-situation, they are unique? Unique, and also, of course, non-obvious so that it is difficult to bring attention to bear upon them in proper isolation—we shall have more to say about non-obviousness presently.

Kant's metaphysicians had often undoubtedly paralogised and mistaken analogic for proper description: but as to what they ought to have done, Kant might have drawn conclusions from his own procedure. For in the positive part of the Critique he is constantly trying to describe unique and non-obvious elements in the structure of 'experience' and uses analogic terms in so doing. But this does not strike him or distress him, so sure is he (and often rightly) that he is writing with his eye on the true objects, so that analogic terms are his servants, not his masters, and do not themselves control the line of discourse. But his treatment of other philosophers may remind us of the danger that in reading a philosophic description with which we are not in sympathy, we may appreciate no aspect but the analogic. There is no such writing against which one could not make a plausible case for its being *mere* analogising, and therefore analogising which mistakes itself for proper statement.

Hegel's name is difficult to pass over here and dangerous to include, so hard is it even for experts to declare what are the dominant principles of his bewildering and many-sided method. Yet we can find in his logic specimens of argument conforming to the dialectic briefly analysed above, and one may detect approximations to the view that the business of analogy is to eliminate its restless and unsatisfying self, and leave us in calm possession of the very object we have been struggling all along to think about; though Hegel seems less concerned with the distinction between proper and analogic, than with that between partial and complete. But the two are not so disconnected as may appear: for if we are trying to describe the whole pattern in terms of some con-stituent or constituents, then *ex hypothesi* we have failed to bring before our-selves the type of unity which characterises the whole as such and is the bond of the constituents; in which case we must be forcing a principle of unity which belongs to the sub-pattern to do duty as that of the primary pattern; and this is to analogise, the unsatisfactoriness of the analogy being used to bring into consciousness that which we have been struggling to express.

(iii) *The Place of Analogy in Thought*

In the preceding paragraphs we have several times shifted our ground from that of an analogical dialectic addressed to others who have failed to grasp an unique object of apprehension already grasped by ourselves, and have taken up the position of men getting clear to themselves an object of which they are confusedly aware. Between these two processes there is no fundamental differ-ence; for unless the person whom we hope to enlighten is also 'confusedly aware' of our object, we shall never make him explicitly so. In this respect the dialectic is like that which sets out to unearth implicit theism (*vide supra*, p. 10). What we do, then, is to provide our friends with instruments to perform an operation which we are able to perform ourselves; by the grace of Heaven, or by the instruction of someone who did us this service.

But the use of the dialectic to ourselves raises the question whether we can in fact ever dispense with it. Might one have got a clear apprehension of the object straight away, without its aid? Or if one has to use it, is it a ladder one can kick down after one has climbed? Allowing that there is such a thing as to reach the top, and that we are not always climbing, may we not still have at least one foot on the top rung of the ladder and enjoy no independent basis?

There is a very plausible doctrine which asserts that every act of thought requires two terms, so that to grasp the character of anything involves com-parison with something else, just as to grasp the context of anything involves relating it with something else. So it has been suggested, apropos of Descartes's (clear and) distinct notion, that awareness of the boundary which separates the object of our consideration from all else must be consequent upon an exhaustive number of acts of thought disjoining it from everything with which it could possibly be confused; nothing can be 'clearly' known as just itself by concentrating upon it and it alone. In the case of the ordinary phenomenal object, exclusion proceeds by genera: a shade of red is a colour, and therefore nothing that cannot be a colour; within colour it is not blue, green, etc. In the case of our unique object, exclusion proceeds by the failure of our experiment in equating it with any of those things with which it could plausibly be confused, or in equating it with any combination of them, or of their elements. Perhaps a sense for red is an awareness of its difference from all other colours, and the more colours we know, the more we know red; and perhaps an understanding of substantial connexion is equivalent in this sense with a knowledge of its dialectical idea.

If this contention is as true as it seems difficult to gainsay, something else must also be true. That relation between two terms which we stabilise in distinguishing them is not a simple relation called 'being distinct from', which remains identical whatever pair we take. Not all things are *equally* different from a thing from which all are distinct, even if we confine our attention to things which are equally relevant in point of logical order (excluding, e.g., crazy comparisons like that between an elephant and a moral virtue). But not only are there degrees of difference; there are modes, and several things are *differently different* from the same thing. So to compare a man with many others is to bring out to ourselves the full flavour of his individuality. But this is not only so when we are dealing with complex terms which share generic descriptions with others. It is also true with simple terms that are 'simply diverse', as with the colours. So in the case of substantial connexion: it must be placed in every significant comparison, if we are to have Descartes's 'distinct' idea of it, an explicit intelligent appreciation of what it is.

But this will mean that even after the comparisons and distinctions have been once made, the object simply apprehended may indeed draw the central beam of luminous attention, but not without a fringe and penumbra of comparison still about it. This will reflect itself in linguistic usage. Those who wish to confine philosophers to plain and proper terms offend against the very form of thought, by which no term is what it is without its fringe. It is a serious fault not to know proper terms from analogical, but to expel the analogical is a cold impoverishment, which makes it a continual strain to remember that we are talking about any real thing, and not manipulating terms of philosophic algebra. Where the reader can grasp the term only by supplying the penumbra, it is strange the writer should be forbidden to assist him.

There will, then, be a descriptive use of analogy in which the dialectic movement is implicit only, when we are speaking of things we know, but supplying them with a running analogic commentary. Since the comment is analogic and not proper, dialectic is implicit in it, and it may be useful to make it sometimes explicit to assure ourselves that our grasp of the very thing is clear. But for the most part we write with much analogic colour, as was suggested of

Kant in his Analytic, but without conscious dialectic. For such writing, positions (6) and (7) above are natural: we use the eclectic method, an amalgam of analogic aspects whose incongruities we ignore.

But if the apprehension of any 'nature' is not without comparison, are we to say that substantial unity itself passed unapprehended, until those subtle philosophic distinctions were made, which surely first marked out its boundary? And if so, how are we to claim that a world of interacting substances is biologically natural, and the scheme of common-sense? To answer this we must return to our biological topic, and table of behaviour-relevances.

What, according to that table, is natural to man in so far as he has reached rationality in his active aspect, has begun to acknowledge the claims of his environment, and ceased to exploit merely? (Not indeed that the pre-rational stage was one of simple exploitation, for there is as much 'implicit morality' in fellow feeling for fellow creatures as there is 'implicit intelligence' in adaptations of habit to circumstances. Both phrases may be condemned as 'metaphysical,' but not one without the other.)

What, then, belongs to such 'active rationality'? Not an acquaintance with the class of substitutibles called substance, as a class and as distinguished from other classes, but recognition of certain differences that fall within that class. If we treat the world, as the savage does however absurdly and superstitiously, as consisting of beings having several values and claims, and in our behaviour show this and have some terms to describe these differences, it is enough. There is no need to consider thinghood, nor, since we take our responsible freedom for granted, selfhood either.

We may say if we like that there is an 'implicit' or 'confused' belief of what has never been considered; but these terms are opaque and we have no need to be content with them, since we can do better. For at this stage we remark (a) voluntary behaviour embodying a principle of choice which is not reflected on or recognised, (b) explicit judgments made in the course of this behaviour which can be seen (by others) to entail that principle, and equally directly to entail a metaphysical generalisation (of substance) along with that principle and as the factual correlate of that principle. If then the factual correlate of a principle of choice by which we choose, and the logical implicate of factual propositions which we assert in choosing, can be called an implicit (confused) belief, then belief in substance is implicit in active rationality as defined. But it does not seem to matter whether we approve the description (implicit belief) or not, since we know in any case what it is we are talking about; and can see now in what way a scheme of interacting substances can be the scheme of common-sense, prior to philosophical speculation.

But it may be asked how, from the standpoint of correlation between behaviour and knowledge, the implicit belief should ever have become explicit; or what behaviour-interests could ever have made the philosophical question a living one? We might counter this by another query: what behaviour-interests have led to the liveliness of the questions discussed by Logical Positivists? On their own showing, it is reaction against rubbishy confusions which have actually accumulated and threaten to silt up the channels of practical thought. Man is a word-user, they think, and has an interest in the serviceableness of his instrument—as one might have in the economical and effective design of a calculating machine. Hence philosophical reflection. There is much to be said for the derivation, and it will suit us very well. The mind has an interest in the clarity of the language which serves its behaviour; and without philosophical overhaul, language cannot be trusted to build itself up unconfusedly. The language or thought system has a native drive towards generalisation, because generalisation is the principle of economy; without criticism the generalisation cannot be trusted to go straight: here then is a fertile source of confusion in the working of language itself. The corrective against crazy classification is the establishment of mutually exclusive genera; and these may be such as are merely implied by the language we have previously been led to use, and explicitly stated first in critical and corrective reflection.

Now it is not difficult to construct a history of mental confusion which will account for the birth of a lively interest in the substance-question by way of critical reaction to that confusion. For the relations of the 'phenomenal' propositions (b) relevant to anticipation and manipulation, with 'real' propositions (a) expressing substantial differences and relevant to choice of aims, are delicate enough, as all philosophical debate witnesses: each type is liable to invade the territories of the other, animism overthrows phenomenal regularity, phenomenal regularity overthrows will and worth, and with each trespass vital behaviour-interests are affected, whether it is scientific manipulation or moral rationality that finds itself denied its proper language and cramped in its exercise. There is, then, no lack of motive to fix boundaries and define the substantial and the phenomenal. Moral interest has never been far out of sight where metaphysical interest has been lively: one hardly needs to mention Plato, Aristotle, Spinoza, Kant to realise that a balance of scientific and moral passion makes the typical metaphysician.[1]

We allow, then, that the knowledge of substance will naturally spring from attention to practically significant differences; but not that the differences involved are of a like transitory nature with these changing phenomena which positivism recognises. We shall see that in substance there is a real permanence, and interest in it can be interest in its continuity as well as in its modifications, as when one person loves another. Substances differ significantly from one another, and not only from themselves in other states. And hence arises a possibility of an interest in God, with whom is no variableness, neither shadow of turning, but who differs from ourselves in a very significant way.

[1] If in Kant the two were liable to come unstuck, that is an index of his ill-success.

(iv) *Definition of Analogy*

It will be serviceable here to define analogy and barely classify its uses; since we have already given descriptions of it (pp. 23, 80 *ff*) and shall hereafter give abundant illustrations of its employment. It would not be of any profit to distinguish all the senses in which the term has been used, some of which have very likely no more than associational connexion with others. It will be sufficient to state the senses to be found in this book.

Analogy is a relation between objects, capable of being classed as a species of 'likeness'. We must say of it, as of likeness in general, that it is not a real relation but *ordo rationis cum fundamento in rebus*. No one can suppose that the mere fact of resembling B is an actual ingredient in the existence of A, nor a condition nor an effect of that existence. If the mind finds the same character in two things, then it does find it, and it is in both places. But the mind itself is the place of comparison; comparability is not a real character in anything. Similarity by itself is not a real structural characteristic of the world, even though apart from it the structural character which the world has would not be possible. Cause and effect is a real structural order, and without similarity—like cause, like effect—it cannot operate.

It may well be the ideal of science to discover the real order which is the *fundamentum in re* for any mere similarity. So Darwin hoped to show that the similarities observed by us between several species of animals made up a cross-section taken by the mind across an actual evolutionary process. It remains, however, that mere similarity as such requires a mind, to take the cross-section. Cross-sections are not a part of the structure of actual being. It is the purpose of theologians to show that metaphysical analogy is an aspect of a real process, the creative act. But this (if we can reach it) is the conclusion. It cannot be put among the premises.

If we wish to define the sort of likeness that analogy is, we had better divide the genus 'likeness', not exhaustively perhaps but so far as the matter requires.

The simplest case is that which is reducible to the presence in the similars of an identical abstractible characteristic. Two figures, at first seen to be alike, are found to be so because both are triangular, even though the one is large, red and scalene, the other small, equilateral and blue. It is really needless to say any more about this; for though some have contested the adequacy of abstractive processes to the representation of any real order, no one can doubt that we in fact think in this manner. Difficulty arises over borderline cases only. For example, we may take our old friend, the similarity between scarlet and the note of a trumpet. We may analyse thus. There is a range of colour-tones and a range of sounds. These, as the sense-qualities belonging to two of our forms of sense, have an identical relation to other aspects of our consciousness, e.g. reflective thought, and this relation can be abstracted. Again, the mere form of continuity by which the colour-tones and the sound-tones respectively arrange themselves in a scale, can perhaps be abstracted, and stated in a purely logical form equally proper to both. We can then say: S is a tone in the colour-scale and T is a tone in the sound scale. But can we proceed and claim to abstract a common character of vividness, clarity and sharpness in the two? Perhaps we may; it seems to belong to sense-quality as such to be clear or indistinct, vivid or dull, sharp or flat. If this is conceded, we have less difficulty with the last point. Both, partly in virtue of their intrinsic character, partly for associational reasons, awake us to certain identical emotions. We may then write the formula: 'S is a tone in the colour scale and T is a tone in the sound scale. They are both vivid, clear and sharp, and they awake a common emotion.'

But not all likeness can be reduced to common abstractible character-istics present in identical form, not even if common relations and relation to common things be added to the formula. We may take the case of two colour-tones. *Qua* colours they are of course identical. We are not speaking of that but of the greater similarity of the tones A and B as compared with the tones A and C, or D and E. This is a question of position on a scale of continuous gradation. A certain red and a certain orange are each simple shades. Because we know that orange can be obtained by mixing red and yellow pigment, or because we have a habit of using red and yellow as standard colours, we may regard the red as pure and the orange as mixed. But this is not really so. Simply *qua* phenomena they are two shades of colour, and one as good as the other. But it just is so that we can arrange a certain series of colour shades from purple through red into orange and then yellow, so that there appears to be a continuous change and no breaks. And in this series the shades A and B are nearer than the shades A and C, for one must pass through B to reach C from A.

The comparison is a little less clear if we compare the interval between A and B with the interval between C and D, when C and D lie on the same scale but not between A and B nor A and B between them. We may of course get a representation of the spectrum and measure the two intervals with protractors. But that is really an external and irrelevant test. *Qua* colour-tasters simply, we may feel that the change from yellow towards green is more rapid and violent than that from red towards orange though both occupy an equal distance in the spectrum. And so, in comparing the width of the colour-intervals A-B and C-D, we cannot be accurate. We may say that the one interval is very narrow, the other pretty wide, but we cannot really say which shade lying between C and D will form with C an interval equal to A-B. We can try to count how many distinct shades we think we can recognise between A and B, C and *n*, and so try to find a partner for C at the same distance as B stands from A. But this again is really extrinsic and irrelevant. Our power of recognising distinct shades in the A-B region may be greater than our power for doing so in the C-D region. To put it otherwise, our sense of the diversity of *n* from *m* need not vary as our power to intercalate terms between them.

The same difficulties arise if, instead of comparing A-B and C-D when they lie on the same scale, we compare A-B and A-C if these lie on a different scale. For we can advance from A (say a shade of red) in several directions, along a scale which brings us to purple, to orange, to brown or to grey: and the degrees of change along these several lines cannot be exactly compared. It is not worth pursuing this subject further. Degrees of similarity in sense-quality cannot be reduced to common characters present here and absent there, nor yet to exact numerical measure. We could not compare them at all, they would be simply diverse, if we had not the notion of continuous scale, so that it appears 'further' from A to B than from A to C.

In thinking about the continuous scale, there are several tricks that the mind adopts. We may take A, say a certain shade of red, as our standard, and regard it as a diminishing ingredient in the scale which extends away through B to C. This is a falsification, for the other shades on the scale are no more composite than A itself: to regard them as adulterated A's is really absurd. And yet, so devoted is the mind to the interpretation of likeness in terms of the presence of an identical characteristic, that we are unable to dispense with it. If the characteristic is not equally present in the two instances—all true triangles are equally triangular—then we will have it that it is present in different degrees of purity or strength; and so orange is adulterated red. There are alternative schemes; we may, for example, in dealing with the similarity of two shades of orange, take neither as our standard, but regard them as both products of a 'pure' red and a 'pure' yellow. The identical characteristic is now not a single factor A but the complex A +B; only the proportions vary. It needs no words to show that this scheme is as artificial as the other.

We do not naturally apply the name 'analogy' to this likeness which lies in nearness on a continuous scale, for it does not seem as though two simples can be analogous when considered by themselves. Analogy supposes complexity in the things compared. Two simples may be reckoned analogous in virtue of their standing in two complexes that are themselves compared, but then it is the complexes that are analogous primarily; e.g. if we say that conscience in a man is analogous to the steersman in a boat. Analogy, then, is of complexes, but the complexes may be vital unities, they need not be mere aggregates. If there are complex metaphysically real entities, i.e. substances, there is nothing to prevent their being analogous to one another in virtue of their 'organic' structures.

But if the two patterns compared exhibit an identical order which can be abstracted, why should we any longer call them analogous? They are identical in that respect, and 'identity' is a more exact and so a better term than 'analogy'. Triangular figures of several sorts may have at first seemed merely analogous, but that was before they were recognised as triangular. We talk of the principle of analogy in mathematics and in physics, but these sciences have in fact no use for the relation of mere, that is irreducible, analogy. The physicist may look out for a vaguely felt analogy between two systems of established physical hypothesis, but it is his business to reduce it to the exactitude of a common formula applicable to both with equal rigour and in an identical sense. If he does not obtain this result, he has achieved absolutely nothing. The scope of exact science, as the modern world knows it, can be defined by the elimination of mere analogy. That to which the rigorous universal does not apply, science neglects, and is abstract for that very reason; since no real event, still less any real being, can be exhaustively described as the instance of general 'laws'.

If we wish to see things in the round, as metaphysicians must do, we are condemned to labour in the field of irreducible analogy unless we are able to refrain from ever comparing one real being with another and a different one. Suppose we compare what it is to be a dog, and what it is to be a man. Well, the behaviour of the two creatures as seen by an observer through the use of his senses exhibits phenomena from which certain highly abstract common patterns can be extracted. And even the psychology of the two, if we think we can have any knowledge of it, presents common orders which can be abstracted in the sense that both sets of facts can be represented by the same diagram, and this may pass as the abstraction of a common universal for the purposes of empirical science. But the metaphysician is interested in the character of the constituents in the two patterns, the character of the relation between them, and the character of the unitary existence or form of life which they go to constitute. But these are all different and merely analogous in a reasoning and an unreasoning creature. Appetite, for example, is not the same when penetrated by intelligence and when not so penetrated, nor is perception; nor is the relation of these to one another or to their objects; nor is the total conscious existence which they go to make up.

When we consider sense-perception-objects as such, we can distinguish and abstract quality and pattern quite satisfactorily; all red patches have some shape, but there is no difficulty about considering their colour and their shape apart. With the actual existences which perception signifies to us, it is not so. That which it is to be a man or a dog certainly has a pattern, an object of study to psychologists and to philosophers. It has also something comparable with quality; the humanness of the man, the caninity of the dog, is a certain degree of elevation in a scale of life, a certain intensity and a specific tone of being, which pervades the whole pattern and all its constituents. But this quality, if we may call it so, is meaningless and quite unthinkable apart from the structure in which it is expressed. Red colour is indeed meaningless apart from some spatial extension and therefore some shape; but it is indifferent to the particular width of the extension and the particular figure of the shape, and therefore it can be abstracted. Humanity and caninity as quasi-qualities cannot be thus abstracted from their patterns; nor conversely their patterns from them. We cannot really think of the relations between the several constituents that make up a human life apart from the peculiar quality of the life which they compose; we cannot regard them as a form equally capable of being filled with human life, dog life, slug life or cabbage life, and in that sense we cannot abstract them.

We can, however, form common diagrams of them, useful to empirical science. The same diagram may stand for the instinctive pattern in human and in canine appetite. But this diagram, whether actually drawn out on paper or expressed in words alone, is spatial and phenomenal in character, i.e. it expresses itself in that medium to which the abstraction of pattern is proper, sensible space. Now this spatial diagram is itself *merely analogous* to the non-spatial patterns which it symbolises; and they are *merely analogous* among themselves. The symbolisation of the many mutually analogous patterns by the one spatial pattern analogous to them all is the form of the abstraction used by empirical psychology.

While real beings and real events have a sort of quality and a sort of structure indissolubly united, it is in virtue of their structural, not their qualitative, aspect that they are properly analogous to one another. Regarded as qualities they may form a continuous scale, and are 'in proportion' to one another; but they are analogous in virtue of their pattern.

But if we take the patterns or complexes, how are they analogous, and what sense can we make of 'mere analogy'? Perhaps there is no difficulty in supposing that the mind scales patterns in degree of mutual approximation, as it does the sense-qualities. Between the circle and any given ellipse there is a continuous series of ellipses which can be graded by approximation to the circle or the given ellipse. Since the formula for the modification can be exactly stated, perhaps we have not in this mathematical example an instance of 'mere' and irreducible analogy. A better comparison might be the case of two crazy figures of different forms which we draw at random and then draw a series of further figures in which the first gradually takes on the shape of the second. For this series no formula could be stated and there would in fact be possible an indefinite number of slightly different series mediating between the two original figures. But none the less, in any of these series we could speak of the greater nearness or remoteness, the greater *analogy* of one than of another to one of the originals, or to any member of the series. What is more, we could compare members of different series in degree of analogy to either of the originals. Sometimes we should be unable to be sure, but sometimes we could say decidedly that one was the nearer. Now we can take a further step: all the figures that can be drawn are open for analogical comparison. We can ask whether a given figure will need more modification to become the figure A than to become the figure B. There may seem to be no answer; but again there may be, and again the answer given may depend upon an arbitrary assumption as to what would be a 'natural' or 'intelligible' direction of change.

This geometrical illustration is at best only one instance of analogical resemblance; and we must not be misled into supposing that it is typical in all respects. For example, to return to the instance of psychological patterns in several animals; we may indeed arrange these in order of approximation to one another, but there is no need to suppose that an absolute continuity of form is here even ideally possible. Between any two figures there is an indefinite number of possible figures: between any two animal existences there may not be an (even conceivable) indefinity of mediating types.

Analogy may be essential or accidental, according as it is based upon the fundamental patterns of two existents compared, or upon the patterns of superficial and partial aspects in them. Again, if these aspects are abstracted and the analogy predicated of them, not of that in which they are, the analogy will then be not accidental but abstract. The essential is of overwhelmingly greatest metaphysical importance, for metaphysicians round things out into complete existences and start from there in their properly metaphysical enquiries; so that essential analogy almost exclusively is their concern. But accidental comparison is by no means to be despised from an epistemological point of view, since upon it is based much of that natural symbolisation with which language cannot dispense and of which it is full; as often when we use something physical for a metaphor of the mental.

It may seem at first sight that the difference between the analogy of complexes and the scale of simples is not of much logical importance. But it is of great epistemological importance, for in the functions of language and thought the analogy plays a far greater part than the scale. It is complex structures that we are constantly concerned to describe to ourselves and to others; very little of our discourse turns upon the correct identification of simple qualities. Now we need, as is elsewhere explained in this book, to express and clarify our meaning by the use of metaphorical symbolisations or comparisons. Our very language does this for us to a large extent without our taking particular pains. And for this purpose it is plain that the analogy of complexes is of greater use than the scale of simples. It is by the complex that we symbolise the complex. Besides, the relation of simples is only with other simples in the same continuous scale, e.g. of colour; whereas the analogy of complexes may leap almost all boundaries; there is no knowing what pattern may not present accidental analogy with what other pattern. Naturally, not all analogies are equally revealing, and philosophers will seek those that are most so.

For example, many analogies of a fantastic sort suggest themselves to the poetic contemplator of time: a reaper, a winged chariot, a running river. But the only analogy likely to be of service to common-sense or to philosophy is that provided by the only other dimension with which we are acquainted, viz. space. This analogy has another important advantage; for since it is through spatial movement that time is measured, there is an active, not only a formal, connexion in our minds between the two dimensions; it is easy to treat the measure of time as the 'shape' of it. But we are not content to treat space in general as the image of time in general. We should then, in fact, have done nothing towards expressing the peculiar temporeity of time; we should merely have said that it, like space, is also a dimension, we should have expressed the common genus, not the particular species, and hardly even the genus, since the knowledge of it as a genus is posterior to the knowledge of more species than one. No, we take within space the most timelike of its manifestations—the single straight line—and we add a rule for the movement of which it is the supposed course, viz. that it must proceed steadily one way and cannot halt or return. It is only such a line, taken as the direction of such a movement, which is our analogy of duration.

Bergson attacks the spatial symbolisation of time, but he does so in further spatial symbolisations. In that there is nothing absurd, for the plurality and formal contradiction of the symbols makes us aware of the unique character possessed by that which is symbolised in them, thus delivering us from slavery to the indispensable symbolic medium. The straight line figure remains the most generally useful, for all that he may say. And in its relation to time there is an element of the merely analogous, which cannot be abstracted. The fact of relation to movement is common, indeed, but *it is not the same relation*. The form of *partes extra partes* is common again, but their manner of collocation is different. That of time cannot even be called 'collocation', and the word *extra* is itself a metaphor from space, so is the word 'part'. The only common properly abstractible form is that of mere numerability. Not even continuity is abstractible, but merely analogous in the two.

In the case, then, of time the class of analogues that are relevant is drastically limited to the several dimensions of space, because that is the only other class of dimensions we have. And of these spatial dimensions one is nearer in analogy to time than the rest. It is much the same with the mental and the phenomenal-physical. These are the only two sorts of concrete existence which common-sense recognises, and so it is in the second that must be found analogues and symbols of the first. But again, not in the whole of it; some phenomenal-physical objects by their apparently 'disembodied' action, breath and flame for example, appear to be nearer to pure spirit.

These examples must suffice. It is not our present purpose to examine metaphorical symbolisation but to show the analogical relation of objects upon which the symbolisation of one by another is based. Where this analogical relation is ignored or exploded, symbolisation cannot be understood. Metaphors are then only relevant in so far as they express an identical abstractible character, common to the symbol and that which it symbolises. It is this character alone which is predicated. But it will be seen immediately that in this case metaphors can signify nothing of the unique character in the reality to which they refer; how, for example, anything physical can suggest the spirituality of the spiritual is totally inexplicable, and so it is an easy game on this assumption to play old Thomas Hobbes's trick of naturalistic reduction and show that the spiritualisers are unable to talk about anything but physical phenomena. On the analogical theory, indeed, the analogue does not actually express or state what is different and unique in the analogate; how could it? But, since the mind can analogise and the direction along which to analogise is suggested by the context, the analogue is a positive contribution to our thinking of the analogate, not a mere conventional or algebraic sign.

In conclusion we may note how the definition of analogy here given covers our theological analysis. Is the finite being analogous to the infinite as one complex to another? Yes, for we distinguish in the creature the complex

pattern essence, existence and the relation between them, and describe the
infinite being as a different and analogous form of this complex (relation between essence and existence not the limitation of the latter by the former, but
its perfect expression thereby).

Analogy provides an instance of itself, for the several sorts of analogy,
considered 'in the round', are analogous to one another. The relation of analogy
between two existents is not the same as that between an existent and a constituent of it, or between an order in substantial reality and an order among
phenomena *qua* phenomena; all of which relations have been illustrated in what
precedes.

(v) *Analogical Discourse*

It is one thing to consider analogy as a relation between objects; another
thing to consider arguments drawn from analogy, or propositions in which
there is analogical predication. In arguments from analogy we attempt from the
analogue to draw conclusions about its analogate, i.e. about that to which it is
analogous. In analogical predication we state of the analogate something drawn
from the analogue, but under the qualification that it applies in such sense only
as the analogy warrants. An analogical predication is the cautious statement of
the conclusion from an analogical argument: the two need not be distinguished
for the purpose of the further twofold division which follows.

As to analogical argument, we have already renounced simple inference
from an unchecked analogical premise as universally fallacious, and do not propose to re-open the topic. We wish only to distinguish two types which we have
used and shall use: we call them negative and positive.

(1) *Negative analogical dialectic* is the type of which we have been lately
speaking, when the purpose is to distinguish an object of apprehension from all
its analogues, so that the ideal appears to be the elimination of the analogues
entirely. This ideal, as we have been saying, is not practicable, since distinctness
is a function of distinction and we have constantly to restore the analogical
context if only that we may distinguish from it again. And it would have been
possible to apply the description 'positive dialectic' to that reversal of the process, in which we build up the analogies; but since this is only another aspect of
the one type of reasoning and the final purpose of the whole seems to be distinction, 'negative dialectic' is a suitable label for it all.

(2) *Positive analogical argument* takes place when we use an analogical
relation already admitted in order to conclude from better known analogue to
less known analogate. Let it be granted that the subjectivity of a dog bears some
analogy to our own. From this unsupported and unchecked analogical premise
nothing can be concluded: we should never know but that the unstated difference belonging to the dog's mode of subjectivity might not be precisely such as
to exclude the aspect of our own which we proposed to transfer. But in the
phenomena of the dog's behaviour we have a certain check. Comparing these

with the phenomena of our own, we are able to analogise as to his consciousness not, heaven knows, within a mile of accuracy, but not wildly or senselessly either. Many of the same limitations will apply as in the theological analogising of proportionality, e.g. that we cannot actually translate into the canine mode the aspects of our consciousness that seem to fit, we can only mark them out from other aspects as having a canine analogate in connexion with this or that detail of the dog's behaviour.

(3) *Theological analogising.* It is often said that theology is analogical in a unique degree. It deals with an object of which the analogical relation to other objects is unique, but this is true of every mode of analogy and says nothing directly as to the method of the science. Its peculiarity may be found in a peculiar combination of methods (1) and (2) in the theological 'proportionality'. For if we compare this 'proportionality' with the case of the animal just taken, what plays the part of check to the general analogical premise? Not behaviour phenomenally evidenced, but the notion of an absolute degree or mode of activity. But this in turn is defined by a most exhausting and difficult process of 'negative dialectic', i.e. the distinction of absolute activity, causality, etc., from all the analogies through which we arrive at our thought of it.

There is here a danger of terminological confusion, which is worth mentioning. The application of our negative dialectic in theology is not the *via negativa, remotiva,* etc., of tradition. What we call the negative dialectic negates all analogues on the basis of some obscure apprehension of the object we are attempting to distinguish, and its purpose is to grasp the mere notion of absolute being. Whereas 'via negativa' is traditionally used of the negative aspect of the proportionality argument in which absolute being is already presupposed; when starting with existence or activity in the full-blooded finite mode we simply strike out (negate, remove) the aspects that can have no archetype in that absolute. The purpose of our negative dialectic is to distinguish the analogate from all analogues, however precise; that of the traditional *via negativa* is to make the analogues as precise as possible by distinguishing their applicable aspects from their inapplicable. It is then essentially the negative precision inseparable from what we call positive analogical argument. We are really concerned with the positive analogical movement which transfers characters found in the finite to the infinite; but the transference is made possible by negation of what will not go across.

Let us hope that this will suffice as some guiding-thread through the mazes of analogising that this book contains.

IX

PROBLEMS ABOUT THE APPREHENSION OF SUBSTANCE

(i) *Apprehension*

WE have agreed that our case depends on some awareness of substantial being, other than a mere awareness of phenomena and of their phenomenal order. It can serve no purpose to place an account of this apprehension among these logical prolegomena. Apprehension is specified by its object, and the possibility of a certain apprehension can be admirably demonstrated from acquaintance with its object, but not from anything else. To make the object evident will be our business presently. Meanwhile a few verbal points may usefully be cleared up.

Is that which we apprehend a *phenomenon*? If 'phenomenon' means something directly given, which 'shows itself' to us, yes. If 'phenomenon' means something superficial, the sign or partial aspect of something underlying, no; for there is nothing more fundamental for us than substantial being. Is it a *noümenon*? If this word contrasts with the second sense of phenomenon, or with *aestheta* as the objects of the five senses, yes. But if it means the apprehension of a 'pure intelligible' in complete independence of any sense-experience, no. We shall in fact sometimes use the words noesis, noümenon in the allowable sense; we shall not find ourselves calling this sort of object a phenomenon.

The same sort of difficulties arise over empirical, empiricist, etc. Evidently we are putting our money on an object of experience: but experience is frequently defined in a narrow sense which excludes *empiria* of such an object, being made equivalent to sense-experience. For this narrow doctrine, phenomenalism and naturalism are convenient terms; for the proper appeal to experience, experiential, experientialism may do.

Apprehension is specified by its object, and so is no separate topic; but the response or reaction without which no apprehension takes place is not specified by the object, though relative to it, and so may be dealt with here. We have already discussed certain aspects of this response, and the practical interests connected with it. The response contains at least an implicit affirmation of the apprehension; if it includes or consists of statements referring to the things, the affirmation is explicit.

(ii) *Affirmation and Obscurity*

We will now ask, what causes us to affirm? At first sight this sounds easy to answer. The occurrence of apprehension and the presence of interest correlative therewith, lead to affirmation. If I am seeing something red, and if there is present interest that makes me attend (without which I should not see at all in the full meaning of the word) then a response occurs which affirms it. When, for example, I am attentively watching the traffic-lights and as I approach the corner they turn from green to red, I cannot fail to respond, even though I override that immediate response by deciding to override the lights.

But suppose the objects of apprehension are not 'clear and distinct'? Then we are back to Descartes's problem. Why affirm, then? Well, sometimes, says Descartes, our judgment is rushed, 'precipitated'; that which is not clear appears so. Sometimes, we will add, a probability piles up so strong that to suspend judgment would be pedantry. Sometimes it is very important on practical grounds to act, without complete evidence. It is not always a good plan to deliberate long whether the sound we hear is or is not that of a car about to round the corner upon us at 40 miles an hour.

Let us consider the applicability of these examples. Is the apprehension of substantial being 'clear and distinct'? It is not. If it had been, the history of human thought would have been very different. It is not simply that, as we have seen, a certain situation is necessary before the substance-question can become a question. Long after it has become so, when it has so long been so that we can hardly bear to hear it mentioned, it is not agreed upon. Very likely the history of human thought allows us to conclude plausibly that there is something above and beyond the sense-phenomena which many people are unable to ignore, yet it is possible for some people to confuse it with the sense-phenomena and deny its separate existence. 'Clear and distinct', or rather 'indubitable' are, or may be, the principles common to any language (system of terms) that we can form and operate, and the voluntary definitions which go to make up a language we construct, and, in the experience-field, sensations viewed subjectively—the fact that such-and-such a quality is being enjoyed; and this holds good, even though we cannot (as some affirm) abstract apprehension from all 'interpretation'; for the fact of the interpretation can be reckoned in.

What is indubitable always lacks existential reference, or rather, the reference is not included in its indubitable content. So much the worse for Descartes. When he asserted that the substance-self was clear, he confused clarity of content with self-evidence of fact. In consciousness it is indubitable that something is given, but for this proposition to be significant we need no sharper definition of 'something' than will suffice to distinguish it from 'nothing', or rather, from something not 'given' in the same sense.

But though we have no indubitable data, we may have probabilities which it would be silly to reject, and we are encouraged in this hope by the parallel of induction. For nothing based on induction can be more than probable: as soon as I go beyond the statement that I am enjoying the view of a paper-like visual datum, and assert that it *is* paper, I am making assumptions about its composition which many experiments alone could verify, and even then I am assuming that a certain thing which satisfies certain tests will continue to yield phenomena of a consistent and law-abiding kind; otherwise the description 'paper' is meaningless. And none of these things is indubitable, and yet it would be silly to doubt them.

In probability of this sort we are concluding to what, in kind, falls within our previous knowledge, for we conclude to the forthcomingness of phenomena such as we have been indubitably acquainted with before. The sort of thing we come to believe in, then, is in no way obscure, as substance is; all that is at all obscure is whether it will turn up in a given context. Further, the principle by which we conclude that it will turn up is not in the least obscure; uniformity of sequence is (a) perfectly intelligible, (b) undoubtedly exemplified in some degree by the 'world'. We do not know, indeed, how perfect the uniformity is; nor whether the rule of uniformity we are applying has been correctly enough stated; nor (perhaps) whether an instance of it is really before us here. But still our acquaintance with some uniformity remains.

In none of these respects does metaphysical 'probability' (if the word can apply) offer any parallel. The thing whose givenness we are affirming is itself what is obscure; the necessity of its givenness is not distinct from its own obscure nature, for if there is a necessity for reckoning all phenomena to substance, this necessity is embodied in the nature of substance itself. If we accept it, we accept it as an obscure epiphenomenon, or epinoümenon rather, upon what is clear; somewhat as 'beauty' has been regarded as a quality epiphenomenal upon sense-data by persons simple-minded enough to take beauty for a quality; if we may quote so damaging a parallel without prejudice. And even then the parallel is not good; for the beauty is supposed to be founded in the sense-data, whereas with substance it is the other way about.

The only good analogy offered by the field of sense-data is the case of the indistinct datum. For then we may not be dubious as to the 'physical thing', as in the above quoted case of the paper; we may be dubious as to whether anything is felt, or what is its nature. Whether, when I think that the scent has changed *for me*, it is so, or I only 'imagine' it; whether the mist shows faint undulations or really looks uniform. Philosophers tell us that in these cases we must have recourse to inductive methods; for example, if I walk the path again by daylight, I may see that there were roses, roses all the way or that the second half of the bed is planted with a different flower. But this only establishes a *presumption* about how the smell was for me and as a smell-datum; the question could only be settled by straining attention at the time, and then not settled certainly, for it is possible to precipitate judgment and substitute 'imagination' for primary sense-experience.

Positivists may try to set this sort of problem aside as a nonsense-question; for how could the answer be verified? If I 'merely imagined', I can never know that this was so, since *ex hypothesi* I have been cheated, and the sole appeal possible is to induction, which we have just ruled out. Positivists are welcome to their terminology; if the question falls under the definition of a 'nonsense-question', so be it. It remains that it represents a real issue, for there is such a thing as intensifying attention and controlling 'imagination' and setting aside

prejudices in the attempt to get a 'pure datum'. Just so, we may be told: faced
with an obscure datum you indulge in certain behaviour-techniques in order to
obtain a different and better datum; as though you brought a telescope to bear.
There is no need to contest this account; it remains that there are sense-phenomena which leave us in doubt (*a*) what to affirm, and (*b*) whether to affirm at all.

This analogy is no better than an analogy, and it happens to be prejudicial
to our case. For sense-phenomena, as we have seen, are often indubitable and
those which we trouble to use are for the most part sufficiently clear; it is seldom
that we have to make life-and-death decisions on our judgment of an obscure
datum, though one can make up a novel to illustrate it if one chooses. More
usually our risky decisions turn on a risky *inference*: e.g. Is it paper or celluloid?
Is it hemlock or fennel? So that the 'obscure sense-datum' suggests something
both below proper standard, and marginal or negligible.

We look, then, for an analogue which is obscure in kind, and does not
have obscure instances merely. Such analogies are forthcoming, but have their
own contrary defect in lack of objective reference, e.g. our old friend 'an ear
for music'. That seems musical in the West which does not seem so in the East,
and some have no ear for music at all. This is, however, a whole type of experience to which non-evidence seems to belong; yet the unmusical hesitate to condemn it as a cheat, because they see what remarkable and elaborate structures
are erected by musicians, and that these are to some extent appreciated by many,
if one can accept testimony.

This analogy has obvious defects, beside simple 'subjectivity'; for is there
really a standard of the musically 'right', except within an assumed system or
style? Yet it reminds us that our obscure object (substance) can be several ways
construed by those who admit the question of substance, and also that what is in
question is not a simple quality but a system: so that the evidence of substance
is not the evidence merely of a quality which hits us so hard that we cannot help
attending to it; it is the evidence of a system the mutual complementariness of
whose parts we strongly appreciate.

This was the argument for what it is worth, used by Descartes, following
Anselm, to show the validity or reality of the idea of God. They treated the
mutual relation of the 'attributes', as indicated by the verbal description, as an
instance of mathematical connexion, which plainly it is not, and a refutation of
the argument is therefore easy. But it may well appear to the metaphysician
appropriate to give 'mathematical necessity' as an *analogue* to the kind of compulsion exercised on the mind by the system of relations in the substance-order.
It is more like the compulsion of pure logic or number than that of voluntarily
formed definitions in so far as assumed. It is not logical necessity for all that,
but the necessity of real connexion as apprehended.

But we wander from our aim, which was to illustrate the *obscurity* of the
metaphysical object, for which the obscure sensum remains the best parallel
after all. But in order to guard against the irrelevant associations of the obscure
sensum, we sought other analogies, reminding ourselves that this obscure

object of ours is obscure as a class—it cannot, so to speak, help being obscure to us; so far as we know, obscurity belongs to it in relation to such an understanding as ours—that this obscure object is not therefore unimportant because it is obscure: that it is not a simple quality, but a structure.

(iii) *Practical Necessity of Affirmation*

We now take up the other half of the division we made (p. 100) and ask how, if the object is obscure, we come to affirm about it at all? For this we need only to refer back to the behaviour-topic. The 'Categorical Imperative of practical reason' has not, as Kant supposed, its sole ground in the abstract character of rationality inherent in the agent's mind. This is, in fact, an absurd limitation, for the very form of practical rationality is attention to and response to real entities according to their intrinsic worth, their need, and also, no doubt, according to the degree in which they enter into the orbit of our own existence. As our contemplative rationality is contemplative response to Being as it is, so practical rationality is the answering of its claims. We shall justify these definitions hereafter.

Now unless we precipitate our judgment of the obscure, we shall not even be able to decide that one matter is a more worthwhile subject to be in active doubt about, than another—that it contains more 'real' or 'likely' questions. And unless we precipitate judgment about the real entities that surround us, we shall not be able to attend to their claims. For it is evident that given a certain degree of probability for it, a reality of which our apprehension is not indubitable can make a claim that is binding. The reason against snaring rabbits with torture is not the unpleasant phenomena nor the nasty feeling those give us, but our strong though unverifiable suspicion that rabbits have a life in and to themselves.

Kant was right when he gave the moral will a leading part in the acknowledgment of metaphysical reality. He had a suspicion that it must, however, be illegitimate to allow will to create fact, and hence his unsuccessful compromise of 'postulates'. When he says that the practical reason is able to affirm what the pure speculative reason would have to leave undetermined, the formula is acceptable—except that there is no 'pure speculative reason' in separation; will and intellect are inseparable though distinct, and the function of the will in judgment is to wager on the non-evident and deliver human life from moral—yes, and speculative—imbecility.

Kant discussed the thorny topic, whether to believe a metaphysical proposition could be a duty, and (as a corollary) whether to disbelieve one could be moral depravity. He denied both: to recognise and perform the dictates of the categorical imperative is duty; and if we perform this duty, we shall undoubtedly assume whatever assumptions are psychologically necessary, for this recognition and this action to take place; including, for the clear thinker, such trifles as the immortality of the soul and the existence of God.

This method of evading the question is not available to us, because we do not think that the mere form of the 'Categorical Imperative' can determine duties apart from the objects recognised to be real. What shall we say, then? That the condition of any duty's being done is in fact the recognition of the claims of entities upon practical reason; but that this can happen with an indeterminable degree of confusion and division of thought, so that no man can say what metaphysical error in conscious speculation may not be compatible with active virtue. Yet error must on the whole cloud and inhibit, especially where there is most conscious deliberation; for we have seen that language is an instrument which is not so serviceable unless it avoids confusion; and there are certain realities or aspects of realities which cannot become objects to the will without a certain refinement of perception and 'interpretation'. We should most of us agree that to refuse to consider a claim because it was not evident, could be a moral evasion unlikely to be innocent, as for example, if a barbarous poacher excused himself by metaphysical doubts about the consciousness of rabbits. And the theologian must make it a serious duty of reflective minds not lightly to deny practical probability either to aspects of the human 'substance' which claim duties independent of *obvious* human satisfaction, or to a supreme being who makes the highest claim of all. Is it fair to claim that we must take our most serious perceptions seriously, even if they cannot be made absolutely indubitable? That to approach existence with the conviction that there is nothing in it, and that debunking is the highest wisdom, is always cheap, and sometimes wicked?

(iv) *Apprehension and Interpretation*

It is commonly held that the dubiety of metaphysics, if it does not completely discredit the science, proves that there is in its working a large proportion of 'mental interpretation'. It is not quite clear what this means. We do not apprehend without response, nor form propositions without words, and the response-habits and term-systems that we have acquired limit the fineness and fullness of our apprehension. To ask what it would be like to apprehend without selecting is to ask what it would be like to be the Infinite Mind. The selection is determined by the limited scope of a given finite existence, and the words are the instrument of this limitation, and not an added defect unless they are unsuitable. In order that they may be suitable, what is required of them? As to 'proper terms', we need enough distinct ones to create the distinctions we apprehend, and we want them arranged in a logical pattern which does not distort the relations in the object. But so far as the terms are 'proper', their significance, and the nature of the relations marked by their arrangement, will *be* our apprehension (or misapprehension) of the objects.

But how can we know that they are simply 'proper', that we have carried the 'negative dialectic' through to the bitter end, and expelled all analogic material from the notion we frame of the analogate? That, in fact, we have eliminated confusion? We cannot know, and evidence suggests that we never completely do. And it results that what we call 'variety of interpretation' is the variety of error or misapprehension, unless it is simply selection. It is a continual mistake in philosophy, than which none is more deadly, to reduce apprehension and misapprehension to equal members of a single genus which they equally exemplify, whereas in fact they are to be compared as the proper and the spoilt example of a species, as (normal) man and idiot. And so we elevate into a general principle called 'interpretation' the dialectical confusion introduced by error in so far as we err, and indeed *humanum est*. But had we not the ideal of eliminating such 'interpretation' and the ability to decrease it we should not even know what error means, except where we can apply the pragmatic test, and that is not in this field.

In so far as error is eliminated, terms do not stand between the object and ourselves: indeed such a view is only possible to a vicious conceptualism like Kant's, if it is right to accuse him of thinking that the meaning of a term was a creation of the mind and applied to the given. But it is not; a term in its real reference is a label tied to some apprehensible to mark it, and the confusion introduced by bad terminology is ultimately a confusion of apprehension, or rather of imagination with apprehension, of which deception, as we have already seen, there is no infallible preventive beforehand nor infallible check after it has occurred. Misapprehension is an ultimate, since of apprehension there is no other evidence but our apprehending, and misapprehension, by definition, appears to apprehend.

The fact, then, of metaphysical dubiety does not impose upon us one particular philosophy before another, except that it denies us the right to assert indubitable clarity, or to deny that men habitually err. If one wishes to see why error is vastly harder to shun and to detect in metaphysics than in the study of phenomena, he must look at the nature of the two subject-matters in the best account that can be given of them, and he will get all the enlightenment that is available. He will also see how we can err in the former without being so simply wrong as the man who thought it was bread, and found it was a stone.

But the problem of apprehension and interpretation comes to a head when we survey the various philosophies of the past. If we attend to their mutual contradictions, we incline towards pure historicism and conclude that any system of metaphysics merely articulates the thought-forms peculiar to its age, or even to its author. If we attend to the merit of each, we convince ourselves equally that it is an instrument of objective apprehension; for we can understand it, can grasp something by means of it, and there is no great system of the past which we can study without our own systems being affected and enriched by it. A solution must be sought along the lines suggested. The singularity of each historical system is the product of selection and misapprehension inextricably fused. We could only separate them completely by obtaining the absolute view of the full and concrete truth. Then we should see that which Aristotle and Kant had partly selected, partly misapprehended. As it is, the best we can do is to form our own system, profiting by the wisdom of our predecessors and standing on the shoulders of better men. Then this system of ours, whether we like it or not, will automatically determine what in them we judge to have been selected, what misapprehended, for the former elements we shall synthetise and the latter exclude. Both selection and error are historically conditioned, and equally so. The 'state of the question' as each philosopher inherits it is dominated by a certain language and certain alternative statements within that language. In these both selection and misapprehension are implicit.

Meanwhile, there is a general consideration from which we may derive a little comfort. The apparent mutual contradiction between the fundamental conceptions of several philosophies need not involve the radical falsity of either or of both, nor yet their real incompatibility; and that for the following reason. No philosophy states itself as a selection from the structural character of existence: for in order so to state itself it must state that from which it is a selection, and then it would no longer be a selection, having stated the whole. No; it must state its selected aspect as the very principle of all existence, and, so stated, this must formally exclude another alleged principle of all existence which is the absolutising of some other aspect. Aristotle, perhaps, tends to panbiologism, Descartes to panmathematicism: the two statements exclude one another, but that does not prevent you or me from recognising that each was describing a real aspect of things nor from stating a more satisfactory central formula which will find room for both aspects each in its place. This formula of ours will itself be a selection, and a partial misapprehension. But that is no more reason for abandoning philosophy, than the impossibility of perfect happiness here and now is a reason to lie down and die.

(v) Conclusion

The philosophical mind tends to be more critical than constructive, and to find its chief motive in hostility to shams. But this hostility itself is faced with a dilemma. On the one side, there is the apparent sham of pretending that we can describe and define the elusive and obscure, such as we confess the subject-matter of this book to be. But on the other side there is the sham of pretending to hold a system of principles which, however clear and precise, cover only a minute area of the actual matter of human concern, and exclude the principles by which we think and act for the best part of our own lives. This is the sham of pretending that the obscure is the unimportant: that if our stated principles do not allow us to give any other account of personality and freedom than an ingenious attempt to talk these things away, this is a trifling matter—we have not yet, perhaps, found the complete reduction, but it may turn up later; we need not worry meanwhile.

Between these two shams every philosopher must choose. We have chosen the former; we are making for Scylla with all sail set: for it seems that this sham can be avoided by modesty, whereas the other cannot be avoided by silence.

And this is our whole answer to those who wish to know why we place such weight on what we acknowledge to be obscure. If they wish further to see both the importance of the elusive and the possibility of reasoning from it, our answer is to be found not in these prolegomena but in the next two sections of the book.

These fragmentary prolegomena have not been designed to show the internal flaws of all empiricist systems or even of one most in fashion. If our objection is that they have left unstated what is important, such a treatment is irrelevant, even supposing we were competent to supply it. Thus there are philosophers who distinguish the object of apprehension from the act of apprehending and consider that object to be something in itself; and yet see no necessity for allowing any but an AND connexion between one real atom and the next. My objection to this substance-doctrine (if it is such) is not that it cannot be stated, but that it does not do justice to what I believe myself to apprehend and my neighbours to live by. The choice of Logical Positivism for some slight consideration here was due to its being the most radical opponent of full substance-doctrine and so most illuminating as contrast and most salutary as criticism.[1] It is not our purpose to write a treatise on the possibility of metaphysics, but to metaphysicise. For 'from existence to possibility the inference is good'. If metaphysical discourse can be exhibited *in actu*, the possibility of it can be left to take care of itself.

[1] Some of my friends tell me that what I have discussed is a debased and puerile wing of Logical Positivism that happens to have made a noise. I readily plead guilty to ignorance of the nobler school. It has served my purpose to explain myself by way of answer to this voice which I have actually heard.

EXAMINATION OF FINITE SUBSTANCE: THE WILL

X

WILL IN THE MORAL STRUGGLE

(i) *Substantial Connexion to be sought within*

THE upshot of our logical prolegomena is this. No valid objection can be raised *a priori* against the attempt to describe or indicate substantial being. But equally, everything turns on our ability to describe or indicate it: if *a priori* considerations cannot block it, no more can they establish it. To this vital task, therefore, we turn; recalling first a previous conclusion, that it is in the common-sense scheme of self and thing that substance is to be sought.

Substances, we have said, are complexes, though perhaps not composites and certainly not aggregates; and that in them by which we have distinguished them is the peculiar 'reality' of the relation which unites their constituents. This relation, then, is what we must first endeavour to make evident. And, of the division 'self—thing', it is the former that offers most promise as a starting-point. For what we have to seek is the most accessible instance. Activity or existence forms, we have suspected, an analogic scale of modes, and we must look for the mode, and the instance of that mode, most known to us, before we can hope to widen our acquaintance.

'Enquire within' is a maxim that seems to apply here. Not that in general we have an exacter idea of what is 'within us' than of what is 'without us'; and that for excellent biological reasons. We are concerned to note the differences in environment with which we have to deal: what is ourself, we take for granted, since that is a self-operating instrument which takes its direction from its objects. Or if free consideration is one of its functions, yet a considering mind is turned wholly outwards upon its objects; we have no more occasion to reflect upon it, than in a cinema upon the projector and the beam of light. We do not look within to contemplate facts, but to listen to the clamour of our desires; and the imaginative content of our desires is itself concerned with what is external. We are, as it were, in a dark room pierced with eye-holes: it may be true that we are in it, but it is much easier to see what is outside it.

The self, then, is obscure, and yet for the search we have in hand it may provide the likeliest field. We seek 'real relation'. Now it seems almost axiomatic that in anything looked at *ab extra* nothing but phenomenal relations can be detected. Take a visible movement. Seen from without, it must be seen as a mere sequence—one phase appears after another, that is all; and though the change is gradual, like that of colours in the sunset, the formula 'mere sequence' is not invalidated; it is a sequence of infinitesimals, or it is a continuous flux, but merely a flux. The uniformity-rule governing its gradual changes is only a uniformity-rule, based on experience and phenomenal analogy. There are none but inductive reasons of the usual kind why it should not be halted or broken or reversed. So that Hume's reduction of causality, so far as outward phenomena are supposed to be the clue to it, has a sort of self-evidence. As much cannot be said about his reduction of it in the self.

For, is there, perhaps, a process which is identical with our conscious existence? Can it reflect upon itself, and enter 'from within' into the very arising of what follows out of what preceded it? Does it not appear that consciousness penetrates a certain span of its own process at once? If, then, there is an activity which really gives rise to events, and does not merely precede them according to a rule, and if this activity can be aware of its own action in so doing, it seems that this might be the only conceivable case in which real connexion could be detected, whether that case is obscure or not.

What has just been written is analogical dialectic; and it is open to anyone to object that its apparent force lies in the analogues 'within, without'; 'an object itself, another object related to it', etc. 'Within and without' suggests the contrast between a view of the machinery from inside and a view of the façade, which plainly does not apply; while the topic of numerical identity and numerical diversity is equally misleading, for an act of apprehension surely implies a difference between itself and its object, and excludes their numerical identity.

But if, after seeing through the analogues, we still feel a force in the argument, it may be because we have the mind's eye on a real analogate which substantiates it. One can only ask for the experiment to be made. But the last point of objection requires an answer. An act can never, perhaps, be simply conscious of itself, but only (say) of its image. And then a dilemma arises: for are not mental images derived from experienced counterparts? Either, then, the act can experience itself, and afterwards the image of itself; or it can experience neither.

But we do not need to maintain that the act can apprehend itself; it can apprehend a sufficient stretch of the process, whereof it is assumed to be itself a phase. If at one instant I can look back through a continuity of my own preceding process I can see the real action by which one phase created the next. 'But' we should be told 'that would be memory, and the same difficulty arises: we can only remember what we have experienced already.' We fail to see any self-evident universality in this formula. It applies to natural phenomena: unless they previously secured a place in the process of our mind, how can we recover them? Though this place, as Leibniz first observed, need not be in the full light of consciousness. But it might be held that it is in looking back along the continuity of our own existence that we come upon these phenomena, where they have coloured it; and that this presupposes rather than excludes an ability to look back along the track of our existence, anyhow to some depth, as in the case of immediate memory, and there descry the experiencing of previous phenomena, and also (why not?) our own conscious act creating its own successor. On Hume's causal-sequence view of the relation between original experience and memory-image, this sort of language is excluded; but then it is not evident that Hume is right, and his hypothesis applies very poorly to immediate memory of every kind.

Our view does not even involve us in the paradox of reducing what appears to be an act of immediate reflection into an act of memory, if by memory is meant such an apprehension of things past as makes possible the apprehension of their pastness. But when (in our hypothesis) an act of mind looks not outward but backward into the active self, there is an object which it comes to first, and that is the voluntary state immediately preceding itself. This is its immediate object. Now we have no awareness of the time-lag between any object that is to our apprehension immediate, and our apprehension of it. Everything has happened by the time we see it happening; but we are not aware of this. We are only aware of 'pastness' when one object of apprehension is past in comparison with another object, not in comparison with the act of apprehending. And so we should apprehend the immediately last will-act as present, since *ex hypothesi* our actually present act by which we apprehend it, cannot apprehend itself. What we have described, then, is an act of reflection that is as immediate as any we could conceive.[1]

In the doctrine of memory we have been sketching, we have fallen again into analogical dialectic, and talked of the active self's past as though it were a tunnel we look back along. But we have used this dialectic for the innocent and negative purpose of undermining an equally analogic *a priori*, viz. that acquaintance with past phases of the active self would have to be identical in a certain respect with acquaintance with previously experienced outward phenomena. Our formula is: The self's past can be apprehended because it is 'there' *qua* past of the self; phenomena, no doubt, because they have been embodied into it through being perceived, but acts in their own right, because they were done. But the appeal must be not to the apparent evidence of the formula, but to experience. We merely remove prejudice against the possibility of the experience we look for. The test is, whether such experience is forthcoming or not, or rather, whether we have acquaintance with its object. If we have, it is enough, whether this account of the mode of its apprehension is proper, or some other. On our principle, we shall expect the object to be far less obscure than the act by which it is apprehended.

(ii) *Will, not Understanding, the Clue*

If, then, we can see a certain plausibility in the contention that nowhere but in ourselves (if there) could we find 'real connexion', we will look for this

---

[1] To talk of dissociation will not help us here: for the act from which the apprehending act dissociates itself has occurred by the time it is apprehended.

in the act of will, whereby common-sense supposes that effects are really produced or created. Not in the act of consciousness as consciousness. Fot it is precisely the abstracting of the onlooking mind by philosophers (i.e. by professional onlookers) that has led to disbelief in real connexion. Apart from the *activity* of our mind, consciousness may be treated as a simple fact of 'reflection', analogous to mirror-phenomena: the 'image' changes gradually, and according to rules, and has a certain temporal as well as spatial extension. But no principle of metaphysical unity is required, any more than with the sunset. The mind, *qua* onlooker, is naturally concerned to eliminate and hide its own activity, as in looking at the stars we are concerned to discount telescope-machinery; the telescope is simply for seeing; and so is the mind's activity in so far as the mind 'looks on'. And this is so, even though our onlooking takes the form of introspection. The perfect realisation of the contemplative ideal in that field is an onlooking that dissociates itself completely from the process it is viewing, and sees the *introspectum* as though from without. The thing can be done, who denies it? Just as the same academic persons have sometimes the curious gift of dissociating a part of their minds, and impartially appreciating their own words and gestures, as from the vantage-point of a fly on the ceiling. There is almost no feat of abstraction that the human mind cannot perform.

But is it an abstraction? That is the question for us. Is there a connexion, a *geistiges Band* that has been artificially eliminated from the scene? The way to answer that question is to look, not for consciousness-data, but for the act of will, to see if there is such a thing. At this point in the argument we are lured by the same old academic temptation mentioned above (p. 71), the *ad hominem* argument. 'Prove to them that an account of consciousness *itself* involves taking account of will-activity.' Well, so it does; but the real objection is not this, but the wider one that *there is will-activity*, and the most straightforward and important argument is that which appeals to its most characteristic and most evident examples. Neither is the *ad hominem* argument even expedient. If men are engaged along the path of purifying and purifying their attitude of contemplative abstraction, if their ideal of knowledge is the perfecting of a filter to keep out the sort of consideration you are offering them, they will not be likely to appreciate that against which they are so excellently armed. Better catch them in the posture of vigorous action (since philosophers, off duty, are agents too) and get them to introspect before they know they have introspected, before they have had time to retire to their fly-pitch on the ceiling.

We will start, then, with the phenomena of free will. What! Make the most singular and erratic phenomenon of all our first clue to an orderly universe? Ah, but that is only how it looks to the onlookers. The pure onlooker has been able to persuade himself that there are no insides anywhere else, but only façade; when he comes to the mind, he limits his recognition of it to a back façade in addition to the front. Only the phenomena of moral free will appear to rebel against this reduction: in a few queer and isolated moments he must confess, or at least suspect, that he is inside himself. But the queerness and isolation of these moments is the creation of the onlooker point of view, they are the last refuge of irreducible subjectivity. The fact that it has been just *possible* to neglect elsewhere all but the façade does not cast any discredit on the phenomena of moral will, because there is no compulsion upon us to accept the façade theory of the rest of the universe; and if we begin by taking the moral will seriously, we shall find ourselves indisposed to do so.

The consideration that there are people to whom the fact (or claim) of moral freedom is an erratic streak in an otherwise façade-universe is testimony to our view that this is the most evident case of real activity and our proper starting-point. What we must do is to examine moral will and try to state its nature as a sort of fact, and see what light this casts on the mind or self as a whole.

(iii) *The Moral Struggle*

The clearest, if not the only, case of moral willing is often reckoned to be that of the 'struggle'; of which the common description runs somewhat as follows. I have two desires impinging on my consciousness, of which one is stronger than the other. The weaker, however, receives the approval of my moral judgment. (So far we are allowed to think of the mental events as following by uniformity-sequence: the desires 'arise' through stimuli internal and external, the approval is called in by 'association', or because the desires act as stimuli to another desire-system whose 'interest' is the applying of rules. So far so good; but now freedom begins.) It may happen that my natural interest in morality [1]—if I am that sort of person—adopting the weaker desire presents a total desire stronger than the originally strong desire. In that case there is no mystery; but often I am sure this is not so—otherwise moral obligation, of which I am intuitively convinced, would be a sham. No, often the moral I, provided with an emergency power-generating plant separate from desire—a sort of starting-engine additional to the motor—puts this extra energy into action and carries to victory a desire which remains the weaker. While this intervening energy cannot act unmotived, it does not function simply in so far as motived; the adequate motive being given, it still may or may not act; and its acting or not acting cannot be referred back to any cause but the free and responsible will. This means that the will is thought of as a potency, not unlimited but restricted to a certain range of acts—*qua* potency it can be defined—but such that no factors external to itself are sufficient grounds for its evocation into act. All that the circumstances do is more exactly to define of what it is *at the moment* the potency; but it evokes *itself* into act, however odd this sounds.

This description is shot through with metaphor from the very start. The trouble begins with the words 'desire' and 'weaker or stronger'. Desire may be an empirical term, but it is by no means a simple one. We may give as its constituents (*a*) a project for some action or course of action, (*b*) a sense of uneasi-

---

[1] or some equivalent object

ness or dissatisfaction, either prior to the presentation of the project or evoked by it, (c) a belief that the fulfilment of the project will relieve the dissatisfaction, (d) emotional reactions to the belief, in heightened present dissatisfaction, pleasure in the anticipated action, etc., (e) further trains of thought (belief) following upon (c), e.g. that the realisation of the project will give considerable pleasure of a certain sort, that it will have consequences beyond itself desirable, etc.

The 'belief' (c) is probably a 'taking-for-granted', unless two projects are in the field; in which case we wonder which will really satisfy, and so arrive at an opinion.

In view of this analysis, what would be meant by the superior strength of a desire?

(a) The project might be more vividly imagined or stated.

(c i) We may believe that its realisation will do more to relieve dissatisfaction, or (ii) we may have a stronger belief that it will really do *something* to relieve dissatisfaction; the other project may promise more relief, but we are less convinced about its power to make good its pretensions.

(d) The emotional reactions, other than that of bare conviction, may be stronger: if I have a stronger habit-interest on the one side, this will happen, even where conviction is equal or slightly less.

(e) I may anticipate more pleasurable experience from the result, whether directly or indirectly; and direct expectation may weigh more than indirect.

One desire—it will be better to say, one project—might be stronger than another in any or in several of these ways; and in each case 'strength' would be a superior degree of something directly present, of which we might be supposed capable of becoming aware. Yet the very multiplicity of the possible senses of 'stronger' seems to set them aside as useless, in any attempt to give an exacter account for the metaphorical description stated above. For while we might be able to feel the comparative strength of two projects under any one of these headings, we could not feel a comparison between a certain degree of strength under one heading, and a certain degree of strength under another; and rival desires can be strong in different ways. Sometimes, of course, it would be possible to feel a clear preponderance; but it is not really plausible to say that this is what we mean when in these vexed cases of moral conflict we assess the strength of desires. For the argument presumes that, other things being equal, the stronger desire will prevail; and if the strength of desires were to be determined in the way suggested, we should be presented with the dilemma of Buridan's ass in all cases where there was any real conflict at all.

It would be better if we could reduce all the headings to one, e.g. (d), saying that the others were only important indirectly as causal factors affecting (d). This does not seem to accord with our experience of the independent force which the others can exercise; and even neglecting the others, it is a grotesque over-simplification of the factors in another respect. For, as is clear from the empirical necessity for psychology to import certain parts of her 'subconscious' apparatus, the stronger tendency to action may not correspond with anything felt: an unperceived habit or suppressed interest may carry the day to our own surprise. The conscious mind is not so self-contained a system as this explanation would suppose.

These last considerations suggest a further sense for strength of desire. Induction from previous behaviour of this man or others may lead to the reasonable anticipation that (apart from the intervention of the free will, presumably) this project under these circumstances is likely to prevail over that. This is certainly good sense, but it will not do in this context. For I do not experience in my own case and in the present instance this inductive probability: this cannot be the superior strength against which the free will is felt to come into action. Our S.O.S. to the free will is surely not commonly: 'Past experience teaches me that I shall succumb to a project of this type (X); come to the rescue!' Admittedly such a fatalistic expectation may be a factor; but it is somewhat sophisticated and secondary, and is not what we normally mean by the felt strength of a desire against which battle has to be done. Were one to say that the anticipation is formed subconsciously and projected upon the present experience as a pseudo-quality of strength adjectival to it, this view would be difficult to disprove. The thing may indeed happen; but we would not be likely to accept it as the whole truth except in despair of another account. The felt stronger pull of one project over another is, we are inclined to think, something known with a more genuine immediacy.

The account which gives the best and most obvious connexion between 'strength' and 'tendency to prevail' is that which equates 'strength' with 'incipient fulfilment'. Between the entertaining of a project and its fulfilment in act, even where the projected action is something simple and, as we should say, immediate, there are no doubt always many steps. Such steps are: the more exact working out in thought of the detail of action necessary to realise the project; the registering of a resolution to act on some future occasion; the innervation of the muscles for the beginning of action itself. What we experience is, in effect, that this project is 'capturing the machine' in spite of the other. It may be that the desire to deliberate interposes a check: but a check is like a grip—its force is intermittent and continually re-applied; and so we feel continually the incipient self-fulfilment of the project, always starting again, always being cut off. In so far as these abortive beginnings cease, the felt strength of the project ceases. There may remain only the opinion that if we dwell on the project, the train of its self-fulfilment would start again; or that certain stimuli if they occurred would rouse it.

Indeed a project is a real project only in so far as it introduces the train of events leading to its fulfilment. When it ceases to do so entirely and in every respect, it is no longer a project. For a project is not made a project by its content, but by its relation to behaviour; and this relation must be actual, i.e. must consist of steps leading to the behaviour, however abortive, however slight. This is not to deny that we can imagine a project; but if it is imagined as a project, it is imagined as thus related to behaviour. In a conflict of projects, even the weaker must be having some consequences, though they are being checked (*vide supra*) by the stronger. If the stronger captures the machine, yet the machine is not so rigidly constructed but that there may be a turning of switches and starting of wheels as for the putting of it to a different use, which, being cut out by a more effective set of initial movements, come to nothing.

The strength of a project is either its incipient prevalence in this moment, or its persistency in re-starting its train of action as soon as some check has relaxed or become withdrawn.

We will now attempt a re-statement of the description of a case of moral free will. The project A and the project B have occurred. While B has been followed by its mental consequences $B_1, B_2, B_1, B_2, B_1, B_2$, A has been followed by $A_1, A_2, A_3, A_4, A_5, A_6$. There is (among the emotional reactions) some sense of discomfort associated with the stuttering of the B-process. Another project C occurs. This is a project not for particular action but for suspending $A_{7, 8, \ldots n}$ while an act of reflection takes place. This project has its full consequences, i.e. $C_{1, 2 \ldots n}$ follow, while A and B, perhaps, both 'stutter'. C_n is a mental event which is a proposition expressing, in the case we are considering, the conformity or nonconformity of A and B respectively to a moral standard which, in this act of reflection, has been taken for granted; or the superiority of A or B to the other in point of the realisation of this standard.

Let us suppose it is a preference of B to A. B now becomes BM, it is both B and the observance of Morality: A becomes $A{\sim}M$, A and the non-observance of Morality. Thus they change their characters as projects. The *de facto* check imposed by the running through of the C process vanishes with its completion: we now have $BM_{1, 2, 1, 2, 1, 2}$ but $A{\sim}M_{1, 2, 3, 4, 5, 6}$, accompanied by a sense of discomfort of a particular kind—a guilt-feeling (or perhaps, acute discomfort-feelings and a guilt-belief) of mounting intensity. Then we begin to have $A{\sim}M_{1, 2, 1, 2}$ (petering out) but $BM_{1, 2, 3, 4, 5, 6 \ldots n}$, where BM_n is the active fulfilment of the project B, or else all that can be done about it at present. It may well be that before the beginning of the effective BM series an event P took place, which might have been a tightening of the muscles, a holding of the breath, or the recurrence of the verbal symbols 'No, hang it all!' It may well be, also, that during the earlier stages of this last and effective BM process, there is a peculiar effort-feeling, which was not present during the prevalence of the A process, the $A{\sim}M$ process, or even the C process—though it *may* also have been present during the C process.

Here, then, we have a naturalistic description of an originally prevailing project, held up by reflection, beginning to prevail again, but, after the rise of the guilt-feeling, prevailed over by a project which the reflection had approved. Not only is this description naturalistic: it is a description of what might well be consciously known during its occurrence.

Inductive science, looking at the same events, may agree that in a pure case of A *versus* B, A might be expected (from previous experience) to prevail.

But, on the same grounds, it might *either* say that a pure case of A *versus* B was quite possible (it would depend on certain further circumstances or the requisite circumstances might be unknown) *or* it might say that in this man any case of A *versus* B was bound to be a case of (A *versus* B)C. Again it might say that by all analogy A∼M *versus* BM would be followed in this man by either the immediate prevalence of BM, or at least (i) the rise of strong guilt-emotions, (ii) the ultimate prevalence of BM. Or it might say that the prevalence of A∼M or BM would depend on further circumstances, and that these circumstances could be stated, or else that they could not be stated.

But so far the peculiar contention of the moralist has not been heard. He says: Even though the result was exactly according to the most exact and definite anticipation of inductive science, it was not necessitated by conformity to the rule. This statement, on positivist ground, is pure nonsense. Nothing is necessitated by any rule. If a case falls in with the rule, it has done all it can for the validity of the rule. To ask more means nothing. So that the negative statement of the moralist negates a piece of nonsense, and is itself meaningless. Positively, the moralist says that its actualisation followed from the self-actualising potency, without whose *ad hoc* self-actualisation it would not have occurred. This is metaphysics, which cannot be naturalistically translated. It is this, hopeless as it looks, that we have to examine.

(iv) *Will defined as Potency of an Effect*

We can at least begin with something naturalistic. However unintelligible the idea of a self-actualising potency may be, a potency is the potency of some actuality, and the actuality may be observable in sense-experience; and to state that will at least delimit the potency. What, then, is the effect of which it is the potency? The discharge of a certain quantum of energy in support of a feeble desire? Such language cannot be given a precise sense. The discharge of energy cannot be observed. There is, as was said, a sensation of effort in what is called the exercise of will, but the immediate effect of willing cannot be the creation of this sensation of effort; which never appears to us to be a positive term in the series which leads to the fulfilment of the project. On the contrary, it seems to be the awareness of some kind of cost at which the willing takes place, and to be, in so far, less an experience of the will's effect than of its obstructions. If on the other hand we place the awareness of effort in an awareness of particular action of some kind, e.g. the innervation of the muscles, then there is nothing peculiar to the exercise of will; we may feel that in acting by psychological automatism. If, again, in this feeling of innervation *plus* the feeling of a physical resistance in the body which is being overcome by it, the *differentia* is once more awareness of obstructions.

If we assume a doctrine of the constancy of energy-forces in the psychological organism—*ex nihilo nihil, in nihilum nil posse reverti*—then we may find it natural to suppose that there is some 'pool' of nervous energy somewhere which the will or moral self draws upon in these cases; and presumably this might be confirmed by physiological experiment. Yet this does not help us, any more than the pineal-gland-theory helped Descartes. There were, he thought, the vital forces—'animal spirits'—in play, and the turning of this tiny switch— the gland—by mental interference, did not create but merely re-directed the forces. Yet to turn the switch in spite of the forces itself required 'force' or else was a miracle. So for us, the essential point is that whatever forces there be available in the organism, the will adds something by rallying or applying them; to do which is to be a will. No help is given, but only improbability increased, by our supposing a secret and separate pool of energy on which the will draws and the will alone. If it draws on existing energies they are presumably those which may be tapped by other releases of activity.

So even if we allow ourselves to pass from observation to quasi-physical construction and to use terms like 'energy', we get no further with our understanding of the will. It remains that the will is the potency of behaviour intended for the realisation of the project, so far as such behaviour lies within the capacities of our 'machine'. 'Behaviour' must then be taken in the widest sense— viz. of that whole train of events 'internal' and 'external' which link a project with its realisation; and which we may call the process of the project. The will, then, as a potency, is the potency of the process of a project which would not have been actualised without it.

The potency of the will, therefore, is defined (i) by the occurrence of such projects in situations of choice, (ii) by the capacities of our psychological organism in given circumstances. Perhaps these capacities are not at all exactly calculable by us; but we can speak of them without introducing metaphysical conceptions. For, according to ordinary inductive thinking, we expect events to conform to rules gathered from induction, and the best statement of any inductive rule is probably a limiting one: i.e. we expect that the event, to which the rule is held applicable, will fall within certain limits, or satisfy a given description. No description can be exhaustive; therefore every description is a limit and no more, even though the aim of inductive science is to draw the limit closer and closer. To talk, then, about the 'capacities of the psychological organism' is only to talk of such inductively established limits, and to assume, indeed, that these limits cannot be drawn so closely as to make the freedom of the will nugatory.

A distinction is sometimes drawn between an ability to will and an ability to act. This cannot be allowed to be a distinction of principle. If accepted it would mean that we must distinguish: (a) limits to the moral heroism of man, such that he cannot will this project even though approved, but can another; (b) limits to the capacities of the psychophysical instrument, such that the willing, though actual, may break down against obstacles. Against this distinction we must urge: unless the willing in (a) has the form of *incipient* behaviour, what is it? But if it has that form, then the psychophysical organism has the capacity for some beginnings of the process of the project. If, on the other hand, the willing is not possible through a limitation, then this incipient behaviour does not in fact occur, or not so much of it occurs—it is a faint 'stuttering' only—and the limitation which prevents its occurrence may just as well be placed in the psychophysical organism. Then the distinction between (*a*) and (*b*) is reduced to a distinction between the capacity of the psychophysical organism for some initial stages of the process, and its capacity for further stages. We might define further, and say that the experience of being able to will, but not to accomplish, is equivalent to an occurrence (through will) of so much only of the process as to lead to some kind of expectation (however instinctive and unreasonable, however immediately disappointed) that the process will be completed.

The distinction being thus reduced to one of degree, a famous problem can be disposed of. It has been asked: *Could* I have acted conscientiously on every occasion? This should mean: wherever a project has received approval, and its process failed to run through for inward and psychological reasons, was this due always to the inactivity of my will? We can now answer: to give an affirmative would simply be to assert that I can never be deceived about the capacity of my organism to allow the realisation of a project. For if we approve a project *qua* project, no doubt we believe it to be in our power, for else it would not be a project. But it is certain that we can morally approve a project in the sincere belief that our organism is capable of it, and then find it is not, even where the incapacity is not of the grossly physical kind (to lift a certain weight, to continue exertion for a given time, etc.). Then the process of the project will break off somewhere; at what point is immaterial to the question.

This conclusion is not, as might at first appear, a moral paradox. We are not denying that in every case of moral decision the agent could have been free from (legitimate) blame. He could always have done what he could have done. Since the word 'could' in each half of the sentence has now exactly the same sense—referring to potentiality for moral effort in a given case—this necessary axiom of morality can be reduced to the comfortable form of tautology: that is to say, it can be made equivalent with part of the definition of the free moral will.

From this digression we return to determine the scope of the conclusion which can be gathered from the analysis of a 'moral struggle'. What we are looking for is the element of sheer will, and this we have found to lie in a mysterious intending of the project supposed by us to be the right one, an intending not determined by anything, but which simply actualises or does not actualise itself and therewith the process of the project.

XI

EXAMINATION OF THE DEFINITION OF WILL

(i) *Is its Scope restricted to Cases of Moral Struggle?*

THE definition of will at which we have arrived may seem to be either tautological or else mythical: the former if we take the words in the most abstract possible sense, the latter if we endow them with any content. There is here, then, nothing to be proud of; the value of the definition depends on our power to give it more exactitude. And first we will examine its scope.

Does the formula at all suggest that free willing is limited to cases of moral struggle? On the contrary, it seems equally applicable to all situations in which there is rational choice, and an alternative is enacted because we think it the right one. This conclusion may not follow, because the apparent wide applicability of the formula may be due to its abstractness and lack of definition. The decision must turn on experiential evidence. Does it seem that the will-act, which we know really causes that to happen which need not have happened and would not have happened else, is limited to occasions of struggle? It does not seem so, and we shall try to show this presently. And, on the assumption that we shall be able, we can at least see why the case of moral struggle should appear to be the most evident.

Elsewhere moral choice is concerned with the question: 'What shall I will?', and in accordance with a principle several times noted above, the will can be taken for granted, and no practical value attaches to an act of reflection upon it. But in the situation of struggle, considered as such, the question is, 'Shall I will (or not)?' This is in a sense no question, for there is no good reason for not willing, i.e. enforcing our rational choice against its obstacles. It is no question, and to reflect honestly on the act of will is to see this and to choose the right. The question is, whether it shall be allowed to be a question or not, whether we will be honest or not. This paradoxical situation will receive detailed examination in due course: it is sufficient here to see how moral struggle provokes a reflection on the act of will, which there, and there alone, has natural and practical relevance (except when the metaphysical question has been raised, *vide supra*, p. 86 *f*).

In the analysis of the struggle already given, we went as far as we could with naturalism, in order not to prejudge in our own favour. But it must be understood that this was provisional; and if as we proceed we see reason to qualify it, that will be no real contradiction. We will begin the good work now, in one particular. For in any account of the struggle such as we gave, natural causality and will-causality are treated as rivals, as possible alternative forces in the same field. But, once we have accepted the voluntarist contention, this becomes immediately absurd. The will-causality is related to the sheer occurrence or non-occurrence of the process willed; the naturalistic interpretation of causality allows no such causes, it simply presupposes the process and discovers rules of sequence that are exemplified in it. As to the occurrence or non-occurrence of the process it has nothing to say; it abstracts from it, and leaves a lacuna of explanation in regard to it; it is a nonsense question for it.

This is not perhaps directly evident. The sparking of the lightning might be supposed to stand related to the occurrence at all of the thunder-noises in my ear; for without the electric explosion (we normally suppose) no thunder noises. Yet this 'without' has a quite different sense from its meaning in the phrase: 'without the willing, no action.' In the case of the thunder, or of any physical process phenomenalistically viewed, we in fact assume the inevitable continuity of the process: *volvitur et volvetur in omne volubilis aevum.* It is not in question, whether the process is to go on or be broken off. Its future we suppose to be only uncertain subjectively and to our ignorance. When we say 'without explosion, no thunder', we simply formulate a law of sequence which has been observed in the past phases of the process, and which the process (if it is to continue constant to its structural form) may be expected to exemplify still; the onward flow of the process, and the character of that flow, being always presupposed, and precisely not called in question. Our ignorance of its future stages we deem an unhappy accident; we form the ideal of the process as an object extended before the contemplating mind in its entirety through the whole of its time.

The case of the will is completely different; the will is to decide whether the process shall be or not. And this formulation can be upheld, in spite of an apparent objection, the objection that the will does not decide whether there shall be a process, but only (within limits) the character that the process shall have; since the human will is not absolutely creative, we do not have to decide whether the events just past in the immediate context of our life shall or shall not be followed by others. Even if we killed ourselves, we should rot, and decomposition is no less an event than any other.

The substance of this objection is incontrovertible, but it only becomes an objection to the formula through an illusion of language. We imagine an outline sketch of the future process. This is already given, and the part of the will is merely to colour the outline in one way rather than another. Such a figure has its uses, but in the present connexion we must remind ourselves of its inaccuracies. The outline sketch on the paper is already something physically complete; the adding of colours is indifferent to its existence. But it stands in this argument as a symbol for a determinable which the will is to determine; and the determinable is as such not a possible existent but a logical abstraction. It is only a convenient way of expressing to ourselves that (*a*) what the will initiates will have certain aspects non-substitutible so far as the will's action is concerned, (*b*) that the will must initiate *something*, even if only negatively by eliminating itself and 'letting nature take its course'. It still remains true that if the process is thought of as *hoc aliquid*, an actuality sufficiently characterised to be an event, then the will is related to the very fact of its happening at all. It is related then to occurrence as the potency of occurrence, whereas all temporal or durational relations fall within occurrence in so far as it occurs.

Naturalistic uniformity, then, is not a rival to will, but an empty form which will may fill one way or another. What, if anything, fills this form where what we call will is absent, is a question which we cannot touch here.

Perhaps we should add that the explanations just given are not supposed to be a solution of the problem: Will and Uniformity. We have merely re-stated that problem, protesting that it cannot have the form: 'How can these rival causalities act in the same field?' but rather: 'How can *such* a living content (will) fill and fit *such* a frame (uniformity)?' It might remain that the question in its second form is no more soluble than in its first. But this, not that, is the question all the same.

(ii) *Of what Project is Will the Potency?*

Will is the self-actualising potency of (the process of) a project. But what is the scope of a project, and so of a single act of will? The man who prided himself on the consistency of his life and the singleness of his aims, might say that his life was the sphere of a single act of will, developed through a highly elaborate process; and the statement would not be altogether senseless. At the other extreme, it seems reasonable to call it one act of will, not only single but also complete, if I overcome my lazy reluctance, and with a combined somer-sault of my whole body, pitch myself out of bed. The act is then nothing but the initial jerk; the rest is the effect not of will but of gravity and inertia.

Our question here is not one of definition; we know that 'act' is used with several degrees of extension and that we could canonise whichever usage we chose. Our business is rather to look at the facts and discover what divisions are to be found in the process of the willed effect. The man who declared his whole life to be one act of will, because he lived for nothing but the deletion of Carthage, was plainly equating the sphere of the act with the sphere of the project. But if we do that, and find that the man dies with Carthage still stand-ing, we shall have to say that he never succeeded in carrying through an act in all his life, since all his efforts were governed by a project, which never was fulfilled. While it is true that no act can be called an act which is not governed by a project, it is not necessary that the act should be of itself adequate to such a project as this, for the project might require the acts of others as well as myself.

It might be proper, then, to treat as the minimum extension of an action, the least process which I will as a single intention relevant to a project—which intention can be regarded as itself a sub-project. The orator who wished to abolish Carthage harangued the Senate to that end, to decorate his speech he threw out a resonant cliché, and to enforce his cliché he punched the desk. If the desk-punching was a separate intention, and not an automatism connected with saying the words 'Delenda est Carthago', then it was a separate act; so far an act and so far deliberate, that he had to overcome a natural reluctance, for he had been used to punching a cushion, and discovered at the last minute that this part of the apparatus had been omitted; but he hit the oak for the good of the cause. We could not find a smaller project than this; analysis cannot here be carried to the infinitesimal. The orator does not *will* each successive stage in the lowering of his hand towards the desk, still less the innervation of his muscles, as a separate act.

We could not take as the measure of the least unitary project 'that which is certainly within our power'. No doubt we must believe it to be within our power now, and we must have some first stages of process actually within our power. The orator willed to hit the desk, although his malicious neighbour pulled it away and he hit his own thigh instead. And though he found that his arm was asleep or paralysed, still certain physical and neural preliminaries took place. If nothing of any such sort happens, there is probably no willing.

We use 'least project' generically, to describe the smallest scope of action intended as a unit in any given case of willing. But the genus contains instances that are less and greater than one another, for the least unit in one 'willing' is greater than the least unit in another; the extent of intention is not a matter of principle, though there are, presumably, some limits. The most perplexing case is that in which the 'least project' merges insensibly into the great project which it subserves, so that it seems impossible to distinguish them. This happens, for example, if my willing is one that sets me to run a mile on a circular and uniform track in a uniform atmosphere without competition and without incident. I do not appear to will separately the separate steps, nor did I originally choose anything less than the running of a mile. I choose this complete process, having an implicit confidence that bodily automatism would fulfil it without further interventions of choice.

There is nothing the matter with this account, so long as we do not conclude that the choosing or willing remains in action throughout the process. I chose to run; but I go on running because I chose, and because the choice has not been recalled—not because I now choose. If I *choose*, I re-enact my choice, e.g. in face of tiredness or of someone's Alsatian wolf-hound leaping about in a threatening manner. I may keep re-enacting in spasms, as we are told that we keep up our hand-grip by spasms, each supervening as the effect of the last fades. To conclude—the act of will may in the case of a uniform project have a long intention, within which no smaller unit can be found which is intended as instrumental to it.   But the act is not correlative with the execution of the long project, but only with its initial stage, by which we actively commit ourselves to it.

The intending of our least project is itself a *state*. So long as I will to hit the desk, it is the single unit of desk-hitting that I continue to intend. This does not prevent my being subconsciously aware that desk-hitting is a process embracing stages; for if I were not, I should be surprised by the discovery that the desk-hitting is not accomplished at the first instant of the exercise of will. But so far there is an exact parallel between will and memory. It is not only in look-ing forward that I embrace a process as a unit, while all the time knowing that it *is* a process. The memory of the immediate past has before it a stretch of process perceived to have extension, yet divided by the apprehending act into chunks which are greater than the most minute analysis possible, and are seen to have stages within themselves.

We have noted this fact earlier where it served as evidence for the thesis that the empirical understanding knows nothing of substance i.e. of 'real divisions'. The memory-stretch can be divided as we like, in many overlapping extensions of various length: it depends on our convenience. And we do not escape from this conclusion by pointing to the act of the empirical understand-ing itself. It is in vain to say that anyhow there is a real unity in the mind's single grasp of the stretch of 'manifold'. This act is, from the naturalistic point of view, itself an event: it can be treated as part of a larger event, or again it can be subdivided; and its 'real unity' only means that it is, as a unit, relevant to a certain sequence-according-to-rule; the running-on of which sequence consti-tutes what is called its 'meaning', as it deploys in expectations and associated images.

But the case of the will is different, once we have admitted that there is will in the real sense. For here 'power' enters in. That will-act which is the exercise of the power to produce the effect, intends the whole as such and is itself one. For we say: It is in virtue of the whole and single intention that the will-act occurs and the process takes place, which otherwise would not be. We could not possibly pretend that it is indifferent, whether we say that I willed the desk-hitting, or that I willed the minute physical stages of that process separ-ately, or the desk-hitting *minus* its culmination, or *plus* an irrelevant extension like the subsequent removal of my hand which was in fact an 'afterthought'. There is, then, an event of which we can say, that it exists or occurs *qua* being a unit of a certain extension and pattern. This event is an event which is willed; and this extension and pattern have a privileged metaphysical position rela-tively to other extensions or patterns that may be found within, or overlapping into, the event; for they have a privileged relation to the *existence* of the event. This remains true, though the full extent of the intended effect is inhibited and the pattern remains fragmentary; for it is then the broken-off extension and the fragment of pattern which enjoy this position.

If this is true of the event, it is equally true of the intention. The intention is to some extent an object of naturalistic introspection. One can introspect the imagery of the intention and whatever else is thus introspectible about it, e.g. the emotions with which it is accompanied; and one can divide these variously, as one chooses. But *qua* relevant to the act of will and the coming to be of what would else lack being, the intention is one, it has a unity which dominates its detail; and the relation of dominance cannot be reversed according as we choose to view it. Here, then, we see the beginning of what we were looking for—how real connexion creates real units relevant to it.

(iii) *The Primary Effect of Will is Immanent*

But it is not evident that the real unit immediately correlative with intention is physical effect, even though the effect exhibits (in an imperfect manner) the pattern of the project, and derives its very occurrence from the project's enactment. Does the will-relation, in fact, obtain between the project and the effect? For we have seen that even the least project may be enacted, so far as in us lies, and yet be baulked of its effect—the effect goes otherwise than the intention; and in the case of the paralytic, it may go wholly otherwise. In such a case, the relation between project and effect appears to be in a manner accidental. It is not from studying such an effect, that we see it to form a unit corresponding to a unitary project, in virtue of whose enactment it comes into being. That which corresponds to the project is *the action*; and the action consists in the project, believed to be possible *now*, and expressed in *some* effect believed to be (part of) the realisation of it. We have a very intimate (though usually implicit) awareness of the states and capacities of our bodies as movable; so that it rarely happens that our actions fail to effect physical changes in some sort of correspondence with our intention. But sometimes we will to jump and do not jump—not through a lack of faith in our ability to cross the ditch—for that is a lack of will also—but through an absolute and incorrigible disobedience of our members. We give a little lame hop instead of the intended jump, without having been able in the least to foresee this disappointment.

The relation, then, between enacted intention and its physical execution is obscure: the effect goes right, or it does not. Usually it goes right, and it is in virtue of an implicit faith in this normal rightness that we can will at all. The faith can be placed within the definition of our act of will, the rightness cannot. The action is an intention (or project) in *exercise*, whether the 'exercise' goes right or wrong. It is in our power to enact the project (put it into exercise) but not to be sure how the exercise will take effect, though we must have a practical faith in the matter.

Therefore the relation is primarily between the mere project and the project put into exercise, that is, the act. Or perhaps we should say, between the mere entertaining of the project, and its enactment. For project has a formal sound; it ought perhaps to be the voluntary analogue of the logical 'proposition', and to describe the content of what is projected; which remains identical in all states of mind about it, whether of approval or disapproval, of consideration or enactment.

(iv) *Continuity of the Project*

One way of conceiving this relation is obvious. The entertaining of the project and its enactment are separate events of which the first precedes the second, and there is a formal similarity in one aspect of them. Or alternatively (it is no more than a different form of statement) we may say that they are two stages of a continuous flux, two cross-sections, as it were, exhibiting a certain similarity of structure. This, Descartes will say, is to consider the two acts 'formally'. Now let us consider them 'objectively', or as we would call it, 'intentionally'. The project which I entertain is the project of an effect dated for enactment at some future time. Were it dated for enactment *now*, I could not be entertaining it, I should either be enacting or rejecting it. It may be dated to a determinate future, e.g. to jump on the bus when the bus comes; or to an indefinite future, e.g. to write a letter to my friend, where I assume that circumstances allow me to begin at any time—and so I am considering when and whether I shall tear myself from my novel and begin. In any case I am considering the project of a future effect, and this effect will be an effect of will.

The act of entertaining a project has, then, intentional reference to that of enacting it; without this reference it would not be the entertaining of a *project*, but (for example) the entertaining of an hypothesis that some future event will occur independently of my will. The *object* of my consideration is, in fact, the (proposed) future action, to which I take up a certain attitude; the attitude called 'consideration of', or, passively stated, 'solicitation by'.

There ought to be made a sharp division between two conditions under which one may entertain a project without immediately enacting it. Either one is entertaining at the same time (it may be more or less explicitly) something which excludes it, e.g. to stay where one is and go on reading. Or physical circumstances have not yet made the action possible—e.g. the bus has not yet arrived. The two states of suspended action proper to these two sets of circumstances are really different. In the first case, the mind is still divided, for nothing but this division suspends the action. In the second case, circumstances do not allow me to know whether the mind is divided or not. For I may feel confident that I shall jump on the bus which takes this corner at 15 m.p.h., yet when I see what this speed looks like, I may find myself thinking twice about it. Or I may be of divided mind whether to walk or ride, until the bus appears and I have no longer any doubt at all that I will to ride.

Sometimes, then, we say that we are merely entertaining the project, because circumstances allow only a *resolution* about future action, not action itself. But a resolution is an action of a kind, and we can be of divided or undivided mind about the resolution itself, and if of undivided, then we have made the resolution; and that is all the action open to us for the present.

Between resolution and action, indeed, there seems to be a debatable borderland. There are many cases in which we anticipate events, taking it for granted that they will befall in a certain way, and they do so. We take it for granted that their occurrence will introduce no objective or subjective [1] factor both relevant to choice and unanticipated. In that case we deliberate about the future act as about a present option, and as soon as the time-space dividing us

---

[1] Objective: the bus is going faster than I expected. Subjective: I hadn't realised how alarming the (correctly anticipated) speed would be.

from the occasion of action appears such as to leave no at all probable field for any change of mind, we appear to have committed ourselves, to have chosen. In such a case it would seem absurd to say that what we are deliberating upon is the formation of a resolution, and that the fulfilment thereof in act will need a separate choice. For on this view we can never really deliberate about an action at all, since up to the moment when we are already acting there *may* always break in a disturbing event. Even in the case of my deliberating about the writing of the letter, it is always possible that a jackdaw may fly in through the window and go off with my only pot of ink.

Well now, but if the unexpected happens, and the jackdaw appears. Let it: it cannot make any difference to the nature of my mental state before its appearance. I was deliberating about beginning to write in the next few minutes, and the disappearance of my ink leaves this process fragmentary, but does not change the nature of the fragment; it does not become (by some retrospective magic) a deliberation about a mere resolution. Here also applies:

> To omnipotence one limit is decreed,
> Not to undo the perpetrated deed.

The nature of a mental state cannot be affected by the future, except in so far as the future indwells that mental state; which it can do only in the form of belief, and belief is fallible.

We take as the perfect case of the relation between the project entertained and the project enacted, that in which the deliberation is about an action assumed to be immediately possible and in which this assumption is correct; the letter-writing plan without the jackdaw. We begin with an act of considering the future performance of the action. As with every other intentional state, it is possible to distinguish (*a*) the imaginative content, *phantasmata*, whether symbols or imagination-images, (*b*) that which is meant through them. For the imagination-image, so far as it is a present reality, cannot be what we intend, for the intention is of a future action. Nor can we seriously mean that the action in the doing will in all details resemble the image, even granting the difference of time.

But it is possible to give more than one account of this distinction, according to the various ways in which the actual intention (*b*) is supposed to be present to the mind.

(I) Along with the imagery we have some sense of what would, and what would not, be a fulfilment of the intention therein expressed. Yet this awareness is always semi-implicit, for were it fully explicit it would presumably give rise to further imagery of a more exact kind alongside the first.

(II) Beside the imagery there is no *particular* intention (*b*) but only the general form of intention, not otherwise particularised than by *this* imagery. I.e. there is the general form of intention to act (in the future) in accordance with a diagram (*a*); and there is *this* diagram. But here again it is possible to ask how far this general form is explicit. No doubt we are intending, and therefore the act of doing so is itself present; but how far are we reflectively aware of the form of this act?

(III) Nothing is present but the diagram, and an attitude towards it (of intending action). We are aware of this attitude only in a general and confused form; it is for us a single item in the situation, and fails to reveal its complex make-up (future reference, creativity, relation of diagram to execution, etc.). We are aware, then, *subjectively* of an intentional attitude, *objectively* of a diagram: the whole business of how the diagram is to be translated into reality is not present to consciousness, but is worked out in a series of events which conform to psychological 'laws'. Our intention is (so far as consciousness goes) 'about' the diagram until we begin to register the sensible effects; which we shall find to be not the exact counter-parts of the diagram, but near enough to satisfy us—or not, as the case may be.

It may be that each of these three accounts has some truth in it, and that situations can be found which are more nearly covered by each than by the others. Yet there are certain general criticisms that we can advance.

(I) puts its money on a fringe of virtual intention, or semi-conscious intention. Now the fringe exists. If, for example, my 'diagram' takes symbolical form, there is present a semi-conscious awareness that I could supply a more concrete phantasma of the act which the words describe; this *phantasma* seems to be felt as waiting in the ante-room of consciousness, or we seem even dully to descry its general outline. The same is true if the diagram is a concrete image, but sketchy; we have the same kind of sub-awareness of the detail with which we should fill it out, were we to let go the whole and bring the parts successively under the microscope of attention.

But against this first description we may urge (*a*) that there are cases in which the image is as explicit as we could make it. Shall we then say that there is no distinction between the image and the intention? (*b*) However explicit and complete the image, it is still a *present* object; and conversely, however implicit it becomes *qua* imagery, it does not advance an inch nearer to grasping futurity.

(II) puts its money on the form of intention as such. But our distinct awareness of this is surely a pretty rare event, and limited to cases of particularly aggravated self-examination, as when I wonder whether I am acting by will or by automatism, or when I am examining the psychological and philosophical problem of the freedom of the will. If we wish to maintain that the 'general form of intention' operates in giving us the intentional project, we had better say that it does so not by being itself present to consciousness as itself, but by projection of itself upon the diagram, so that the diagram appears decked with the form of future event. But even this way of putting things may appear perverse; since the (subjective) form of intention is itself unintelligible and inexpressible unless the notion of a future act is presupposed and the intention directed towards it: so that the futurising of the diagram results not so much from the projection upon it of the form of intention, as from the attribution to it of an objective futurity without relation to which the form of intention is itself impossible. Yet on the other hand, in so far as the contemplated act is not only future, but an act (i.e. voluntary), the form of intention may enter into its conception; though not *qua* general, but as particularised by this diagram.

(III) takes its stand on the negative fact that the content of the project, if demanded, is never put forward except by means of *phantasmata*. Everything which makes a difference between one project and another seems referable to a difference of *phantasmata*; and thinking appears to be concerned with significant differences.

But this view, as it stands, cannot be accepted, for the reason that we simply do not think *about* the *phantasmata* but about the future act. Thus the general forms of futurity and of intentional action must be ' applied' to the *phantasmata*, as suggested by our criticism of (II) above. But to speak of 'application' is a ridiculous understatement. You cannot '*apply*' 'futurity' and 'intentional action' to *phantasmata* and they still remain *phantasmata*. If these forms enter into the object to which attention is being paid, that object ceases to *be* the *phantasma* and becomes something else, which is thought through the *phantasma*. It is the same problem as with memory. In both cases, the *phantasma* may be compared with the film running through the projector, which accounts for all the differences in what is seen on the screen; but what is seen is not the film. The remembered past or intended future reality is not seen in the form of a present *phantasma* but in its own.

It is not necessary, for our purposes, to carry this discussion further, so long as it is admitted that the tentative intention (consideration) of a project grasps it as a future act distinct, in existence, from my present state. If, then (to return to the Cartesian distinction mentioned above), we consider not 'formally' but 'objectively' the relation of the project-entertained to the project-enacted, we can say that the project remains identical in content in the two states. In the former it is intended as future; in the latter it is caught up with, and enacted as present. It is of this moment now present that we were formerly thinking as still future. The objective, in a sense, remains constant; it is we that change in relation to it. But if the objective does so, then so does the project, which is nothing else but our objective in so far as intended by us.[1] The distinction between objective and project would not be needed but for the possibility of error and failure in intention.

(v) *The Change from Entertaining to Enacting*

For a description of our change in relation to the constant project, it may help to contrast will with expectation. In the case of expectation, we anticipate the event, and (if anticipation is correct) catch up with it: the event does not change, but our position relatively to it changes, and this change is not due to us. In the case of will, taking the perfect case defined above (p. 124), the

---

[1] The relation of project to the act of which it is the project is analogous to the relation commonly established between proposition and fact.

intended action indeed does not change, when we pass from consideration to enactment; what is intended remains the same. But we do not merely change position and obtain subjective certitude in relation to something whose occurrence is objectively certain. It is not only our condition which changes, but that of the action itself. It becomes at the same time an actuality and a certainty, from having been a mere candidate for these qualifications. In the case of correct expectation, our subjective attitude—confident belief about a continually nearer event, then experience of it—is dictated by the change in the factual situation. But in that of successful will, this relation is reversed: our subjective attitude by changing creates the new fact—the action.

If we were allowed to use a Humean confusion between the interior object and the mental attitude, we might say that the project, identical in content, through being intensified passes into act. But it is not proper to say that the project is intensified, but that our attitude to it is; or perhaps not so much 'intensified' as 'simplified'. To intend is an attitude *sui generis*, and to intend simply, without qualification, when the conditions for enactment are already present, is to enact; there is no need to intensify intention, but merely to purify and simplify it, to let it be itself. We may use 'to intend' as a verb covering the two species 'to entertain' and 'to will', so long as we understand that these two species are not related as horse and dog within the genus mammal, but that the first can be reduced to the second as to its 'principle', being the imperfect state of the second; 'entertaining' is obstructed, divided, tentative willing.

The project, then, *objectivè consideratum* is, let us say, simply identical as entertained and as willed. The intention (in the sense of the intending) is not simply identical, nor yet simply different in the two moments: the same intention passes through phases, till it reaches that of simplicity or purity—till it is made absolute. This development is the actualising of will. We may give the name 'will' to the last moment (of enactment); yet this is a point without magnitude, and by 'willing' we commonly mean the movement we make from 'entertaining' to 'enacting'.

If will passes from the tentative to the absolute enactment of an identical project, do we not seem to have run the concept of active potency to earth? Have we not discovered it to be an object of immediate experience? Is it not from here that we derive the notion? For the intending of the project in its phase of 'entertaining' is the potentiality of the phase of enacting. This statement can be analysed as follows:

1. The project is identical (*objectivè consideratum*).
2. The entertaining of the project needs only to be simplified or absolutised to become enactment.
3. This simplification requires no outside factor to actualise it.

It is the third of these statements which is of course difficult and is liable to land us in unprofitable dialectic if we are not careful. 'No outside factor'—no factor external to what? To the entertaining of the project? But we can perhaps speak of the 'entertaining of the project' in two senses.

(*a*) Abstractly, as a clearly marked stage in the process leading on (when it does lead on) to will-enactment; as the name proper to this phase as such. Now plainly, *qua* the aspect of 'entertainingness' formally considered, it excludes what is not itself and cannot of itself be thought to give rise to that which is not itself. If the entertaining of the project is thus thought of, then surely some factor outside or beyond itself must be the active potency of what follows. For the entertaining of the project in this sense is the abstract *terminus a quo* of the movement which this active power achieves.

(*b*) The entertaining of the project may be thought of comprehensively, as describing all the reality there present, not only the phase *qua* phase, but that which is having this phase: not (in an outworn terminology) the mode *qua* mode, but the *ens qua* modified. And then it seems proper to say that the entertaining of the project attains simplification and hence passes to enactment *of itself*, without any factor from without.

This dialectical opposition cannot be accepted as it is stated. For the *ens modificatum* suggests a metaphysical *Unding*, an occult character other than the modification, and itself the (supposed) ground or potency of the enactment which follows the modification. But of this occult character we know nothing, nor can we conceive its relation to the enactment to which it gives rise, except by the analogy of the relation thereto of this very modification which it is invented to supplement.

No; but we must say: 'Entertaining' or 'tentative enactment' can be described in the round, without abstraction, if we describe it not as a motionless point, a *terminus a quo* of the vital movement, but as movement. There is a movement, which may remain still as 'marking time' remains still; it is 'consideration' because it does not run straight through but repeats. It is this which is the intrinsic power to set aside rivals, overcome obstacles, and go ahead into enactment.

But we have not yet succeeded in 'describing in the round' and avoiding abstraction. That which 'marks time' is not simply the movement which is, in 'entertaining' of that project, destined to be fulfilled in act. In that case it would not 'mark time' but go straight to its aim; for what would inhibit it? It is a movement which oscillates between rival projects, and does not commit itself to one except at last by enacting it. The weaker form of existence which intention has in the phase of entertaining excludes it from realisation, but confers upon it the ability to coexist with other intentions that are in the same weak state. The vital movement of the will mimes these intentional attitudes in turn before playing out any one in earnest. Potency is always a potency of opposites. When we reflect afterwards on the act of will we see in the earlier phase the potency of that which was fulfilled; but this potency was itself many-faced, and its other facets were potencies of unfulfilled actions.

That which is *potential* enactment of a project is itself *actual* entertaining of the same project; and is related to the actual enactment as temporally prior to temporally posterior. There may be a long series of phases from the merest entertaining to full enacting. It would be tempting to say that these form a continuity or actual infinity, like the series of mathematical points in a physical movement from one position to another. Yet it is doubtful whether this suggestion rests on anything better than this physical-mathematical analogy itself. Bergson does not tire of remarking that what science measures as a progression through a multitude of points, life wills as one act; and if this is true of the acts willed, so it is of the process of coming to will. We make acts of considering, each of which as reflectively analysed may be a process having detail within itself, but each of which is made as one; until we come to make the act of will proper, which itself, when at last it is made, is made as one.

APPENDIX TO CHAPTERS X AND XI

DIALECTIC OF THE WILL

(i) *Idea of a Dialectic*

In describing the act of conscious choice or will, we found ourselves guarding against 'unprofitable dialectic'. And this we did, by concentrating on description of the process, that is, of its phases and aspects. We did not avoid the use of analogic terms, but perhaps ideally we could have done so. There is nothing impossible in the plan of giving a technical name to each element we are able to distinguish, and to each of the relations obtaining between the elements; and, by the methods discussed above (pp. 80 *ff*) leading the reader to discover to what it is that our technical and proper terms attach.

It is not possible, however, to avoid dialectic if we allow the question to be asked: 'What kind of a relation is involved in the real arising of a state out of a previous state?' For the answer, as we have seen, must be that such a species of relation is unique, if indeed it ought to be called a relation; so that to carry the question further is to fall into analogies. The most profitable method is to build up the whole complex and context of the will-act in the hope that it may be apprehended clearly in itself; this enterprise we have begun upon and mean to continue. And in fact 'willing' is not intelligible unless all its elements are stated; or, if you like to call it a relation, until all the terms are given between which it obtains. For it is not a two-term relation, and if we try to treat it as such (as in the question just quoted) we shall not get very far. The authors of 'The Meaning of Meaning' discovered that no progress could be made so long as that word was taken to describe a relation between symbols and things—a third term was required; if you shut them up to the two terms they would refuse to play your game. So in the case of will: if we think of a relation by which a later state (enactment of the chosen alternative) arises out of an earlier (entertainment of several alternatives), we can make no sense of it; the preference is arbitrary. But that is because we have abstracted from a further term, viz. entities as objects of apprehension. It is because the multiple relation of will embraces these entities by apprehending them, that decision can have the nature of a reasonable judgment.

In spite of these warnings, we find it almost impossible to restrain ourselves from asking the above question, and taking a plunge into dialectic. And, if we do not allow ourselves to be fooled by it, but remember what it is—a negative clarifying of our term by comparison with analogues—it may have its use. Let it be granted that willing is not covered by a two-term relation; yet in so far as through it something arises from something else, it offers an aspect comparable with other sequences. We will take a turn on the dialectical ice; and if we find it impossible to stand in any position, but that we are always driven

into another to save ourselves from falling, we will not imagine that it is necessary to keep it up until we reach an equilibrium—as soon as we have had
enough of it we can get back to terra firma by the simple expedient of stepping
off the rink, and abandoning a dialectic which cannot in the nature of things
get us anywhere, though it may improve our skating.

(ii) *Examples of Dialectic*

Let us start from the description arrived at in the end of the last chapter.
There was a movement which, after playing with several alternative projects-
entertained, runs out into the enactment of one of them. The motive here
stressed was the continuity of movement; it seemed all-important for the
moment to escape from the notion of a sheer state which is itself and can give
place to nothing else except by a miraculous jerk. No, we said, there is a continuous unresting movement, which runs in several rhythms or figures successively, but is the same movement running on through them all. Well, that is very
nice, and to insist on the continuity of the will's activity may be quite proper.
But have we not obtained this advantage at a high price? Have we not reduced
the will to a process which simply flows—*volvitur et volvetur*, etc. (see above,
p. 118)? We have suggested that it must flow on in some meander or another,
and that it observes certain formalities in trying figures tentatively before working
them out; but this is a mere principle of uniformity in sequence, as is observed
elsewhere in nature. But so long as this rule is followed, there is nothing that
gives any account of real creativity in choice; one figure happens to be made by
the meandering stream, it is a simple fact, there is no more to be said about it.
Sheer continuity, therefore, will not do. At every point where a decision
is made, we must think of the movement as having checked and summed itself
at that point as the Jordan did above the Israelite march, in order that it may
voluntarily add to itself some next stage rather than some other. It identifies
itself with a point or phase, in order to fix the next point or phase beyond itself. Only by the scheme of a point related at first indifferently to two possible
subsequent points, then really to one of them as actualised, can we represent the
notion of will.
So willing is a series of will-phases, in which an earlier selects a later
though not according to any rule, nor as a mere consequence of the nature of
the previous phase. But here we are up against an old difficulty; for how does
the previous movement, or phase, select the later? In so far as it endures, and is
itself, it is not the willing of the successor's existence, but is its own existence;
the seeds of the successor may be in it, but equally so are the seeds of alternative
successors, which, scarcely sprouting, are nipped in the bud. Willing appears
to be rather the substitution of the successor for the predecessor, and a relation,
therefore, between a given term and several alternative terms, to whose individuality it is of its nature indifferent, yet posits one of them.
But is it not a paradox, that willing should be a *relation* or have its seat in

a relation? Perhaps not, since we have several times said that it is a *real* relation and quite likely the only one of which we have experience. It is not, then, the mere relatedness of its terms—for if so, how could it be the cause of the existence of the second of them? It is a reality, a content filling the form 'existence', and its metaphysical singularity can be expressed by exhibiting it as a thing no less than as a relation—as a *quale* no less than a relation of one *quale* to another.

Let us try the form of description which hypostatises it. It is, then, a power in action, by nature indifferent to the several phases which it realises successively. It places one, and that one prescribes a class of possible successors, of which the will again places one in actuality.

Still, even if we are prepared to hypostatise it, we may wish to draw the line at making it simply transcendent, a separate substance. It does not dwell in the great inane, sufficient to itself, throwing off actions when it feels disposed. It is bound to its successive phases and must go on adding more. It is identified with the phase of the moment, but not wholly so, it transcends it in so far as it reaches forward to add the next phase.

But once we have given will-power a hypostatic continuity, there seems to be no motive any longer for the staccato representation of the phases; that arose from the previous description, in which they formed the terms of which it was the 'real relation'. It is now a permanent power which 'relates' them, i.e. adds new terms to succeed the old. It is a power, then, which generates and directs the continuous process of terms, yet is inseparable from them in its existence; it is a double or shadow which accompanies the process in its flow, rising above it and always a little ahead of it in so far as it is always creating the subsequent phase.

It is a short step from this to the conception of it as the potency, the shadowy pre-existence of the process. For in what mode does the shadow exist? Surely in the mode of 'active potency'; it is the same content which is to exist (or that along with other possible rivals), the mode only is different; it is potential simply.

Yet once we deformalise the will, and identify it with a 'matter' of potency, we are faced with a dilemma. *Either* the potency is limited to what will happen, in which case the will must determine the potency itself if it is to be free; and in that case it may as well determine the events directly, the potency serves no useful end. *Or* the potency is potency of opposites; in which case the character of will as such belongs not to that which is these potencies, but to that which chooses one before the other.

We fall back, then, from material potency to the notion of an abstract power; that is, an undetermined potency of action, able to enact any of the material or full-blooded potencies presented to it by the march of events. Events as they pass present to this will a fringe of possibilities, as the film running through the projector presents a fringe of sound-record to the noise machine; but here the figure breaks down, for the will may enact which it will and cannot enact all.

But, it is objected, in the last description as in several preceding, the will is emptied of content and presented as a mere form. Is not this the most obvious of abstractions? Unable to conceive free will, we hypostatise the abstract form of voluntary action, emptied of every content, and pretend that it picks its content for itself. . . .

(iii) *Solutions of Dialectic*

Will this do? Have we had enough? Shall we step back on to firm ground, and see what positive statements of real worth correspond to so many dialectic positions? We can express them in far fewer words:

(1) The analogue of a continuous physical process as viewed from 'without' is proper to express the continuity of freely willed activity. But the mere supervening of the later phase on the earlier is precisely characteristic of the 'outward view' (*vide supra*, p. 106), and so can have nothing to do with the inward.

(2) In so far as will projects a new phase it takes the present phase for granted and discounts any activity therein. It also envisages the new phase as a unit (*vide supra*, p. 121), and so the scheme of two related terms has an application here.

(3) Will cannot be identified with the present phase (though that is its *locus*) any more than with the relation of passing over into another phase. Both of these formal elements belong to the will; it is neither.

(4) Term (a *quale*) and relation (of succession) each express a certain aspect of will, in so far as it is both reality and movement.

(5) Will is 'hypostatic', nothing more so, for '*esse est operari*'. But it neither transcends its constituents nor identifies itself with them but organises them in a unique manner which shall receive proper treatment presently.

(6) The notion of potency is meaningless, and a bastard metaphysico-naturalistic concept, except in so far as it reduces to the relation between an inchoate stage and a later complete stage in the same will-act (*vide supra*, pp. 126*ff*).

(7) As to the dilemma expressed in it—that will must either be the pre-existence of its actual effects and so determined, or an empty form and so abstract and incapable of real existence—this rests partly on the old dilemma of the Hen and the Egg (how is real growth possible?), partly on the sound observation that to find an analogy for the reality of will-activity we must take a phenomenon with full content (phenomenally concrete); to find an analogy for its freedom, we must take a determinable (phenomenal abstract).

This dialectic thinking (if personal experience may be quoted) has a purging effect on the mind; until we have done plenty of it, and seen through the tricks, we cannot trust ourselves to talk about the will without paralogising. It is to be recommended as an exercise, and we have given enough to convey the formula. So we will end here with the conclusion of the old ditty:

'If you want any more, you can sing it yourself',

for dialectic is like one of those rigmarole songs, which, if their structural principle is followed, can add fresh stanzas to themselves for ever.

XII

THE SCOPE OF WILL

(i) *Automatism, Desire and Will*

WE took up the examination of will, because we hoped to find in it a real connexion fit to be the bond of substance—and primarily of the substance in which it is, that is, the self. This raises the question of the universality of will in the field of the human subject. We began with will in the moral struggle, and saw no reason to limit its existence to that, its most evident instance. Where there is rational choice, there seems to be will. But how wide does that make the extent of will to be? 'Proportionately pretty narrow', might be the deliverance of common-sense, or rather of one mood of that self-contradictory oracle. It seems that we act by automatism, impulse, desire, will, and that if we allow will its even fourth of our behaviour, we are much overstating its effective sway. But if so, how can will be the bond of the self? How can that hold the beads together, on which only every tenth is threaded?

We know that psychoanalysis seems to make the will flow underground like the River Mole, only occasionally emerging to sparkle in the sunlight of full consciousness, and treats automatism, impulse and desire as phenomena which mark and express its hidden course from time to time. This hardly solves our problem. For however practically useful such language may be, there is a heavy dose of metaphor in it. Does it mean any more, than that behaviour, even when not consciously chosen, falls out as though it expressed a continuous line of purpose? The psychologist is interested in uniformities of sequence, and discovers in the life of the mind certain typical patterns like, or identical with, those which we at other times make the projects of conscious will. But now if we can say, 'Will always aims at and enacts schemes of the type A', it by no means follows that the proposition can be converted, to give 'Schemes of the type A are always the enactments of will'. Nor, if we do assert the second proposition, is it at all clear what we mean by the will which can go underground in this surprising fashion. It cannot, evidently, be something to which running above ground is of first importance; and so the consciousness of the (conscious) will begins to look accidental to it, and we have prejudiced the question of the will's nature before we have examined it, and prejudiced it by an unverifiable hypothesis. To explain *obscurum per obscurius* may be unhelpful, but to obstruct the explanation of the obscure by the identification of it with the unintelligible would deserve a harder name.

However this may be, it is proper to philosophy and to our enquiry to start with the more intelligible, and to keep on the level of consciousness at first, however far we may later have to travel into the dark, in trying to do the facts of empirical psychology justice.

Automatism, impulse, desire, will. Automatism seems to be physically necessary, impulse and desire psychologically necessary, and will not necessary at all. To speak thus is to speak from the will's point of view, and to use 'necessity' in a negative sense. What is at the bottom of automatism and desire, we do not pronounce; we simply state that will does not get a chance to direct them, in so far as actions follow from them simply, and not from will. That will may approve or modify impulse and desire, is of course admitted. But in that case the action becomes an action of will.

Automatism is physically necessary. In using this definition we assume that the functioning of the body proceeds, by whatever forces impelled; and assert that the action or reaction which we class as automatic takes place without the formality of projects *pro et contra* coming before consciousness first. There is, then, no question of will-control. We do not need to say the *class* of action is such, that in no instance of it could its project have appeared in consciousness before it was performed. There are such classes of automatisms, the digestion of our food and the beating of our heart. But there are others, e.g. the doing up of buttons, which were consciously directed once, and can become so again on occasion. But in a given case either there is a project of them or there is not, however hard it may be to draw the line between the presence and the absence of it.

Impulse and desire are psychologically necessary—or would be so if there were any pure cases of them. In these cases a project of the act is given; the question for and against it is superficially raised, but at the beginning of the first stage of reflection the case against it is cut straight out. There was no case. The opposite is equally possible; there are projects which present themselves, yet so that on a given occasion it is impossible that they should establish their interest to the point of my acting upon them. These would be psychological impossibilities, to set over against psychological necessities. It is impossible that (in the given case) I should not jump out of the way of the bus to save my life, equally impossible that I should pick up a penny lying on a live rail; though in other circumstances both might be possible, e.g. if I were crossed in love or distracted by a problem of algebra.

In the common case of impulse, the presence of a project is not connected with the question, 'Is this what I want?' but with the question, 'Is this what I want *in the circumstances?*' For if a project is of other than the most elementary kind, a cursory glance round the environing facts is needed. E.g. it may be axiomatic that I want pennies, but not from live rails nor if dropped by people who will fight to recover them. But the question of the mind is only a scarcely explicit 'Any objections?', and unless one immediately occurs we go straight ahead, without the least motion in the direction of looking for trouble, or making particular enquiries. It would indeed be more proper to say that the presentation of the project is itself the implicit question, but that unless an objection suggests itself there is no question of which we are conscious; our adoption of the project is itself the implicit answer.

In the case of desire, it is equally taken for granted that the project is one to be aimed at, but the means of immediate attainment are absent. Were the difficulty such as to make us ask whether we want the objective at all, it might become a case of will. But we assume that this has not happened. In respect, then, of the entertainment of the desire itself, there is no willing, it has simply happened to us.

Between the psychological necessities and psychological impossibilities there lie the open possibilities, with which will is concerned. Yet necessity or impossibility does not immediately become an even possibility as soon as it has crossed the border line. Possibilities are in degree, and so might be called probabilities and improbabilities, so long as we do not allow ourselves to be led away by the naturalistic associations of the words. Natural probability is either supposed correlative with ignorance of the determined (the usual view) or is taken to express a measure of actual hazard in things; and it is possible to think of the probability of projects in this way, as when we take bets on how someone else will react to a proposal we are going to put before him. But we are speaking of the probability of projects as relative neither to ignorance nor (supposed) chance, but to a free will. Some choices are a great deal easier to make than others, and the project easy to prefer is probable. Not necessary, however, for I may be so wicked that I do not carry out the very small degree of reflection required; or so heroic that I prefer an alternative that was *a priori* improbable because of the stupendous demands it made on effort of reflection and subtle rectitude of judgment.

The pure cases of desire (or impulse: the distinction is not relevant) may not be many, or anyhow it seems impossible in most instances to say which they are; so that it does not appear likely that the popular use of the term corresponds to the class of pure cases, or even rests on a clear conviction that there are any. Do we not commonly mean by action from desire, action in which the solicitation to the will was strong and the project probable, so that we abstract from the possibility of choice? If approbation was implicit, or quickly granted, its occurrence does not seem worth considering—it 'made no difference'.

All these distinctions fall within the scheme of the relation between solicitation and response; so let us consider that.

(ii) *Solicitation and Response*

The nature of interest (i.e. interestingness) is to solicit activity: the nature of will is to respond to the solicitation of interest. Neither is intelligible without its correlative. Interest causes movement 'as does the object of love', will is moved 'as is the lover' (κινεῖ ὡς ἐρώμενον—κινεῖται ὡς ἐρῶν). But the two are not equivalent in the sense that interest solicits in proportion as it is positively responded to, i.e. accepted, or that will responds positively in so far as it is solicited. The measure of solicitation is the bother made by the will about it, whether this bother takes the form of enthusiastic acceptance or heroic refusal, or any mixture that you like. There is indeed no solicitation without some tentatives toward positive response, for unless the besieger has some friends within the fortress, there is no bother made even about his non-admittance.

We can say more than that solicitation varies directly as the bother made over it. It is that bother; for the Aristotelian tag we have just quoted puts us in mind of the philosopher's purpose in writing it; which was to show that solicitation is not an event in what solicits (unmoved mover) but in that which is solicited (the moved). Solicitedness, not solicitation, is the event, and is a state of tentative response or responses rather; while that to which solicitation solicits, viz. adequate response in the enactment of the project which interests us, puts an end to solicitation itself.

If interest can be said to exercise solicitation, it exercises it in the will, as the 'final cause' in the will's concern about it. And therefore it cannot be proper to say that will responds to solicitation or we shall have it responding to itself. It is to interest that will responds (where interest is taken to be a character or characters in the object). And so 'solicitation' is not an event preceding another event, 'response'.

All the same it may be said that there is a first moment at which the response is not a voluntary response but a reaction simply necessitated by the stimulus. But this may be an error due to the fallacious supposition that a point has magnitude. The voluntary increase in concern begins from the beginning and not after a moment of passivity, or a moment at which the degree of attention is static. 'But even so, though there may not be a time during which the will is purely passive, there is still a sheer passivity of the will in respect of this selection of the object of interest. The will may actively respond from the start, but the object was given.' No. If the 'first point' has no magnitude, then the response of the will, if it did not actively develop itself, would have no magnitude, i.e. there would be no response, and so no solicitation.

We may make this clearer by starting from another place. The matter of interest 'causes movement as does the object of love'. And yet this 'activity' of causing movement is surely no proper 'activity' in that which exercises it. The stag is not active in determining the lion to pursue him. The lion has an interest (in the subjective sense) which determines itself upon the stag. It might be too much to say that the lion was looking for stags or stag-like things, but it is far truer than to say that the stag was out to attract lions or lion-like things. We defined will as real potency of effects, and if it is wholly latent until possibilities for its exercise arise, yet when they do, they arise in it and not in the conditioning environment, and it leaps upon that environment, not *vice versa*.

Here, as in all descriptions of the will and its relations to other things, we are the victims of analogy in any case. If we allow ourselves to use the word 'stimulus' of the object of interest, the will immediately becomes a sleeping lion, which the stag pricks into active response with his horns. If we say 'causes movement' of it, the will perhaps is a lump of metal which moves when a magnet is introduced into its environment. But if all language is analogical, it need not be all equally misleading, or at least we may escape slavery to one analogy by balancing it with another; and so let us consider a different and contrary lie.

The scholastic doctrine of the will describes it as determined to seek a universal object *a priori*; the lion is out for food, if not out for stags; the stag merely provides an actual will with a practical particularisation. That this is a lie, we can see from the following considerations: It treats all will as identical in structure with a particular case of will. I do sometimes seek a universal object (e.g. something to eat) explicitly, and then particularise my desire. But this explicit and more universal object is not always present to us when we accept a new project. The difficulty may be met by making the difference one of degree; the universal is sometimes more explicit, sometimes less so. We may then have the modern psychological doctrine of instinct, sentiment, etc. But even so, the doctrine plainly will not do; for it would either assume that will is essentially for the universal in which case its particularisation is accidental to its aim—what the will is out for is any instance of a wide genus. Or else, if one particularises the intention of the will *a priori*, the will contains implicitly and potentially all that it will ever do, and therefore an implicit knowledge of its own destiny, and its history is only the unwinding of this, and is logically independent of any bit-by-bit determination by its environment—the extreme form of Leibnitianism.

These absurdities arise because the will's relation to the environment from which it chooses is treated as a case of its relation to an already chosen element from within that environment. Until a choice is made we cannot say that the will is 'out for' anything relatively to what is new in the choice; it determines itself then and there in this respect. Yet an instance of will may be the best clue to will as such, and if we say that will is out for life and activity and so actively seizes objects of interest, we shall at least be able to admit the *ab initio* activity of the will in response to solicitation.

Indeed, we might think it best to abandon entirely all 'solicitation and response' terminology and to speak instead of 'tentative selection' and 'final selection' respectively. But that would have an equal danger on the other side. 'Selection' suggests either an *a priori* principle of selection in the selector, or in the absence of it, an arbitrary choice. If we speak of 'solicitation', it at least suggests to us that the motive for the action lies in the worthwhileness of the action; 'it moves as does the object of love.' Not, doubtless, the worthwhileness of the project *qua* project, the empty shell of the action, the mould into which the substance of my activity has not yet been poured, but the full-blooded reality intended. And this will be not other than me, but myself in action. But even though the project, translated into action, will become the mode of my own being, it is not adopted because it will be me, but because it is of such a kind, and therefore (if one likes to say so) because it will make me to be of such a kind; it is worthy of adoption because of its own essence (though viewed relatively to myself) and this is well expressed by the 'moves' and the solicitation.

(iii) *What Solicits?*

Let us say, then, that the will is an explorer, and that what its exploration reveals solicits its action; as soon as it begins to explore it looks one way rather than another, and the response to what solicits it must partly take the form of further exploration along that line. But now, what does it explore and what solicits it, and to what does it respond? For this rôle we might suggest the following candidates: projects, possibilities, facts, entities.

It seems first that the will is solicited by a project. Intention may not out-run action by more than a hair's breadth, but it seems it must outrun it if there is will, and the intention is directed upon a project of what is to be done. Yes; but the project is only the subjective grasp of a possibility. Because 'subjective' it may be erroneous, and what it proposes may be in fact impossible; but its *raison d'être* is to be the instrument by which possibilities are grasped, so that we are not moved by the project except in so far as we believe it to be the apprehension of a possibility; so that ultimately and properly it is possibility that moves. Further, it appears that the project, being subjective, is itself the child of will-activity and so of response; it is the objective possibility which draws the will absolutely.

Yet, to go further along the same line, it seems odd to speak of possibilities as given objects for exploration. It may seem that what we explore are facts, and we explore them with an eye to construing the possibilities they offer to our several modes of activity. The possibilities are of and in us, and we, by our inductive thinking, construe them from the facts of environment and of our own bodies. Still, on this view, the facts solicit in virtue of the possibilities they reveal, and the possibilities are 'objective': it is or is not the fact that something is possible to the will at a given moment. So that whether we prefer to say that facts or that possibilities solicit, is a matter of definition only.

It is another matter when we come to consider the last suggestion—that entities solicit. Might this be the suggestion contained in the famous 'moves as the object of love', anyhow in its most spiritualised form? If 'love' for God moves the spheres, it is not only that their 'intelligences' see in the fact of God the possibility of their own imitative action, through the suggestion that His being makes to them of tranquil and continuous movement. They are interested in Him, and therefore are drawn to contemplate Him, and fulfil their own revolutions merely as the living diagram through which they think His eternity. Or can we say that this is only to shift the possibility which attracts, from that of movement to that of contemplation?

Well, that depends upon what the interest of the contemplation is. If merely to clothe one's thought with a certain form, as one might be said to clothe one's movement with a certain form in dancing, yes. But if to grasp an independently existing Being, then no; the activity is for the sake of the object, and not *vice versa*. And whenever the formula can be applied to exploratory or creative activity, then we can also say that it is the entity and not the possibility which solicits. Above all, no doubt, in altruistic action; the man is solicited by the other's being, and the possibilities of its continuance and its enrichment. Here again are possibilities, but in the other, not for oneself, and themselves dependent on the intrinsic worth of the other as a being.

The solicitation of one's own possible action and of the entity need not exclude one another. Perhaps neither ever is without the other, yet the one may be primary. Apart from the interest in God as existent, there would be no interest in contemplating His idea, or else quite another interest—that of mental chess-playing, or of metaphysical poetry; and these again may have some relation to being. And perhaps all activity has at the least some reference to oneself as an existent to be perpetuated and enriched. But be that as it may, so far as fully conscious interest goes, it seems we may be interested in and solicited by an entity not a possible act, or a possible act not an entity, or by both.[1]

(iv) *Will and Desire not Opposites*

Our purpose has been to illuminate the notions of solicitation and response as correlatives. An object which simply determines a reaction does not solicit, but dictates it. A response which has no freedom does not respond, but follows as an effect. But on the other hand, an object which obtains no responses cannot even solicit, and a will which undergoes no solicitation cannot will.

What is the bearing of these conclusions on our original question, the relation of desire and will? We were unable to distinguish action by desire from action from automatism, psychological from physical necessity, without treating desire as a prevalent solicitation which, in a given case, runs on into enactment because no real opposition puts in an appearance. Yet solicitation which dictates is not solicitation, and the active spontaneity is from the subject not the object. The analogical conception of the will as *a priori* active, as 'out for life', will help us again here. For if the exploring will hits upon a treasure whose value it cannot but take for granted in the determinate circumstances, it will grasp it, and there will be no lack of responsive activity in such a seizure. And this is so; whether the 'taking for granted' is the project of rational conviction or of blind preoccupation, whether it is immediate or the result of previous doubt and debate; whether it is an implicit new choice, or the mere application of an old one.

If this view is right, the difference between action from will and action from desire seems almost accidental. In the best of all possible worlds, deliberate choice would (as it were) hold a watching brief, and intervene when it was required, but then only; for it seems as important that deliberate choice should keep out of the way when it is otiose, as that it should intervene when it is necessary. This is not the best of all possible worlds, or at least we are not the

---

[1] The ultimate derivation of all solicitation from entities is a metaphysical rather than an experiential fact.

best of all possible men, and we do sometimes act from superficial desire when deliberation would have been well advised to weigh against it the claims of a deeper interest; the case goes by default which should have been sustained. But this does not mean that desire as such limits the sway of will, for it is essentially the expression of will appropriate to certain circumstances.

Though this conclusion be allowed to be in accordance with our will-consciousness and to contain in itself no absurdity, it is nevertheless extremely difficult to hold fast; as soon as we have thought it out, it begins to slip from us, and we find ourselves treating desire and will as exclusive of one another; so inveterate is the habit of using the naturalistic and voluntary modes of interpretation alternately and not correlatively. Some of our acts are willed, we think, while others are the simple effects of stimuli. The reason is not far to seek—our old friend, the principle of practical interest.

We saw previously that the absorbing interest of the moral struggle, where the issue is whether we will 'take trouble' or not, makes the terminology of will current coin of everyday thought in that connexion. This was the strongest case. Less strong, but still not negligible, is the case of any deliberation which distinguishes itself as 'choice' against a background of what (by contrast) appears not to be choice; for the scheme of common sense is not that of analogy (several degrees or modes of choice) but of simple opposition (choice and not choice). It is interested not in continuities but in practically significant differences. And when choice is made without trouble and there is no problem of it, there is no practical inconvenience and much economy of terms in treating as empirically necessitated a self-orientation which is taken for granted. We are interested not in the choice of the object, but in the object chosen and how to cope with it; we do not begin to think about it until the choice is as good as made, and once it has been made there is no practical interest in remembering any other factor in the choice except the attraction of the object. This we continue to bear lively in mind, since it is the continuing motive of our continued interest, as expressed in our present thought about the object. This attraction is regarded, therefore, as acting simply, and therefore as an empirical cause determining its effect according to rule. I like oranges because I am made that way, and this is an orange....

Yet even that common-sense which is devoted to the habit of alternating the voluntary and empirical interpretations of behaviour reveals at other times the inconsistency of this division, when interest directs it in a more speculative direction. If you tell the man who says he acted from desire that he could not, therefore, have done otherwise, he will often, unless he has an axe of immoral self-excuse to grind, deny the consequence. As it was he was content to act from desire, but he need not have let himself do so. This means that in effect the desire was reviewed and passed by the censorship of will, which is only a misleading way of saying that it was chosen. We spoke above, indeed, of deliberation's holding a watching brief, and intervening when required; but deliberation is a phase or function of will, and what we meant would be better expressed by saying, that will or choice goes into a deliberative phase when occasion demands, but otherwise elects *nemine contra*. The party which holds the watching brief, if any does, would be better identified with particular interests vested in memory or habit; it is either they or the immediate contrary solicitations of other objects which call for a trial and oblige the will to go into council.

The unsuitability of the censor or constable theory of will to what normal common-sense believes is shown if we take the complementary and positive case. For as common-sense takes responsibility for many regrettable but undeliberated actions, so it allows merit to much spontaneous virtue; and these two attitudes ought surely to be referable to a single principle. But the censor-theory covers the former alone. I am guilty, because the constable *could* have put in a word. But I cannot be meritorious because he did not need to, on the view that non-deliberate desire is a brute fact which simply determines action.

The illusion which commends to us the policeman formula is simply this: we have been treating the empirical account of choice as adequate, and surreptitiously charging it with the superempirical content of real agency. The will, when we have to introduce it, is *de trop*, and gets conceived therefore as a rival cause on the same footing as the others, and capable of interfering with them; as the policeman is a causal agent of the same type as his suspects, distinguished only by skill with the truncheon and a hypnotising name. Apart from him, they are capable of going about their own business, to which his normal attitude is merely permissive. Once it has been seen that an empirical rule and a voluntary agent are not causes in the same sense, the illusion vanishes. The will can permit the actions of another agent only; in its own sphere what it does not reject it chooses and enacts.

To follow further the common man's refutation of his own division: this is more evident with regard to future than to past acts. For he cheerfully undertakes for the future, which involves the effective control of the will over the great mass of his behaviour. He knows of course that he might be wicked and misuse his will, but in that case the existence of will as power relevant to the failure is admitted. Or again, he knows that he might forget his promise; but that is not absence of will but absence of a particular basis for choice; it may be a division of the sphere of the will's action—action in watertight compartments —but it is no absence of will. He knows also that he might perform automatic acts, but he assumes that these will not be important or interfere with his duty, and he would be far from equating them with what he would normally call actions of desire.

Be it understood that we are not here attempting to show that the positivist or determinist can give no account of the reasonable and verified persuasion that we keep our own promises. The 'censor' can be treated empirically as the working of a psychological rule, and mental machinery may give rise to reasonable anticipation, as may the uniformity of physical nature. But we are speaking of the 'common' man who alternates voluntarist and determinist language, but who certainly does not take a determinist view of responsibility and the 'censor', and we are showing the untenableness of his compromise. He might perhaps say that the act of promise, itself voluntary, sets up a censorial mechanism which fulfils its purpose deterministically; but he does not in fact use this explanation, and if he did it would make as great nonsense of the will as any other. If the will is anywhere it is everywhere.

(v) *Will the Clue to the Nature of Desire*

So far we have carried the war into the enemy's country, demolishing the hard division of will and desire. But it is time we considered the defensibility of the position into which these operations have brought us, for fear that we succumb to the first push of the counter-attack. That attack will take the following form. We have argued that action from desire must have the character of response, and that it is the nature of response to be choice, to be voluntary. 'Please tell us then', the enemy will say, 'what you mean by this choice which does not deliberate, this implicit willing which seems just to happen. You set out with the resolve to remain on the intelligible level; you were not the people to take refuge in the dark. The clue you followed was to be an act of perfect consciousness, upon the form of which you could reflect. And this you found in the act of deliberate choice, which you analysed with some parade of accuracy. But now you say that this is only one mode or expression of will, and almost accidental to it. But this is the very language you used of the position which treats psychoanalytic metaphor as true philosophy. You used it and you meant it to sting. Have you not in turn identified the essence of will with the unintelligible?'

Well, yes, in a sense we have. But there are two ways of doing it. You may take the unintelligible as your standard of what will is, and add its occasional intelligibility as an 'accident'; or you may take the intelligible as your clue to its nature, and treat the 'unintelligible' examples as not the substratum of the intelligible stripped of its intelligible aspects (which would be to think nothing) but as something analogous to the complete intelligible instance. And, since we do not think nothing, it is more likely we do the latter.

When confronted with the question, why will in its explicit form is more accessible to our apprehension than other modes of agency, we formerly replied: 'Because we happen to be it; at this point, and this point alone, we can see agency and not merely its effects, because it flows from us and as our existence.' But this answer contains only part of the truth. For it assumes that the limitations determining that which 'we' are, are clear, distinct and evident. They are not. Let it be granted that 'we' are some sort of agents, anyhow. Yet it is a nice piece of definition, whether we are to declare the agency which maintains our pattern of bodily functioning in all its detail to be us or other than us. But suppose that it is we, as St. Thomas taught, then it is a level of agency which is more obscure to ourselves than are the minds of beasts. We see, then, that whereas we began with explaining the intelligibility of will proper, by the coincidence of its sphere with that of ourself, we end with defining the sphere of ourself by its intelligibility to us as will.

Let us then correct our statement, thus: The intelligibility to us of will proper is due to two reasons: (*a*) that it is a form of *our* subjectivity, (*b*) that it is the form of our *intelligent* subjectivity. Will is correlative with intelligence and intelligence with will. I will, in view of an intelligent grasp of facts and possibilities; my intelligence grasps facts and possibilities with voluntary attention. The truth of our first reply was, that the mind understands will because it stands inside it. But it is as mind that it must stand inside it. What does this metaphor of 'inside' mean? It means that intelligence by a reflection on the form of its own act discovers will as the form of that act. This act of reflection is perplexing and unique, and its object evasive; subjectivity is precisely that which is no object, and as soon as we have fixed it we have stepped outside it and objectified it. The attempt to intuit it is the attempt to catch ourselves out, and reminds one of the fairy-tale. The child was only visited by his fairy-relatives in dreams; his companion was to wake him suddenly, that he might surprise the fading vision with his waking gaze.

But this paradoxical reflection, however imperfect, must be carried out by the *intelligent* process upon itself, and not by any other, nor by this upon any other. We earlier insisted that the object of reflection must be a typical act of practical choice, because there (we said) the form of agency is most evident. We now insist that it must be an act embodying the explicit structure of intelligence, in order that it may be penetrable to intelligence. We are not here asserting in its objectionable form the doctrine that everything, to be understood, must be 'akin to mind'; but merely that our sadly limited mind has an inward understanding of its own principle of action, that it can have of nothing else's.

And yet, even if we put our money on intelligibility, our way is not clear. For it seems that we shall have to take the instance of deliberate choice for our clue to its less accessible analogues, and obtain clarity at the price of incompleteness. Yet is even this a possible procedure? That about which we want clarity is the real relation that holds together a substantial complex; and this relation is both unique and many-termed, so that we shall not understand it unless we can state the types of terms which it combines. For its pattern is not, like a spatial one, expressible as the mode of a neutral medium (space) but in relation only to the several sorts of terms it relates. But now one of the things to which deliberative will stands essentially related in ourselves, is the act of simple desire. An all-deliberate life is presumably unthinkable. We shall show this in detail later.

That, then, of which we hoped to have clear apprehension without analogic mediation, that which was to be our clue to its darker analogues, will shine after all with a qualified clarity. Though there may be something clear in its pattern, there will be irreducible surds among its constituents; there will be no entity, not the most accessible, which we can claim to comprehend even in respect of a complete non-substitutible structure. But that does not neutralise the importance of the act of conscious will. There is nothing to prevent our having a clearer understanding of one structure of act, even though it embodies as constituents others that are dark. For that structure is not the mere resultant of the natures of its constituents. If it were, we could not know it any better than we know them. But since it is also something in itself, it can be the first object of knowledge, even though this knowledge is never properly cleared up until we have analysed (but we cannot) its correlative 'matter'. Nor need we go to the extreme of asserting that we have no distinct inward sense whatever of the less deliberative and non-deliberative acts, but interpret them simply by analogy from the deliberative, as we interpret the interior acts of animals from our own. The line between the deliberative and non-deliberative is not sharp enough to make such a view plausible. But as we descend the scale from the deliberative, our apprehension becomes confused and dark, and so that it is incapable of clarification. If we clarify, we find that we have substituted for the immediate object the image of its higher analogue. Is this perhaps what Hegel meant when he called the higher or more explicit states the truth (*Wahrheit*) of corresponding lower and more implicit forms? For truth appears to be correlative with clear apprehension, and so no 'truth' of the lower is obtainable by us until they have been 'raised' into the more explicit state either in fact or in imagination.

It would not serve us, however, to attribute the whole image of the higher form to the lower, for we should have lost the differentia and substituted analogue for analogate. We are inclined, therefore, to use the formula of dilution—the proper form of explicit will is a diminishing quantity, tending towards a vanishing point, in something which has some other constant character; or, the form of explicit will continues down to the bottom of the scale essentially identical, but gets 'buried', goes out of sight, is hidden from itself. But it is plain that the form of (conscious) choice is not the same when its consciousness is removed or impaired; a form whose pattern contains reference to self as an essential feature is not the same with this feature removed. It is not necessary to waste more words on these simple tricks of the mind.

XIII

THE RATIONALITY OF WILL

(i) *Appetite specified by its Object*

LET us hope that we understand a little better now the paradoxical position of that 'most intelligible real activity' which we are making our object; so setting aside for the present all questions about its wider context, let us concentrate upon the nature of this ὡς κυριώτατα ἕκαστος, this truest self.

We have distinguished between implicit and explicit choice; of which the most perfectly explicit form seemed to be found where we consider the intrinsic character of objectives, and make that determinant. For then we seem to choose absolutely, and not to leave any surd, as we do if we accept the mere fact of desire as an ultimate.

A choice either presupposes an appetite, or is free. This does not mean that there are choices in which appetite in every sense is absent. This never happens, and appears to be nonsense, as has been only too often demonstrated. Thought alone moves nothing, we cannot know the good for us except as what aspiration jumps at, after it matters not how much consideration of the object and searching of the heart. The good cannot be defined without relation to appetite on the whole, but the appetite need not be presupposed particular and determinate. If we take for granted an appetite for stewed prunes or meta-physical curiosities, then the presentation of the appropriate object assures its seizure, as with the sea-anemone; and this is often what happens. True, any view of human choice goes beyond the sea-anemone, but the principle that transcends might still be merely the vulgarest and most selfish form of prudence, the aim harmoniously to satisfy as many sea-anemone appetites as possible in the long run. Particular determinate appetites may still be presupposed, and there is no rationality or freedom in our ultimate choice itself—unless that choice is a choice to presuppose the appetite; but then what is the motive of it?

For an object to be chosen there must be a point of contact with a de-siderative disposition itself developed from the fundamental directions of instinct. But the talk about 'sublimation' etc. itself shows that the existence of the particular determinate desire does not alone account for the selection of the object; the object comes into the line of vision, so to speak, as being 'marginal' (*vide infra*, pp. 176 *ff*) to the already fixed track of the desire. But why does the desire branch out and seize this marginal object rather than that? It can only be because we develop here and now an appetite for this object as such.

Now a new appetite for a new object may be in a sense subjectively deter-mined, i.e. from existing desires and not from the object. If I am led to desire resinato before I have tasted it, I may desire it simply out of curiosity, or in the mistaken hope that it will provide experiences analogous to certain I affect, e.g. the consumption of sherry. But in that case I do not desire it as itself, but as an object of gastronomic curiosity or as a sherry-like substance. Or one may suppose a determinate existing instinctive desire which has not previously found expression and of which I was not conscious. This would be the case with the first stirrings of sexual interest; where the object may well be selected by the determinate appetite, and desired in the first instance simply as an appropriate object of that appetite, even though the appetite awakens now for the first time.

By contrast, if we are sufficiently romantic to believe this, there may be the case where the sexual appetite as existing does not fully determine the choice of the object; but an objective contemplation of the beloved evokes a specific sexual passion for such a woman rather than for any other; whereas if the contemplation of the woman's quality had led to our valuing her less, a specific sexual aversion for the type might have resulted.

Can we then suppose that appetite may receive its last and decisive specification from the perceived merit of the object? That, in the last resort, the desire becomes such because the object is perceived to be such? At least no other account can be accepted of moral approval and disapproval. Our moral prejudices and principles already fixed may partially specify our judgments. But what they still leave open, what we recognise as a new case and painfully reflect upon, we believe ourselves to judge by an informing of our appetite (or aversion) by the object itself. And though we do not suppose our judgment infallible, we believe that in principle it can be done, or else must abandon every belief in ethical judgments.

This doctrine can be expressed (if anyone prefers) in the form that will, as such, is an appetite for the highly generic object 'that which is good', so far as examples of this object fall within the margins of our already formed appetitive tracks. Any such description is highly artificial, since such an appetite is not *a* (determinate) appetite, any more than the good is a genus of object. We cannot say that the (rational) will is an appetite for the good rather than for the bad, and that this is a determination. For we shall have to say of the good that it alone can evoke an appetite which is not determined to particular sorts of object; so that our description of the rational will turns out to be the description of an appetite as undetermined, as unspecified, as any appetite can be. And in rational choice we seem aware of the effort to de-specify appetite in order that it may be specified by the object alone. Conversely, we might describe the goodness which attaches to ends thus: 'the character of an object whereby it is fit to specify [1] appetite in so far as unspecified subjectively.'

If, then, the characteristic of good is to specify appetite, and this cannot be inverted, then the appetite is not specific until it has been specified, so that the goodness of the object cannot depend on its relation to *this* appetite as such,

[1] This lacks accuracy, because all the activity and process of the specification is from and in the subject; *vide supra*, p. 137f

nor can its fitness to specify appetite depend thereon. We must conclude that it is equally specificatory of *all* appetite.

(ii) *The Object qua Rational is Universal*

But now in what aspect of an object does its goodness lie? Whether or no its goodness is identical with its character, it is founded therein; anything is good because of *what* it is. But character (= quality in the etymological sense) is in principle universal. Or even if we held the metaphysical opinion that the character of everything is ultimately unique, we should find difficulties about founding the practical effect of goodness upon the uniqueness. For those who hold the opinion have to admit that the human creature is capable of no more than an inaccurate and generalising reaction to the unique realities; our reactions, our appetites are directed towards the analogous apprehended under the form of the class universal. Even, then, if the goodness of everything is distinct and unique, it will specify our appetite with a broadness which will leave us capable of reacting analogously to an analogous object. Let our opinion be what it may about the metaphysical status of real species and genera, it will remain that the nature of the objects of rational appetite is to be *universal*, whatever fullness or thinness our general philosophical position enables us to give to that term.

Now the superficially natural conclusions to be derived from the last two paragraphs would be: (*a*) that which we know as good is always a (real or apparent) class of objects, (*b*) this class is always good to every free appetite. Which conclusions are palpably false.

(*a*) It may be true that what we react to as good is never so completely specified as not to be theoretically capable of reproduction elsewhere. But it does not follow that it is, or will be, so reproduced, e.g. what we can grasp of the character of a given human being.

(*b*) That which is good may be so only in a certain position as constituent of a whole, and the only thing excluded *a priori* from the composition of such a whole is the very appetite which the good evokes. And undoubtedly an act may have certain sorts of goodness as constituent of one man's pattern of life, but not of another's. In that case, however, what is good in itself is the pattern not the constituent, and the pattern is theoretically universalisable, i.e. it is conceivable that a life characterised by this pattern could be found elsewhere; and if it were, it would then be good in virtue of it.

These considerations might appear to rob of all practical value the doctrine that will is essentially the appetite of universal objects. For we might say: if in fact the essences for which we form rational appetites never recur, the appetites will be in effect completely singular. And if every man's whole of life is his own, and the excellence of his objects may be relative thereto, then no two men need have the same objects, and the theoretical universality of will need never mean any practical agreement between wills.

These conclusions would not be just. To take the second point first: the life of every person other than myself is something complete in itself and presented to me as a unity [1]; and not to be valued for the way in which it fits or fails to fit into the pattern of my own existence. It then commands the 'rational appetite' of you and me and others in an identical manner, so far as we are rational. To proceed to the first point: even though good essences should not recur, there would remain individual essences that have a considerable measure of constancy over a time, and if I have appreciated the excellence of any such once I have appreciated it for always; and this introduces an attitude of constancy into my relations towards it. In particular, if I have approved for myself a pattern of life not relative to circumstances that change materially within my life-time, I have approved that also once for all and shall continue to observe the norm.

And in fact we may claim that there are many 'characters' or 'patterns' judged excellent for themselves, or relatively to mankind in general, which do recur and make up the membership of classes, anyhow to our apprehensions. Beside this, it is a fact, that our 'rational appetite' spreads itself beyond classes and strict generalisations to analogy. Things approved as uniquely good—e.g. works of art—are found to stand in a scale of analogy with one another. Works of art belonging to the same medium are always in the end analogous and yet never strictly classifiable; and it is these two facts together which make the inevitability and yet the torturing elusiveness of aesthetic criticism, in its search for principles which always turn out not to be principles.

It will be remembered that the solicitations of will might be variously described as projects, possibilities, facts, and entities (p. 139, supra). Of these the last were independently real and presupposed; they solicit our activity to contemplate them or to defend and enhance their being according to its own law. The first three reduced to one—facts solicit us by the possible actions they imply, and these possibilities are called projects in their subjective form as conceived by the mind. If these possibilities are not reviewed with relation to the needs of entities outside ourselves, then they are possible behaviour for ourselves and relative, if to anything, then to the constructed and constructible pattern of our own behaviour; they become constituents of our project-self. Now in so far as this project-self is a project-self which we are to actualise, in so far as circumstances leave us free, and in so far as we are rational, the project-self is the choice of our rational appetite. And, being rational, this choice, once made, is made for always whenever it is made; and being made can continually actualise itself. Here the mind's universal does not have to wait entirely on a world of process outside its control in the uncertain hope that it may discover itself. We ourselves, in so far as in us lies, intend and actualise the universal form which is the object of our rational appetite.

[1] This statement does not assert monadology, but simply that, however dependent on its environment it is, the self is enough a real centre of being to have some value inherent in itself when taken in its environment, such that all perfectly instructed angels and men would agree about it.

(iii) *Illustration from Kant's System*

It is impossible here to avoid a comparison of our doctrine with that of Kant, and this on three heads: (I) the distinction between universal volitions and particular appetites, (II) the relation of volition to possibilities and entities respectively, (III) the distinction between the place of the Idea in the theoretical and practical spheres.

(I) The practical philosophy of Kant is built on this distinction. The immorality of the particular appetite is its merely given character. It is a brute fact that I have the desire for this and that. Just because the desire is presupposed, rationality cannot penetrate my choice of ends, but merely show me how to realise them, or what to realise them will cost in pain, or in the incidental frustration of other ends. It is no answer to Kant to say, that not all brute desires are for selfish satisfactions, that one may have a simple impulse to relieve a beggar. So far as it remains a simple impulse, we are the victims of it, and its being selfish or otherwise is a consideration extraneous to our will.

Kant sought, therefore, an end which should not be chosen by a presupposed particular and determinate appetite. We know that he found this in the much derided form of pure universality. But it is worth noting how many of the essentials his doctrine contains.

(*a*) Cognitive apprehension of the end must precede and form 'appetite'. And so, for Kant, the good man must first on rational grounds make the right end his object, but then may obtain an *interest* in it which issues in satisfaction when the object has been gained.

(*b*) If we allow ourselves to think of the rational will as an appetite with a determinate object, this object must be conceived as highly 'generic', i.e. only very imperfectly determinate after all, as we have seen (*supra*, p. 147). Indeed we saw that it is not really even generic, since 'the good' does not deserve the name of genus. And though it has certain 'marks', like that of universality, these 'marks' are *conditiones sine quibus non*, but not in themselves a description of a character with which the 'rational appetite' is correlative. Kant may be credited with appreciating the high generality of the rational objective. Our complaint is that he did not go far enough; he still tried to regard it as an actual genus and so fell into the mistake of attempting to treat the marks of the good as that, the presence of which in a project motivates rational appetite for it.

In so doing, he succumbed to the error of transcendental subreption which he so frequently denounced, for he imposed upon the rational 'appetite' the form of the particular appetite; he treated it as a determinate appetite presupposedly correlated *a priori* with a generic 'character', in this case the universalisability of the maxim of the project. Thereby he denied to the will that which above all is distinctive of it, its indeterminacy *a priori* and power of estimating its objects, not by its own measure, but by theirs. In view of Kant's general position, it is of course in no way surprising that he should find no place in the practical sphere for the supreme truth which he had already denied in the theoretical: that mind, in its perfection, eliminates its own forms and becomes a view of the object, while will in its perfection eliminates its determinate appetites and becomes a response to the object.

(c) Kant's 'subreption' led him into difficulties with the rational appetite itself, considered subjectively. We have seen that the essence of the matter is that appetite is specified by the object, and that Kant allows this in some sense by allowing the good man an interest subsequent to the adoption of the right project for its own sake. Now for us, the will is undetermined *a priori* and the choice of the project is all one with the formation of an interest, or particular appetite, by the project as seen. If we speak of the will as being in general an appetite for the good, this general appetite is related to its specifications by particular 'goods', as the genus mammal is related to the several mammalian species. It is not something actual alongside of them, but becomes actual in them. For Kant the reverse must be true. The rational appetite is a determinate appetite for a particular genus, viz. that of project-whose-maxim-is-universalisable: it is its action *in this form* which leads to the selection of the project, and our particular 'interest' is something subsequent, separate and inessential. Then it has its own subjective form, and this is 'awe'. So the righteous man is (1) moved by awe, respect for righteousness, to prefer the universalisable project, e.g. of saving the child from the canal, and (2) may subsequently develop an interest in line with his moral choice, an interest in the safety of the child. The absurdities of this position have been often enough dwelt upon.

(d) Kant is by the same principle led into error with regard to the relation between particular appetites and the rational appetite. For it turns out, of course, that the principle of the moral will, while it is a true motive, is not a sufficient motive. A man cannot initiate an act, unmotived except by the universalisability of its maxim; and only very rarely by the non-universalisability of the contradictory maxim. Particular appetites for particular ends are presupposed in the only intelligible form of the Kantian doctrine; and the principle of the rational will becomes a principle of choice between these, viz. that only those should be enacted whose maxim is universalisable. But if so, the will is shorn of half its glory, and there are no objects (unless we allow the case mentioned above) which are rational without qualification.

This doctrine has to be contrasted with that which we have proposed— of the marginal freedom of choice which lies along the fringes of the paths of formed particular appetites. Though, as Kant saw, the particular appetites are the basis for freedom, they are not so only in the manner he supposed. The will can seize a marginal possibility for its intrinsic value, i.e. its whole appeal to us is as an object of rational appetite, and its position in the margin of a track of desire is accidental to this.

(II) Kant's theory presents an interesting analogy to our statement, that the solicitant of rational choice might be regarded as either a possibility or an entity. For he is able to present the form of the categorical imperative in two ways: we must act always so that the maxim of our act could be willed by us as law universal, *and* we must treat all men always as ends-in-themselves and not as means only. The first form determines our action by reference to the project for that action itself; the second by reference to already existent entities which make a claim upon us.

But as the mind is incapable of grasping individual worth in a project, still more, for Kant, is it incapable of penetrating the individual worth of another self, which is a 'thing-in-itself' so far as our minds are concerned. Our motive cannot be, then, to cooperate in building up or defending the peculiar excellence of this individual person, nor to explore his real being. I can only know him under the abstract form of a rational will, so that respect for such a self-legislative entity is the only attitude of which I am capable *qua* rational being. So the first precept commands me to act in a form suitable for universal autonomous legislation for and by wills; the second commands me to act in a way which will assist or not impede wills in so legislating and practising. The first precept assumes that rational appetite is correlative with a determined generic project; the second that it is correlative with a determined generic entity (i.e. aspect of an entity).

To accuse Kant of legalism, i.e. the belief that the determinant in ethics is the rule, appears to be not wholly just. He knew that morality had reference both to (projected) actions, and to entities (persons); he took a formalistic view of both, but did not set one absolutely over the other. He gives a rule, indeed, for the treatment of persons, but not as a case of the moral rule (i.e. as a universalisable maxim) but as necessarily correlative with it. And, conversely, we can say that the sanction of the moral law itself is not independent of the fact that it is the very form of rational personality in action. So Kant was by no means the intuitive legalist who is content to say that the sanction of the moral law is the testimony of the moral conscience. He founds it upon being, the nature of real entities, the self that I am and the selves that others are; indeed, upon the only aspect of real being which, according to his philosophy, can be known; viz. the principle of universality or rationality itself, as constituting the nature of spiritual agents whose actions issue in the phenomenal realm.

(III) Kant saw that the applicability of the universal, the 'law', holds in the shaping of voluntary action a place different from what it holds in the direction of theoretic enquiry. For the exposition of this point of doctrine, we must first set aside the *a priori* universals. These are contributed to the phenomena by the sensibility and understanding. They are the alphabet into which the percipient being mysteriously decodes the hidden reality. It must be then that whatever appears appears in these forms, whose universality signifies nothing even indirectly of the realm of the real.

By contrast, the Ideas of Reason, if taken as constitutive, would signify something of the nature of the world, viz. that the hidden reality contributes to the phenomena such material and such only as to yield, when decoded into the percipient's alphabet, none but complete and perfect 'sentences'. And even if these do not, in any given experience, make up a complete and reasonable story, yet an experiment capable of making the experiences appropriate for filling in the gaps could (we should be assured) obtain that complete reasonableness. Now such universality as this, Kant sees, can neither be imposed nor assumed by the mind, nor can the apparent discovery of it ever yield final certainty, in the cognitive sphere. The mind may guess, may form hypotheses, but must wait on experience to confirm or refute them.

But for the will, it is otherwise. The principle of absolute rationality is no longer a dubious clue, but an imperative law; in so far as the will is free, it makes, and can rationalise its action in so far as it can make it. The phenomenal effect of what I do, because phenomenal, will automatically appear in percipience under the *a priori* forms of sense and of the categories—that can be taken for granted here also. But above and beyond this, I can secure to my action a universality of form which I can never be perfectly assured of in nature, the perfect rational universality of its intention. We need not go again into Kant's errors with regard to the nature of this universality, but we can underline his adherence to the truth that, however dubious may be the will's constancy of response to environment (for the constancy of environment itself cannot be guaranteed), it can be constant in the effort to realise its ideal for itself, so far as that ideal is a practicable one.

The purpose of this shamelessly perfunctory criticism of the great philosopher has not been critical, but to show how firmly he held some of the essential elements of a true doctrine of the universality of will, though frustrated at every turn by the fundamental error of the Critical Philosophy.

(iv) *Two Relations of Practical Reason to its Object*

Since we have defined practical reason as an active and voluntary response to the worth of objects, it may be expected of us to take sides on the moralist's favourite problem—whether morality is to be placed under the flag of sheer obligation, or under that of the noble ideal. Is it to be duty, or aspiration: law, or creativity: deontology, or ideal utilitarianism? But it would be hard for anyone who has read Professor de Burgh to engage in the attempt of reducing either to terms of the other; he has made it so evident that both are original and natural forms of experience.

It is a more useful aim to derive both from the same objective grounds, in such a way as to account for their difference; and such a solution is provided by the principles outlined in this chapter. For there are two relations in which we may feel ourselves to stand towards the object which makes a claim on us. We may consider it as something existing, which needs our action to uphold or complete it. In that case our experience will be cast in the mould of duty. Or we may consider it as something not existing nor absolutely demanded by anything existing, but as one among, presumably, an indefinite number of enrichments that existing beings could receive. And then our experience will be that of attraction by the best ideal, the most worth-while project, known to us.

Duties are commonly supposed to be owed to persons and to laws. Persons exist, and so do laws, as established working patterns in the lives of persons. What the justification of laws may be, is another matter, but so far as we accept them as existing, we feel under obligation to uphold them, as we do also the contracts into which we have voluntarily entered. And so long as we keep our eyes fixed on what is, not only on existing obligations, but also on the absolute demands made by innumerable souls on charity and justice, we shall have small leisure to consider the noble ideal, and free creativity of the simply best. And yet again, unless we turn the other way, we may lose the knowledge of what charity and justice are, for it is charitable to help men to the attainment of what is good for man, and most just to make an even division of the best things; and what these are, is revealed to free aspiration.

The two types of rational attitude intermingle with an infinite variety of complication, and it is very much a matter of accident in most cases whether we view a project *sub ratione boni* or *sub ratione debiti*; since what at one time appears a free enrichment of an existence not suffering from any shameful privation in this regard, may at another seem a necessary expression of that existence if it is to be itself. At one extreme you have the Kantian legalist, who perversely transforms free choices into duties towards his own rationality, merely because it would be unreasonable to choose otherwise: at the other, the utilitarian, who sees in the discharge of a duty of faithfulness a free contribution to Utopia. Perhaps this dialectic can be escaped by none but God Himself, for whom there are no established claims existing *a priori*, since He is the Creator, and wills all things for their good.

However that may be, human oscillation between the two positions is due to ignorance of fact and partial viewing of particulars, and not to any obscurity of principle. Each attitude expresses practical reason in relation to a type of object. It is unreasonable to take up towards a privation, e.g. of breath in a drowning child, the same attitude we adopt towards the mere absence of something desirable, say of an interest in opera among the inhabitants of our suburb. It is not that the one affects our will more strongly, which in the instance taken it may happen to do, but that it affects it in a different way. For the value of the existing child is axiomatic, and the saving of its life follows as a corollary; the value of the opera project is not yet axiomatic, nor a corollary of the axiomatic.

For the reduction of discordance between the two attitudes, religious contemplation is recommended, and rightly; yet it seems that consideration can assist, even without theological reference. It is only necessary to dwell upon the intrinsic worth of the axiomatic (because existing) values, for our service of them to become the object of aspiration and interest, as well as of debt; as when we take trouble to remember that we care for a person, to whom we find ourselves suddenly under an inconvenient obligation.

(v) *The Act of Bad Will*

We have been treating of the rationally-responding will, as though its response were simple and infallible. The abstraction was convenient, but it is time we reminded ourselves that the response was a judgment, and may be erroneous or insincere. Of error we have already treated; it remains to consider insincerity.

Every actual conclusion of a 'practical syllogism', every practical judgment, has an action as its ultimate expression (until we act, neither we nor anyone else can know certainly what our belief is—i.e. our belief about the value of an objective). If this proposition could be converted, all will and all action would be rational and 'good'—if, that is, we could say: 'Every voluntary action expresses a practical judgment.' We cannot say this without qualification; the 'bad man' does not act upon a genuine judgment of value. But neither can we assert the simple contradictory, that he acts without any sort of judgment at all; since, if he does, his action would not be voluntary nor come into the forum of moral judgment. In fact, just as misapprehension is *sui generis*, and yet bears some relation to apprehension; so failure of practical judgment is *sui generis*, and yet bears some relation to practical judgment. To fail to judge is a sort of act, as it is a sort of act to misapprehend. Every kind of error arises in epistemology from the attempt to treat misapprehension and apprehension as equal species of an identical genus; and just as much error in the philosophy of will, if we try to treat the sincere practical judgment and the bad quasi-judgment [1] in that same manner.

It is notorious that Aristotle asserts the two extreme positions—the intemperate man simply holds the erroneous judgment that things really evil are good: the incontinent does not really judge at all in relation to the universal practical propositions he *appears* to believe; they are dissociated from his present act, which is in fact an implicit practical judgment on other principles. And these two solutions he applies to different men—or to different elements in the behaviour of the same man. This shows his sensitiveness to the problem, though the true solution must lie between his extremes. We are not denying, of course, that there are intemperates in Aristotle's sense—men suffering from 'invincible moral ignorance'—and incontinents besides, whose non-judging is due to mental dissociation. But the Philosopher was apparently trying to deal with responsible moral will, and he failed to do this.

The modern or anyhow the Christian reader's reaction to Aristotle is usually the bold assertion: 'Nonsense! The very nature of moral iniquity is to judge one thing, and do the reverse.' But this is much too simple. For, as we have seen, the practical judgment is not complete without an act; I have not willed until I have (in my own sincere expectation) committed myself, and then only in so far as I have committed myself. The bad man may have formerly

[1] We cannot say 'misjudgment' because that would be understood to imply simple error (misapprehension) and not practical (moral) failure.

judged the good to be good by enacting it, but that does not give sure evidence about his present judgment. Or he may now have a 'stuttering' (*vide supra*, p. 113) of the process of the good project; but this is not a complete judgment so long as the stuttering continues.

Let us start in another place. The bad man, we feel, goes against moral 'evidence'. It is he who must confess: 'Video meliora proboque: deteriora sequor.' But what is the nature of this evidence? It is not knowledge, nor is it a formed opinion of probability. A man who saw, by mathematical demonstration from accepted *data*, that the materials he had would not reach to span the river, could in defiance of this knowledge attempt to build a bridge out of these materials alone; say, to keep up his reputation of obstinacy. A man who concludes to the high probability that the weather will be foul to-day may yet start on a picnic, because he chooses to take the risk. Action against 'moral evidence' has no resemblance to either of these cases. Moral evidence is not an accepted probability that something should be done; it is a solicitation to the formation of an irrevocable judgment that it must. An empirical judgment of probability is a formed opinion complete in itself apart from the practical judgment which we may or may not base upon it. I think it will probably rain; that is an expectation of what will probably happen, whatever I do or do not do, and in view of it I may choose to act in several ways. But moral evidence is a solicitation to *one* action, and the state of the man who has not begun to act is not one of opinion but of solicitation—solicitation at once to act (practical aspect) and to accept the claim of the objective (theoretical aspect). We have already seen (*supra*, p. 137) that the nature of solicitation is tentative response.

Let us put the contrast in another way. Empirical probabilities are based on facts (or propositions taken for granted as though they were facts). From these the probabilities follow by rules already known. Moral solicitations also follow from facts or things taken for granted—e.g. that it is open to me to act in a certain way. But the belief that so and so must be done does not arise on already established grounds, but out of the influence of the object on my will. Or if it arises from a moral code, that code itself must rest ultimately on no other basis than such an influence; and the code itself, or its applicability here, is called in question in so far as I hesitate about acting in this instance.

Practical (moral) judgment does not proceed, then, from facts to inferred probabilities, nor from an addition of probabilities to a firmer probability. It proceeds from suasion to persuasion, from tentative to final response. The bad man, then, who holds out against moral 'evidence', instead of making the act of sincere and objective attention which draws a rational suasion on into a persuasion, forms his persuasion from suasions which are not rational, by wilful concentration upon them until they have filled the mind and captured the machinery of action.

(vi) *The Bad Man's Maxim*

We have already said that true will is perspicuous, intelligible, because it is an act of intelligence, and can reflect (with some success) upon its own form. The perverse moral judgment is in so far unintelligible because unintelligent; it is a 'surd' and must remain so, and this was what made Aristotle's puzzle. The perverse judgment is not simply the response of a formed disposition to its appropriate stimulus; it is the resolve 'I will do this (which gratifies formed appetite) rather than that (which claims to be worth while on objective grounds)'. This is not instinctive behaviour; it is a quasi-judgment, and since it sets aside a rational claim, it can do so only by opposing to it a quasi-claim. The woman in Juvenal replied to masculine dissuasions: 'Sic volo, sic iubeo: sit *pro ratione voluntas.*' The poet is very philosophical and very exact. The lady makes 'acting upon impulse' into a quasi-*ratio-agendi*, into a bastard 'maxim' in Kant's sense.

The bad man, in fact, endows certain types of action with a privilege: things which concern one's worldly welfare, or that are the objects of certain formed desires, or that are strongly desired while being of small consequence and unobserved (so that it would be pedantic to enforce rule upon them), or whatever class of project it be, these are made sacred or absolutised as ends. Such quasi-maxims, then, become legislations of the will for itself, and borrow as far as they may the character of universality; and so the bad man has policies of badness—not merely policies instrumental to the attainment of given aims, but policies about the choice of aims; and the life of the strong bad man (e.g. Napoleon) attains to a truly terrifying consistency. The explicitness of these 'maxims', and the degree in which an attempt is made to justify them, may vary infinitely. But maxims or policies of a sort there must be; for there is no such thing as 'mere' selfishness, there are several quite distinct policies open to the selfish man, and the choice between these, though it may waver a while, will settle one way presently. For if we have chosen once this way, why should we not next time accept our own determination of what we want?

Will, then, even when degraded by wickedness, does not lose the whole form of universality, but tends towards some unification of life, though imperfect, and though the unity which it intends be of a kind which is bound to break against the facts of our own nature—as it would be comfortable, with Plato, to suppose.

What the form of the bad man's maxim will be, is a question which cannot be answered simply. We must first distinguish between 'rationalisation' and that which is rationalised. It is evident that rationalisation can take an infinity of forms, which it cannot concern us to detail. He may tell himself simply that his actual bad principle is good—e.g. that self-expression without regard to others is noble and free. He may tell himself that he acts from policies other than his actual—e.g. the tyrant who tries to view himself as a patriot. Or there is the pretence that one's bad (and really perhaps most significant) acts are psychological accidents irrelevant to one's main line of conduct. Or there is the cynical form—these are the things which in fact one 'has to' pursue, being but human—and so on.

Perhaps the bad will, when reflective, is never without a trace of rationalisation; and this may have complicated the problem for Aristotle. E.g. our first form of rationalisation above, if taken seriously, would present us with Aristotle's intemperate man, whereas the third would appear to agree with his account of the incontinent; the fourth is a piece of self-deception about the general character of man's existence, the second of self-deception about the character of our particular acts.

If now we ask after the 'real' form which the rationalisations misrepresent, it is not perfectly clear what we are asking about. Are we asking for the explicit 'maxim' of the most sincere bad man in the moment of his badness, or for the implicit maxim as it appears later upon penitent reflection? We have indeed to assume that even under the rationalisations there is at some stage such a feeling of their probable falsity, that if good will had followed this clue, the man would have acted right.[1] But the clue might not take the form of an explicit awareness of the real maxim—only such a half-glimpse out of the tail of the mind's eye as to suggest the propriety of looking further.

Let us make a fresh start. The agent is facing a (rational) claim that something should be done or not done by virtue of its character, because it is *tale*. 'This—being such—is to be done.' If he repels this on the level of rational will at all, he must surely repel it by another *tale*: 'But this—being such—is what I will to do.' One cannot compare a *tale* with a mere *hoc*, as such. Even if I appear to do this, and say, 'But I want to do this other thing very strongly', I am advancing a *tale* of a kind—though the 'character' does not belong now to the object, but to the subjective situation relatively to the object. What I am saying is, in fact: 'Where my already formed desires are as strongly concerned as this, I set aside objective claims of such and such a sort.' This expresses a 'quality' in certain situations, in virtue of which I oppose them to situations of solicitation by certain objective claims; and is the implicit formulation of a policy. We are by no means always clear to ourselves how wide or how narrow is the 'quality' or class of claims that we implicitly reject, nor how wide the rival quality in virtue of which we do reject them. Yet in so far as we formulate in the vaguest or most implicit way an opposition between two solicitations, we must oppose a 'such' to a 'such', and if we do not, there cannot be a choice which concerns the moralist.

The essential maxim of the bad will would appear, then, to be 'Of such a kind is the thing I will to do'. Not 'I think good to do', or the man is merely in error; nor 'I desire to do' or there is no expression of will at all in the proper sense. No doubt in fact the choice of the bad man always does minister to instinctive desire or to dispositions which happen to have been formed on the

---

[1] Otherwise the case would be one of theoretical error merely, or psychological compulsion.

basis of it [1]; but his maxim is not a maxim of desire (could one have such a thing), for were it so, it would not be a maxim of will, even bad will.

In so far, then, Aristotle's first position is justified. The bad man, like his intemperate, has maxims, though these ought not to be described as 'the apparent good'—unless 'good' is given the nugatory definition 'whatever is aimed at', in which case 'apparent' is *de trop*. Otherwise 'the preferred good', the good which is selected by (arbitrary) choice, would be better. But Aristotle's second position also has justification, for the man who rebels against his 'better judgment' never rebels against it in a complete state; Aristotle was right when he said that it is an unendurable paradox that reason should be dragged about, because my reason is myself and when fully formed it is my action; if reason can be 'disobeyed' by other elements in our nature, what becomes of the unity of the person? [2] Clearly reason must betray itself; instead of completing its own process it turns into paralogism. And so the two Aristotelian positions meet: for the principle asserted in the Incontinent's paralogism is the 'maxim' of the bad man.

[1] Even though the worse choice be a free and rational choice but on grounds more partial than the right alternative, my *preference* for the more partial is what has to be explained and this must be referred to instinctive or dispositional bias.

[2] Once again, disunity is possible, but if so, and in so far, the agent is not responsible.

XIV

THE FREEDOM OF WILL

(i) *Modes of Freedom*

WE have made a distinction of more and less in the freedom of actions, for the more explicitly conscious choice appears to be more free in being more an action. Again, we have made a quite different distinction between the use and misuse of whatever freedom of choice a given situation allows us. It seems natural to enquire next, whether in cases where freedom is not misused and is of equal degree, there may not be several modes of freedom. We are inclined to suspect there may be, from the variety of doctrines about the free choice that have obtained. Some may be false, and others due to confusion, but it seems likely that others have been partial, and true in what they asserted, and erroneous by omission alone.

If there are several conditions necessary for free will to be realised, now one, now another may be present in greater perfection, or at least be more fully utilised by the will. Will you object that this is not to distinguish modes of the will itself, but simply ways in which it may be impeded, by the sufficiency or insufficiency of instruments; that to judge freedom by this is near to the banality of judging it by the presence or absence of handcuffs? But this will appear less so, if we reflect that there are certain conditions relatively to which alone free acts can be made at all. If the vanishing-point of these conditions is the vanishing-point of freedom, then their development may well be the increase of freedom, and the development of one the increase of it in one way, that of another in another; so that we may say that one act is freer in one way, another in another, and this in virtue of its immediate conditions and not of the energy displayed in exploiting them.

For the sake of clarity let us begin by setting aside several senses of freedom, according to which the more and less may be predicated of it, but which do not belong to this topic.

(*a*) The higher (more explicit, more rational) levels of will can be called freer than the lower.

(*b*) The good, rational, sincere act of will may be called free, in contrast to the bad, selfish, irrational act, which is enslaved to partial appetite. (Whether this is a contrast of more and less or a simple opposition may be disputed.)

(*c*) The (sincere but) erroneous will may be thought less free than the enlightened.

(*d*) Certain purposes being assumed to be universally human, we may call a man more or less free as his circumstances or mental and bodily constitution allow him to attain or at least hopefully pursue them. Endless variations are possible on this theme, according to the purposes supposed—whether universally human, or actually entertained by this man, or believed to be those through the expression of which alone he could 'realise himself', etc.

We are dealing with none of these distinctions. All the acts which we proposed to consider may be assumed to be free in the senses (*a*) and (*b*). (*c*), stated thus baldly, hardly refers to the will in itself at all, but to a relation between it and absolute standards, which it, *ex hypothesi*, is unable to know, or it would not be in error; it is an extraneous consideration, and not a condition of will for the agent who wills. (*d*) is 'handcuffs' again, and does not deal with the varying form of will-acts actually made, but either with the possibility of translating certain wishes into acts of will, or with the chance enjoyed by will-acts (once made) of producing the physical effects intended in them.

(ii) *Rationality, Choice, Creativity*

We turn, then, to the immediate conditions of actual willing, and take:

(I) Objective motivation. Since rational volition is specified by its object, and not *vice versa*, an act may seem to be more free in so far as the object is qualified to specify it by (*a*) clarity and (*b*) worth, and less free in so far as the object fails in these respects; if it is hard for us to grasp what is presented to our choice, or if that which is presented, however clear, is trivial.

A further subdivision may be made, according as the inadequacy of the object *qua* presented is due (*a*) to what is external to us or (*β*) to subjective, though not at this moment voluntary, factors. What is obscure in its axiological bearings may be so for any human mind, or specially for this mind in view of its history. So far as the special obscurity is due to special ignorance of facts, that does not require more than mentioning. But equally the obscurity may be due to a lack of moral 'faith'. For in proportion to our making of relevant moral choices in the past, will often be the firmness of our judgment in this case. As with obscurity, so also with triviality; if an object appears to have no great importance, it may be because this is so, or because I have not developed the moral 'apperceptive machinery' to grasp the importance it has.

This sense of freedom—the liberation afforded to the will by the adequate presentation of an adequate object—has, of course, a distinguished history in theology. The will that has lacked full activity through the lack of a sufficient object is presented with the vision of God, or of the purposes of God; and this object, being in itself sufficient, is made subjectively to appear so by the mysterious operation of the Holy Spirit in the 'heart', preparing an appercipience capable of the object. And so God's service is perfect freedom, and the question of the will's freedom of *choice* is talked out of court. How can the will want anything better then to embrace Perfection? And if it has seen Perfection, what has it to do but to embrace it? For the Will of God Himself (the theologian may continue) to be presented with the adequate object and to embrace the object is all one, and there is no liberty of indetermination. Well, then, we ought 'to live the life of gods as far as we may'—we can hardly become less free by being placed in a situation of will which approximates us to God as closely as possible.

But when the position has been carried to this length there is sure to be a revolt, which may rally round one or more other conditions of willing, of which we will signalise (II) open alternatives and (III) creativity.

(II) Open alternatives. It seems that the will is in real exercise, is really doing something, where there are serious alternatives, and choice is momentous. The defenders of the position we have just left may say that this is to make perplexity into freedom, whereas it is evident that the perplexed will is bound, and only escapes into action when one alternative has drawn it. To which it will be replied that perplexity is indeed bondage, and therefore is the *dignus iudice nodus*—the *iudicium* of will shows its discretionary power in cutting the knot, but not in virtue of the plain superiority of one alternative, or no knot would be there. To be simply drawn by adequate objects is not the full exercise of freedom. And for the other party to protest that after all we are always free not to follow the evident object is frivolous; it is a physical possibility indeed, but psychologically it is unreal through lack of motive.

If there is to be a real act of will, then, there must be a measure of obscurity in the object—if not in the one alternative considered by itself, then in the whole situation presented to choice. We cannot say then, the more evident the objective clarity, the greater the freedom.

(III) Creativity. This condition of freedom seems to be in opposition to the first, though in a slightly different manner from (II). For now it appears that the supreme condition of a truly free act is that it should be aimed at the shaping of a state of affairs which is unique, and of which the design is born in the brain of him that shapes it. This is not intended to make moral activity equivalent to aesthetic creation. It is recognised that a moral act as such is not aimed at producing a thing by itself, like a work of art, but is a responsible contribution to the total edifice of human life; that it must be an appropriate response to conditions; that it must conform to certain principles, embodying certain 'values', etc., etc.

It remains, however, that the true shape of my destiny and of theirs whom I can influence or affect is not wholly prefigured in the present facts, even to the most morally enlightened eyes. I do not simply grasp an object or project, I design it, and this not by a pure mental exercise prior to action. The first design is sketchy, obscure, tentative, at the best a prophetic inkling of the true way; it has to be acted out before its value is known; and even then what we obtain is a fresh prophecy embodied in a new project. Act is the only full revelation; all intending is uncertain and dark.

This position has a simple retort to the 'live the life of gods as far as we may' of the first. God is above all else creative; if it is true that He knows His object with clarity and chooses it without hesitancy, it is also true that His object does not pre-exist Him, is not presented to Him from without, but is the project formed by His own mind. But we are not, as He is deemed to be, free originators of all that is; our primary object is a world of perplexing variety already existing. If this simply dictated our response (so far as we act rationally), we should have no creativity; if we are to be creative in view of a complicated and unpredictable environment, our visions must be dark. Or if *per impossibile* they were clear, they would not be clear as an object simply presented and demanding certain actions, as (I) seemed to suggest. They would be presented as what we make, where the existing states of affairs fail to lay down a complete guide to action.

Before proceeding to a further condition of freedom, we may pause to tidy up the relations of these three. No one who has followed the preceding discussions with any measure of sympathy will need to be shown that they are not mutually exclusive. As to the first and the third: an object which solicits the will always calls for the creation of something by the will, and never absolutely prescribes its character; and conversely, for human minds there is no such thing as creation *ex nihilo*, nor without a foundation in the existing state of affairs, and in the claims this asserts. Besides, though my free behaviour is not a mere selection from the possibilities presented by the state of affairs, but is a design of my invention, this design is a project, which can be valued for the intrinsic worth it is honestly expected to have if realised. It must be worth while in other than the selfish sense. So we do not escape from objective motivation.

Again, as to the opposition of the first and the second: this appears to be less sharp in practice than on paper. For a great and commanding purpose, however clearly grasped, involves us in cruel perplexity about the proper form of its realisation here and now, or about the circumstances which allow it to be furthered, and those that demand that it be (for the while) set aside; so that Aristotle was able to treat this as the typical case of moral choice. And even though there are cases where we choose between aims that appear to us to be simply diverse, and not alternative means to an agreed end, we cannot allow that judgment cuts the knot by an arbitrary choice, or that if it does so, it is free. It may be that there is a struggle in choosing; but either the choice is not rational and free, or else the struggle is a struggle to apprehend the real superiority of the one alternative; in which case we attain to increased perception of the objectively real by our efforts to choose. And so the choice appeared more really a choice, because as an act it was enriched by something which was lacking to the man who simply recognised the good when he saw it—a development of perceptive power, accomplished through our own endeavour. But in that case the prize we obtain is an additional aptitude for (I), for being adequately determined by adequate objects.

In spite of these harmonising considerations, it does not appear likely that one can find a single act of will in which all the factors are present to the highest degree imaginable. Typical acts of exploration with a view to enlightenment are not identical with typical acts of response to that enlightenment when obtained, even though the types interpenetrate to some degree—for one cannot explore till one has some lights, and acting upon enlightenment always reveals something fresh. Every act is toward light and every act is from light, every act is objectively motived and every act is creative, but one characteristic preponderates in one act, another in another.

(iii) *Moral Effort compared with the previous three*

(IV) Moral effort may appear to be the essence of freedom. We are not free because we can choose how to act for the best, but because we can choose whether to act for the best or not. If 'the good will' could be presupposed, the choice between alternatives would be like the working of a sum when we are already interested in obtaining the correct result. If I already want to know whether the money in my pocket will pay my bus fare to X, and bring me back from Y, it requires no effort of the will, worthy of the name, to work the sum. And even though my stupidity is such that I tear my hair and bite my nails over the mathematics involved, it is still only pain and delay incident to a process already chosen; if there is effort, it is not effort concerned with choice, and free will appears to be concerned with choice. If choice enters, it will be because I begin to ask myself whether it is worth while pursuing this line of activity after all, at such a cost. But—if I can presuppose good will—this is only another calculation in making which there may again be effort and delay, but always incident to a process already chosen—that of arriving at a correct answer. Real choice, then, appears to be confined to cases where I choose to act for the best or not to do so, when I have seen what the best is; it is confined, in fact, to situations of temptation.

According to this thesis, the three-cornered argument between the three former positions is irrelevant. The temptation may arise in relation to any of the three factors: I may be tempted to refuse the best when seen for the sake of the satisfaction of a particular and formed desire; I may be tempted to withhold the effort needful for the solution of a perplexity; I may be tempted to 'create' irresponsibly or to acquiesce in a non-creative, routine way of life. Yet of all these forms of temptation, it is the first that is typical—the case in which I see the better, and prefer the worse. For in the second case also, I see that intellectual effort is required, and prefer the pleasure of indolence; in the third, I see that I ought either to regard social values or to liberate myself from herd dominance, or whatever it be, yet prefer to do otherwise.

What shall we say to this thesis? Let us admit that sincerity of intention—the 'good will'—is at least a latent issue in all free willing, and sometimes the most prominent issue. Who, in fact, would continue in strenuous and sincere well-doing, without a sustained and active turning toward the good and away from the baser ends? Let us also admit that the issue between 'good' and 'bad' will is what gives full value to any choices whatsoever. The choice of selfish prudence, in any of its forms, is not a choice but a calculation; the choice between diverse ends by the arbitrament of various formed desires is not a choice but a dog-fight; the choice of the rational will incapable of suffering temptation would be a simple intellectual vision, and would reduce will to identity with an intellect which uses action as an instrument both of exploration and execution.

But these admissions do nothing to justify the contention of this thesis, that the second and third factors can be reduced to the first; that only the vision of the good is relevant to moral choice, and not perplexity about the good nor the free creation of one's own life. To take 'perplexity': we have already seen in our discussions of the bad will, that we have never completely judged the superiority of the alternative which we sinfully reject; so that a certain 'perplexity' characterises every temptation-situation. Not perplexity, necessarily, in the sense that there is a genuine problem for good will, could good will be supposed; but a sort of perplexity for this imperfect mind in its as yet unresolved state. But further, the moral issue penetrates *true* perplexity-situations; for we can never take for granted the purity of the judgment that we exercise, so that the effort at solution is just as much an effort at sincerity as an effort after exploration. Indeed it is in perplexities that the content of our habitual moral judgment itself is formed.

In the thesis which we are busy qualifying there occurred several times the phrase, 'if good will could be presupposed.' This phrase may be taken in such a way as to cover a huge unreality, which has done not a little to mislead the philosophy of the will. Kant's system, for example, provides the good man with a direction of the will *a priori*, before all particular objects and actions— the intention to work only upon universalisable maxims; and the application of this intention to particular situations he supposes to be evident. Kant, then, could fairly talk about presupposing good will. But for us, good will must mean the following of the best objects we have seen. If, then, I am approaching a new situation—and all situations, in fact, are new, and especially those causing perplexity—I cannot address myself to it with a formed intention which is certain (like that of the Kantian man) to cover the case. I can only come with the highly general resolution 'to act for the best I can see'. Let us look at this word 'best'. What does it stand for? It stands for an empty scheme of comparison. I believe myself to have seen in the past that one aim was objectively worthier than another. But the relation of superiority which any aim may have over any other is not a constant relation; superiority differs materially for every genuinely different pair of things in which it is exemplified. Thus, in resolving to choose 'that which shall be seen to be superior' I am not giving my will a really positive direction; I cannot really commit myself by signing a sort of moral blank cheque. I have not already resolved (let alone willed) anything; I have only warned myself 'Look out about being sincere'.

But in so far as the choice is a new one—in so far as we are presented with a superiority which has never yet imposed itself upon us—our will cannot be fortified against temptation in advance. Even if we had never sinned, or even never been tempted, until this moment, that would be no guarantee for this moment, because we have never made this choice before.

This is, perhaps, to overstrain the argument a little, for there is such a thing as analogy between situations of choice, and if the guarantee above could not reach to considerable probability, there could be no such thing as character. But it remains that every moral perplexity, *qua* perplexity, calls for a fresh specification of moral judgment, and presents us with a new moral choice between a better and a worse unfaced before. This choice has to be made and constitutes a temptation-situation.

But instead of the phrase 'Good will being presupposed' we might usefully write 'in cases where it happens that already formed dispositions make the right the psychologically easier alternative'. Then indeed the only temptation may belong, not to the choice between the perplexing alternatives, but to the choice whether or no to take the perplexity seriously and think it out. But in so far as the perplexity is really perplexing we can never know beforehand that the right alternative is going to be the easy one, or *vice versa*. So that every moral perplexity has to be approached with a certain moral wariness, and this wariness becomes part of the mood of honest moral perplexity itself. Enough has been said, perhaps, to show that the situation of open alternatives and the situation where good or bad will is the issue, interpenetrate one another.

Now as to the third factor, and its relation with the theme of moral effort. This is, in effect, far more intimate than the moralising thesis admitted. No doubt various aspects of the will's 'creativity' can be placed under headings which have been already dealt with. In so far as we formulate 'creative' projects they fall under judgment in respect of their intrinsic worth, or their relation to other worthy ends; and if we have alternative projects, we may have perplexity. Or, as the thesis noted, we may require the self-exhortation to take the trouble of applying the constructive imagination to the business of living; or to curb its irresponsibilities.

But there is more than this. Moralists from Aristotle downwards have noted that province of virtue which lies outside prescription and rule. While doubtless a man ought to test his behaviour by conceptualising the intentions it expresses and judging their merit when so presented to his own mind, this salutary check is a check, an interfering control, which cannot itself create a satisfactory whole of activity; we know the moral pedantry and social inhumanity which arise from the abuse of reflection in the sphere of conduct. The more we come down to the detail of life, the more absurd it is to think out and judge our projects; action and thought and judgment lie in one another; we think and judge in acting. But this does not mean in any sense that formed desires and habitual dispositions take control; we may create the individual structure of conduct for its worth. Or, of course, we may not.

Here moral effort is not that of fidelity to truth seen, nor of sincerity in explicit judgment between given alternatives. It is the effort of imagining and realising what is worth while, where imagining and realising are on top of one another—the imagination is bit by bit acted upon and the action bit by bit directs the imagination. That moral effort is possible in this sphere is a matter of experience; yet to describe its form is distressingly difficult. We are reminded of the place of constructive imagination in Kant's system. He knows of the (explicit) understanding, which conceptualises 'experience'; but believes this would be impossible—the order corresponding to the concepts would not be there to be 'grasped under' them—unless the matter of experience had already been worked up by the same principles which the understanding will conceptualise. This underground working of the principles—an inherent orderliness in the way in which the memory and imagination arrange their content—he calls constructive imagination.

Without expressing any opinion on the soundness of Kant's view, we may recognise a valid parallel to it. Kant may have been wrong in assuming that the order in the natural world, as we think ourselves to apprehend it, is constructed by us. Perhaps it is just *there*. But anyhow our behaviour appears to be 'constructed' by us. And if the good man can occasionally pause and reflect on his behaviour and test the rightness of its direction, then it may well seem that the unreflective will which creates that direction must be animated by the same principle as is explicitly and more clearly expressed in the reflective judgment.

It might be, indeed, that the control exercised by reflection upon action were external, like discipline sporadically imposed by force on untamed beasts; or it might be that all the right direction in our behaviour was due to the mechanical operation of principles sanctioned by previous acts of reflection, and of dispositions correlative with them. These two suggestions are both, perhaps, conceivable, but neither commends itself as true in fact. We make the most serious choices of our lives, sometimes, in strenuous and unreflective action; and when we reflect on them in a cool hour, it is not to apply rational choice to something other than itself, but to give a better chance to an essentially identical process which has had to be fulfilled in a cramped and hurried manner. Nor should we ever dream of saying that temptation is proper to moments of reflection, or that the only temptation to arise at other times is concerned with faithfulness to accepted rules, or with the duty to pause and reflect.

When, therefore, we are using constructive imagination to sketch out our lives in advance, or when we design and execute the design piecemeal as we proceed, it is possible for moral 'good will' to animate and direct our construction, prior to all reflective judgment; or alternatively, for this good will to be lacking. Creativity appears to be a certain identity of judgment and action, whereby we do not judge actions or projects as they arise, but express our judgment in making them what we make them.

This is to be distinguished from that other identity of judgment and action which caused us to say that action is the conclusion of a true practical syllogism and that apart from action no practical judgment is complete. There we clinch by our action a choice between alternatives which is not otherwise final. Here we make a project, or form an act, which is itself an implicit choice from an indefinitely wide disjunction. We shape it, discarding moment by moment all that we do not use in its construction; so that the number also of implicit acts of preference is indefinite.

The implicitness of the good will in such activity may easily lead to a sensationalist or emotionalist interpretation; we shall say that right conduct in this kind is a matter of the 'heart' or of 'feeling'. But it is difficult to see how a practical attitude can be an emotion, even though it may be normally accompanied by an emotion.

The right account appears to be that judgment and execution, which must separate for perfect clarity and efficiency, must unite and interpenetrate to the highest degree for creativity; clarity can only judge of, and efficiency execute, what creativity presents. Morality has three forms, proper to the three: honesty in judgment, loyalty in execution, and in creativity an implicit form which contains the germ of both, and appears to be nameless, being the sustained effort towards the creation of what is best, either in itself or as a contribution to something more.

(iv) *Conclusion*

In the light of the preceding discussion, we may formulate the description of freedom as follows.

It is as though rational and fully voluntary action were developed by the specialisation of acts which lay formerly in one another, or, to speak more properly, were once aspects of a single form. The primitive sense of the verb *to do* would describe an act containing the following aspects: Behaviour is shaped in a certain way in being executed; it is so shaped in view of facts; its shaping thus and not otherwise excludes alternatives; the execution of it brings other facts into view.

From this form the following specialised four emerge:

(I) *Designing* is separated from doing; we construct an imaginary experiment.

(II) This is in order that we may *consider alternatives* before acting.

(III) The activity of *exploring the facts* is likewise specialised.

(IV) *Execution* is specialised, as a merely practical effecting of the plan already sketched.

These specialised forms are all forms of *act*, and are all characterised by the common form, with one aspect disproportionately developed; and all approximate themselves to this and that of the other specialised forms more and less from time to time, by developing the appropriate aspect. All are voluntary, and morality (i.e. the active preference of the better) has its expression in them all. And so has objective determination, which appears not to be a specialised form, but a common form—except when it is identified with determination by the existing state of affairs, and then it becomes identified with (IV). Thus morality and objective determination are really universal and correlative, while exploration, creativity, choice, execution are forms in each of which both are exemplified, and which may belong to actions good or bad. And so our original problem is solved. The rival freedoms of creativity and open alternatives are the characteristic excellences of forms of act (I) and (II), that of action upon sufficient evidence belongs to (IV), while the purely 'theoretic' activity (III) has its own freedom, naturally enough omitted from the argument in the present 'practical' question. In all these types of activity objective motivation ought to be determinative, and in all moral vigour is required in order to make it so. Of forms (I)-(IV) none is ever completely absent, though all but one may be latent. Objective motivation is variously related to these several types, but present simply in proportion to the seriousness of the action; moral effort in proportion to the temptation offered by some alternative course.

In so far as the specialised forms fall back into a primal unity, morality becomes implicit—as it does in design also—and were the primal unity perfectly reconstituted, without even the marginal activity of the specialised forms —or, let us say rather, without even a margin of specialisation to the central activity—then a level of will would presumably be reached which is not sufficiently explicit or rational to allow of moral effort in the directing of it.

This topic, then, of the specialisation of will-functions needs to be joined on to that of levels of will, which at the same time it qualifies; for will cannot retain its own altitude in the scale without continually falling back into its implicit form, as Antaeus renewed his vigour by touching mother earth.

(v) *Summary of Chapters on the Will*

The purpose of these chapters has been largely descriptive: we have wished not to establish a mere table of conclusions about the will, but to familiarise ourselves with the view of it. And this purpose could best be served by a somewhat discursive treatment. Still, since in what follows we shall build on the material of these chapters, it may be useful to tabulate results and sketch the main line of the previous argument.

The moral struggle is the most evident instance of an act of will, because in it we are concerned with the choice of willing or not willing. But this is no reason for thinking that willing is restricted to the moral struggle; and the definition of will which we extract from an examination of that struggle does not suggest any such limitation. For it defines will simply as the self-actualising potency of a project.

A closer examination of the act so defined leads us to see that will actualises the project not primarily in the sense of bringing the corresponding objective into existence—this it may or may not succeed in doing—but by initiating behaviour believed productive of such a result. And this happens simply by the will's committing itself unreservedly to the project believed realisable by its own effort here and now. The enacting of such a project is a unique type of act irreducible to any other, and it leads to behaviour whenever it is simplified, i.e. freed from that division and hesitation which makes it an act of mere 'entertaining'.

Such an act has a unique metaphysical importance. The question of substance is the question whether there is ever any sense in saying that a complex exists *qua* complex rather than as the several elements which occur together in it. The act of willing provides an answer to this question, for it posits its own final phase as a complex; it is such a complex unit that is willed; except as such a whole it would never come into existence at all. Further, the process by which it is enacted has a certain complexity, of which the several elements again would not ever exist unless the whole pattern were there to be the form of an act of will.

The unity of will therefore is the unity of an act, and not of something else. An act is neither an object nor a relation between objects, and an unavailing dialectic discussion arises if we try to assimilate it to either. Since it holds its elements together in a real unity and adds its later phase to its earlier it is the cause of real relations between its constituents; which relations, stated by themselves in abstraction from the act, are indeed abstract and so metaphysically intelligible only as redintegrated into the act, in which alone they have their being.

Acts of will constitute a rising and falling scale; not all are equally acts or equally will; to the lower levels we give other names, 'desire', etc. The lower levels are opaque to our apprehension, because in them an explicitly rational act cannot reflect upon its own form. We are justified in using the highest and most intelligible as our clue to the nature of the lower; for it is the only clue we conceivably could have, and the scale is continuous.

We can justify the statement that the act of a high level is intrinsically intelligible; for it is the act of 'practical reason', of rationality in action, and its principles are therefore perspicuous. The act of false or bad will is unintelligible in proportion as it is wicked, but with an unintelligibility other than that of the low-scale act.

But if we examine the rational act, can we indeed gain insight into its voluntariness, i.e. its freedom, its creativity? We left this quality as the subject of an unexamined assertion when, on moral grounds, we established the fact of freedom and then turned aside to analyse the structure of its act. We now examine freedom as such and its several modes, and are able to make some general assertions about it and to solve its more glaring paradoxes. And this completes our examination of the single act of will. It is already a complex unit with a unity that is metaphysically real; but we have done nothing to establish its relation to a larger complex, the self, which common sense suspects to be also a real unit, though not perhaps of a unity so close. To this question therefore we now turn.

EXAMINATION OF FINITE SUBSTANCE: THE SELF

XV

UNITY OF SELF IN UNITY OF BODY

(i) *Bodily Bias of the Will*

So far we have examined the act of rational will in its character as a single act. It was of course obvious that no such act stands alone; there is a series of them strung across our life; and they are surrounded by a context of less explicit choices and acts, which, we have concluded, are lower analogues of them, and in some mysterious way subject to their control. The total complex of acts both higher and lower, in its extension through time, we call our self, in one at least of the current senses of the word. But we have still to examine how this complex coheres in a unity, and many acts form one self. Yet it was this very question that we set ourselves to solve; we concerned ourselves with will, not for its own sake, but because it was suspected to be the thread of unity in a self.

If we ask for the unifying principle of the many acts, 'concern with one physical body' seems at least part of the answer; so we had better look at that. It requires some careful definition, for it is not obvious at first sight how the bodiliness of the will is to be squared with the rational freedom which the last two chapters have expounded. The distinction is now not merely between explicitly rational will and obscure or implicit choice masquerading as 'desire'. It is between two sorts of intention. For a will concerned with a body seems to be tied to the intention of operating that body's vital pattern of functions and promoting its fixed interest; and this remains, however explicit and deliberative the will's choices are. Whereas the total and rational will of the last two chapters was endowed with the ability to construct its own aims and attempt the promotion of good wherever it saw it. How, on this level of intention, do we accommodate to one another the angel and the animal within us? If the rational will wages war on the body's interest, it will frustrate itself; and if it comes to terms, how can it remain free?

What we have to see, is how rational freedom is related to natural necessities. Let us start with the assumption that there is a truly free will having its own rational interests, and ask how and why these will be fulfilled through nature.

To begin with, the will is constrained by hypothetical necessity. Must one quote the platitude that nature is commanded by obedience to her laws? Nature meets us in the uniformity of process belonging to our external environment, to our own bodies, and to our minds also, in so far as the word 'mind' is used to denote a mechanism to think with; it has its rules. Whether, then, the will chooses its ultimate aims by any principle or none, it cannot achieve them except by modelling its use of the instruments on the mechanical law of their working; and this may be applied to the whole relation of the will to the body. Let us suppose the extreme case of a man who has gone so far against the body as to choose the policy of selling his life in killing the tyrant. Yet he can only achieve this purpose with his body. Even suicide is committed by the body upon the body, and a life of extreme asceticism, while it 'denies' the body in some aspects, uses and cultivates it in others, whether the ascetic knows this or not. So that whatever our aims, a certain care of the body is, up to the moment of self-destruction, hypothetically and instrumentally necessary. But what is hypothetically necessary to every aim whatsoever is necessary absolutely, the only 'hypothesis' required is that the will should be exerted at all.

But if the welfare of the body (in the simplest sense) is the strongest case of hypothetical necessity, there are many skills and aptitudes developed by habit, and many rules of action and of thought, which have a very high degree of it. The majority of the purposes which we have observed men to embrace, or have conceived ourselves as ever likely to embrace, either demand them as instruments or at least are facilitated by them. In the civilisation that we share there is a very high 'hypothetical necessity' for the possession and use of money, and there are many aptitudes in which we confidently train the young, in the belief that they are of general utility, e.g. reading, writing, and arithmetic.

The libertarian may find it pleasant to place the body's claim on the will under the light of a hypothetical necessity for purposes not otherwise determined than by the limitations of the bodily instrument *qua* instrument; but this view is artificially simple, for at least two reasons.

(*a*) The interest is certainly not given in the form of a hypothetical necessity. Our desire for self-preservation, or rather our repulsion of dangers to it, is experienced as an end in itself; and though it may be set aside by other aims, it is not even then set aside as an inappropriate instrument is discarded, but as one attractive purpose is sacrificed to a more attractive. Further, our choices of the repletions which supply the body are not made as instrumental to the preservation of it but for their own sake. This is so far true, that a child or childish person can employ freedom solely for the purpose of preserving the body and satisfying its appetites and keeping its senses and members in comfortable exercise, so that the body and the appetites are the principal aim and not instrumental to any other aim.

(*b*) The bodily bias of the will cannot be said to keep the direction of its inclination within the limits of what is instrumentally necessary for any purposes whatsoever of which the embodied will might be capable. The strongest of the passions inclines us to spend our forces in an act contributory to a purpose which we, as individuals, might not be inclined freely to choose—the propagation of the race. From this and other kindred facts the false conclusion has been drawn either that there is a will of the race, or that the individual will lacks reality and independent unity. To this it must be replied, that the 'purposiveness of the race' is reducible to an empirical rule relevant to the solicitations experienced by many individual wills. The will is no less active in unearthing and responding to these solicitations than any others. We know nothing of any will but our own. It concerns us to discover how that will is related to the necessities which press it; not certainly to waste our time complaining that it is less a will than we supposed; for if it is not a will, what is? Certainly not that unintelligible monstrosity, the will of the race.

To examine in detail the 'bodily bias' of the will would be to make an excursion into the psychology of instinct, which can be safely left in the hands of the empirical psychologists. It is no doubt extremely hard to say what belongs to this fundamental bias, and what to the secondary dispositions developed by race-wide habits which are in fact almost universal but might perhaps have been otherwise if men had once chosen otherwise. But in principle the distinction is good, whether or not we can make it out; there is a bias of the will which springs from biological roots, and this is instinct, and there are embroideries upon its theme superadded by behaviour—we may call them dispositions.

(ii) Instinct determines the Finitude of Will

It is our business to explore the essential relation of instinct to will as such; and we may put forward the formula: instinct determines the finitude of the will. In order to develop this thesis we can hardly avoid the somewhat unreal procedure of attempting to describe a will which lacked this sort of finitude. This is of course an analogical and dialectical argument, aiming at a *reductio ad absurdum* of alternatives which turn out to be no alternatives, and at a clarifying of the intuited singular relation in which will does stand to instinct. Even the formula itself has no meaning out of relation to this dialectic. 'Instinct determines the finitude of will' can, on its own merits, only mean 'Instinct is something to which will is relative'. Equally artificial is the apparent teleology of the sort of argument we are about to use. 'The will had to be made relative to instinct in order . . .'—in order to be what we can and do grasp as will! This is not teleology, but a dialectical method of arriving at the definition of our intuition.

Well then, how can we think of an infinite will?[1] It is not restricted to, or in any way identified with, one place in the world rather than another, nor one selection of facts rather than another. It is aware of all the facts there are, and of all the alternative possibilities for subsequent states of affairs allowed by the rules of uniformity. And its action is not limited to one mode of activity rather than another; it can enact any possibility of any kind which it has seen to be possible, in any place. In order to present our hypothesis with the greatest purity, we must suppose that there are no finite wills in this world to which the infinite

[1] This 'infinite will' is not God, for it is infinite only in the scope of its operation, not in and nature thereof; and it is supposed to have space-time-events for its proper field.

will is related. Its world is an ocean of process, the process of perceptible events, or event—for it is no more one than many, no more many than one (*vide supra*, p. 66). We cannot say—as theists are given to saying of the divine will—that it makes the existence and well-being of finite substances its aim; there are no finite substances, for there are no finite wills nor anything analogous thereto.

What will be worth while to this will? Truth, beauty, goodness. Truth *ex hypothesi* it has: the adequate knowledge of the present state of the kaleidoscope of being, and the possibilities of its alteration according to rules of sequence. By shaking the kaleidoscope it could obtain no more. Beauty it might obtain by realising certain combinations; though if it has adequate knowledge of them in possibility perhaps it will gain little. Let us remember that there is no form of the whole, no dominant design; the multiplicity is perhaps actually endless, and it can be read and actually is simultaneously read in terms of all the overlapping patterns that can be found in it by an omnipercipient mind. Goodness can mean nothing. Nothing that this will may do can perfect his own form, for he has no form. He has only the abstract form of awareness and of agency; for positive form he is thrown on the objects of his knowledge and the effects of his act. But there he can find none. The 'world' is no world; it is no more one than many, nor many than one; there are no real forms in it, every form is a cross-section across a whole of process which could be as well cut in an infinity of other ways. It can confer no unity on him, nor he on it; for neither has any to give.

Watching the water swirling from a weir, I tire of following with an impartial and embarrassed eye the detail of the moving pattern; the netting and re-netting of the lace of foam, the winding, dissolving and re-winding of the maze of the eddies. I fix my favour on one little whirlpool and sympathise with its affairs. I would, if I could, energise it to withstand competing twists of current, to re-form its broken round where a twig has fallen upon it, to hold its identity as it drops away into the effacing calm of smoother waters. I pretend both ignorance of its destiny, and ability to influence its determined fortunes. With some such game our infinite will might mitigate the boredom of never-ending variety, fixing an arbitrary favour on some element of pattern in the current of events. But he can do better than I; he need not merely watch his favourite's ephemeral history; he can, within the rules of uniformity, enact the possibilities which help its continuance. It is the King in his game of chess, and he moves every piece to stave off a mate as long as he may.

Even so, his absorption in the game will suffer from a too extended knowledge; knowing all the facts and all the alternative consequences, he is like the too experienced master-chess-player, who—anyhow in the novice's imagination—knows too much for real enjoyment, and whatever opening he plays is merely expressing on a visible board one of the almost numberless variations which he had already in his head completely worked out. Besides, it remains a game, a trifling amusement; he cannot convince himself that the maintenance of this pattern is of any importance, when there are infinite others with which the same game can be played. What interest it has depends on the illusion that the pattern is not an empty form, but a reality which is something to itself, so that it would have meaning to speak of 'what it is to be that pattern'; the illusion indeed that it is a self, that it is *him*self who fictively identifies himself with it.

There is only one way to turn this illusion into reality—the will can give the pattern selfhood by becoming it—or, if it is nonsense to talk of a will becoming pattern, let us say, by limiting its knowledge and action to the scope of it. If the pattern is to be of vital concern, it must be vital to that which, in our hypothesis, can alone have concernment—the infinite will. Its infinitude, then, it sacrifices, and this is its salvation.

But we have just used a phrase which requires explication. The will was to 'limit its knowledge and action to the scope of the pattern'. What can this mean? To begin with action. The will will only enact those possibilities which lie in the pattern itself. This will have no meaning if the pattern is absolutely fixed; it must allow of several arrangements of its parts, such that their alternations do not infringe its structure. Indeed a pattern which is to be the vital and continual concern of a will must surely itself be deployed in time as well as space, it must be rhythm as well as pattern, so that the will is continually active in enacting it; a rhythm and a pattern, therefore, as is the form of a figure danced by many performers.

The will, then, has two concerns: continually to enact the constant and cyclic rhythm over its due pattern of space, and to enact those 'permissible variations' of the rhythm, which affect environment in a way favourable to the constant aspect of the rhythm-pattern. For the environing events are related to the events of the pattern by rules of uniformity in sequence.[1]

Of these two concerns, that of enacting the constant rhythm-pattern, in so far as uniform, is one act and requires no attention. It is not chosen from moment to moment, but accepted as the very condition of finite existence; not selected and enacted, but co-selected and co-enacted implicitly with every act and choice. It was once enacted by the act of incarnation, and constantly enacted only in so far as the 'will' constantly wills its own limitation, its determinate mode of being. But the variations are willed, because they are new, and of them and the facts that motive them there must be detailed awareness. But how extended an awareness? If the principle of finitude and unity is to be maintained, an awareness of the environmental forces in so far as they impinge on the pattern, and in that selection of their aspect which is relevant for the choice of 'variations' which will defend and support the constant rhythm.

(iii) *From Fixed Pattern to Free Super-pattern*

So far we have pursued the downward path, the path of narrowing and concentration. The finite pattern imposes on the will *an* interest, a place, a

---

[1] It is really necessary to suppose that the infinite will has not identified itself with one form only, but divided itself by many such identifications, in order that there may be active principles in the environment also.

direction of activity and a filter of knowledge, and all these belong to one another and stamp one dominant unity on what is done and what is known. The will is particularised; from now on we may attempt the path of re-ascent. We grant that the selective unity of experience and action finds its principle in the existential needs of the pattern. But, this principle being once established, is it necessary to stop there? Is the will obliged to act only for the preservation of the rhythm-pattern in its constant state? Might it not, as the mind and will of this rhythm-pattern, and within the limits so imposed, set out to conquer to itself as much of the world as it can? As will, it is essentially ordered toward the actualisation of being. If it had to limit itself in order to realise this aim—in order to introduce into the world any being that *is*—it does not follow that it has achieved all in the limitation itself, and therein must acquiesce. Cannot the being of the pattern, without violation to its own determinate form, be itself enlarged? Cannot it attract into its unity some of the riches of its environment? Let us see if any precise sense can be given to these rhetorical phrases.

There seems to be no reason why the interest of the will should be strictly limited to variations which defend the constant pattern. If, indeed, it is to dispose of any margin of safety, it must possess itself of a range of knowledge wider than the number of facts which it will ever actually need; and have open many more possibilities of behaviour than it is ever forced to enact. But if this is so, then in order to be utilitarian it will have to pass beyond the consciously utilitarian. There may be some facts about which one can be sure that they will never have a practical bearing, but this negative assurance is itself the product of advanced reflection, and it will be a good rule on the whole to push discovery in all directions, with the tracks of known or anticipated utility as one's basis; like a party of men who, in passing through a forest which holds they know not what of hostility or treasure, will take their principal direction from the track which they know they must follow, but scout the wood on either side to such a depth as is feasible. And if this is true of exploration, it is equally true of the activity which is directed to the production of changes in environment. It is necessary to develop practical aptitudes which may or may not be required, and to build up around oneself actual systems of defence against attacks which may or may not be delivered.

The will, then, must dispose of a margin of knowledge and of action; but though the limits of the margin cannot be exactly defined, there is no question of the will's losing thereby its saving finitude, or the reality of its identification with this pattern and this place. For explore as widely as it may, it is always exploring the world in so far as it impinges on this organism with pressures of such sorts as can affect its existence. The world is still seen through a filter of relatedness to self, which reduces its infinity to a certain form of unity. And the action which organises environment is always limited and determined by the pattern of the physical self and its vital needs, however widely it may go beyond them. It is still *this* knower who is trying to possess *his* world by a knowledge of a sort and scope that is *his own*, *this* agent who shapes *his* environment by *his own* type of activity, and into forms which are extensions of *his own* design.

The upward path is not yet complete: indeed the essential step has not yet been taken. We have provided the will with an exploratory activity directed, within limits, by a random curiosity, and with a constructive activity aimed, within limits, at every sort of re-arrangement of environment; the limits in each case being (*a*) the intrinsic capacities of the organism, and (*b*) the need of constantly returning to the strictly utilitarian track. But as to the interest which directs these two marginal activities in so far as they are marginal, we have said nothing. Both might be still implicitly utilitarian; both might be carried on by the 'you never can tell' principle, on the model of the man who collects old candle-ends and crooked nails and scraps of wood and wire, in the belief that they might 'come in somewhere', and that 'he who keeps a thing seven years will find a use for it'. This is certainly one of the principles of marginal activity, but there is no need for it to be the only one.

Let us consider the words 'utility' and 'utilitarian'. We have used them so far in one sense—to describe a relation of conduciveness to the preservation of the vital pattern of the organism. But it is possible that the organism might develop a voluntary super-pattern, in virtue of a form that is voluntarily imposed on its marginal activities; that it might take an interest in the super-pattern, second only to its concern with the basic pattern; in concern no doubt second, but first perhaps in attractiveness to conscious attention most of the time. If this were so, then there would be a new sort of utility, viz. of conduciveness to the construction and maintenance of the super-pattern.

But what would this super-pattern be? In knowledge, system is already of utilitarian value in the lower sense. But that will not prevent its becoming an end in itself, and knowledge being knowledge, and not something else, its system must be that which is to be unearthed from the objects, in so far as they pass the 'filter' of the finite self. My intention will be to grasp my body as related by principles of uniformity to an environment of events in which uniformity holds sway. My knowledge extends its system by discovering what my system is, and what its systematic solidarity with its environment. In constructive activity, I am less limited in the choice of form. We used dancing above as an analogy to illustrate the basic pattern of the organism. But in fact we know that dancing is an activity voluntary in the sense of optional, its pattern is made up and woven by ourselves, and we find a satisfaction in it, in virtue of a varied and moving formality congruous with, though not determined by, our vital pattern. And this may stand as an analogy for the system that we impose upon our behaviour, and upon the instruments through which we extend it.

Here also, system is of utility in the lower sense, but that does not prevent our cultivating it for itself. Orderliness is an element of efficiency, but that is not the motive of our love for the decencies of civilised life. We build a house to resist the weather and to house with convenience the departments of our domestic economy, but that is not a complete account of the shapeliness we look for in our home.

We must call a halt: there is no natural end to this description, and it cannot be useful to spin out a banal morphology of human interests. The relationship of sociality alone must barely be mentioned. For if the infinite will has not identified itself with one form only, but distributed itself by many such identifications into as many independent finite selves, then there will be elements in the environment of each having an intrinsic value for contemplation, and an intrinsic interest for an activity directed to assist them; and community of action with them will give a further super-pattern which can become an end in itself.

It is time that we tried to extract the moral from our mythus. We introduced it with the aim of determining the place of intrinsic concern for the body and its needs in the process of the will. The mythical exposition expresses the fact that concern with the body is not related to the will's freer projects as concern merely for an instrument without which these projects could not be realised. The vital pattern of the organism and the needs of that pattern give determinate form and scope to the super-pattern of free act. The super-pattern is bound by the necessity of being a marginal pattern based upon and woven round the vital pattern and its requirements. Apart from this necessary relation to a given nucleus its possibilities would be insufficiently determinate. We can make no sense of a will turned loose in the world to enact whatever possibilities can be realised by the means of a given instrument. Only on the hypothesis that the world already contained more fully determined selves for this self to assist and to explore, can we assign him any intelligible ends. Otherwise an angel limited by the necessity of using a body as his tool would be faced with the same embarrassment of indefinity as our supposed infinite will; whatever he did would be arbitrarily chosen, and he could escape from meaninglessness only by committing himself to one arbitrary choice among the patterns of action of which the instrument was capable, by making that his life, and only then developing variations on that pattern—in fact, by further limiting himself, and completing his incarnation.

To put it otherwise. If the will is to be significantly free in the shaping of the super-pattern, it requires as a basis the pattern in relation to which it is not free; only in a middle state between these two can freedom as we know it operate at all.

(iv) *Several Modes of Bodily Bias*

The relation between the two patterns is not so simple as this language suggests. While the super-pattern can only arise as an embroidery upon the basic pattern, it can, once established, operate against it. For the sake of a voluntarily chosen system of life, a man may act dysbiologically. He may take physical risks which on biological grounds he would not take, he may deny the body satisfactions which would contribute to its perfect well-being; he may, for the sake of a brief realisation of his voluntary projects, take action to-day which will end his life to-morrow; he may, for the welfare of others or the maintenance of a social pattern, sacrifice his life here and now, knowingly and willingly. It is this possibility of turning (though not always with impunity) against our own biological basis, that caused us to speak of concern for the body as a bias, rather than a fixed direction, of the will. We can choose to risk kicking away the ladder on which we stand—we may take the risk, but successfully avoid the evil. We can also choose to kick it away, and do so, but when we do, we fall.

But there is another sense of 'bodily bias' which we must distinguish from that just given. As we have used the term, 'biological prudence' might stand as a description of its tendency. A man might choose to regulate his life by this principle, and some appear to do so. It must be very dull; and certainly it is too ascetical for most of us, and involves putting a good deal of constraint on what are usually called bodily desires; and these in their form of simple and immediate solicitation might in another sense be called the 'bodily bias' of the will.

How in fact does the body make its claim upon the will felt, at the level below reflection, the level on which reflection is all to be built? Undoubtedly by instinctive solicitation, of which emotions are the sanction. And this solicitation is of a violence and immediacy quite other than that exercised upon us by a contemplated ideal, e.g. of human character, however much more effective the ultimate influence of the latter may be in a given case. Now the instinctive solicitations, being pre-reflective, work by a gross rule and are prudent only on the whole, and enlightened bodily prudence requires a peculiar effort to set aside their letter in the interest of their spirit. It is true that to some extent the habitual correction of them leads to the correction of the incidence of the immediate solicitation and its emotional sanction, so that our dispositions formed by training and self-training become 'second nature'. But this is only so to a certain point. It is much more difficult to transfer the emotional sanction to that which lies more remote from the original bodily desire, to poetry than to pushpin; more difficult to transfer it to that in which the habitual element is small and every fresh act is essentially novel in type, e.g. the study of philosophy.

It is therefore fallacious to use against pleasure-seeking the following argument. 'Anything that we choose becomes an object whose attainment is attended with satisfaction in proportion as we want it for its own sake. Therefore the search for maximum satisfaction cannot be the criterion of choice between one object and another.' In so far as satisfaction is the filling of a want simply, the argument is excellent. But there is emotional satisfaction which is not proportional simply to the degree in which we have set our heart on our objective, but proportional partly to this and partly to the analogy which the objective bears to the objects of bodily desire. It is a perfectly intelligible policy,

then, for a man to choose to confine attention to the more childish sort of projects, in the reasonable expectation that he will be able to interest himself in
them, and so attain the maximum of emotional pleasures, with sufficient variety
to avoid the boredom which otherwise destroys them. Here is another prudential development of 'bodily bias', but with a principle quite different from
that which informed the first, and capable of running contrary to it.

But the conclusion that concerns us here is that pleasure-seeking of this
sort is a voluntarily chosen policy alternative to others, e.g. obedience to a
pharisaic code; and the same is true of biological prudence in any unmitigated
form, though some measure of the latter may be said to be natural when compared with the former.

(v) *How Instinct limits the Will*

We set out (*supra*, p. 171) to discover what sorts of order and necessity
the will, though free, accepts from its incarnate state. We pointed out the
'hypothetical necessity' of choosing means in accord with natural law, once ends
had been chosen; we proceeded to the examination of bodily bias and hope that
it has now become in some measure clear how this is related to the free scope of
the will. But we may still be asked for fuller precision. What, it may be asked,
is effected by will, and what falls outside it? Is bodily bias a constraint upon the
will, or a direction of the will itself? In answering, we must avoid being deceived by the teleology of our myth. For we dreamt there of the volitions of an
infinite will, which willed certain things in order effectively to become a will.
This is an evident figure of speech. What the will wills in order to be a will
cannot in fact be willed. It is a way of describing certain states of affairs to which
will as we know it is essentially relative. These states of affairs must simply be
for the will and are not the matter of its choice one way or the other. The man
who said that he had chosen (or rejected) his biological basis and its necessary
relation to any superstructure whatsoever, would deserve more scorn than Car-
lyle expended on the lady who had made up her mind (at last) to accept the
Universe.

But this is not the only pitfall our answer has to avoid. There is another,
provided by the dialectics of the 'scale of will-acts' (*vide supra*, pp. 143 *ff*). If we
take 'will' to be coterminous with the highest expressions of explicit rationality,
the question, of course, answers itself: only such acts are willed, and the bodily
bias of will is left to be operated by some other mysterious power. If, on the
other hand, we are prepared to extend the name 'will' to cover all the activity
which is in a manner continuous with will in the narrow sense, the question
answers itself again; and the whole biological pattern is operated by will.

But the second of these definitions is so wide that no one is (in fact) going
to accept it; for 'will' appears to be a certain mode and level of activity, and not
activity as such, nor even biological activity as such. And yet if we retreat to the
first definition, it seems nugatory, and in particular it has no useful relation to

our myth, since it takes no account of the 'condescension' and 'self-incarnation' of the will.

Let us try a third definition, which is drawn on the analogy of that of a thing having 'form' and 'matter', though the analogy is not perfect. This is the parallel. If I conceive of a thing having a dominant pattern which organises a multiplicity of constituents, I think of it by means of its dominant pattern primarily, since it is this pattern which makes it in my eyes a unitary thing of such a type. But I do not think of the thing as *being* this pattern; I think of it as having also whatever plurality of detail it must have in order to exist—even though much of this detail is irrelevant to the form of the pattern, and very likely quite unknown to me. I think of it as the embodied actuality of such a pattern.

So with the will; we may be thinking of the rational activity, together with whatever backing it needs of less rational process in order to exist. We are thinking, then, of a whole activity whose distinguishing mark and principle of activity is, for us, rational will. The parallel with the 'form and matter' relationship is not exact; for the particles of bronze, for example, out of which the Mercury is cast, have each their own interior organism, to which the Mercury-shape is completely external and accidental; and so, too, the other way about, for the shape could exist also in clay. Not so with the several levels of the will, which are continuous, and between which there is continual interchange.

Another parallel could be the non-botanical person's way of regarding a plant, say a nasturtium. For he has no idea of the plant as a whole; he knows only the flower, and thinks of 'the nasturtium' as just that flower with whatever roots, stem and leaves are proper to its existence. Here there is more continuity between the specifying part and the rest; but we have not the essential obscurity which belongs to the lower grades of activity—it is a mere accident that one should know the flower better than the leaves or the root. And, which is the most serious defect, the analogy gives no expression to the governing position of the fine flower of rational choice in the tree of will. It is that which alone can give any philosophical importance to the middle definition we are advocating. The will, however embodied or embedded in lower levels of activity, can act as itself—and, as we have been suggesting, precisely because so 'embodied'. We can consider it as an activity in and through its 'embodiment'.

If this definition is taken, then, once again, the question answers itself, but in a less insignificant manner. The will is that which operates the super-pattern on the basis of the necessary bodily pattern. Whether we call the will the active principle of the bodily pattern in so far as it develops free action in the expansion into a voluntary super-pattern; or whether we call it the real potency of the super-pattern, taking initial direction from, and throughout influenced by, bodily bias: we have given complementary expressions to the fact that the bodily pattern is in a unique manner which we have attempted to describe, the *terminus a quo* of the self's intelligent and intelligible freedom. This *terminus a quo* determines the will to a finite place and form. The manner in which it does so is studied in the psychology of instinct. Somehow, this study assures us, any development of behaviour and interest must be linked to and developed from the instinctive interests of the bodily pattern. The formula is vague, and cannot be made precise. It cannot be said *a priori* nor by the light of any clear and universal principles established by induction, what interests could, or could not conceivably and in any circumstances be derived from the instinctive basis, through 'sublimation' or some equally mysterious connexion. We can at the most claim that (*a*) the connexion could always be traced *a posteriori* through gradual stages, (*b*) the departure from the instinctive line cannot be infinitely great. We may represent the position of the will by a revised version of the myth of Sisyphus.

Sisyphus is chained to a stone ball, and the ball stands at the bottom of a hollow, into which uneven rocky land descends on either side, less steep at the foot, steepening towards the precipitous as one ascends. The place is dry, and the bottom porous; such rain as there is has worn a system of channels converging on that spot, and there it soaks away; the channels unite as they descend and where they meet at last there are only seven. Sisyphus cannot drag the ball out of these until he has gone some way up, where they are slighter; he must start by one of the channels. There is no saying what are the exact limits to which he can climb, but it is certain he will not get clean out of the hollow; and wherever he gets to, it will always be possible to see that he got there from one of the channels, and how. If he uses worn channels as far as he may, he will save his strength and get further, than if he turns off early on to the rougher rock; but he may do which he chooses. He is not, as in the Homeric story, cursed with immortality; he can get round about into places from which the ball and himself will fall and smash, whether by accident or design.

Such, then, is the indefinite yet inescapable bond which holds the will to its instinctive tracks; it is a *terminus a quo*, but one that is never left behind, it limits the directions and distances of our travels. And in so far as the bodily basis limits, it simplifies and unifies human purposes; this does not need to be further illustrated. For in fact it constitutes 'human nature', as we use the term when we are taking the universal forms of intellect and will for granted, and noting the actual limitations on their direction which are common to mankind.

It was the genius of Plato to invent myths which he did not feel the immediate need to correct. We are not so blest, and must hasten to acknowledge the sharp contrast between this myth and the preceding. The Sisyphus figure suggests that to be incarnate is to drag a chain, while the other suggested that it is the beginning of worth-while existence. Either valuation can be allowed, according to the point of view. If we think of will as such, then incarnation is a limitation, as it is a limitation to be determined to any finite essence, and only God is free. But if we think of our mode of will, then to be incarnate is proper to it, and its fulfilment. This, however, tells us nothing as to immortality; since that state is not nakedness, but such a still unknown medium of existence as it shall please God to assign.

XVI

UNITY OF SELF AS UNITY OF PROJECT

(i) *Unity of the Chosen*

In the last chapter will began to assume the form of a self, having obtained in the bodily pattern a unitary base from which to operate. But if we are going to be able to show that will is the bond of unity, we must prove that it makes for unity itself, and is not merely restrained from dissolution by the unity of its base. It is true that according to the doctrine of the scale of will, it is will of a kind, or an activity analogous to it and continuous with it, that operates the bodily pattern and thus creates that basic unity. But this activity is dark to us, and we are hoping to understand it so far as we can by the analogy of a more explicit and intelligible operation. Unless we can find in conscious will a principle of unity, we have understood nothing, and the unity of basis could be externalised and treated as a phenomenal pattern that happens to appear so.

If the unity of self cannot be found in the bodily basis alone, it is natural to look for it in that voluntary super-pattern which on that basis the will erects. Is not the essential unity of a self its unitary scheme of voluntary behaviour? This seems plausible, and agrees with the bewilderment and dismay we feel when confronted with radical and unresolved discontinuity in the aims and tastes of a neighbour; he seems to be not one man but many.

But if we place the unity of the self in an expressed unity of enacted project, we expose ourselves to anti-libertarian dialectic of a familiar kind. 'The form which makes you a distinct self, and is the principle of your being, is the form of project(s) which clothes your voluntary activity. Very well; this is your specifying form, by it you are you. But now either you are, or you are not. If you are not, it is no use talking about you; but if you are, your existence is determined by your specifying form, for else you are not you. Your specifying form, then, must be given with your existence. But in that case you cannot be free to enact it or not to enact it. The formula of your so-called voluntary projects is already written in heaven; all you can do is realise it serially in the medium of time, as the film story, all contained together in the roll, is serially projected on the screen. Subjectively the will appears to be free, since it does not know its own formula, and the enactment of the next stage prefigures itself in a mental struggle; a struggle in which the will attains gradual conviction what is her destiny. She struggles from ignorance through doubt into the knowledge and realisation of herself; and this is the only freedom.'

This argument is an old friend, and may be fathered on Leibniz. It may serve as a warning against placing *the* unity of the self in an expressed form of project. But even though that unity is to be sought elsewhere, it seems reasonable to allow that unless the will does make for unity in its projects, it can hardly be the bond of unity in a self. Let us, then, examine what unity of project is to be found in its operations, and what is not.

If we adopt the Leibnitian dogma, it is enough to find our unity of life in a transcendent form which, being demonstrated *a priori* by the philosopher and known *ab aeterno* by the Deity, has no need of empirical verification. But if we are free of the dogma and look at the intentional content of a man's life, in what are we to find this unity? A quasi-aesthetic mutual complementariness of parts has been a favourite with many; but this seems to belong to the view of an on-looker, whereas intentional unity is as it is intended by the subject. But how seriously does the subject intend a unitary design? How considerable is the rôle of any dominating plan? Where is the totalitarian soul, in which all the several interests are *gleichgeschaltet*? In which the different instruments never play except to fill out the harmony of the one orchestral symphony?

No doubt there are dominant patterns in the lives of all sane men; but these seem to control and regulate merely, not to dictate and organise. It is often sufficient to avoid practical conflict of interests, to see that certain general principles are not infringed, to observe on the whole and over a fair period of time some sort of balance in the types of our activity. Even such universal aims as the love of God and one's neighbour are general, and cannot beget out of their own generality the particular intentions in which they have to be embodied, with however great sincerity they come to be embodied in them.

It is unnecessary, then, to maintain that the will makes for a unity; it is sufficient to say that it makes for unities. As for the unity between these unities, it can be ordered by positive principles, but need be of no more than a negative kind—compatibility, an absence of mutual interference either in physical effort or in psychological operation.

And even the negative unity may, in fact, be most imperfect, although that need not prevent our claiming that will as such makes for it. For do not conflicts arise? Do not psychologists reveal the most surprising phenomena, and have we not all heard of divided personalities? One must not concede too much to the psychologists—the girl who thought she was two was wrong, as wrong as the man who thought that he was the Shah of Persia; it is inadvisable to forget that lunatics are mad. But if we placed the unity of person simply in that of project, then a will which had seriously dissociated two systems of project would be in so far two wills; and this is sufficient evidence that even negative unity (compatibility of projects) is by no means always realised.

But even if we are content to claim that in the normal case will makes for some loose complex of unities, we must still concede that this is not realised as it is intended. If we take the 'least project', we find that it may easily be frustrated, so that we have willed and acted, but what is effected is a fragment of the process, and this conduces in fact to a state of affairs other than what was projected. The intention, then, even in its most immediate form, is willed indeed but not effected. But it must be the intention, not the (in this case) irrelevant effect, which is the objectivised form of the will and the self; and this intentional unity is continually shattered against the hard rocks of environmental necessity, and when revived must be re-shaped, and in so far discontinuous with its former self.

Of course the content of intention cannot be limited to the least project willed; for while it is true that nothing is willed nor intended in the solid mode of intention until some least project is actually willed, yet this project would not be willed at all but for the larger project it subserves. The intentional form of will is, then, the motivating project of the actual least project. Here there may be self-deception; it is hard to say how much of the supposed 'greater project' we solidly intend to promote by our least projects. But setting this doubt aside, let us suppose a will with highly developed and unified intentional content.

Such a will, then, intends a unitary pattern of life (this phrase is extremely vague, but it may serve for the present). This policy, we must suppose, is not a pure *a priori*, but a project or complex of projects formed in awareness of facts, and believed realisable. If several aims are included, they must be expected to harmonise—i.e. not physically to frustrate one another, not to cause psychological chaos. And there will be certain general principles and dominant aims to which these are all supposed to submit. The field of these projects cannot be infinite, and must in fact be very small compared with the extent of the life the agent hopes still to have before him; we cannot plan for our whole life until we are as good as dead. We may have projects of indefinite scope, e.g. to become engine-drivers when we grow up, or to love God and our neighbour, but they are also of indefinite content, and some of them (e.g. the engine-driving) are known to be subject to revision. As to the less sketchy and more immediate projects, we have presumably the confidence that they will not hedge up the road which leads to further projects which we might, in their season, strongly desire to adopt; but this belief that we are not mortgaging the future, that our present actions are not obstructive of, but perhaps even conducive to, the probable future projects of such creatures as ourselves, is a most uncertain expectation and little better than a pious hope.

It will probably be allowed that this is a pretty generous account of the will's unitary intention for life at any given period. Still, such as it is, it has no hope of surviving intact; it will be smashed on the rocks of fact, and have to be re-made from day to day. It may seem tempting to claim that the facts teach us to find what it is we really wanted, but this is rather too good to be true. No doubt what we wanted was the realisable and not the unrealisable, but we wanted the realisable with a certain content, and we could not get it, and we have to begin wanting something else. The satisfactions which the exile on St. Helena began to aim at when he had given up the hope of recovering his crown were not what he had really wanted while he continued to wear it. It sometimes happens, no doubt, that the school of disappointment teaches us to aim principally at certain universal goals of which no facts can disappoint us; and that when we have learnt this lesson, we declare these projects to be alone worth while and to have been all the substance there was in the mixed and contingent aims of our former years. But if we do say this, we must admit that we formerly sought these things in error and ignorance of what we sought; which in plain English means that we sought something else in the belief that it was the thing to seek, and that we were wrong, or only so far right as our projects overlapped the true aim; as frivolous companionship may overlap Christian charity.

(ii) *Policy of Choice*

If, then, the will makes for unity, it does so in the form of its intention; but this is not the unity it effects. It is not merely that events turn out otherwise, but that our interior operation, pressed by those events, changes direction, so that our great projects never get embodied in the series of 'least projects' which alone could give them reality. If there is indeed a consistency and sequence in our lives, it is thrashed out in a conflict between intention and circumstance, and intention is only one factor in it. And even so, it might appear to be an accidental cause. If we speak of the unity of a man's life, we speak of something extended through time, a consistency which binds together his earlier actions with his later. But this consistency is one which was not intended by the man at any time whatever. He staked all on projects which failed; took up others, which succeeded, but disappointed his heart in their success; and so chose new ventures. We, looking at him from without, may find in him a consistency which runs through the three periods, but this certainly never was a pattern intended by his will either before or in them. If his life, then, has the unity of an epic, his will traced the plot accidentally and much against intention; and if we say that none of the earlier willing was lost, but that it guided through acquired wisdom all the later, then the intentional unity his life achieved was the project he had for living in the moment when he died.

The paradox in this conclusion is due to the two senses which 'intentional unity' might have. If it means a unity of plan actually intended in a single act of the mind—or rather in a connected and mutually completing set of acts—then the conclusion follows. But it might equally well mean a unity of direction between several separate acts; and though this unity is never the formal object of an act of will, it would be absurd to call it an accidental by-product of will. If, as we have said, the actual sequence of our lives is worked out by the interaction of intention and circumstance, the intentional unity (in the second sense) which can be found in that sequence is the effect of the former factor rather than the latter. Will, having taken a direction, tends still to follow it. Though circumstances impose a change of objective, there is a profound analogy between the old intention and the new. Though conversion invades the very shrine of subjectivity, the sinner reappears in the saint, however transformed. The former volitions may be redeemed, that is, their successors are holy, but they are their successors none the less and would not be what they are but for their serial position.

The will, then, makes for unity in two senses which are not independent of one another, the second reposing on the first. It is because our single acts, or act-complexes, have a unitary intention and a will to constancy, that (*a*) there can be intentional analogy between several of them, and (*b*) the dynamic is present which produces this analogy.

(iii) *Intentional Unity imposed by Nature*

In the preceding discussion, the world of external fact has been made to play the villain's part; it has been represented as a rugged and unsympathetic obstacle to the fulfilment of man's designs, and as therefore a factor of disunion in his executed projects. Yet this is only half the story. For in so far as the man learns by experience and attempts the possible, nature serves to unite or at least harmonise his projects, since nature presents herself to us as an orderly continuum of events. Which half of the story we prefer to tell, will depend on our assumptions. If we assume a unified subjective project, we can trust nature to disturb its *a priori* neatness. If we assume a chaos of projects, we can trust nature (granted prudence in the agent) to reduce them to some kind of harmony. By forcing us to alter them, no doubt; but still she harmonises them.

Rational will enacts that which, to a mind with some scope of understanding, is good on the whole. This is no more than a generalisation of the notion of prudence. But it means that the will enacts in a law-governed universe an effect which is intended as a modification of the world, and one that will work itself out into its proper consequences. In so far as will is intelligent, it is then allowable to say that what it wills is not this effect but the process of environment as modified by this effect. We do not will an abstraction, we will things 'in the round'. But in the most significant parts of our behaviour, environment is not related to us as uninhabited country to a solitary traveller, who moves on every day. Every beast he kills, every stick he cuts, every fire he lights, every piece of rubbish he burns, affects his environment with incalculable consequences, but never the environment that matters; for he moves on every day, and he is not going to return on his tracks. On the contrary, our actions shape the world in which we have to live, and, in so far as they are rational, they must shape it consistently, into a machine which will work and which will satisfy as many of our aims as possible without intolerable conflicts. And this imposes a systematic unity on our acts themselves and their immediate aims.

We say that our action is the shaping of our world. But in this world must be included ourselves, in so far as that description covers the psychic mechanisms built up by and for habitual action. These also must be constructed by us as the by-product of our acts in a way whch will not frustrate our further purposes.

But, further, not only does a certain subservience to the machine's demands impose order on our voluntary acts; even in so far as we are masters of the machinery and using it for purposes independently chosen, it is plain that only consistent purposes can be subserved by the machine, so that our position of mastery over it is itself a control on us. Unless our purposes have such consistency and continuity from day to day that we can hew a law-bound world into a shape which will tend to foster their success, we shall have to fall back upon a form of will which comes short of what we defined to be its full rationality, viz. the enactment of changes in the world which make it such as to favour our purposes on the whole. Our purpose is not itself that of creating a machine for ends presupposed, our ends may be freely chosen; yet they must be such as to form a system at least in this sense, that a uniformly-working world can be shaped to promote them. This principle is, of course, only true to the extent that it is true; to some extent the figure of the lonely traveller fits us and we can neglect the modifications which our acts introduce into their environment; and even where we should not feel free to do so were we omniscient, yet in fact we must do so because we are ignorant.

We speak of shaping our natural environment by our acts, of willing not the single effect, but nature as modified thereby; yet what we are often principally concerned with is not nature, but the quasi-nature of a social pattern. The running (let us say) of a railway is a system sustained and fulfilled by the voluntary endeavours of many agents. Yet so strong is the interest of them all in the functioning of it, that we depend upon it as upon nature itself; and what I will when I set out to catch a train is this piece of quasi-nature as modified by the presence of my body in a third-class compartment on the line between Oxford and Paddington. To say that man is a social creature and to say that these quasi-natural formations are necessary to human purposes is to say the same thing.

This quasi-nature, taken in its full extent, resembles the true nature by having a complexity and breadth which exceed the individual's grasp, so that in willing modifications in it, or it as so modified, we are willing what we understand in outline only. Nature it resembles also in not being fully amenable to the action of my single will, and in pre-existing that will. Yet these characteristics do not make it anything high and holy, since it shares them with inanimate nature, and it was the most revolting paradox of Idealism to have absolutised it, and equated subservience to it with the moral aim. Its true status is that which we have assigned it—that of a machine of which we cannot but will the modifications, if our willing is reasonable. But the revolutionary may will revolutionary modifications; he is only bound in that (a) he must will modifications of what is, and (b) must will some reconstitution of social mechanism which itself will work. To act with simple disregard of 'the system' is irrational and immoral, but the serious purpose of 'smashing' it may be the highest duty. The system does not define the ends of will, but is an instrumental and material necessity to them.

(iv) *Intentional Unity imposed by Reason*

But in this whole discussion of the will's tendency to unity, are we not absurdly neglecting the most obvious factor, the very rationality of will in choosing—so far, that is, as it is rational and fully a will? Have we not seen that rationality means a constant and consistent valuation of ends? We have. But we have also seen that rationality as such appears to be impersonal and discarnate, being directed to the realisation of being whensoever and wheresoever, so that there is nothing in it to prevent the individual from aiming at a number of good and in themselves worth-while possibilities, without any interconnexion to speak of; and this hardly seems to provide the unity of a self.

But we have already entertained the suspicion that all these worth-while possibilities can be reduced to the claims of substantial entities; and it seems that were this so, the unifying tendency of rational will would be enhanced, for it seems then to be directed solely to the actualisation or completion of units. Ought not the hypothesis to be considered?

On this question we may say first, that undoubtedly we sometimes make entities our aim, as has been sufficiently shown by the way. We sometimes act for the sake of the continued existence of others, or the continued realisation of their chosen path of life. Or again, we sometimes act with a view to the realisation of our unitary ideal of ourselves. In the second place we may of course say in a certain sense that all our rational actions have relation to the realisation of our self or someone's self. Our myth of the infinite will turned on this very issue. Nothing can be of value except to a being that is something to and for itself. And unless aesthetic (say) or cognitive experience enriched a mind or sensibility, it would not be chosen. But in these cases it may well appear that the self enriches itself simply by seizing its environment in its very otherness— *mens fit quodammodo omnia*. Even so, the mind, in its limitations, acts as a filter and a boundary-line to the world that it can receive, and imposes on it a sort of negative unity. But it will hardly do to say that this unity is the intention of the mind in cognitive exploration. Its intention has reference to an unit, viz. itself. But its intention is not the unity of the unit, or the construction for it of a more widely extended pattern-structure. On the contrary, the intention of *mens* is *fieri, quantum potest, omnia*; there is a genuine movement towards 'dissipation' even in rational will, which receives, no doubt, a check in a contrary movement of concentration. Yet there is no more reason to say that we dissipate only in order to enrich our concentration, than there is to say that we concentrate only to keep pace with our dissipation.

Let us write a conclusion to this whole topic of intentional unity. In a world such as that imagined by Spinoza, in which there was one great pool of mind, and individual selves detached themselves from it simply by their inner coherence, the human mind could hardly keep its individual status. For it could hardly claim to be one 'idea' if by 'idea' is meant 'project-system'. Spinoza only upheld such a conclusion by a deterministic dogmatism which reduced the super-pattern of conscious activity to a necessary function of the basic bodily pattern, and roundly declared the mind to be the idea—i.e. consciousness-aspect —of the body. But if we do not share this dogmatism but admit a freedom which on the fixed bodily basis weaves many and varied patterns of intention, we cannot claim that these form a system, but merely that there is some degree of unity or compatibility between them, and this in two ways: (*a*) in the projects we explicitly or implicitly entertain together at any one time, (*b*) in the analogy or similarity of policy between our projects at several different times throughout life.

APPENDIX TO CHAPTER XVI

PROBLEM OF CHARACTER AND FREEDOM

(i) *Character as Policy and as Disposition*

CHARACTER appears to be a continuous direction of choice, not itself chosen, and yet forming our choices throughout life. Now we have already been at pains to show that, though not a direct project of any act of will, such a tendency is the expression of our will. But there is something else that needs to be shown: viz. that in proportion as character is formed, it does not remove liberty or strangle the voluntary nature of the acts that take place in accordance with it. Here again we encounter a venerable piece of anti-libertarian dialectic. It argues that libertarianism must either make the very existence of character unintelligible, or else make it exterior to the act of will—a psychological compulsion from which we occasionally escape to perform a free act. Whereas it appears to common sense that character is the expression of will, and (in another sense) will that of character.

In principle our solution must be that *character is the policy of choice.* It is of course foolish to suppose that the word 'character' is used in a simple or consistent sense by the British public. It may be used to cover a great deal that is below the level of intelligent will; and if, as we have suggested, there is a real continuity of will from the 'form (i.e. active pattern) of the living body *qua* living' upwards through all gradations, then a similarly scaled use of the word 'character' may have its philosophical justification. But it is character at the highest level of will that must concern us, and this we declare to be the policy of choice. In so far as a direction of conscious behaviour is merely inherited or inculcated, and continues to operate without being either adopted after criticism, altered, built upon, or rejected, it is not character in this sense.

But if 'character' can follow 'will' through its several levels, it will be natural for us to attach most importance to that definition of 'character' which fits the middle definition of will, i.e. that which takes the name to cover the whole of activity in which will of the explicit form occupies a predominant place, in so far as this whole serves as the 'embodiment' of such will (*vide supra*, p. 181).

'Policy of choice' is as ambiguous as 'intentional unity'. It might perhaps mean (*a*) 'a chosen policy'; but more probably (*b*) a policy which is exemplified in our several distinct choosings. It is (*b*) that is more particularly meant when we call character 'the policy of choice', and it is the relation of this to free will which appears somewhat mysterious. In dealing with intentional unity we were content with a provisional conclusion, viz. that policy is at least a direct result of our conscious acts of will; but the nature of its relation to free choices was not defined. Can one, for example, regard it as a dead deposit, left by former living and free actions, in such fashion as to restrict the possibilities which are psychologically open to future choice? If so, we have surrendered to the attack made on libertarianism just above, have made character external to freedom and freedom characterless.

Let us take up again the theme of our discussion concerning the good and rational appetite. In the case of rational action, we said, there is indeed appetite, but the appetite is not specific *a priori*, it is specified by the object. This suggests that the good seen and responded to can create a disposition which will function in future as an already specified appetite prior to objects; we begin by doing what is good because it is good, we come to get a taste for it. Is character then simply the body of such dispositions? Certainly such dispositions are often included in what we call character, but that is not the whole of the story.

We must distinguish here. The resultant specific and dispositional appetites (even if in some inchoate form they always arise) are not that appetite whose immediate specification by the character of the object leads us to call the object good. That appetite is none other than our voluntary action, considered in one of its aspects. It begins indeed as incipient action; but unless it proceeds to full and self-committing action, it does not carry a full judgment of the excellence of the object. But why call action appetite? Because all action is appetitive, wherever I act, *appeto*, I am out for something, and if the appetite is not prior to the act, then it is developed in and as the act. We call the act appetite, then, in order to stress its character of 'finality'.

We declared: 'Thought itself starts no movement (οὐδὲν κινεῖ); we cannot know the good for us except as what aspiration jumps at, after it matters not how much consideration of the object and searching of the heart.' This may seem to suggest that 'aspiration' (i.e. rational appetite) is a brute force, and that we judge of the good by (*a*) considering the object, (*b*) standing aside and watching which way the cat (of aspiration) will jump, (*c*) recording the result of this experiment by labelling that animal's landing-place 'the good'. This was not our meaning, and it is not true. For we (as judges-in-acting and agents-in-judging) are ourselves the cat; we jump at the object as being the thing to jump at (τὸ φύσει ἔφετον) and if we afterwards record the fact that we have jumped, we do so by an act of reflection on what *we* have done. To say 'we cannot know the good for us except as what aspiration jumps at' is like saying 'we cannot know fact except as what judgment accepts'. In the long run, there are no grounds for theoretical belief except the 'evidence' of the object, the fact that it 'persuades' the best judgment we can apply. And in the long run there are no grounds for practical belief, except a similar evidence—the fact that the object is chosen by rational will, when we are being as careful and honest as we can. We are not assured of the excellence of the object first by our reflection on the fact of our choice; we are assured of it by the choice, and that choice is not actual without action. All that the reflection does is to raise a vain question (What is the exterior criterion of judgment?) and to remove it by denying that any such criterion is conceivable.

It must now be clear what is the relation between pure rational appetite and dispositional appetites arising therefrom and generally regarded as 'virtuous'. The latter are in their nature simply dispositions, and only rational by accident. The man who has a taste for certain forms of amiability or generosity and performs actions of this kind simply because he has a taste for them may not be moral at all. In fact it is constantly necessary to check these virtuous 'tastes' by genuine choices. On the other hand, the mere fact that one has a taste for certain virtues by no means debars one from the real and concomitant exercise of live rational appetition. For example: The Lady Bountiful who has a taste for charity may be inclined thereby to take up 'cases' of need; but that will not prevent her from interesting herself in the human beings concerned objectively and on their merits and devoting herself to them. In so far, the initial disposition or taste leads on into the act of real freedom which is motived by its objects. Her taste for charity would stand in the way of free action only if she allowed the gratification of it to remain her aim. The condition of rational freedom is objective interest, and that can never be the mere operation of subjective habit.

The function of dispositions, then, is to subserve freedom; and to admit that they *are* character would be to admit that the constant element in our life is something necessarily less than rational. They are or should be a sort of habitudinal and emotional shadow thrown by rational character itself. And here, by the way, is the solution of the famous paradox: 'Only the man who dislikes virtue can be actively virtuous.' It arises from a plainly insufficient analysis, assuming that an action is a simple event arising from a simple cause. 'If I *want* to do an action (through a pre-formed appetite) then this appetite is the "cause" and "motive" of the action, and there's no more to be said.' But there is a great deal more to be said. If the action is to be complete and sound, it is often the case that subjective motivation can only take us in the direction of the object, and must then hand over (so to speak) to genuine objective motivation, and once this change-over has occurred, nothing will be easy or automatic.

(ii) *Character as Active Belief in Previous Choices*

But we must turn to the nature of character itself in its most active or most rational form, and this we declare to be 'active belief in the rightness of our own practical judgments': a formula which we offer as a gloss upon 'the policy of choice'. When we are to act, that is, explicitly or implicitly to make a practical judgment, we have not to do so *in vacuo*. It is impossible to erase all that is written on the slate of memory and judge the object simply by itself. We judge in the light of our previous judgments. This is possible because of the universality of practical judgment (*vide supra*, p. 148); the new object is recognised as at least analogous to previous objects. Doubtless we have often occasion to correct and reverse previous judgments, but in correcting some we build on others. If the reversal or conversion proceeds beyond a certain point, we do not hesitate to speak of the change of character.

The matter may be made clearer by attempting to suppose an 'intuitive' self[1] which had complete and immediate grasp of the nature and worth of objects, as they were presented. To speak of 'character' in such a self would be unmeaning; every active response to the world would be necessarily right, and each one would be independent of every other. Independent, that is, so far as subjective motivation was concerned; none would serve as a rule for the direction of any subsequent response. Previous acts would simply form part of the body of facts in view of which the new 'intuitive' judgment was made; this self's own acts would be on a level with those of others in this respect. There would be an actual harmony of direction between the later acts and the earlier, for all would (ex hypothesi) follow the right principles. But they would not do so by borrowing them from one another. Even though the 'intuitive' self were concerned not only with response to environment but also with the selection and construction of the pattern of its own activities, this would not give it particular character in the sense that we are considering. Its view about the proper function and structural individuality of its life would be equally intuitive and certain, and each detail and step would be independently seen (with the 'independence' we have just defined). So that it would create an individual object in creating its own form of life, and this object can be called a 'character' if we like to call it so; but it would not show *subjective* individuality, of the sort called character, in the creating thereof.

In contrast to this stands the self which we know and are. Its response to objects is by no means 'intuitive' but full of darkness and ignorance; the whole of its life is one grand experiment in practical judgment, of which the best we can hope is, that the more we try, the more we shall go right. We cannot hope for a blinding flash of clarity by which the single object should of itself alone fully illuminate the understanding. We must build on our previous judgments (that is our acts *qua* rational) and construct a system of practical belief which, we hope, more and more approximates to a true response to the real nature of things.

Now it may seem that to call character even in its most voluntary, most rational aspect a system of belief, is to give an absurdly narrow definition. But this objection arises from the identification of our 'system of belief' with the verbal formulation we could give of our principles of action. Such a formulation could only extend to general principles, in which several men might agree. But the 'system of belief' which is our character includes much that is intimately particular, e.g. the value for a person placed just as we are of another individual person related to us as this one is related. It includes the value we attach implicitly, by voluntary action, to every element in our environment which has a sufficient stability for us to have a 'policy' towards it; every set of possibilities which are sufficiently analogous to be treated practically as a class. There is nothing here, indeed, which is incapable of verbal formulation; but the verbal

[1] i.e. one gifted with the powers of Kant's imaginary 'intuitive understanding'

description of one man's character would be almost endless, and few men if any ever attempt such a formulation of themselves.

Characters differ not only by the different responses they give to the same things and sorts of things. Equally they differ in the things and sorts of things to which they give responses of any kind, either positive or negative. For our policies of choice (not to mention our bodily and social starting-points) determine the path of our activity and our attention, and thereby determine the marginal area on either side of the path within which all possibilities for this will are bound to be found.

Let us return to the contrast with the intuitive will. The intuitive will simply knows, in the realm of value (i.e. propriety of response) as well as in that of simple fact. Now we have concluded above that there is no sinning against fullness of light, though sinning is always against sufficient light. It follows that the possibility of moral failure is bound up with, though distinct from, ignorance. The non-intuitive self, then, because non-intuitive, has the capacity of badness, which is always, alas, in some degree realised. And this fact makes 'policy of choice' a better description of character as we know it than 'active acceptance of our own practical choices'. And it seems that if we wish to describe character in its most voluntary form—the highest and most voluntary stratum of it—we ought to describe the highest stratum which is actually found, not the ideal for that stratum. But what is found includes reason and paralogism, good and bad will, inextricably interpenetrating. The two are more inseparable, less fairly divisible into two strata, than the voluntary and the analogous lower levels of the semi-voluntary. For it is reason itself which chooses to paralogise, and otherwise there is no responsible wickedness. And, in so far as the reason does paralogise or the will sins, character may also be expressed, but not as an 'active acceptance of our own previous practical choices', but rather as the same perversion of judgment and confusion of act which we have previously committed.

Let this suffice, then, for a statement of the essential relation of Character and Will; from which we gather that will on the level of rational freedom is related to character on the same level; its relation to the character on lower levels is part of its relation to the will of lower levels. The demonstration we are concerned to make is that there is no opposition between character and freedom, since freedom in a non-intuitive self supposes character.

(iii) *Formation of Character No Simple Decrease of Freedom*

It is sometimes maintained that (on the libertarian view) the progressive formation of character must decrease freedom. We reply that it only does so in so far as the character is of the lower, dispositional kind and in so far as these dispositions are incommensurate with and independent of character in the higher sense. It is the function of dispositions (if we may be allowed for the moment to speak teleologically) to mechanise our approach to the objects that our character chooses. In a mine or quarry it is possible and useful to lay railway tracks because, although the points of excavation are always changing as we dig, they move gradually and we know in what sort of direction they will do so; so that the system of rails can be kept adapted to the digging. So with the dispositional machinery. If we begin to make it our object to fill the trucks where they run with rock, irrespective of its quality, or if our points of excavation vary erratically because we can never tell where the metal will turn up; in either case the rail-system is a nuisance rather than a help. It is needless to point the application of the parable. A man must (a) keep his objective interest dominant, and (b) have an environment sufficiently stable to allow of the useful functioning of formed dispositions. The first condition lies in his own power, the second does not. The most pathetic instance of 'character cramping freedom' is that of the old man who is suddenly flung into a new world.

But then it is not normal for old men to be flung into new worlds; if it happens, the teleology of Nature (if we may mention it again) seems to be overthrown. There is a course of normal development in which freedom does not decrease with advancing characterisation, or not until the point is reached where vitality itself and activity decrease, and move with a slower beat.

The freedom of youth is the freedom of choice; it is rich in the ability to choose its own principal directions, but poor in the criteria of choice and in the power to attain fully specific objects. The prime of life is poorer in choice of principal direction, but richer in choices which are fully specific and effective; there is less variety in the direction, but more detail in the matter, of choice. A later age does not so much choose between objects as concentrate upon the choices it has made, and actualise them with a vigorous serenity. For choice, as we have seen, is an act of judgment, and our acceptance and further definition of our direction is a sort of faith, which cannot reach its maximum of conviction and solidity until that direction has been in a large measure specified and defined. On the other hand, faith never can become simple certainty, nor action upon it automatic; the concentrated and serene enactment of it towards objects already in principle chosen is an exercise of freedom which has its own privileges as compared with less mature phases. The vigour of age which prefers to enact its principles rather than to relapse into laziness may be said to enjoy the advantages of a simplification of choice, without any relapse into indefiniteness (for the choices of youth may seem simple, because they are vague). The choice of age, we suspect, is the choice to believe and to do, with less choice as to what; its course is set.[1] And therefore, in a manner, it has a full possession of its ends.

[1] The elderly often say that they find life immensely complicated and the issue less and less clear. But does not this mean that *practically* they confine their intentions to the world in so far as they have defined and assimilated it? Their judgments are fixed; but the application of these to a changing world involves a more and more complicated casuistry.

Or again, being unprepared for fresh creation of systems, they react more passively to things as they are; trying no longer to *impose* new unities on them, they find them acting upon their own established unity with all the variety of wild nature. It remains that the choice of principles (values) is made; the application to the infinite variety of things calls for moral

Now it is perverse to pretend that any of these periods is 'freer' than another; all are essentially related to character, the earlier more to its formation, the later more to its exercise. The freedom of one age differs from that of another; each, if made the measure of the others, will condemn them. There is no common measure of freedom by which they can be scaled; there is one common character of freedom, which is expressed in different modes. These modes cannot be numbered, but form a continuous scale of modifications from one extreme pole to the other. Childhood, in so far as rational volition is not yet developed, and extreme age, in so far as volition ceases to be exercised, lie outside the scale at either end.

Such generalisations as this awake a just suspicion of superficiality, especially when they seem directed to the justification of what is. But even though (for example) age were usually a tragedy, because environment fails to provide fine weather, because society has not found out how to allow the elderly to be their age, but confronts them with the alternatives of competing with their juniors on ground not their own, or else of being simply immobilised, it would remain that there is a mode of freedom possible in age and most probable then to be realised if at all. And that is all that is needed by an argument directed to show that the specification of character does not of itself destroy freedom. For there is a supreme freedom in the simple act of adhering to a good that we have fully specified. Whether and how far this is exemplified in the advancing years of human creatures depends on a great number of other factors. For age is not simply the specification of choice, it is many things beside: 'aret latus, hebet pectus, minuuntur gaudia. . . .'

energy, expressed through intelligence, rather than for moral (practical) choice. It may also be that this bewilderment of age arises through the veteran's trying to do the things that are not suited to him.

XVII

UNITY OF SELF AS CONCENTRATION

(i) *Project and Background*

In the last two chapters we have considered that unity which is imposed on a self both by its starting-point, and by its aim; and neither appeared to give *the* unity of a self. For the self's starting-point can hardly be the unity of that self, *qua* activity and *qua* free; whereas the aim, though it has more claim to be the form of the self, turned out not to be a unity. We have found what we seek neither in the basic pattern, nor in the super-pattern; which need not surprise us, since we have placed the self's activity between the two. And so it is natural to turn next to the form of the act itself. We discussed this before, when we were defining the will. We discussed the single act; but may it not be that activity is continuous, or that the form of the single act stretches wider, and embraces a whole self?

Our account of the act described it as a process which, containing within it the entertained projects of several operations, enacted the one, and excluded the other(s). In virtue of what, we now ask, does the one obtain preference, when there has been a real balance between them at first? If one knocks the other out, as the one boxer knocks out the other with whom at first he seemed evenly matched, but whom he has now succeeded in out-tiring, that is an odd account of reasonable will, and one which would rather fit the case of persons whose psychic life was extremely discoordinated; for indeed the very difference between such cases and normality is the open conflict in the former, and in the latter some common factor or factors whose mediation awards the palm and persuades the vanquished.

It might be that the projects themselves, at first balanced, became unequal through consideration of the nature or consequences of what is intended under each. But then the projects have changed in content, and that which triumphs is not that which was held in suspense. Whereas the perfect case of will-choice is that in which objective consideration of projects is finished, and both in their final form make their appeal to the will.

Well, but after all examination of projects is over, we may have simply to contemplate them, in the effort to appreciate their value; we may have to make a moral effort to overcome our fear of error, or our wish to have it both ways, or our cowardice in view of a superior project which involves more trouble, or our selfishness in view of the renunciation of a cheaper satisfaction. All these biases may need to be set aside. Yet the process of making up one's mind is not simply moral, nor simply an examination of the immediate projects, nor simply a combination of these two factors. The will seeks wider grounds, and canvasses the votes of other interests, and extending tentacles back into its own past, becomes the focus of a self.

We have called will 'self-actualising potency'. This description has two parts: the potency, which, formally viewed, is some sort of 'character' or pattern, or complex of such; and the self-actualising thereof. The first requires description; about the second, perhaps, little can be said; it is the unitary and unique fact of freedom, it cannot be further analysed. When, therefore, we try to give a description of will which is to satisfy us, it is not in the analysis of freedom as such that we can expect to be satisfied or dissatisfied. At the most we can compare freedom with other things to get quite clear what it is *not* and to sharpen our perception for this unique object of intuition.[1] But on the other hand the mind can hope for complete satisfaction, when the 'character' which is (self-)actualised has been analysed and adequately exhibited.

The centre of this character is found in the (entertained) project. But from this centre it is necessary to proceed forwards and backwards. Forwards, by shewing its formal relation to its own fulfilment, and so its character as potency (for the idea of potency involves relation to actuality and so looks forward). Backwards, by showing its relation to further characters which support it, and which by their addition make it the adequate ground for its own actualisation in will. Adequate, not as the Sufficient Reason of Leibniz is adequate, viz. fully to determine the effect, but adequate to be the ground upon which a free act can take action. The characteristic mark of the narrow ground is formal identity with the effect. The characteristic mark of the wider ground is completeness or sufficiency for the effect. In the Infinite Mind the two would not have to be distinguished; in the finite mind they are distinct the one from the other—the centre from the background, the project from the self, the particular character from the substantial essence.

The background is not to be confused with the metaphysical *Unding* attacked above (*vide supra*, p. 128)—the *ens* of which the particular character (entertained project) is a 'mode'. Of that we could say, that (*a*) its contents, (*b*) its relation to the effect, were wholly dark. It was introduced to be the real cause of the effect and as such to replace the entertained project. But the background does not replace the entertained project, but reinforces it; and not in an unintelligible manner, nor by 'doubling' the relation of the particular entertained project to its own fulfilment; but in its own observable way, and complementary to the other. Nor are its contents wholly dark, but can be to some extent detailed.

What then is this background? It is memory in the widest possible sense of that term; it is what we suppose our minds to 'contain' even when we are not aware of such contents. Bergson has produced a marvellous profusion of metaphors to describe how all that we ever perceived, or did, or dreamt, or thought penetrates and virtually indwells the present moment of consciousness. In the moment is its whole past background, but a principle of selective oblivion

[1] *vide supra*, pp. 80 *ff*, 130 *ff*; and *infra*, ch. xix

curtains off what is not relevant. The past throngs the gate of the present, but (in a healthy mind) the least-wanted members of the crowd are on its outskirts, and these indeed are always the vast majority; those more concerned are in the forecourt, ready to come to the front; while on the very steps the subconscious mind has marshalled the witnesses she expects to see called. These nearest, Consciousness looks in the face and recognises, of those next she is dimly aware, and the more distant make up a featureless crowd: for of memory-consciousness there is an indefinite number of degrees. Sometimes she is content with those directly before her, sometimes she calls forward some more remotely descried, and sometimes she institutes a search for the missing witness in the indistinguishable mass behind.

In this crowd are not only contents of past experiences, but also habits and formed desires and previous resolutions and tendencies of action.

(ii) *The Concentration of the Background*

This crowd, then, throngs the gate of the court house where the case between the two rival projects is being tried. And the will allows that project to proceed which is best supported. Neither project is ever considered as unsupported, or in pure abstraction, but at the beginning of the case the support for each may well appear equally strong. But then a concentration takes place; further apparently relevant witnesses push their way or are summoned in; and the whole crowd becomes more closely pressed, so that voices too distant to be heard come within range of hearing.

'The will allows that project which is best supported.' But 'best-supportedness' is not a simply given characteristic, as though, for example, one were to count heads and approve the candidate that wins most votes. This would nullify the freedom of the will; and we have already established the fact of its creativity, the fact that it devises and invents its future on the basis of the past. The will needs, however, sufficient grounds on which to choose and construct. That 'best support', which gives superiority to a project, is adjudged best by the practical judgment, and is nothing but the sufficient materials for the formation of that judgment.

It has been an accident of our procedure to go back from the particular project to its supporting (or opposing) background; we assumed that the case was being tried, and then looked outside the door for the throng of witnesses whose added voices would make possible a decision. This presentation was artificial. No doubt, when a trial has in fact begun, it may be necessary to look for fresh witnesses, because (as we assumed) the cases *pro* and *contra* seemed balanced at the first. But evidently the witnesses play a part not only in deciding the case, but in bringing it about that there is a case at all.

The ultimate factors which are the grounds of a choice must be reducible to two. On the one hand, potential objects of apprehension; on the other, mnemic contents and forces. We call the first factor 'potential' objects. There are certain events taking place in such a manner and such a position that they could become the objects of our attention were it bestowed, through whichever it be of our apprehensive organs or powers. Will the attention be bestowed? That already depends on the mnemic content, which disposes us to attention in one direction rather than another, because certain elements of memory are pressing closest to the gate—the gate this time which looks out upon the world. To bestow attention is already to be solicited by a project, if only by the project of bestowing it further. Already there may be a case for and against, and a mnemic witness be called. For the initial solicitants of attention and action are too numerous by far and must be weeded out, and for this purpose a more exact testimony is required from the witnesses than the casual cry that this or that appearance fleeting past the door looks worth catching at. Cases arise, some of which can be settled by summary jurisdiction while others demand formal trial.

And when a formal trial arises, then, we have seen, there is a certain mnemic concentration, a massing of forces until one project prevails. Of this concentration we gave above an oversimplified account; for we suggested two possibilities, (*a*) that the witnesses push themselves forward, (*b*) that they are summoned by a central authority of consciousness and will. This has some initial plausibility because we often seem to discover (*a*) that the active prominence of mnemic factors is determined apart from conscious choice or even contrary to what full reflection would have chosen, (*b*) that conscious search is made into both mnemic contents and dispositional desires—as though we were discontented with the order of the crowd at the gate and set about marshalling it for ourselves in accordance with true relevance to the matter in hand.

Yet even if 'pure cases' can be found of the two extremes (*a*) and (*b*)—a fact which we shall have presently to question—it would remain that there are innumerable mixed cases between the two, as we can see by observation. The effort to remember a relevant fact or recapture an attitude of will is often a process to which we contribute voluntary attention, but only of the vaguest kind—we do not 'look' for what we want, but only encourage it in the most general way to emerge; we concentrate by a voluntary act, we rally the forces of the mind to the point in question, but we do not in any way direct what it is that shall come to the front; or we suspend action and intensify the concentration which is anyhow taking place.

And further, if we take the extreme cases of (*a*) and (*b*), we never find them in fact to be 'pure'. To take (*b*) first. Who searches for what he already has? It is an easy metaphor which speaks of 'summoning this or that witness out of the crowd'. The metaphor is misleading, for it distinguishes sharply between the witness and his evidence. But in fact the witness *is* his evidence; he is a relevant fact or rule or tendency. If I have seen him sufficiently to summon him, then I have his evidence. I may of course, having seen it out of the 'tail of the eye', judge it to be relevant and retain it for more complete and attentive investigation. But if so, it must have come near enough 'of itself' to be in the line of vision. Or again, I may throw out general feelers, as when I tell myself that

I want a memory-fact of such and such a sort; but it still remains for the fact to emerge in response thereto. The point does not need labouring; the application of mnemic data to situations by voluntary recall is never a voluntary pheno-menon of the same explicitness and simplicity as the enactment of the fully formed project, when I know what it is that I want and proceed to do it. Indeed we can be sure almost *a priori* that the operation of rational will towards the 'background' of the project cannot be of the same character as its operation towards the formed project itself; since it is by their several relations to the will that the two are distinguished.

Now to take (*a*). The witnesses, we say, sometimes present themselves. Does this mean, simply, that mnemic data often come to bear on our conscious choice which we neither expected, nor threw out feelers for, nor (on subsequent reflection) judge to be useful or relevant? If so, it cannot be disputed. But this does not justify the metaphor 'they present themselves'. Are we seriously pro-posing to personify the several mnemic elements? They do not present them-selves fortuitously, and it seems much to credit them with individual intelli-gence, of however rudimentary a kind. Is there not, then, a quasi-purposive principle of the whole which directs the order of concentration? The hard-bitten empiricist will always wish to avoid this conclusion by supposing there are some 'rules' of association which adequately account for the appearance of mnemic data exactly when they do appear. Doubtless whatever principle pro-duces them, does so not without rules, as indeed all purposive activity uses rules; to deny associative rules in memory would be insane. But that these rules are not a total explanation may be argued in two ways.

(I) As by Bergson, that in fact the rules do not and cannot cover the functioning of memory.

(II) That it is impossible to draw a sharp line between voluntary recall and 'automatic' memory, and the former at least (on the grounds of our general position about the will) we know to involve principles of free choice and pur-pose. Here, then, also will belong the topic of the analogical scale of will-acts, which we set forth above (*vide supra*, pp. 144 *f*). Of 'concentration' also there will be a scale, rising from blind will to the most rational. But there will be no reason to personify or even to atomise the mnemic materials of concentration in its lower phases. If we are to proceed by analogy, we shall say that what concentrates is the (rudimentary) central 'force'—or, let us say, it is a self-concentrating concentration; not a centripetal activity of the elements. In distinguishing conscious voluntary concentration from its less conscious substratum, we are not distinguishing between the centre and the elements; but between central activity of several levels, the more conscious and the less.

(iii) *The Pre-existent Grounds of Concentration*

The only key we have to the structure of concentration is that which we derive from its most explicit, conscious, rational, voluntary levels; and this must be applied to the more implicit and blind, with an analogical difference which can never be exactly determined. But now on the conscious level we established an important fact. The support which this or that mnemic element lends to a project, it does not lend of itself, but in virtue of the relevance recognised in it by the active judgment. But if relevance depends on judgment, then judgment is the principle of concentration. It seems to be the purpose tending towards the particular act which, striking root back into the mnemic soil, collects and orders concentration, and is its principle.

But this statement seems to be in danger of leading us into a dialectic argument. For it provokes the reply: How can the purpose tending towards the particular act be the principle of the concentration, when it itself arises in the process of concentration? For, as we have seen, nothing but (a) mnemic contents, and (b) actual events which are potential objects of attention, etc., can be simply presupposed. These, then, must either be the principles of the concentration, or contain them.

This antithesis bears its dialectical character upon its face, and no doubt springs from an illegitimate application of the topic of the prior and posterior. But to dispose of it we propose to take a more constructive path than the unmasking of the fallacy.

(I) Concentration and active choice are anyhow aspects of a single process and neither is without the other. To choose a project we must concentrate the background, and conversely, to concentrate the background we must have the (formation and) choice of a project in view. We can treat the process as a unity, having a certain characteristic structure, no part of which can be dispensed with. The problem then can be simplified. How does this single process arise?

(II) It is indeed plausible to say (as the antithesis above suggested) that it arises from (a) mnemic contents, and (b) events which are possible objects of attention. The second (b) causes no particular difficulty; but of the former (a) we must ask: in what manner do the mnemic contents exist prior to concentration? For they only become matter of consciousness or springs of behaviour in so far as they tend towards a concentration, and outside of all concentration appear to exist in a state of 'pure potency', which is as much as to say that they do not exist at all. How can an 'active tendency' exist except as the shape of some actual present movement, and how can a matter of awareness exist with no awareness had of it at all? This is a very venerable problem.

Before we consider any solution, let us remark that if the mnemic matters have lapsed into (so far as we can know) a state of 'pure potency', then they do not seem to enjoy any privilege as compared with the concentration which, by being actualised, could summon them back into more full-blooded existence. This too, may be said to be in a state of 'pure potency'. Its actualisation is bound up with theirs, and theirs with its; and conversely, one supposes, its state of potency with theirs in the same mutual relation.

What is it, then, that gives us the illusion that *their* potential existence is more solid than *its* potential existence? No doubt that their form, *qua* potential,

appears to us to be more determinate. Concentration indeed has form, and we
have been studying it; but this is a form common to all acts of concentration.
The particularisation of this form to a determinate project (and determinate
choice concerning the project) is not without the operation of freedom, nor
without envisaging of the circumstances which may from moment to moment
arise. Thus the concentration which can be thought of as sleeping and waiting
to be evoked into actuality is unparticularised. There are indeed limits within
which we can be sure that its particular form will fall, but more than that we
cannot say. Whereas the mnemic contents even *qua* potential are particular; the
man who has the potential memory of Magdalen College Tower has the
potential memory of Magdalen College Tower, and to become a complete
image this needs only to be actualised, but not to be further determined. Now
that which needs to be in some aspect determined as well as to be actualised
appears more potential than that which needs to be actualised alone, and is so
if by 'more potential' we mean requiring more sorts of operation upon it (as it
were) to make it real. But this distinction leaves untouched the fact that the
same process (viz. the occurrence of an actual concentration) performs all these
operations; it both actualises the one, and the other actualises and determines
as well. So that both are equally potential to the occurrence of the concentration—in the sense that both are merely potential apart from it, and both fully
actual in its occurrence.

But (it might be objected) this only holds good if we allow the absurd
supposition of 'pure potency' in describing the state of mnemic matters before
concentration. This, as well as being absurd in itself (since pure potency is
absolute non-existence, and non-existence is the potency of nothing, or equally
of all), runs counter to empirical evidence. For

(*a*) In any concentration there are mnemic matters on the fringe of that
concentration which exercise a dim half-actuality; which seem to be holding a
watching-brief and threatening to become fully active should the direction of
the concentration touch their interests.

(*b*) Psychologists have advanced a great deal of evidence in favour of the
doctrine of subconsciousness, i.e. that mental elements keep themselves alive
in trains of quasi-consciousness of which the effects can be detected and even
the direct memory subsequently recovered.

(*c*) Our doctrine of the scale of will-acts extending from the fully voluntary, rational and conscious down towards the merely biological level allows
that mnemic matters may be low-degree activities which evade consciousness.

And so, we may wish to conclude, it seems likely that, *apart from any
actuality of concentration*, the mnemic materials for concentration keep themselves in being by a very low intensity of activity, below the level of what is
conceivable to us.

But the evidence adduced has no tendency to support this conclusion—not
at any rate unless the italicised clause is struck out. Always alongside of the
low degree of mnemic actuality we find a low degree of concentration equally

present. In (a), the holders of watching-briefs are active in relation to a 'case', i.e. the concentration—and we can just as easily reverse the metaphor and say that concentration holds them in readiness (and in actuality) because of their supposed possible relevance to itself. In (b), the mnemic elements are never inferred by psychology as active in isolation, but always in a concentration of low degree. While in (c), the low-degree concentration is our very ground for positing the low-degree mnemic matters.

Indeed, this evidence points (if anything) in the opposite direction. All the evidence shows is that there are low degrees of concentration to be found, either marginal to higher degrees, or occurring on their own; and that the human creature is never (perhaps) without concentration-processes of some sort. But the evidence by no means tends to show that the innumerable contents of 'habitual' memory are all continuously actual, even as watching-brief holders, in connexion with the concentrations that are there. We might con- clude that concentration-process is always actual, but the mnemic contents are simply potential to it and from time to time actualised by it.

As to the way in which mnemic matters 'are' in the habitual memory, perhaps it does not greatly matter how we conclude; and it may be that the difference between several solutions is likely to be purely verbal, since we are *ex hypothesi* dealing with what falls outside the in any way observable structure of psychic life; and this might be an instance of a metaphysical opposition which implies no significant difference, and fair game for the Logical Positivists. To catalogue a few possibilities:

(I) The mnemic matters exist *qua* our past experience, behaviour, wishes, decisions, etc. For the past in so far as it is our past is an immediate object of memory-awareness, and this awareness is directed by our present concentra- tion; which can thus be said to range over the field of our previous life and collect into itself what is relevant. The problem is then (in Bergson's amusing phrase) not how we ever remember, but how we ever forget.

(II) The mnemic matters do not exist in any psychological mode nor as objects to consciousness of any sort, except when they enter into some concen- tration or other. For the rest of the time what exists is their 'physical traces' in the nervous system, and these are the ground of the evocation of the mnemic matters when they are wanted; somewhat as the gramophone record is the persisting ground for the evocation of the music at such times as it is evoked.[1]

(III) In spite of appearances (*vide supra*) the mnemic matters are all actual at a very low intensity in concentrations which are also of a very low intensity. For we know that when mnemic matters do come to be evoked, they are evoked through already formed systems of association or interest. Let it be

---

[1] The physical must also be reduced to real activity and not e.g. 'matter' or 'extension' and so the difference here is of two relations between those grounds of consciousness and occasional consciousness of them: (a) as 'matter' to 'form' (subordination), (b) as root to flower (continuity); see above, p. 181

supposed, then, that these systems are themselves low-degree concentrations, holding watching-briefs as regards the central and fully active concentration of the moment; while *it* is a process that really proceeds, *they* are processes that continually repeat, or mark time. The mind may be thought of diagrammatically as a map, with main thoroughfares and side alleys of interest and association, to which the particular mnemic matters are adjoined like particular houses and buildings opening upon them. There is one such diagram which represents statically the usual relation and proportion of our interests through a period of our life. But to represent any given moment, we shall need·a diagram which makes central that concentration which is actually then the centre of consciousness and of action, and maps the rest as radiating from it.

It does not concern us here to discuss whether these three forms of statement exhaust the possibilities, nor whether they are different in substance or in figure only. They all allow the same function to present concentration, and all describe the mnemic matters which—so far as their full activity is concerned—are potential for entry into some fully actualised and central concentration.

Let us now return to our account of the manner in which a concentration arises, and what can be presupposed to it. It seemed that we could presuppose (*a*) mnemic matters, (*b*) actual events such as to be potential objects of attention. But now we can say: the mnemic matters cannot come to bear in order to select the objects of attention and give rise to a concentration, except in virtue of a concentration. We cannot suppose a situation in which the whole content of memory in its passive state simply confronted the actual events which are its possible objects and selected some for actual attention and for active concern. There is always some concentration already actual which *sets* the mind in a certain way towards its possible objects.

For some voluntary activity is always proceeding in the self, and if not voluntary in the fullest and highest sense, then quasi-voluntary and belonging to the bottom of the scale; and wherever there is voluntary activity of any degree, there will be rudimentary concentration with the structure that we have detailed. The irreducible minimum of such activity is that which operates the fundamental bodily pattern; and this is already operative in the womb, and again during sleep.

(iv) 'The Soul and Her Faculties'

We meet here the ancient problem, what essentially is the soul or self? We are tempted indeed to describe it in terms of its faculties: *res cogitans, volens,* and so forth. Yet these faculties have a real distinctness from the soul, since it can exist, without energising in any given one of them; it has, but is not, these powers. And it seems very just to say that it *is* the actuality of the form 'living body', since this always persists, and it is difficult to see what else does.

But life is a pattern of movement, and the activity of this movement is a low-grade voluntary activity. What makes this mass of organised matter the living body of a man is the rhythmic pattern which runs through the whole. And the problem of 'the soul and its faculties' is the problem of the relation between this basic activity and the higher and intermittent activities. The Thomist solution declares that we know the soul through its faculties, and can predicate of the hidden essence only that it is the active potency of these faculties, without knowing what it is in itself in order to be this. Descartes, on the other hand, boldly declares that the mind is a *res cogitans*, and that it is always cogitative; for how could it exist without its distinguishing attribute? And how can this attribute exist, except in act?

Descartes appears to be absurd in defying fact; while on the other hand we have to approve his demand for a common denominator of activity running through the whole existence of the self. This demand can be met, and the facts squared, if we admit that the soul's *cogitatio*—we prefer to say its *voluntas*—can be degraded and elevated up or down a continuous scale, so that the lower is the potency of the higher. For the downward path is not continuable *ad infinitum*; we reach at length a minimum of voluntary activity which is the self-energising rhythmic pattern of bodily life. This is the redoubt into which life retires, and from which she makes her sallies.

On this view it might seem that the higher is the potency of the lower, as well as *vice versa*; for the common factor—voluntary activity—can fall as well as rise, so that what was in a higher mode, comes to be in a lower. But this is not really so. We may talk of a common factor, viz. activity, but that does not mean that there is a single quantity of energy now displayed in a higher, now in a lower mode. The bodily pattern does not cease to operate because I philosophise. The bodily pattern is continuous, and develops temporary activities from itself, as some base organisms throw out temporary tentacles for immediate uses, and re-absorb them afterwards, without ever suspending their central functions.

We may go on to ask—how is it that the baser activity can flow out into the more elevated? And in what does this power reside? And how can that which is baser be a vehicle of continuity between acts of higher will? But this question cannot be answered in the terms in which it is asked. Let us remember that we are not out to find 'sufficient reason', since that is the denial of will. We are only seeking adequate grounds for will, that is for freedom, to operate upon. Just as we cannot find in the particular mnemic matters a complete determination of the course voluntary choice will take, so we cannot find in the activity already operative an already complete form of the higher concentration such that it needs only to seize the matter appropriate to it. There still remains a sheer coming into being of what was in potency only, viz. of the higher form of activity; and it is a primary deliverance of the moral consciousness that we are responsible for rising or failing to rise to a higher form of act, in cases where it has begun to dawn but is pushed back into darkness. Laziness, rather than perversity, is the radical sin of the mind, and laziness is acquiescence in the lower level. Freedom, then, can raise itself from lower to higher concentrations;

yet it cannot raise itself from nowhere, and hence the need for the continuous activity, though of lower grade.

It is not meant that the intermittent higher activities all arise from the 'bodily pattern' by acts of conscious freedom; it is evident that they often do not, and not evident that they ever do wholly. By the time I begin to act with truly free choice I have already come into a state of consciousness—I cannot, for instance, choose how I shall direct the attention whose beginning marks the end of sleep. The volition is there, at a low level and fairly closely determined by habit and the immediate perceptible environment.

The problem 'how does the higher arise from the lower?' is not so singular when once we have realised that the 'bodily pattern' itself is not all active at once, but is a rhythm spread through time; e.g. we are not always asleep, and our lungs, when contracting, are not expanding. We have to accept the fact that the present phase of the rhythm 'carries' the potency of others, which are latent in it. And so are the higher activities, when they are not in exercise, latent either in one another, or in the lower.

To return to the 'faculties'. These represent the sorts and structures of act which are possible for the self: higher, lower, and variously specialised at the same level. They are possibilities which voluntary and quasi-voluntary activity can fulfil, and what they are is known from experience. In any moment of full consciousness a certain minimum of structure is evident as the form of it, and the necessary form, in the sense that without it such consciousness cannot be even conceived; for consciousness *in that sense* it is a non-substitutible formal element, while the particular matter of perception, intention, etc., is substitutible by other such matter. But at a given moment of full consciousness it is not evident how many other modalities and levels of consciousness and subconsciousness, will and quasi-will, are possible. This has to be collected by observation and appears purely contingent.

But if the faculties represent sorts and forms of possible act, the mnemic matters operate as part-determinants of the manner in which these acts will be exercised and these forms be filled. In their 'potential' existence they may be reduced to rules governing the matter, direction, etc., of such concentrations as may from time to time arise, and the problem of their existence *qua* potential (above discussed) can be then disregarded.

XVIII

ASPECTS OF UNITY IN CONCENTRATION

OUR purpose in describing the wider context of a project's enactment was to see whether the unity of the single act could be stretched to cover the self as we commonly think of it. And now it does appear indeed that the unity of the present act strikes roots back into the past and seizes it, binding it into its own unity; or (an alternative form of statement) that the mnemic matters concentrate into the present project for the purpose of its enactment. This complex has a structure, or perhaps several overlapping structures. It might be a good plan, therefore, if we called a halt here, and catalogued the unities that we find in the act-self. And for this purpose the Aristotelian 'causes' may well be applied. It will be hardly necessary to repeat here that these are not 'causes' in the sense of full determinants, but factors in the situation in which free activity takes place. This freedom is not itself numbered among the four 'causes', however proper it may be to insist that it alone is really the cause.

(i) *Unity of Material Cause*

If we consider the unity of the self in a single moment, the material cause can hardly be made a principle of the unity; for the material *qua* material is rather the principle of a plurality which the unity is able to dominate. No doubt any material plurality which enters into a formal unity must be made up of constituents which are amenable to grouping within the formal pattern, and some forms can be imposed on that matter only which has already received sub-forms; as the form of a Commonwealth (if that is a form) can be imposed on physical matter in so far only as the latter has received the sub-form of 'human being' in a plurality of examples. But we are discussing what makes the central unity or unit of selfhood, and it is irrelevant here to ask what material sub-unities and orders that implies. No one in fact supposes that the materials, i.e. the events that go to make up mental life, are completely without order or orders apart from the single unity of the self; selfhood is not like the magnet which grasps and interconnects an otherwise unorganised mass of iron-filings. It may indeed be that there is this much resemblance: the interconnexion of the filings is not independent of the action of the magnet, and the groups, complexes, etc., of psychical matters are not independent of the central unity; they do not pre-exist the unit whose system they serve. But this is not our problem, and we will not discuss it.

But if the 'material cause' has nothing to contribute to the principle of unity while we confine our attention to the single moment, it is otherwise when we embrace the tract of time. Hume, whose atomism dispensed him from considering formal causes, supposed that we mean by the unity of a self little but the unity or rather identity of its matter through time. The mnemic matter of what we call an individual mind has some constancy through its history. Some may pass into oblivion or at least be effectively swamped by later acquisitions, for if there are not losses, there certainly are additions; yet our eyes are not always looking out for difference within a given area—it is sometimes the identities that strike us; as sometimes we note the mark of passing years in physical appearance, and sometimes prefer to see the constancy of feature beneath the ravages of time.

Hume was right in concluding that material identity, taken by itself, would yield only a relative unity—no more many than one, no more one than many, except in one respect arbitrarily selected. We have pursued this theme already almost *ad nauseam* and will not repeat. By itself, then, material identity gives nothing worth having; and yet it is the necessary condition of any identity whatsoever. The mnemic matters are the deposit of former experience and action, and were it not that they had a tendency to re-present themselves, if they were not there for the act of concentration to find, our own past would not be for us, so that no question could arise of our actively appropriating and voluntarily continuing it; and this consideration covers both the representative and the dynamic functions of memory, both 'contents' and 'tendencies'.

(ii) *Unity of Formal Cause*

The formal cause *is* unity, by its very definition; so that here we can consider unity in the single act, as well as over a longer stretch of time.

(*a*) In the single act. This is the citadel of unity, and its formal cause is the structure of the act, embracing the set of relations between background and project (concentration) and between project entertained and project enacted (realisation). This has been enough described above. Here it is to be noted that the unity of this pattern (like the identity of mnemic matter) would be no more than *a* pattern of sequence to be found in the forward flow of process, were it not experienced to be the form of the voluntary act, and the form without which that act cannot be conceived.

(*b*) In several acts. In so far as there are many voluntary acts, there is a formal identity between them all; for the act has an unalterable structure. Yet this structure is specialised into several sub-forms—those which are predominantly practical, predominantly theoretical, etc., and these can be at several 'levels' (*vide supra*); though as the level sinks, they tend to lose their speciality and merge in the common form. In so far as there is a common form visible even in the specialised forms, and in so far as there is a limit to the number of these themselves, a certain formal identity accrues to the self throughout life.

(*c*) Over a span of life. It is perhaps possible to talk of a form exemplified not in the single act but in the succession of acts one upon another, if there are certain rhythms or sequences to be observed here. There is, for example, the alleged behaviour-cycle, proceeding from the discovery of dissatisfaction, through diagnosis of its cause and prescription of its remedy, to action for its removal, with the result of temporary quiescence. Such systems by their recurrence imprint a certain uniformity on life; and—like the single cycle from birth to death, and the repeated cycle from sleep to wakefulness, and many others, less obvious, to be found in psychological treatises—are referable to bodily causes, that is to say, to the necessary pattern of activity from which all others are outgrowths (*vide supra*, p. 207). But these are not formal causes of voluntary activity as such, but rather stand outside it, guide it in spite of itself, sometimes interfere with it, sometimes are profoundly modified by it themselves. Or again, volition may consciously adopt these structures, model its plans upon them and assist them. Is not this a clue to their nature? They may be made a part of conscious teleology; but otherwise are they not the blind teleology of the subconscious will, presenting themselves sometimes as more, sometimes as less external to the conscious will? If so, they are the low-level analogues of final causality, and should be discussed under that head; since the blind striving of the subconscious will seems to be for the fulfilment and maintenance of the vital pattern. Yet the distinction between formal and final causality is notoriously difficult; in so far as the pattern aimed at is necessary in order that the being of which it is characteristic should be at all, we may say that it is formal as well as final, or rather the former than the latter, final causality belonging to those variable outgrowths and modifications which arise for the sake of it. Yet these formal and final causalities belong as such to the lowest level of the will and almost to biology; and as they appear external to the conscious will, belong to the material causes of the latter. We here come up against the dialectic of the levels of will, their identity and their distinctness. This has been dealt with and need not be repeated.

(iii) *Unity of Final Cause*

(*a*) In the single act. First among final causes is the project itself, for the unity of the act both makes and depends upon that of the project. The project is marked off from all else by being the aim of an (incipient) act; the act can be one act because what is so marked off has an internal coherence that makes it the possible intention of a single enactment. The project can be unitary because it is abstract, and its detail is therefore not infinite. What I will is always *such* an effect, and this 'suchness' can be exhausted. No doubt in order to become actual this 'such' must qualify an actual set of events, and that is what I intend. But I assume that it can do this—can provide itself with a matter that will support it; the detail of this matter, which in fact is always perhaps infinite, I do not intend.

(*b*) The single (least) project even in the moment has a background of further projects. It is seldom enacted for itself alone; and beside the project for the sake of which it is enacted consciously, there are others which just make themselves felt as allowing, welcoming, questioning the immediate project from the point of view of their own interest. These indeed are the correlatives of the mnemic matters, projected on to the screen of the future and expressed as virtual intentions. In the moment of act, trusting the mnemic mechanism and our own past choices (so many as are still uncancelled by later decisions), we assume that the guidance of our semi-conscious mind is to be trusted, and that we should be actively choosing (had we leisure to run over it) all that this semi-conscious mind suggests to be our choice: a mass of projects dimly descried at present, and requiring perhaps an indefinite future for their execution. And so not only an indefinite future, but also an indefinite past enters into the final causality of the present act; the future as the sphere of our many projects, the past as the feld in which all these have been seen, experimented with, adopted. To will the single project is, for a rational will, to place it in the system of a future which we intend, and claim for ours. To intend this future is to adopt the past, in which that future was bit by bit projected. We make that venture for which Descartes required divine assurance, and trust our memory to tell us what we were; not only so, we take her word for it that what we were we are, that what we intended we intend. We cannot claim the future without admitting the claim of the past; not the whole of our past as it fell out, but so much of it as is the effective organ for the grasping of the future we intend.

We may speak of a totality of our intentions, since there are many that make themselves felt and are adopted by more or less implicit choice. In this totality is there a unity? Or is it an aggregate simply? In fact there seem to be several unities.

First, there is the unity imposed by reference to the single project actually willed here and now. It is only in so far as they have reference to this project that they enter into the act. But the unity given to them by concentration on this one point is of a purely formal kind. Some are subserved by it, some are kept waiting by it, and so on. These relations are extremely various.

Secondly, there is the unity of a single teleological system. This may be more or less actual; our aims may or may not form a practicable—let alone a rationally ordered—whole. We may have a more or less developed system of general ideals or rules, and these again may have more or less actual influence on the form of our particular projects.

Thirdly, there is the unity imposed by our organic needs and physical basis, the unity of the root from which all our intentions spring, however tangled and confused they become in their remoter branches; the unity of whatever system and pattern of our being we in fact take for granted and everywhere impose; for the 'necessary' system of the body obtains many accretions, and habit becomes second nature.

What is the relation of these three to the act of freedom? The first unity is directly conferred by the act, and is the fact of concentration seen under the aspect of finality. We do not find a single project *in vacuo* a sufficient claim on action; it must stand its ground in the whole company of our (virtual) projects. The free act is the active choice of it in such company.

The second belongs to freedom under its aspect of teleological reason; the third returns to that borderland of the rational and the sub-rational, the final and the formal, which we dealt with under the last-named 'cause'.

(c) Teleological unity over a stretch of time. We have already seen that the narrowness of the present moment forces us to use the past (by the channel of more or less implicit memory) as our sensorium for that future which in the present moment we envisage. And this means that we in fact continue in the lines our past resolves have drawn for us. But the negative fact of inability to revise all our decisions at once is not the sole cause for teleological continuity, as though we regarded them as makeshifts and quite expected to have to reverse them entirely if we had time to overhaul them. The possibility of learning depends on the principle that, other things being equal, we trust our past judgments; the possibility of growth in wisdom of choice, on the principle that we trust our past decisions; so that we are bound to accept the most part of our past, and always do so. We have dealt with this above (pp. 193 ff).

How is this related to Freedom? As the necessary precondition of its advance, and its effective attainment of ends above the lowest. It shares, then, the privileged status of the free act *qua* rational. It belongs to rational freedom to have *some* past.[1]

(iv) *Unity of Efficient Cause*

The *efficiens* has as its mark to pre-exist the effect and to be complete and to be 'in act'. Well then, it may be said, to seek the efficient cause of the act of freedom is either to deny that freedom is free, or else to ask for a transcendent substance, or perhaps both.

This conclusion need not follow. If freedom is to be free, we must certainly demand (a) that the *efficiens* be not outside the self, (b) that it be not a total determinant. But if these conditions be satisfied, it does seem reasonable to try to meet that common sense which demands an agent for an act; and intuition, i.e. introspection, seems to reveal something of the sort.

The *efficiens*, then, must be declared to be the immediately past act. The man who comes to act is always (*vide supra*, p. 206) in some 'active state', he is concentrated in some direction or another; the vital movement is continuous in some sense, even though it proceeds by spasms.

The unity of the *efficiens* may be considered in two ways: (a) in the single moment, (b) over the tract of time.

(a) The unity of the *efficiens* in the single moment. If this could be claimed to be absolute, it would mean that the mind's life is a completely one-track affair, so that at any moment it is set in a single direction; the point from which a new concentration started would always be indeed a single point. It would mean that the mind moves in a single line from concentration to concentration.

---

[1] Here is again the paradox of growth. Our early years develop rationality, and by the time they reach it, have a considerable past in a scale rising up to the present.

This cannot be made out. Apart from the evident fact that we must dissipate in order to concentrate—must relax concentration in order to allow all sorts of mnemic 'evidence' to make itself felt—we cannot even maintain that the points between which we dissipate are themselves single concentrations. At its lower levels we know that will undoubtedly collects itself at many points to perform at once many operations. At the most, we can establish the principle that the higher the concentration, the more unitary; that higher concentrations either are closely connected and tend into one, or else the one depresses the other and drives it to a subconscious level. There is undoubtedly a tendency to simplification, and this is sufficient to provide the new act with a determinate starting-point; it is from a will-state that we proceed to an act of will.

It is odd how any coexistence of will-acts is felt by our imaginations to be an infringement of personal unity. Perhaps this arises through the simple dialectical process, which identifies the self with the *efficiens*, and proceeds to conclude: if the *efficiens* is several at once, there are several selves. Yet in truth there is no more difficulty about different contemporary acts, than there is about different successive acts. The self identified with the act *a* is aware of the past act *b* as his own and as conditioning his present act. And the self identified with the act *a* is aware of the (present) act *b* as his own and as conditioning his present act *a*. In fact, no doubt, what we are aware of is always done; the self in act *a* is aware of the self in act *b* as having acted up to the point which the process *b* has now reached, and *vice versa*. Well, but the self in act *a* may not be well informed of the self in *b*'s proceedings. Granted; but equally there may be a failure of awareness about a *b* that is past. Memory is not infallible; the unity of the self through its several acts is not complete in the sense that there are no disconnexions between any act and any other act.—It is easy enough to make these elucidations; and yet the imagination is devoted to the idea that the identity of the self is the identity of one person that puts on successively several suits of clothes; it cannot be satisfied, if he has to wear two suits at once.

In fact, then, the *efficiens* is the system of act to which the new act stands immediately related, and constitutes the act-situation in which it takes place. This situation is partly constituted by completed acts, partly by acts of which the process is contemporary with the new act, in the manner above suggested. The unity of this system is not the simplicity of a single act, and it is irrational to make it the principal ground for affirming the unity of the self. This is better sought in (1) some general teleological unity of the whole pattern of the self's acts, (2) the concentration of the whole system on particular projects, whether these concentrations take place successively or contemporarily.

(b) The unity of the *efficiens* over a tract of time. Since we have already disposed of the one-track will, this unity can only be the continuity of vital process. There never is a time when an act has to build itself on no will-situation; the will may recede into the merely bodily area, but never ceases to act (*vide supra*, p. 207).

The givenness of some *efficiens* is a precondition of any act of will; we know will only as advance from will-state to fresh act, neither can we conceive otherwise. The mystery of the origin of a new life, or self, is hidden from us. We know that lower levels of will have given rise to a will-situation by the time that any rudiment of conscious will can act. The origin of a new train of conscious will is inconceivable to us. One could write a Kantian Antinomy on Traducianism and Creationism. It is not worth while.

(v) *Successive Concentrations not a Mutually External Series*

What right have we to speak of that 'continuity of process' by which we define the action of the *efficiens* through time? Have not we found the unity of will to be concentrated at a point? Can continuity—in a strictly metaphysical view—mean any more than that the present act had predecessors serially related to it?

From the previous discussion we can cull the following propositions:

(1) There is real unity in that act which raises a project-entertained to a project-enacted.

(2) This unity takes in, as its necessary periphery, an (implicitly) intended future and an (implicitly) remembered past.

(3) If the future is intended and the past remembered, that means that a future is anticipated, consisting of acts which will be mine, but are not my present act; and a past believed, as consisting of acts which were mine, but are not my present act. These acts were, or (if they occur) will be, as much acts as the present act, it has no privilege. And so we proceed to the view of a self displayed in time and actualised serially in acts outside one another, of which the present act happens to be one.

The third division of this progress seems to be as necessary as the two first. And it seems to break up, or escape from, the unity which is established in (1). The unity expressed in (2) appears after all merely a subjective unity due to the viewing of the rest of the series from the viewpoint constituted by one term of the series. We may concede that the series is bound together by a very intimate set of relations between its terms; but each act, each concentration, is itself and they are all outside one another.

To this we shall reply: The phrase 'merely a subjective unity' will not pass. It is about subjective unity, i.e. the unity of a subject, that we are talking and no other unity or discreteness has any interest for us here. We have realised from the beginning that it is only within the subject as agent that unity is to be sought. Now when we think of the series of acts displayed in time, none of them possessing a privilege over another, we are taking up the attitude *either* of a second person reconstructing his neighbour's supposed inner history *or* of one recollecting (or anticipating) several of his own acts together *or* of one viewing his acts—the present act included—from the imaginary viewpoint of a fly on the ceiling. We say 'imaginary', for this view cannot in fact be achieved; we

simply imagine a group of acts as displayed in memory and assert that one of
these is our present act. But the assertion remains purely nominal and exterior,
the presentness cannot be incorporated into the act to which it is alleged to
belong.

In short, acts which are viewed as all on a level and side by side are being
seen in the form in which they enter into the concentration which is another act.
It is the concentration which gathers them and places them side by side. Side-
by-sideness, in fact, belongs to acts *qua* ingredients of another act through
memory or anticipation, and not *qua* acts in their own right. No doubt in so far
as acts become ingredients in another in the mode of explicit memory, there is
assigned to them a ghost of self-being—we are aware that in their time they
were each *the act*, in which other acts could appear only as ingredients, never as
equals. And, if we go further and try to recover the self-being of the past act,
we can dramatise ourselves into the position of that past act; it becomes a
pseudo-present, all else becomes its past and future. We are then, of course,
aware that this pseudo-present is a *pseudo*-present, that there is another present
which is our true present; and yet this brings us no nearer to an ability of rank-
ing the pseudo-present and the real present side by side in one series. If we
attempt it, what happens? We simply have recourse to a third imaginary
present, for which these two 'presents' are reduced to the level of ingredients.
But in that case, *as represented side by side*, they lose their presentness.

A concentration, as such, is the focal point of the whole world, and two
focal points cannot be realised as focal. To grasp two, we must concentrate
them in a third, and then the two cease to be focal. We can then, of course, take
a fourth for all three, and so *ad infinitum*. Now the business of 'science' in the
ordinary sense is to eliminate the observer, i.e. the focal point, the concentration, and to consider things abstractly as matters for concentration. But for this
reason, such science abstracts from metaphysical reality, which can be seen only
in the concentration, i.e. the act.

Is this argument heading for solipsism? By no means. We believe in the
reality of each act which enters into the concentration of another act. It was,
is, or will be, itself an act. But our business is to distinguish between mutual
externality, manyness, and true unity. The world is substances; there is a
difference between the relation between two substances, and the relation between elements grasped together in the unity of one substance. Elements only
enter into a unity in so far as they enter into a concentration. It is the ghosts of
the past, degraded to ingredients, which enter into the present concentration.
Viewed as acts, the several acts which become ingredients in a fresh act are
simply external to one another, and to attribute to them *qua* acts the unity
which they have as ingredients is to commit with a vengeance the fallacy of
projection. The external side-by-sideness of acts is no real mutual order; it is an
abstract scheme of correlation between the orders of matters in several actual
or possible concentrations; it is *ens rationis*. Substances are really related by
entering each into the others, under the form of ingredient.

To conclude: we have no need, therefore, to say that memory and (true) anticipation imply a real external order of series which, if taken seriously, sets aside the internal order of ingredience in a concentration. What they in fact imply is a mutuality of 'internal' order. The mutuality is not indeed strict. If I remember an act, it does not involve that, in the past act, I anticipated what is now my present act, nor even that there was a real possibility that I might have done so; but only that the past act had its own ingredients, some of which also enter into my present act, and so forth.

Therefore substantial unity is to be found in concentration, and the past and future have unity only as ingredients in a present. The past was, the future is not yet, only the present is, and it embraces them according to its own manner.

It is easy enough to say: Yes, but all the same the several concentrations do co-exist somehow, and it is only because they do so already that they can enter into one another, or side by side enter into a third. Well, that depends upon the sense we wish to give to 'co-exist'. What is co-existence, apart from interaction of any kind? It reduces to the conjunction 'AND' between two sentences, each asserting existence and each true. A is, and B is. But the co-existence of A and B is neither a temporal nor a spatial relation, unless they enter into one another, or both into a third.

We pause to recover the drift of this argument. It had been suggested that memory and anticipation imply that the self's past and future consist of acts external to one another and ranged in a series of equal terms, among which the present act appears as one. To this we have now replied: So far from this 'external series' being the most real articulation of acts, it is not in itself a series or articulation at all, but a form into which acts enter in becoming ingredients in a third, which is then the only actual focus. Complete (non-abstracted) reality when and where it is, is always a concentration. What was, was, no doubt, but it has no actual relation with the present except as entering into it.

(vi) *Continuity of Concentration*

We have established that it is useless to seek the continuity of the self through time simply in the series of acts as supposedly visible to the fly on the ceiling (even if we endow that insect with powers of telepathic introspection). But neither can we be content to find it simply in the entry of former acts into the present while it is present. For, if we allow ourselves to think of acts which, *qua* concentrations, are absolutely distinct existences, their entry *qua* ingredients into one another will not give us a continuous self. For the concentrations *qua foci*, are simply present, there is no continuity between them; their identity is generic, not numerical, and consists purely in the sameness of the material they concentrate. We need also a fluxion of the *foci* into one another, so that what we have is a focalising process with nodal points which we call *foci*, rather than a series of *foci* externally related.

But can we make this out? In our original description of the *efficiens*, we went no further than to say that every act has an immediate background consisting of the directly previous act or acts, by which is determined the voluntary attitude out of which the new act arises, and which could be treated as its 'efficient cause'. But we were careful to reserve the independence of the act which emerges on this basis; and so it might appear to be, after all, a 'distinct existence', into which the previous acts enter indeed as ingredients, but remain *qua* acts and *foci* perfectly external to it.

We were restricted by the topic of 'efficient causality'. For this involved thinking of a single effect, or element of form, as the product of something previously actual and separate from itself; and this excluded the thought of a continuous activity passing through phases of greater and less concentration. Having taken the single concentration as our 'effect', we were bound to treat it as a unit; and justifiably so, for it can be distinguished from its antecedents in a certain respect, viz. by its project and by the structure of concentration around the project.

But if we put such ideas out of our heads and try to describe the process of mental life over a period of continuous consciousness, there are two schemes which appear equally applicable and mutually complementary. There is the scheme of the 'many', which we have been working with, and the scheme of the 'one', which sees concentration as continuous, as an activity which specialises itself from moment to moment in acts.

Introspection, like every other activity of the mind, attends to the marking of differences within the field it has taken for its sphere; and so a number of people taken by a psychologist into his laboratory and told to introspect for concentration-data of a sort indicated to them, will find these in particular situations which contrast with others where they are absent. Yet in a conscious state of the utmost relaxation compatible with consciousness, there is always concentration because there is always attention; the mind is always brought to some sort of a 'point', for attention is never without activity. Active concentration is a constant factor, which varies in respect of (*a*) intensity and (*b*) direction. If we are examining (*a*), we are inclined to oppose activity to inactivity; if (*b*), we find it equally natural to take activity for granted while we observe its several objectives.

It is not possible, therefore, to regard successive concentrations as simply distinct existences succeeding at intervals of time. They overlap, and not merely by accident. When attention passes from one thing to another, there is a brief concentration which holds them both, for else how should it be seen that the one is (however superficially) more worthy of attention or pursuit than the other? Such a concentration may be shallow, and when our senses have received a new and sharp impression, the switching of attention to it may appear to be automatic. And automatic it is, if this means simply that we had no real choice in the moment not to have attended. But the 'automatism' works through a concentration; there is an act of mind in which (on the superficial level represented by the activity of that moment) the claims of the new object to attention appear manifestly superior. This is taken for granted, it is voted *nemine contra*; but unless the object successfully claimed attention, we should be unaware of it, like the ticking of the clock which is cut out from the start for its unimportance.[1]

Further evidence of the continuity of concentration can be obtained, not this time from the succession of acts but from their subdivision. If I start with a wide project, e.g. to construct a garden fence, I concentrate on that; but now attention must be focussed on detailed means to my end, to the buying of wood and nails and the digging of holes for the posts. But the principal project never completely vanishes nor sinks into subconsciousness; and so one concentration can bracket together many concentrations.

It seems, then, that concentratedness runs on continuously. Admittedly, it must go underground sometimes, we are not continuously conscious; but we have already found reason to suppose that will itself goes underground. And if the continuity of concentration is the character of will as we know it, we can but suppose some analogue in its subconscious operations.

But let us remember that the stream of concentration can be divided at any given time. Thus it will not do to find in the continuity of concentration the very unity of the self. It is simply a formal element of unity, like any of the others we have tabulated. We can at the most say that continuous lines of concentration link every particular act to a system which is ultimately grounded in the more or less fixed rhythm of the bodily pattern. From this the lines of concentration run out, but may then branch, re-unite, or break off leaving no successor. But still there is continuity somewhere, anyhow in the bodily pattern, which does not break off till death.

We have justified the thesis we proposed—that if we take a line of continuous will-concentration, the dialectic of the 'one and the many' may be applied to it. We may treat it as terms (will-acts) in a series bound together by relations of successivity. Or we may recognise that the succession of one 'act' upon another is itself willed, so that the change in will-direction appears to be the characteristic expression of will. And then it becomes natural to elevate this succession-principle into an hypostasis, a continuous activity, which specialises itself in its successive forms which are 'acts of will'. Either then we have a series of modes to one hypostasis or a series of terms interrelated by a relation of will-succession. The two schemes are equally right and equally wrong. The unity-in-plurality which will actualises cannot be exhibited by any scheme of terms and relations, but only be intuited *in re*. It is not a logical order, it does not arise through the dominance of the one factor or of the other.

In so far as it belongs to will-acts to have a past,[2] it belongs to them to have a past with which they are continuous in this manner, and this is one of the ways in which we observe the unity of the self.

[1] *vide supra*, p. 135   [2] *vide supra*, p. 215

XIX

THE UNITY OF UNITIES

(i) *Id quod Unum est*

In our search for unity in the self, we have found only too many answers, and still have to ask, what is *the* unity of a self? We have traced so many unities, that is, elements of unitary form; and each one, while we have looked at it, has tended to impress us as *the* unity of the self. And yet none can maintain the impression. We have found their focus in the act on which they all bear, and, as subserving which, they are mutually complementary. But the self is none of them, nor is it the sum of them; it is that ENS which they characterise, the unit of whose aspects these unities are the abstractions.

When we are asking to be shown the unitary self, what are we, in fact, asking for? That there is diversity in the self we know before we start. We have been presented with a wealth of unity-forms in this diversity; so subtle, so multiform, is the web of the self's structure. And we have seen that this system is not just one way of grouping the multiform data; it is the grouping through and in which they come to bear to determine real activity. It is in so far as the system—material, formal, final, historical—meets in a situation, that this situation is one of will; or, to speak more properly, it is in so far as the force of will orders the multiplicity in this pattern, that will-acts can and do take place. But now what is the self? Not this structure, but the will that wills and lives through and in this structure. We here return to the place from which we started. We agreed that in the nature of the case self and will must be indescribable, except by metaphors, which are always wrong. And therefore we were driven to turn our attention towards the structure, which can be described to some extent. We find that structure to be systematic and continuous, though not fixed; and it is filled and vivified by a will itself continuous, forming it and formed by it. This will, taken in its extension, we call the self; in its focussed expression, the will.

It cannot be too often said that the function of the intellect is always to mark significant distinctions; and from this it follows that if we want to become aware of the self as a unit, we shall be always baffled if we look within the self. If we take the self for our field, we can find nothing but significant distinctions within the self; we may grasp the elements of a pattern one by one, and even see, by a constructional synthesis, how they supplement one another and are ordered towards a unity. But it is another thing to be aware of that unity in its unitary character, to intuit the *unum*, and this cannot in the nature of the case be done by exploring the self; we never get beyond the 'unity of composition' when we see distinct elements and see their mutual adaptation and relation. We may then pass on to regard the form of unity which binds them, the pattern into which they enter, as a quasi-hypostasis, which we mark off from the plurality which it organises. But the self is certainly not a distinguishable element within its own field; the unitary being of the self is not an aspect of the self, but the self expressed in all its aspects.

Hence the inevitable and even salutary illusion which arises when we look within the self—we are convinced that something essential has been omitted, the very thing indeed, and so we find ourselves assuming a transcendent unit, the self in itself, the pure subject, unanalysable and related externally to the data which we have been industriously analysing. Empiricists then complain that this self is nothing but the ghost of the total empirical self viewed externally and taken in the lump; and they are right (with a reservation on the sense of the word 'externally'). But their inference is wrong. They say: 'We analyse the self, and you admit the analysis; you only save the self from disintegration by re-stating the still unanalysed datum as a metaphysical *Unding* transcending the analysis.'

We reply: the illusion of the transcendence is indeed an illusion. But to appeal from the analysed 'many' to the pre-analysis 'one' is right and necessary. Analysis applies the form of thought aRb, which rules out the apprehension of unity from the start; and any Hegelian challenge to achieve a synthesis transcending the divisions with those divisions as our data, demands the impossible. Such a synthesis can only show the mutual adaptation of elements and aspects; everything is there except the one thing needful, *das geistige Band*. We must shift our ground, therefore; aRb must symbolise a distinction-and-relation of terms one of which is the self, the other something which totally excludes it; and that can only be another self or quasi-self (every substance which exists as itself being a quasi-self, i.e. some analogue of the self). As soon as we do this we are in no difficulty at all as to the intuition of the self's unity. When I experience myself as coming into action against another self, substantial unity is something that I am aware of.

We shall here, of course, be accused of the most ludicrous naïveté, in hoping to put so open a piece of psychological legerdemain upon the public. Naturally, if one does not look for distinctions, one does not observe them; if we treat any bundle of things as a unit for the purposes of a particular argument and place it under a single term and turn our attention to its external relations only, we shall find it easy enough to take its substantial identity for granted.

This objection, it will be noted, simply reverses our argument. We said: the form of division precludes the apprehension of unity. They retort: the form of unity precludes the apprehension of division. Very well; and we may allow that it does. But what follows? The objectors are, in fact, simply re-asserting the absolute nominalism of the positivist position. They say: in so far as we place a group under the subjective, verbal form of unity we group it as a unity; there is no other awareness of unity than this.

It is this position that we have all along contested; we have claimed that there is an intuition of the unitary self as unit. We are not abandoning this but saying merely that this intuition, in order to be realised, must be allowed a thought-form appropriate to it. This intuition does not in fact arise wherever this thought-form is used, but only when myself falls under it. To see a star one may indeed require a telescope, a microscope will not do instead. If we saw the star whichever way we looked, we might justly suppose it to be painted on the lens. But if we see the star by looking in one direction and one alone, the suspicion is unfounded. We do not mean by the intuition of the self's unity an unawareness of distinctions, but an awareness of unitary selfhood; and this positive awareness is not present when I treat a bundle as a logical unit, even though there is a complication here through the slight tendency of the mind to hypostatise, i.e. endow with selfhood whatever it grasps in one.

But about this we can make the following points:

(a) Hypostatisation is a positive business and does not consist in unawareness of distinctions or treatment of many characteristics as one *characteristic*. It adds something above all characteristics and this something probably comes from somewhere; why not by transference from the self?

(b) Hypostatisation can be seen through. I can by attention realise that this hypostatical character is not a datum but a projection. The self's hypostasis, by contrast, stands solid and claims to be 'perceived'.

Even if our position could be granted so far, it might still seem pretty weak. Are we to rest all on the perception of a unique positive unity about which no more can be said; which can be grasped in the lump only, and (inevitably) disappears if we try to analyse it? One might well protest: this awareness of a unitary characteristic may be a fact, but if it stands by itself and defies investigation, then almost any explanation may be equally well offered for it, or none; and it seems excessive to claim that it demands of us one metaphysic rather than another.

To this we reply, that the impossibility of analysing this unity is only asserted in a certain sense. We can indeed analyse that in which the unity is perceived; what we cannot do is to attend to the intuitable unitariness of it while we are applying the analysis to its parts. But when we analyse, we are met with a structure of a very close-knit kind, manifesting an order concentrating on a point, and being the necessary background for an event of unique metaphysical importance—free activity. This being so, we can say that the analysis, though it cannot exhibit the unity, accounts for it in the only way in which any analysis could, and so affords the only justification possible for our acceptance of the intuition, beyond the force of that intuition itself.

When it is said that the self is that unit of which we are directly aware in an act of mind which opposes its own self to another, it is not meant that all the analogical descriptions of the self which in such an act arise by way of comment, are to be accepted. We may find ourselves commenting on the perception of self with the crude figure of a perfectly constant group of physical characteristics enduring through time and yielding perfectly regular reactions. Such an analogical commentary may have its use at the moment, to point our awareness of the self's permanence; which may he all that is then demanded or indeed relevant. But as an account of the nature of that permanence it is worthless. If we wish to examine the modes in which the unity of the self is expressed, we must turn to analysis of the type which we have been attempting in what precedes.

When, in fact, the nature of the self's unity comes up for discussion, it is commonly with a view to some particular question: for instance, the sense in which a man is now morally answerable for a crime committed long ago, when he was not what he now is. Any such question is a question about a particular aspect of the self's unity; and cannot be answered from a general assertion of the reality, supreme importance, etc., of that unity, but only by reference to those parts of the analysis which are directly relevant. We can never, then, be content with asserting unity in general; we must discover what sort or aspect of unity is involved. There are questions which can be raised which can only be answered by denying that the self has unity in the sense that would be relevant to the point at issue.

(ii) *Dialectic of the Self*

We have used the dilemma: either we look into the self, and so analyse; or else we oppose the self to another, and so take it as one. This dilemma does not in fact express a complete disjunction. There are many other possibilities, and their actual occurrence in our minds creates a dialectic of the self and misleads us from the true path of discovery.

It was noted above that analysis of the self leaves us dissatisfied, and that the ghost of the unity we are dividing returns to haunt our minds in the form of the transcendent self which stands above all analysis. And this indeed is the natural form of illusion when we take up the attitude of thorough-going analysis, so that all constituents are set by themselves and none can claim to be the home of substantial totality. But we may stop short of this; we may leave the bulk of the self unexamined, and content ourselves with picking out a single constituent or group of constituents. It is then natural for the ghost of totality to take refuge in what remains, oblivious of the fact that the same principle of analysis which takes apart these details is capable of taking apart all the rest. The residual whole is then 'the self'. In practical activity it is never of interest to us to consider the thoroughgoing application of analysis; it is sufficient always to attend to a single desire or set of desires, to one pair of rival projects, or whatever it be; which thus become my objects, while the rest of my (unexamined) being remains subject.

Here again the formula aRb applies. a is the (residual) self, b the selected constituent and R the relation. And hence the form of thought which treats the self as a substance actively engaged about an (interior) object; and this might be the form of Berkeley's thought, as contrasted with that of Hume. Or perhaps Berkeley belongs more to the 'transcendent subject' school. It is difficult to tell.

Probably there is always a certain contamination of the two; for once the believer in the transcendent subject relates it to its (interior) object by any conceivable relation, he will have to degrade it to the position of residual subject. For the relation, to be conceivable, must be one that obtains within the structure of the many-one self.

This form of thought (we said) gives rise to a dialectic; for the division between the residual self and its interior object can be drawn in an infinity of places according to the direction of attention, or as the dialectic chases it from position to position. This dialectic must proceed for ever, until it is recognised that analysis is a universally-applicable formula and that unity belongs to the whole, not any residuum.

In so far as this form fits the mind in practical activity, it has a significance beyond the forms of merely theoretical dialectic. It is indeed true, as has already been remarked, that we can only call in question one of our intentions at a time; the rest we must take for granted as being stable, as constituting *our* character, *our* intentions, while we consider whether the intention we are criticising is to pass for *ours* or not. But this may lead to the illusion that the rest simply allow or disallow the criticised member, so that 'I will,' 'I choose' means simply 'the single desire is adopted by the many'. This is in fact false, as we have seen. 'I will' means something far more mysterious; it means 'as a total concentration into which all the relevant elements are drawn (so far as in me lies to draw them), *I will* this particular project'. The choice need not accept every other constituent already established in the self and present to consciousness—it may negate it, but it must take account of it.

The common-sense 'residual' self, in spite of its practical employment, cannot be taken seriously in a theoretical view, because it leaves out the present act—which it treats as a relation to the project, action, object of interest, etc., with which the self is at the moment concerned. Thus it leaves out what is most actual, most alive, most the self; and so it provokes a dialectical antithesis, which we can leave to the reader to construct for himself.

Can we perhaps find a 'best' dialectic of the self—one that is less unreal than any other? For to exclude all dialectic is to condemn the analytic view to the dead enumeration of the parts of a structure, and the total view to the recording of a single intuition. Whereas we should like to be able to read into intuition some articulation of structure, and into the structure some intuition of actual unity and of life. Well then, the most essential dialectic might be that which is concerned with the primary distinction within the self, and this distinction be found in the opposition of the circumference to the centre in concentration. For the very principle of the unity of the self is its focussing upon a point. We may, then, give preference to a dialectic of the three following positions:

(*a*) The self is all that is there for concentration, active in focussing itself in a new single act.

(*b*) The self is the central act or interest, active in collecting and exploiting the mnemic matters.

(c) The self is the form of activity, always there from moment to moment, active in grasping the mnemic multiplicity on the one hand, and the particular new projects on the other.

(iii) *First Experiment: Externalising the Objects*

There is a certain form which the dialectic always seems to employ, however we draw the distinction within the self. Always there re-appears an agent, something he is concerned with, and the act in which he deals with this thing. And it would be odd, if this scheme, so variously misapplied, had no place in which it properly belonged. As to the unitary agent, we have already seen what his proper place is; he is a totality which covers all the constituents of the self's life of action. But if so, the proper direction of his act must be outwards and the matter with which it is concerned must lie in entities other than himself.

Suppose then that we make this whole scheme the framework of our analysis. Will it be possible then, perhaps, to get an analysis which embraces the thought of totality without being dialectical? This may not be possible, but it seems worth considering. The principal reform will be to abandon the interior object for the exterior object. We found ourselves distinguishing projects from objectives, by a distinction equivalent to that between propositions and facts. And no doubt it is proper to distinguish the subjective intention from the actual effect intended, since the effect may not occur, or may fall out otherwise. This distinction is necessary, but it is no excuse for treating the project as that at which we aim. In truth this is always a reality, supposedly destined to be what the project means. The same type of re-statement, applied to the mnemic matters, will make of them references to particular past facts, to states of affairs believed actual, to supposed general characteristics of the world, or (if they are habitual intentions) to effects or classes of effects which we mean to produce.

The self, according to this description, 'contains' nothing but acts of cognition and will, virtual or actual or tentative. The 'material constituents' vanish; they reduce to mere contents of intention and belief inseparable from the acts themselves. It will be still necessary to place mental images, descriptive or symbolical. As events, they may be located in the body; the mind of course it is that perceives them and refers their 'meanings' to the remembered past, the believed present, or the projected future, i.e. to the outside world. The self is a bundle of concernments with that outside world. These concernments are at various levels of rationality (explicitness) and actuality. One or few of them are in the state of being present choosings; the remainder condition the choice in the many ways that have already been described.

If, on this view, the self appears as a bundle of mutually-conditioning acts, which, though interpenetrating, remain a plurality, this will be due to the piecemeal way in which the mind grasps the past, anticipates the future, and intends effects. We may, if we choose, attempt to treat this as accidental. The business of the mind, we will say, is to grasp the continuous past, forecast the equally continuous future, and intend a total scheme of behaviour which shall be continuous. A mind capable of doing this immediately would have one memory-content, one anticipation, and one project, though each one would be a one-and-many. The acts of remembering, anticipating, willing, would each be no more than one; they would derive their manyness from the diversity within their continuous objects, their unity from their concentration at a point; the point at which memory and anticipation focus, and from which issues will, modifying and extending its project on the basis of their information. The history of change in such a self would be nothing but the gradual lengthening and altering perspective of the past, the gradually shifting prospect of the future, the continuous act by which the project of behaviour is developed in consideration of their continuous modification. About such an 'intuitive self'—to adopt Kant with a difference—it would never occur to us to ask whether it is truly one or not. It has the only unity that there is, apart from the unity of an indivisible point: viz. the unity which focusses many in oneness, and out of oneness projects many. The many that it focusses and projects are deployed in time, and the focussing and projecting are always at a moment of time; and so the multiplicity has a temporal form both subjectively and objectively.

In fact the self is not so; the mind proceeds by separate acts of grasping and projecting. The description we have given is dialectical. And yet it is not a piece of pure nonsense; and the reason it is not, is that it describes a real aspect of the mind abstracted. To some extent the mind is able to rise above the piecemeal manner of its own operations; for although I cannot grasp the world in one continuous awareness nor project my action in one continuous plan, I know that what I grasp does, and what I project must, add up to make a continuity of fact. And this knowledge of mine makes incomplete the statement that the mind is a series of separate reactions to a continuous actuality. The piecemeal working is, in a sense, a medium through which the awareness of continuity passes on its way to the projection of continuity. Thus the more we emphasise the outward action of the self, the more does the unity of that action come to light.

To return to the self of many acts—this new way of looking at things illuminates the 'interpenetration' of the acts; this appears now to be their entry into a unitary activity embracing them all. And yet this unity cannot be seized and brought before consciousness; it always lies just outside our reach. It is the principle which determines our acts' mutual conditioning of one another; and yet it is not a mere frame or system of relations which falls outside our intentional activity, but enters as an 'idea of reason' into the intention itself. This is most mysterious, perhaps, in the realm of project. For so far as apprehension is concerned, it is more easy to suppose that the elusive continuity belongs to the object in itself, not to our grasp of it; and that our consciousness partakes of that unity in so far as informed by it and reflecting it. But in the case of projection, the unity cannot belong to the object in itself, for the object is not in itself, but is to be what we shall make it; so that the unity, so far as it informs our projective activity, is 'placed' by our acts of intention apart from which it would not be. Thus we intend it, although we cannot grasp it in one; and it is a fact, however strange, that nothing we can grasp or express in one or present together before our minds, ever can adequately inform us of our whole actual intention, which makes itself felt only by obscure inhibition or support accorded to what is presented to the mind. And when we explore that support or inhibition, we drag into consciousness some other limited intention only; and once again there is that conditioning background, felt but not explored. (This is not to deny that the single objectives of single acts can be assessed *to some extent* on their single merits, or we should have no rational control of our lives whatever.)

So far as apprehension is concerned, it is easier to suppose that the elusive continuity belongs to the object itself. It is easier to suppose it, but it may be further from the truth. The somewhat Leibnitian trend of the argument will have prepared the reader for the conclusion that in full metaphysical rigour the continuity of the physical world in itself is *phenomenon bene fundatum* and no more. Reality so far as we know is *in* finite substances whose existence is indeed determined and qualified by the focussing of their neighbours in each one. But we know nothing of a real unity apart from that focussing, unless it is the unity of some other one focussing. So that the form of the world's continuity as apprehended is the form of a relation between the world (i.e. other substances) and the self. The world is to this extent a unity, that it is a plurality *such as* to be focussed as unity in any of its parts, and to be focussed in a given order. To explore further would exceed our present purpose; we must be content to state as probable the conclusion that the continuity implicit in apprehension cannot be referred to the objects apprehended, in themselves; like the continuity of what is intended, it belongs to the self or is not without the self. Here, then, the unity of apperception belongs. It needs to be paired with a 'unity of projection'; and is then the revelation of a formal identity of self through time.

What conclusion can we state, as the result of our experiment in externalising the objects of the self? The conclusion that the self is left as a very function of unity, whose life indeed proceeds in a pulsation of distinct beats, yet not so that the unity is removed.

(iv) *Second Experiment: Externalising the Acts*

When this point has been reached, a temptation is felt of proceeding to an apparent logical extreme. Cannot we somehow throw the whole weight of plurality upon the objects, so that the self remains simply identical, even through time? For time itself is a form of plurality. Can we not say that the self then and now differs from itself merely by relation to this and that, so that time is outside it? No; the self may be mere act, but it is not Pure Act; it exists in and as its active concernments with this and the other object or project. The timeless self is a mere logical 'pole' and empty form, a determinable, an hypostatised abstraction. The self is its own life, which has, but is not, enduring identity.

The dialectical plausibility of the rejected error arises as follows: We conceived of the self as a term related to other terms, and the 'focussing' of these terms in the first as a set of relations accidental to all the terms. But the externalising of the objects does not mean this, whatever else it means. It means rather the extension of the self over the universe, than the expulsion of relation to objects outside the confines of the self. Concern with objects, objects not internal now but external, remains the nature of the self.

If atomists and naturalistic empiricists wish to hypostatise the several moments or events of successive time, it is useful, as a dialectical antithesis, to frame a case for the hypostasis of the continual 'present', the 'now' of immediate consciousness. But this has a merely controversial value. Neither is by itself. What is, is not a third form of which these two are misrepresentations, but is the actuality having these two forms, itself not a form. The self's activity or actuality has always the aspects of continuous presence and of successivity; but the subject of these two properties is that totality of characters to which both belong and which, as a totality, is the object of a simple intuition (*vide supra*, p. 220). The distinguishable forms to be found within the totality can indeed be exhibited as mutually complementary, as a 'pattern', and so, two being taken, others can be found which in a sense mediate their union by exhibiting further relevant elements of the structure which is that union. But this does not mean that the two forms of 'continuous present' and 'successivity' have a mediating term in a further *temporal* form, for on this principle we should have to proceed *ad infinitum*. We can understand their union only by appreciating the structure of activity in which both find a place. To endow this activity with a further temporal form called duration or anything else is a dialectical paralogism. (The term 'duration' has of course its uses, in reminding us that the successivity of life is not the successivity of clocks. But this is a domestic issue inside successivity itself.)

It is time formally to answer the question asked some pages back (*supra*, p. 225). Can we, by externalising the objects, apprehend the unity of the self while detailing the pattern of its form? The answer is, as we expected, a negative. We can appear to do so only by externalising acts as well as objects, so reducing the self to a logical monad. The advantage of externalising the objects is the reduction of the self to acts. And this makes it easier to appreciate the organic interconnexion of the details of the pattern which a self exhibits.

(v) *Summary of Chapters on the Self*

We took over from the chapters on Will the doctrine of a voluntary act having a real and complex unity and capable of greater or less altitude in a scale of such acts. We proceeded to consider how the many acts of this kind cohere in one self, if indeed it is truly and metaphysically one. We considered first the physical basis of self, and saw how this provided a unity of the *terminus a quo*. For the many acts of will spring from a continuous implicit action which enacts the unceasing rhythm of physical life. The many free and explicit acts must develop themselves as marginal embroideries on this given theme.

Having observed by the way that such constraint upon freedom does not remove it but is the very condition for the exercise of the sort of freedom we can alone understand, we proceeded to see whether the many acts were united in their aim as well as in their starting-point. A certain intentional unity is imposed by natural environment, and also by the form of reason; but equally by habit and our tendency to follow still a line of purpose formerly adopted. Yet such intentional unities are incomplete and cannot yield *the* unity of a self.

If the many acts are not united by an overruling unity of project, we ask next whether they are united by the focussing of them all in each act successively. This hypothesis holds good; for in each act when it occurs a plurality of matters are found to be concentrated. These matters, until they are effectively concentrated in the present act, have an equivocal and ghostly existence; but they are media through which the past acts enter as ingredients into the present act.

After making a summary of aspects of unity in the concentration-self, grouped under the Aristotelian 'causes', we turn to the paradox of unity through time. Time exists only in the real present of each real being, and so the past acts and the present act are not a real mutually external series. The past acts exist only as ingredients in the present. Neither is the succession of acts upon one another completely *staccato*. The concentration which makes the act has phases of intensity and relaxation; the self is continuous activity though not a continuous act; the activity intensifies itself in each particular act.

Here again, then, we have two structures of unity. *The* unity of the self is neither the focussing of the many acts in the single act, nor is it the continuity of activity from one act to the next. Both belong to the unity of the self, which is neither. It is itself indescribable; it is not a structure or pattern but that which has these. A good reason is found for its elusiveness in the very form of thought. The unity of the self and its structural complication cannot be grasped in one; yet they imply and support one another. The unity is best seen when the self is opposed to external things, not to its own constituents. The experiment of developing this form of statement only results in a clearer apprehension of the thesis already established—that the self is a continuous intellective and creative activity which proceeds by concentration into successive particular acts. It is the substantial connexion provided by activity as such and studied under the name of will, which holds together the self as well as the act. For the act is not even as an act self-sufficient; its boundaries extend to embrace the totality of a self, which is thus metaphysically, and not just phenomenally or logically, one.

Armed, therefore, with such a description of the self we turn to the examination of substance in general, to which we have hoped that the self may provide us a clue.

EXAMINATION OF FINITE SUBSTANCE: GENERALISATION OF THE SUBSTANCE-FORMULA

XX

KNOWLEDGE OF THINGS

THE self is the only substance which can be described in any proper sense, and this must be our excuse for dwelling at such length upon it; for it is the foundation-stone of all metaphysical knowledge, and the quarry from which the materials of all further metaphysical thinking are drawn. As it is a direct object of study, there is really no end to what can be said about it, but one must stop at last, and we have placed the limit here. About other substances one may as well write with great brevity and a drier abstractness. For our knowledge of them is schematic and in a manner empty, it is a mere piece of extension-machinery by which we project the knowledge of the human substance upon them. This logical scheme it should be possible to seize and to state in a limited number of words, and no purpose could be served by multiplying them.

In the order of reality, the division 'self—other substances' would be absurd; to place God and physical atoms under one heading, and human beings under another, is really preposterous. But in the order of our knowledge, the division is intelligible, for it is a division between objects immediately and objects not in the same sense immediately known. God and physical entities are both known abstractly and with the aid of analogy, even though the form of abstraction and the principle of analogising are different.

(i) *How do we know Things?*

There are evidently two main problems: What is a thing? and, How do we know things? It may be easier to take the second question first. We will approach it by stating certain apparent data, and then the problem to which they give rise.

(I) It seems that we are aware of things, for we instinctively attribute self-being to the constituents of our physical environment.

(II) The self is not easily intelligible without supposing things; it appears to us that we exercise physical activity and that this is a real operation, and that it is concerned about and necessarily interacts with other physical activities which are somehow *in pari materia*.

(III) Our knowledge of things is abstract, and this in the highest degree. Not only have we no inspection into their true natures; we cannot even divide them numerically. What I am aware of, then, is rather 'thinghood' as the character of the physical reality I meet than 'things' as its identifiable constituents. I do, no doubt, habitually divide; for example I may regard my chair as a thing. But I do not take this seriously. It may be that physics can suggest the proper division; yet many of us are ignorant of physics, and it is not plausible that we first came by our assurance of thinghood through physics.

. These are the data, which could be much developed, but shall not be here, since they will be in the course of the argument. (I) and (II) merely say that thinghood is apparently known both for itself and as something to which self is relative. But (III) suggests so great an oddity in the manner of its coming to be known, as to make us wonder whether it can be apprehended after all. For here is the problem: How can something come to be apprehended which is not apprehended in an instance or instances? But if thinghood is apprehended in instances, how can we fail to distinguish the instances?

For thinghood is the notion of a determinate unit; it is not the notion of a form of continuity, like space, nor of an extensible quality, like colour. However phenomena ought to be divided, we can appreciate their spatial character, and we need not make up our minds where the red ceases to be red as it fades, to know that in its centre and outwards there is red. But we could hardly be said to have apprehended triangularity from our environment, if we had never perceived even roughly which particular extent of figure was triangular; and this is the parallel for thinghood.

And it will not do to say that we know it simply by interpretation, from the analogy of our own substantial being. For analogy cannot be applied at random. Unless we perceive thinghood in some manner in the object, we have nothing to interpret by our analogy. Berkeley said that the phenomena thrown by other selves are so like those thrown by us ourselves, that we conclude to the other selves from ourselves by analogy. He did not extend this argument to material things, and truly it would have been quite without plausibility if he had.

The solution that we shall propose is a causal solution: we know things as they condition or affect our vital operation. The reader who has been nicely brought up ought to shut the book at this point. Do not we know that causal theories of perception are ruled out? Did not Locke stray up this cul-de-sac to his lasting discredit and the eclipse of realism for two centuries? Be it understood, then, that we do not intend to rehabilitate any theory which takes the perception-phenomenon as a complete fact, and then tries by some causal inference to reach that reality of which it is the phenomenon. Our view will have more contact with Spinoza's theory. My affection by another being is concretely experienced as an interaction of beings; I feel the form of that other as an ingredient in the interaction, so far as the interaction expresses it; and that may be very abstractly or incompletely.

Before we proceed to explain this dark doctrine, we note the formal solution it proposes for the problem. The apprehension of a form with such abstraction, in an instance of itself perceived as itself simply, seemed impossible. Now it is suggested that the concrete datum is not of an object having the form, but of the interaction-event, and that it is from this that the anomalous abstraction is made; and then, perhaps, never without the *help* of analogy from our own substantial being.

It is usually supposed to be the duty of philosophers to start from 'hard' data, immediately presented objects, and not to take for granted any historical or scientific hypotheses. We propose temporarily to abandon the path of logical rectitude, and to consider evolutionary theory and biological probability. Let us keep lively in mind the enormity of what we are doing, and not attach any value to the result until we have succeeded in confirming it from direct experience.

The biologists assure us that the five senses are the development and specialisation of some more rudimentary and common feeling. Sensitivity to the impinging of other processes upon our vital pattern of activity is something older than awareness of colour, noise, taste, smell or touch-quality. No doubt we may call the primitive sense 'touch' since it worked through contact, but there is no reason to suppose that the object was appreciated in the form of our touch-qualities, as silky, bristly, warm, cool, etc. These specialised qualities, in this as in the other four senses, are instinctively taken by us as signs of things in our environment with which we have to do. You do not have to teach a child the category of thinghood, he assumes it from the start. It would be biologically odd if the primary form of experience were awareness of groups and classes of sense-qualities, for what would be the practical use of such an awareness? Our clear and sharp experience of the 'qualities' seems to be a sign-language whereby nature directs our obscure and groping consciousness of the beings with whom we interact. Now it is a plausible view that the common sense from which the particular senses are developed by specialisation continues to mediate between them and to provide that 'thing'-awareness for which they act as signs and pointers.

Let us try the experiment of reconstructing this common sense in isolation from the five senses. In order to do this we must introduce great artificialities. We must suppose a being with no sense but this, and yet with the intelligence of a highly reflective man, able to analyse his experience and give an account of it. This is plainly impossible. A man totally blind, totally deaf, with perfectly insensitive palate and nose, and with the whole superficies of his body so numbed as to have no feeling, would be a complete idiot. Let us, however, postulate the absurdity and see where we get.

The man still has a will. The immediate expression of will is action. When I cease to think with images of bodily movements, and begin to think with and in bodily movements themselves, then I am acting. I cannot will that of which I am unaware, and so the man must be aware of a rhythm of movement described in space by his limbs when he moves them. It would be possible to imagine him, perhaps, as always swimming in a perfectly smooth medium which offered no variety of resistance to movements slow or fast. In that case, his awareness might be of nothing beyond the pattern of movements he himself performed, and the field of space with which he was acquainted would be simply that covered by his own movements; and these would be the only features in that field.

But here there is a complication. For if he is aware of his movements as though *in vacuo* they cannot be completely *in vacuo* or they will not be movements. If he extends his hand, he is extending it from his trunk outwards and unless the trunk remains as a point of reference, a *terminus a quo*, throughout the operation, there is no movement. Even if we suppose that he is moving all parts of his body simultaneously, yet the several movements are particular. The mind or will identifies itself not with a whole of movement but with each movement separately, though contemporaneously; the mental-physical act of will which is the outstretching of the hand is other than the act which is the curving of the trunk. The trunk, even in being curved, remains the point of reference for the hand in the hand-stretching movement, while the middle and two extremities of the trunk are points of reference for one another in the trunk-bending movement.

But in fact the man is not swimming in a perfectly featureless medium; he is walking the earth among all sorts of obstacles. It might be thought that his consciousness of obstacles would be purely negative; he finds his steady forward movement broken at the place where we see a brick wall, but perhaps he does not know whether the break in his movement is due to a sudden inward paralysis or to an opposing outward mass. But it is otherwise with the ground on which he walks, or any other physical object which he makes the basis of a voluntary movement. The very act of walking is relative to the ground over which one moves; this act can only be performed in a field of space containing this feature.

This man's consciousness, then, is of his own movements in a field of space and of other things as constituting the features in that field which make it the sort of field for movement which it is. It is, primarily, his field, the field of his action, and it is the extent of his action that determines the extent of his field. The other things only enter the field in so far as they modify it for him. They may have activity and so have fields of their own, into which he will enter as a feature, but that is another story.

We have based the man's consciousness of other objects upon the relativity of movement. For a movement is relative to at least two terms; the formal description of it is the alteration of their mutual situations. From this it may be wrongly concluded that no movement can be the expression of an operation centred in the one term rather than the other—perhaps it just happens according to a uniformity-rule (i.e. it is a pure phenomenon), or perhaps it expresses the operation of a mysterious whole embracing both terms, and so we are in for Spinozist monism and conclude physical space to be one substance. But the conclusion does not follow if we allow that the operation though centred in the

one term embraces a field which reaches to the other. Then if A repels himself
from B he can do so because the distance between A and B is a fact in the existence of A, and his action consists in the modifying of this fact. So if A and B
change their relative position we can significantly ask whether this was due to
the action of A or the action of B. It may be that B is attempting to repel A
while A is attempting to attract B. Their positions may then remain the same
or one may prevail. In such a case, or if A is completely inactive in regard to B,
A will experience a passivity on his own part to the action of B, a modification
and conditioning of his own action-field apart from any activity on his own part.

The physicists assure us, and it is absurd to dispute it, that our bodies
never absolutely touch other bodies; and indeed if bodies are to be regarded as
systems of action creating patches of force in the fields of other agents, then the
notion of absolute contact is actually meaningless. Thus all interaction of substances is 'at a distance', and it is only a question of more and less. When we
speak of action by contact, we are thinking of a standard 'nearness'. Every
active being is concerned with the maintenance of a certain pattern of movement, the vital functioning, for example, of our human body *plus* those voluntary and additional patterns such as walking or jumping which we are able to
weave round the basic plan of animal operation. Such a pattern of movement
moves relatively to the features of its field. But not all the constituents of the
universe are equally effective in determining that field. Perhaps all the substances in the universe affect my movement in some way, but either very
slightly or else not individually: e.g. all bodies may contribute to the gravitation
of each, but if so they add up and cancel out and present one pull on balance.
But the nearer bodies have their own fields of immediate operation covered by
their own patterns of movement and from these they repel mine. Such mutual
repulsion is called contact, and we acquire a natural prejudice for regarding it
as the standard type of interaction.

Let us return to our man endowed with none but the unspecialised and
basic 'sense'. If he moved in a perfectly smooth and featureless medium, that is,
a field filled with minute bodies at equal distances and yielding to his movements without any noticeable alteration of pressure, he would then have no use
for any awareness of that medium at all. He would fulfil his own pattern of
motion without any incident. The features of his field only become features and
so perceptible in so far as they disturb and diversify the field. And so he knows
'the other, relatively to which I operate' only in so far as it varies the disturbance of his field—he knows it as a class of disturbances. Now the separate disturbances do not coincide simply with separate individual substances. A single
disturbance-effect may just as well be the movement of a block of substances at
rest relatively to one another, or even the several movements of many substances which produce for him a block of disturbance, their differences having
cancelled out and produced a general effect in the conditioning of the man's
movement. Again, that which by moving is disturbance for him may move
partly through its own operation, partly through the movements of things to

which its operation is relative. Of this distinction too the man will have no awareness.

In the case of this man, then, we find no difficulty about the paradox with which we started—our being acquainted rather with 'thinghood' than with correctly distinguished 'things'. For the distinctions he draws between thing and thing vary arbitrarily with the variations in the combination and division of disturbance-effect; whereas the mere sense of thinghood is derived from interaction—the immediate experience of being up against that with which we interact in some manner on a level and which must thus be known as to some degree *in pari materia* with our own activity and being. *Qua* things in themselves and according to the form of their own operation, they must be supposed to have their own field of space concentrated upon themselves as centres. And the holy angels, viewing us and our interagents from without, may see an interaction of operations, and so of fields, as it were in one field. The physicist does in a manner take the angels' point of view and constructs one neutral analogical diagram which can be interpreted equally as the plan of the space-field of every interagent in the system. But we can only maintain the angels' view at the price of diagrammatic and analogical abstraction. As soon as we wish to give it concrete interpretation, we must return to the centre of our own field, or by imaginative projection pretend to occupy the centre of another's.

(ii) *The Status of Sensation*

We stripped our man of the five senses. Now we may as well restore them, and try to show why they are necessary to the actual consciousness of things which he has through the basic or common sense. We saw in a previous discussion that consciousness is possible only with a time-gap between awareness of facts and effective reaction to them. If I become conscious only of the circumstances to which my vital pattern of operation reacts, and only in its reacting to them, consciousness has neither sense nor function. The reaction which the consciousness should direct takes place in the occurrence of the consciousness, the awareness that this was prussic acid in the struggles of my dying organism, and that this was milk unsteadily placed in my spilling of it.

Therefore if perception is to occur it is necessary to suppose luxury-activities, not themselves parts of our vital behaviour, highly sensitive to environmental disturbance and reacting thereto with merely conventional reactions which we can interpret as a guide to our action proper. There is such an activity in the organs of hearing; it responds to environmental disturbances with a conventional operation differing as the disturbances differ. Now this operation of the organs is, like any other operation, relative to its field, a field which extends to embrace the disturbances to which it reacts. Thus the operation is directly aware of the 'out-there-ness', the spatial externality of the disturbances, even though such awareness is vague in the case of this sense and is supplemented by interpretation based on experience.

The operation of the sense organ is continuous, but we have no interest in its continuous regularity. In so far as in it lies, it would always be the same, but this sameness only exists for the purpose of being modified by the objects. So in consciousness of the interaction between the organ and the objects we count the organ out and attribute the modifications to the objects, thus viewing them, by projection, in terms of the conventional reactions which they occasion. And so sensations are both conventional in their matter or quality, and veridical in their thing- and space-reference. But this is merely a particular case of what is common to that basic 'sense' of which they are but particularisations. The basic sense also interprets things in terms of its own reactions, or, more exactly, in terms of their conditioning of its action. It is only in so far as it acts that it feels the conditioning. What is peculiar to the five senses is that the reaction is absolutely conventional, has no interest of its own, and serves as a sign simply, so that there is no biological utility in distinguishing the sign from the thing signified, and projection is complete. But the basic sense's interpretation of objects in terms of disturbance is just as 'subjective' as the eye's interpretation of them in terms of colour.

The natural scientist reduces the data of the five senses to terms of the data of basic sense, and then by very careful observation of mutual disturbance-phenomena he arrives at more precise divisions of the objects and even attempts diagrams of their operations.

The reader will complain that nothing has been said that casts light on the venerable problem, how an operation or physiological functioning of the sense-organs and nerves appears in consciousness as the sense-qualities. I make a voluntary movement and (though not without the assistance of interior feeling-qualities by which my limbs are present to me) I experience it as a movement, as what it is. But for a perception of the minute movements and functionings in the sense-organs is substituted an awareness of broad states of sense-quality. About this anomaly we have nothing fresh to say, and perhaps it is not really a problem at all. The principle of the union of consciousness and physical opera-tion is already given in the 'basic sense', i.e. the consciousness of movement itself. That there should be a movement of which the whole purpose is to issue in a 'mental' result, i.e. of which the teleology is mental, not physical, we can see in the case of language habits. That the mental result should take the form of sense-quality-presentation is of course unique, but how could it help being unique?

Sense is itself and neither intellect nor physical act; but it is fair to insist upon its analogy or affinity with intellect. The mind grasps in conventional and static units the moving multiplicity of real existence; and sense translates into smooth expanses of quality-state the continual repetition of real operation. This is perhaps the final argument for the 'subjectivity' of sense-qualities. To be blue cannot be a mode of existing for it cannot be a mode of operating and therefore not of being. To see blue can, for it belongs to the mode of conscious-ness to hold together a stretch of continuous process under a static unity of idea. So we can justify Berkeley's metaphysical objection to the objective existence of 'inert' qualities or 'ideas'. In order to apprehend things we must conventionalise them under the form of static conditions for our own active existence. The things themselves can be no more static than this existence of ours which they are seen as conditioning.

(iii) *How do Things exist?* (*a*) *Problem of Analogy*

We are not primarily concerned with the status of sense-qualities, if these do not declare to us the manner in which things exist. It is our concern to determine how they do exist. In attacking this problem it would be absurd to be sanguine. We may approve and have already implicitly justified Leibniz's distinction between *phenomenon bene fundatum* and the real order of existence, between our manner of representing things as an external order of *partes extra partes* coloured with the qualities of our senses, and the manner in which things exist each as the centre of its own 'field'. But we cannot follow his optimism about the possibility of describing the existence-order correctly and independently of our subjective perversions. The philosopher is not such a magician. It is, in a sense, his business to clear up and distinguish the 'confusion' of common experience, as Leibniz says. It is for him to unravel the several strands in our thinking, to lay them out in separation from one another, to show their nature and what they are good for and how they are interrelated and why, as twisted together, they do not make up a proper and consistent unity. But he cannot himself recombine them in a perfect order, so as positively to know any reality that is hidden from the common man. He can at best hint at the general form of an experience impossible to us, in which the several strands would properly combine and things could be seen as they are. Of that divine knowledge we enjoy no more than a spoilt copy and confused reduction, from which the perfect archetype cannot be reconstructed by us.

When we try to analyse our thought about the existence of things, we come first to the distinction already noted between the fact of their self-being which qualifies them for interaction with us, and the various ways in which we distinguish and divide that being in terms of their conditioning of our activities. It is evident that the two sides of this distinction do not really fit together in the way in which common sense fits them. We have said enough about the second side and will let it go in order to concentrate on the first. How do we and how can we think of the mere existence of things as interagents with ourselves? This question raises two problems: (*a*) of the analogy of existence, (*b*) of materiality.

(*a*) The problem of the analogy of existence is obvious. I know my own existence as I am conscious of it. But I am not conscious of all aspects of it, but only of its most human, most voluntary, operations. My lower operations I do not enter into so as to have an understanding of their active being. I experience them passively, as objects, through feelings interior to my body. I cannot travel down the scale of existence even to the bottom of myself, that is, of the physical rhythm which appears continuous with the pattern of voluntary action; how much less to the level of atomic existence. We are shut up to the merely negative procedure of marking off certain aspects in our own existence which appear apable of having some analogue in merely physical existence from others that do not. If we regard the residuum as the description of a complete real existence we fall into a double absurdity. For first, as Berkeley complained, we set up abstracted aspects for a concrete reality, a scaffolding for a building; and second, the abstractions themselves are borrowed from an activity different in mode and degree from that to which we apply them, neither can we supply the scale of difference by which to translate them. The absurdity would indeed be complete if we thought that our shadowy outline described a complete existence. The same difficulty, *mutatis mutandis*, arises in the rational knowledge of God. To strike out the aspects of our being which do not positively express His is not to seize that completeness of His which synthetises into a living unity the supreme analogues of the aspects that we leave standing.

But how much can we strike out? The acceptability of our thesis is likely to turn on this point. For the following criticism will have taken shape in the reader's mind. 'You make self the clue to thinghood, and the real bond of self you declare to be real operation, which actually prolongs itself in existence, or (by an alternative form of statement) in which the earlier phase actually produces the later. But the clue to such operation you made to lie in the will, the act of intelligent choice. Is this not as much as to say that baser activities have or are some analogue to consciousness and to choice? We are not going to believe this. For even if it be true in fact (and almost anything might be true in fact, for example that certain physical atoms are, by an order unintelligible to us, constituents in the bodies of angels) none the less it has no positive plausibility in your system of ideas. For you claim to tell us how we in fact think about physical things, when we attribute to them existence in themselves. But we do not think this, whatever we think, except in certain silly imaginative moods. We are then, we must be, capable of a thinner abstraction of activity. Shew us how, on your hypothesis, this is possible. But you will not be able. You have taken choice as your clue, and you cannot let it go out of your hand. You have taken up with panpsychism, and you cannot drop it again now.'

Here is the opportunity for an indiscreet friend further to discredit our languishing cause. 'Have you not heard', he replies to the last speaker, 'that there is indeterminacy among the electrons? The physicists are clear that their laws are statistical averages only, as one might establish a law that a certain percentage of Londoners crowd down to the Underground at five o'clock. But this does not bind the individual Londoner. He might stay above ground and go to Lyons' shop. So with the electron. Which way will he jump? The law does not make up his mind for him; he must do it of himself. Among the courses of the electrons there are great searchings of heart. Now is the time to revive the delicious speculations of Malebranche and Pascal—the infinitely great: the infinitely small. What is size? It is merely comparative; why not a universe in every drop of water? Why should not the least constituents of matter be *homunculi* with everything proper about them?'

No. That is not the way. If the physicists are working with statistical averages, that need mean only that their rules do not directly result from the essential principles of the least operations, but from averages arising out of the accidental effects of these principles. And we do feel ourselves bound to show that we are under no obligation to attribute quasi-consciousness to electrons. The challenge of the first speaker must be taken up.

Why did we take conscious choice as the clue to activity in general? Not because this is the only type of activity that could act; but because this is the only type of activity which we can properly know. We can be inwardly conscious of activity only where consciousness penetrates the real causality of the act, where something *fit voluntate*. But voluntary operation is not reducible to its conscious-choice aspect. *Aliquid FIT voluntate*: the real force, the doing, is not the explicit voluntariness; a sense of real doing can be strong when the automatic functions of the body are working against obstacles, for instance with impeded breathing, although no choice is in question. Choice declines as we sink through the scale of activity within our own being, till we can presage its vanishing point, though *ex hypothesi* we cannot reach it with any interior understanding.

Free choice itself is a development from bound activity; instead of simply doing the one thing we pause to deliberate between two doings, and this seems to show that to do, or to operate, is not simply to choose. For what we choose is an operation, or, choice is a contest of operations; and in so far as it is simplified, i.e. in so far as the choice-situation is eliminated, we act. So that though choice is required to give us an inspection into activity, though we do not know the structure of activity apart from choice, the fact of choice points to activity which is not choice; both in its root, and in its fruit.

We may fairly claim to be in a happier position than Leibniz, with his 'perceptive' but 'non-apperceptive' sleeping monads. It was his fundamental error to make consciousness rather than activity his primary notion; for he reduced activity to the modification of consciousness instead of making consciousness awareness and direction of activity. And so he is reduced to the absurdity of making the essence of thinghood a consciousness at such a level that it cannot be conscious, or, otherwise stated, a consciousness existing in the mode of mere potentiality which is tantamount to sheer non-existence. We on the other hand can give as that essence an activity at such a level that it cannot possess consciousness, and this, though admittedly unknowable in concrete fullness, is not a manifest contradiction.

But though we may strike out or negate that aspect of our activity which is its being penetrated and directed by consciousness, there is another aspect of great importance which we cannot strike out, viz. reference to a vital pattern or essential form which it is the activity's business to fulfil through changing circumstance. In the lower physical being we may suppose this pattern absolutely to determine the activity; and from this it seems a natural conclusion that such beings work by simple automatism. But this is an error into which we are led by the false analogy of a macroscopic view of man-made machines. A machine may be constructed to yield a fixed number of reactions, and it seems that the limited number of possibilities are actualised in turn according to an absolutely simple rule; for every A stimulus an *a* reaction, for every B stimulus a *b* reaction, no stimulus in the A to N series, no reaction.

But the relation of a real physical operation to its conditioning environment cannot be supposed to be anything like this. Let us suppose that it is the vital concern or 'law' of this operation to maintain a perfectly simple continuous motion—say circular. Its circularity will be relative to the features of the field in which it operates, and these features are neither uniform nor stable. The path of its movement, then, will be circular in relation to a sort of balance struck between the positions of the several moving entities by which it is surrounded. Well, you may say, environment presents this total result, and in relation to it the movement mechanically gyrates. No description could be more misleading. How can the several entities that compose the environment conspire to produce this miracle? This field exists as a field only in being the field of this movement. It is itself the only real point of synthesis; it strikes the balance, it makes the abstraction of a total position or frame of reference from the many moving positions and pressures of the others; it makes its movement circular by always relating itself differently to each of the constituents in its environment. Nothing could be much less like what we suppose to be the principle of mechanism. It is not that we required a principle of active choice over and above the mere principle of circular movement. On the contrary, the latter principle is fully sufficient, but the manner in which it determines the operation varies continually and is as remote from mechanism as from conscious choice.

This description is of course purely mythical and describes no real operation. Its value is dialectical and negative and its utility is limited to the explosion of the mechanistic error. It gives us no positive information about the manner in which primitive physical entities are or operate.

(iv) *How do Things exist?* (*b*) *Problem of Materiality*

(*b*) We must now consider the second problem concerning the conception of physical existence, viz. that of materiality. If we take our own activity as some remote clue to prime physical existence, we meet an obvious difficulty. Our activity concerns itself with the manipulation of subordinate entities. Even though we extend the scope of that form which we are, to embrace the whole functioning of the living human body, this pattern of function is still only that of the great organism and does not embrace the individual patterns of the cells; still less the patterns of the physical constituents in the cells themselves. And so the only activity and movement with which we have any acquaintance presupposes organs and something which is moved. But we cannot proceed *ad infinitum*. Somewhere we must come to an entity which is either inert or is an activity without any matter subject to it. Neither hypothesis is intelligible to us. The inert substance is indeed completely meaningless, being the mere hypostatising of a relation. Some substances are inactive (or appear so) in relation to certain other operations, but the conception of a being which is inertness is not the positive conception of anything. So we must make the best we can of the second unintelligibility of activity which is its own matter.

The supreme consideration here is that our own activity is something positive in itself, even though it never to our knowledge exists by itself. It is not a mere set of accidental changes in its subject-matter, but is itself the author of the changes, and organises and holds together that matter; without the general life-pattern even the cells dissolve; they are dependent upon it and not it simply upon them. Thus if the human being is said to be 'compositum ex materia et forma', this is a real composition in the sense that the 'constituents' have equal physical and dynamical reality, or certainly not the form less than the matter. It is a very different case from that of the statue 'composed of a Mercury-shape and bronze' when the form is as nearly nothing as it can be. We know that St. Thomas felt able to assert that the human form is even capable of separate existence. To this we may at least append a *non liquet*, and if we hold for immortality prefer to suppose that the form is capable of re-embodiment in a different medium which it pleases God to assign it. Still, St. Thomas's position may serve as an extravagant statement and over-emphasis of the truth that our operation is *something*, and that there is nothing of which we have proper knowledge which is *something* in the same degree of completeness.

In another way it may seem to us that physical entities are more complete and more truly *something* than our soul, because we take them, as we take our own embodied being, as a sum of all the subordinate forms present in this and so as *ex hypothesi* complete. And this begets a prejudice in favour of mere sense-quality as the presentation of real being and against our interior knowledge of it through our own operation. For sense-experience, just because of its convenient 'confusion', can be treated as the apprehension of a sum of all the forms necessary for the actual existence of a complete being; whereas when we begin to analyse in terms of operation we realise that we have no positive conception of any operation which is not existentially incomplete. So much the worse, we may say, for intellect and so much the better for sense. And so there is a certain naturalness about the use of τὸ ἀντίτυπον, the thing you can kick, as a type and symbol of solid fact. But to kick reality is not to understand it.

The problem of materiality is obviously insoluble, if it is taken as the problem of finding any conception of a prime or lowest operation. We can only add to our conception of our own activity the negative 'having no lower operation as matter subject to it'. Such lack of matter is not to be confused with that traditionally attributed to pure spirits. Their immateriality is supposed to be a sovereign freedom with respect to all existents, enabling them to apprehend and to use these as they will—it is an abundance of active relation to all things—they have the universe for their 'body'. The lowest operation is 'immaterial' for an opposite reason—its poverty in active relation to anything; it cannot even annex and control that small organism of inferior entities which constitute a 'body'.

The reader will see how far we are from pretending to a knowledge of physical being beyond the common. We are simply criticising what common-sense does, as it alternates between the assertion of self-being and stolid confidence in sense, as it defines some physical realities (e.g. wind) in terms of activity, others (e.g. stones) in terms of inertness. Yet even the stone, when we think of it as existing and being something, we think of as somehow positively sitting there as though it were a frog and not a stone, or as though it were I sitting in my chair. Yet the frog's sitting, and mine by which I interpret his, is a positive business and I am dimly aware of several activities which contribute to it. Such a fancy, Heaven knows, is in need of drastic criticism—the stone *qua* one lump does not 'sit' nor indeed exist, it has no vital form; its molecules cohere and are perhaps the first patterns to which we come, and they have interior and exterior activity. Yet such criticism enables us to add nothing to the animistic interpretations of common-sense. We can only qualify them with the negations which common-sense itself implicitly applies.

One most fertile source of prejudice against our doctrine of self and thing has still to be mentioned. This is the confusion of the phenomenal behaviour-pattern with the real. For in the case of creatures which stand nearer to us, for instance living things, we believe that from the phenomenal pattern traced by their operation in our world we can construct the diagram of their essential activity, and this seems to be the ideal also, however unrealisable, of physics. Then we come to see that the phenomenal pattern is expressed in the medium of the sense-qualities, as Berkeley will stoutly and rightly maintain; and these cannot be attributed to the things in themselves, since to look blue is not an operation. Apart from these qualities, the pattern is the pattern of nothing, unless of a real operation which the thing has or is in itself. There is in a sense an identity of the pattern (in so far as an ingredient in my existence) with the same pattern (in so far as the principle of another's existence): but in so far as it appears to me, it is filled out and coloured with sense-qualities, and must be translated into another medium and supplied with another filling in order to be in itself.

If we neglect the distinction, what results? It seems that in order to exist, the (phenomenal) pattern needs no addition; as when the events on the cinema screen seem sufficient in themselves and one forgets the vital part played by the projector. Then any thesis like that we are defending seems a gratuitous addition to what is already complete. 'What are we up to? If we *add* the notion of activity to that which can do so well without it, we are evidently personifying the impersonal.' For it has not been seen that in order to exist at all, and not simply appear, the pattern must be the pattern of an activity; so that activity is not the distinguishing mark of persons, but of whatever exists.

But we have not yet got to the end of the error. For when the mistaken view of the thing's pattern has got established it carries the war into the enemy's country and assails the self. The interior phenomenal series, as open to that abstract introspection of the dissociated mind, of the pure onlooker at his own states (*vide supra*, p. 109) is equally supposed sufficient to its own existence; and choice and purpose, sucked of the marrow of real act, become nothing but particular phenomena of an odd type occasionally turning up in the interior order. If the victims of this sort of error hear talk of the thing's activity, and of the self's will as the analogue and clue, what do they suppose? They can only suppose that we are attributing to the thing an introspectible phenomenal subjectivity like our own. And this is so silly, that it does not seem worth talking about, and indeed it is not.

(v) *Overlapping of Substances*

As we have just mentioned the belief we all hold that we can recognise the vital pattern of living things to some degree, let us make a fourfold division of substances according to the sort of knowledge we think we can have of their existence.

(*a*) Our self, of which enough has been said.

(*b*) Beings whose pattern of operation we can so far seize, and so far interpret by its closeness to our own, that we have some notion what their existence is like to themselves—for there are conscious creatures, other men, some animals—it is not possible to say where the line is to be drawn.

(*c*) Beings whose operative pattern we grasp to some extent, but as the diagram only of an activity whose nature we cannot conceive. For most of us many inferior living things come in this class.

(*d*) Beings whose operative pattern we cannot distinguish, nor, therefore, their number; we take them in the mass. For most of us, everything below the level of life. Perhaps physicists can extend class (*c*) at the expense of (*d*); or perhaps they cannot.

Of these classes (*c*) creates an apparent difficulty for the doctrine of substantial units, which we ought to discuss. For we made it a cardinal point that the notion of thinghood is the notion of a unit, so that the thinghood of mere things (*d*) which cannot be discriminated into its units, provided an apparent paradox. But when we look at the vegetable creation, for example, does it remain plausible that operation is marked off into clearly divided units? No doubt if we take the oak and the ivy, they are substantially distinct. The problem arises with regard to the oak itself, or the ivy itself. Is each one unit of operation or many? We are not asking whether there are not subordinate units held together and organised by the unitary operation; of course there are, as there are cells in the body, and physical constituents in the cells. We are asking whether the supreme pattern of working, which makes the plant to be a plant and to be ivy, is one or several over the extent which we should call that of one ivy plant.

It springs indeed from one root, but each of the limbs appears to be complete, has rootlets of its own into the oak, and, if it finds sufficient soil, is capable of becoming an independent plant. Or if we start from the whole: the number and extent of its limbs makes no difference to its being ivy and exhibiting its proper form.

It would be absurd to labour so evident a consideration. Life at a certain level seems to be so organised that it is ambiguous whether we ought to call it a unit or a group of units, an ivy or ivies. Exact investigation would presumably enable us to draw certain distinctions: there are operations of general scope, like the circulation of the sap; and others whose form is particular. And the same will be true in our own bodies; we must regard them as covered or organised by a whole hierarchy of forms, superimposed, as it were, on one another; of which at least one level is organised on the ivy-plan, or else generation would be impossible, since it proceeds by the separating off of an element having the same specific character as that from which it separates.

But does this ambiguity about the spatial boundaries of substantial operation need to distress us? It is time we referred back to the account we gave of the self's unity. That unity was centred in the act; in that alone it was actual. But it was found to have a complexity of pattern by which certain constituents or ingredients were concentrated in the act; and the act itself to have continuity with previous acts, forming with them a prolongation of act which, in its working, was related to an essential form of working. Now there is nothing in this description against which the ivy-phenomena rebel. The notion of substance with which the instance of the self has supplied us is not a notion which has anything to do with tidy spatial boundaries. The boundaries it has are those of the field of an activity-complex, and fluctuate with its changing extent.

If, then, we take any given operation in the ivy, it has always its own form, and continuity with previous operation, and 'concern' with some essential pattern, viz. of some ivy-unit; and this is all that is needed for substantiality in our sense. It is vitally related, very likely, to other operations having a different scope, a wider or narrower essential pattern. But why not?

We are reminded of the mediaeval controversy about the unity or plurality of forms in one thing. And so long as the 'thing' is regarded as a spatial block, the problem is insoluble. For on the one hand a thing must have, it seems, one form according to which it is that thing. Yet on the other hand it is not plausible that all the operations in the supposed independent spatial block characterised by this form should be reduced to either (a) operations of the one form, or (b) operations of sub-forms organised by it (its 'matter'), or (c) accidents due to extraneous influence. The thesis here maintained provides a solution. Unity is found in the operation, and that must be determined by one essential form, plurality of forms would be nonsense. But as to the spatial overlapping and interweaving of activity-forms, and the several sorts of interrelation they can have, we are in no need to dogmatise.

But of all moments the most perplexing remains that of generation or division, when operations which began as developments under the same essential form are found to have split the form between them and established mutual independence. This is dark to our understandings, because we never experience it interiorly; and it could not be interiorly experienced. We do experience interaction, because as conscious agents we interact with others; and we experience a formal and actual continuity, because as conscious agents we have it with ourselves. But we do not experience generation; and therefore, in a theological connexion, we denied that this was an intelligible relation, or applicable as an analogue of any profit.

The ivy has clung too long about the argument, for these considerations probably apply with far more force in the purely physical field. For there, one would suppose, essential forms can be of much greater simplicity and divisible more readily; so that (if any one is helped by the metaphor) substance in that field is almost more linear than complex or extended. It is vain to talk where we cannot understand, and sufficient to conclude as follows: Whatever fluidity we must attribute to physical substance has no tendency to overthrow our contention that thinghood is the notion of a determinate unit. Whether we have to fence off an area or merely to trace a line, it remains that we must distinguish operation from operation to know substance. One operation does not fuse with another, however they interweave with or are generated from one another. And each operation, with what is concentrated in it, continuous through time as the expression of a determinate essential form, is substance.

(vi) *Conclusion*

It does not concern us to follow the articulation of thinghood into further detail, and indeed we have probably already overshot the mark and fallen into developments which betray absurd ignorance of the positive sciences. But whatever errors of this kind there may be will not invalidate the thesis. For the general nature of thinghood as known to us results not from those sciences but from the primary relation of the 'self' and the 'other' immediately known. It was only necessary to show that this can be accommodated to the particular conclusions of the sciences; a fact which is really evident *a priori*, but can be exhibited in instances. And whether these instances relate themselves to contemporary, outworn or never-held positions they will equally well illustrate the method of accommodation. Scientific conclusions change from time to time; it is not through them that we came by thinghood.

This attitude to the sciences implies no disparagement of them as methods for arriving at truths of fact. For we do not wish only to know thinghood, we wish to know how it is organised and distributed, to know the types of things; and in so far as the sciences approximate towards diagrams of real operations, they give us information on this topic. But this does not mean that the philosopher would be well advised to start from these data. It must always amaze the readers of (say) the late Professor S. Alexander's *Space, Time and Deity* that he should construct from the bottom upwards with so little recognition that his elementary entities are personified abstractions which cannot really be thought about, analogies derived negatively from our own being. It is not enough that a writer who pursues this method should confess with his lips that his elementary being is hard to think about, that the poverty of our language drives us to metaphors drawn from the level of consciousness. For if he made serious work with this reflection, he would not dream of beginning with the less known in order to build up the more known, nor expend the sweat of an Egyptian bondage in rearing a pyramid, merely to crown it with an apex which would stand more handsomely upon the ground.

The knowledge of other finite substance has relevance to the rational knowledge of God, in spite of Descartes. For (a) one type of analogical and causal knowledge prepares us for another yet further removed: (b) the existence of several sorts and degrees of substance prepares us for the possibility of a quite other degree, the absolute: (c) we use of necessity the analogy of distinct sorts of substance and of their external relation in thinking of God and the world related: (d) the plurality, variety and mutual externality of finite substances reveal by contrast the unity and necessity of God's being, and so constitute a springboard for theological dialectic, additional to that provided by the mere metaphysical finitude of the individual self: (e) the demonstration that all that is, is substance (or at least that we have no grounds for thinking otherwise), enables us to understand everything, and not our own conscious being only, as dependent upon the creativity of God.

XXI

METAPHYSICAL ANALYSIS OF THE FINITE SUBSTANCE

WE have described the finite substance in some manner, but, if we propose to pass on into theological dialectic, we shall require first to re-describe our description in more abstract terms. For in the theological analysis with which we started, we decided that the idea of God is bound up with the very finitude of the creature, i.e. with the real distinction of its essence and its existence. Now nothing we have so far established about the finite substance has direct bearing on this distinction, and very little upon the notion of metaphysical finitude. We have been engaged in describing the form of the finite substance, as far as that is possible, with the purpose of showing that there is such a substance and that it has some kind of a form. It is possible to ask a question of a higher abstractness; not, 'What sort of form is it?' but 'What is it to be a form?' and, as a corollary, 'How is form related to that which it determines or limits?'

Since we have received rational theology in an Aristotelian garb, it is natural to approach this task by an examination of the Aristotelian concepts of form, essence, and substance, in order to see how they and the relations of which they are the terms will be interpreted by us.

(i) *Form*

Aristotelianism reduced time to the measure of movement (i.e. change) and movement to successive states in substances, or at least in some 'subject' (ὑποκειμένου). The primary 'subject' admitted change from substance to substance, but this only under the influence of an already existent substance. It could not then be asserted without qualification that all the changes studied by 'physics' had substance for their 'subject', but it could be said that they were concerned with substance, whether by modifying it or creating it. But in so far as a substance contributed to the causality of a movement, it was itself already actual. A substance, then, once it had come to be, was essentially out of time because out of movement. It might indeed undergo changes, either in a nominal sense by the changing of other things relatively to it, or more intrinsically by the alteration of its matter or of its accidents. But these changes, though they were of the substance and had the substance for their true subject, still left something unchanged, and that was the form. The form either is or is not; if the form is, the thing exists as such a thing. Change (and therefore time) is a horse which the form has to ride; but so long as it keeps in the saddle, it is not subject to change nor therefore to time. Some day it will fail to manage the beast and fall under its feet. One could then say that it had had a ride for its money, and that this had covered a 'period'. Yet this period was, for the form considered in itself, without any intrinsic measure; for time is the measure of changes, not of existence.

Whatever in the history of a substance belongs to it as a substance of such a character, is referable to the influence of its form; and so whatever in the life of a man bears the stamp of his humanity is referable to that form as its cause. But if, in fact, we try to describe what we can observe, we can give no account of this existent identical form; it must therefore be declared to be unknown, but to be the ground of that essentially human pattern which we find exemplified in the life of the human creature. The unknown form has to be posited on the strength of an allegedly self-evident metaphysical principle. This principle we have already treated roughly and traced to its dialectical origin.

The form which 'rides' change but is not a form of change was proper to Aristotelianism. Aristotelianism is a system which allows God as cause of changes only; so the being of finites must be grounded in themselves, they must be 'mortal gods'. Thomism escapes this atheism and holds fast the participation of finites in a being derived from God by the distinction of essence and existence (*vide supra*, p. 33 *f*): this is sufficient, and it would be absurd to charge the system with atheistic pluralism of principles. But it is still possible to ask whether, once the distinction has been made, the time-transcending finite form is worth retaining; it would seem to become a question for observation, whether (granting the metaphysical principle) the previously-actual ground of characteristic activities is to be found within their own substance; and if we make an unknown form this ground, it cannot be established by observation.

On the other hand a certain givenness of the pattern is necessary. The finite will is only intelligible—i.e. so far as we know, possible—in relation to some basic pattern which it is concerned to fulfil, and which for it is simply a datum (*vide supra*, p. 178). If we can treat the Aristotelian doctrine as simply a way of stating this fact—if the 'existence' of the form is no more than its bindingness upon activity—then that doctrine can be accepted. But this is not what its upholders have meant.

While the Aristotelian doctrine can be reproached for introducing a 'surd' of explanation in the unknown form, it will, in another sense, claim intelligibility as its very principle. This form is only occult to us; in itself it is perspicuous to reason, and even to our reason the general notion of the form as such is clear. The form is a subsistent character, a character which has obtained the full conditions necessary for its existence; and a character is that which is intelligible, *quod mens percipit*. And if anyone objects that this fails to differentiate substance from attribute, it will be replied that attribute is an incomplete character, having reference to a complete character which is a substantial form. Not only does this theory treat the fundamental unity as an intelligible character, it treats the further aspects of it as further such characters added to the first; so that the whole remains clear.

But for us, that which exists is not character, but activity according to character; so that we are under no necessity to posit an enduring and hidden character in which the successive rhythm of perceptible character is founded. The complex of apprehensible characters is directly inherent in the functioning of the continuous activity, and requires no other foundation. We have seen in what sense and why both activity as such and the substantial whole or unit of activity are indescribable, though not inapprehensible; it is structural aspects which can alone be set forth in detail, and are 'intelligible' in the sense of the Aristotelian doctrine. And so that doctrine appears as a dialectical error, which arises through demanding of the whole the sort of intelligibility which belongs to the partial aspect, and the 'clarity' of the notion of a substantial form is sufficient evidence against its pretensions to be the basis of existence.

The rhythmic principle of an operation cannot (obviously) be a formal cause in the Aristotelian sense, and yet it is necessary to the existence of the operation. An operation having no structure of succession is unthinkable, for it would have no continuity even for an instant; the world would no longer be made up of operations, but be one absolute chaos of operation, in which no line of continuity could be traced. Form is not the foundation of activity but the rhythm and direction of activity, and without these there is no activity.

We must apply the topic of form to our topic of the 'four causes' previously discussed. Which of these enter into that form which specifies an active substance? Not the material, nor the efficient; but the formal, which determines the structure of our activity or activities as such; and the final, though only in so far as it consists not of purposes that may be adopted and left behind but of purposes we cannot escape—that is, those of the body, and any others inevitably founded on these by the sort of rational apes that we are. It may seem odd that the form should not be simply identical with the formal cause, and it might be neater to define so. We found the boundaries of formal and final cause difficult to determine, and necessarily so, on our hypothesis; for the final, as we descend the scale of acts, takes on a formal air, till what was purpose above becomes law below. And so there seemed to be an advantage in a different division: by 'formal cause' we meant the structure of activities as activities of such a kind, by final cause the particular direction taken by the activities, whether they could be thought to exercise choice or no in adopting it. Perhaps it would be most exact to define the inescapable among them as formal cause of the self, but final cause of the activity considered in abstraction.

However that may be, a self is not sufficiently specified or limited by the formal cause (or causes) *of its activity* (or activities); for these, as we have seen, require a particular pattern determining their direction, which is as it were chosen for them, before they can begin choosing variations for themselves. And this pattern belongs to the form *of the self* as specifying it to be such and such a substance rather than one of a different kind.

Since the limit accepted by the individual appears to be more particular than that of the species, we may as well admit the form to be individual, even though within that form itself a further distinction can be taken between what belongs to the species and what is accidental to the species though intrinsic to the individual form.

(ii) *Form and Essence*

'Essentia' was the general notion of the form, taken together with all that is needed for its actualisation: the form *plus* its existential requirements described in universal terms. For example, if 'reasoning animal' defines the human 'form', then to have some flesh and blood belongs to man's essence; but not to have the particular flesh and blood of Peter or Paul, or the special type of these constituents found in Europeans or Negroes. Such a definition can still be applied by us; if we have the notion of a specifying form, viz. of a limit and basis accepted by activity as its charter, we must also have the notion, however indeterminate, of what would be an actual filling of this limit and development upon this basis; and this whether describable or indescribable in particular, is the notion of the essentia of this substance.

In attempting a description, we should have to begin with the form and proceed to the attributes it demands. The mediaeval notion of the form in its relation to other essential characteristics was based on the supposition that there are certain nuclear characters, the subjects of the definition, from which other characters can be derived. This does not seem to have any place in our doctrine. But we can allow an analogous distinction, viz. between the limiting form of the individual *qua* focus and mode of focussing, *qua* project-centre and mode of projecting, and on the other side the class of matters which are focussed and projected wherever *such* a form is operative. Stated as belonging to the essence, these matters will appear as general relative predicates belonging to the centre, and naming the class of this substance's concerns. Further, the essence must include the notion of an uniting living will operative within the limits and on the basis so defined; so that it will include the notion of the whole as open to unitary intuition alone (*vide supra*, p. 220) as well as that of the structure such a self must have.

According as we start from the form of the individual or that of the species, we shall develop the individual essence or the specific. In either case, the notion of the essence is the notion of an object of investigation, which we have never learned perfectly to know, and perhaps never could. It is certainly not a set of clear and definite ideas possessed by the mind.

(iii) *Essence and Substance*

The distinction of 'essence' and 'substance' is not a distinction of characters connoted; but simply that while essence connotes all characters proper to an entity of the given form, substance connotes no additional characters but rather the additional fact that these same characters are instantiated and have each of their open blanks filled with one or other (it is not stated which) of the appropriate substitutible 'accidents' of which the essence connotes the class.

It might seem that substance does connote additional characters, if it is used to refer to a realised entity known *a posteriori* by its history, while essence is used for the same entity as describable *a priori* from a knowledge of its mere form. Then the entity referred to by the two terms would be the same; but the essence would not only be abstract, it would also be poorer in the characters directly connoted by it.

Yet it would be odd to use the term 'substance' to cover a total description of the life spread out through time; we could call nothing a substance till it was dead; besides, a substance seems to be the object of a definition or at least a description; and one cannot describe a life-history, but only write it. And yet in the process by which the essence (as known *a priori*) gets its blanks filled, further enduring characters are added; some of the blanks are filled with elements of structure, and not with passing events.

We have seen that free will operates by the construction of character; and some parts of character are 'second nature'. We could say, then, that at any given moment in the life-history of the self the limit imposed on possible action by the self's 'nature' is more definite than the charter of being with which we deem it to begin. We are not only making the banal observation that a particular situation restricts the possibilities of action more closely than does the essence of the agent alone. We mean that the possibilities for the whole of remaining life are more closely defined every year that we live. And this is not an accident of our ignorance, as though with sufficient knowledge we could have foreseen all this from the beginning. No, character is formed not without the use of freedom, and might have been otherwise. Thus the intrinsic limit changes, the charter of our being receives additional clauses.

But this will give us—if we like to call it so—a constantly expanding *form*, in the sense we gave to the term; and, from the form, a constantly changing definition of the essence. But no especial place for 'substance' appears; so that it would be best to give to this latter term the sense simply of οὐσία ἐνυπόστατος, an essence not taken in abstraction but as exemplified in fact, with *particular* accidents filling all its blanks; as was said above.

(iv) *Can Essential Characteristics be the Object of Free Choice?*

Character is partly second nature and the delimitation of our future scope. But partly also it is a pattern of existence now freely willed, the fruit, not the bound, of freedom, the system of our projects so far as they express an order of our own existence as agents, a rhythm imposed on our own activity. Have we here a yet further form, and essence? This question is not merely verbal. It means, have we here a formal principle unreducible to any others, or can the reduction be made? The ancients would, I take it, be for reducibility. They would analyse thus:

(*a*) The specific form (man)   }
(*b*) The individual accidents (of this man) } *in actu primo*

(*c*) The external realities open to exploitation by a being of such a form.

(*d*) The exploitation, *in actu secundo.*

The positive formal principles involved in (*d*) would be (*a*)—as hindered or assisted by (*b*)—and (*c*). Human behaviour, teleologically considered, is the exploitation of situations and objects (e.g. a chance for bravery in battle, or God as an object of contemplation) by the human 'nature'. Humanity might be inhibited or distorted, as expressed *in actu secundo*, and so act with great diversity, but so far as it was right, it was one—'They are one way good, and evil every way.' Excellence thus consists in (1) being human, and (2) choosing the best objects and exploiting them.

In this scheme (*a*) can do double duty as a formal and final principle. Manhood, diluted by its particular accidents, gives us the individual as he is *in actu primo*, and the possibilities that lie before him *in actu secundo*. But again, as a principle which leads him to master, as may be, the limitations imposed by the same accidents and develop his second act in the direction of the norm, it is the principle of the ideal as well as of the real. This very neat scheme has of course a proper application. At the merely vital level, it is proper to view the stripling oak as the typical oak-form conditioned by certain accidents, and again to view this form as the final principle which governs the further growth of the tree so far as this is not referable to extrinsic causes. And this way of viewing things is not bound up with an unhistorical belief in the fixity of species. Species may change, but at a given time a certain phase of the species is in force, within narrow limits of variation. The question is, whether such a scheme will do when we leave the vital for the rational and voluntary level. Can we say that rightly used freedom aims at (*a*) activity 'according to nature', and (*b*) an appetition of the best extrinsic objects which our nature allows us to reach? This means to say that the pattern we impose on ourselves or on society is shown to be either (*a*) an expression of the human as such under given conditions, or (*b*) merely instrumental under given conditions to the exploitation of the best objects open to us under given conditions. Since the objects open to human exploitation exceed what each man can grasp, specialisation may be good to some extent, as instrumental to the fullness of life. But in no case can we regard it as a reasonable intention for its own sake to imprint any other order on our activity than the order of being human; the individuality of a single character or of a national culture has no *formalitas* which it is right to shape or to preserve for itself.

We can approve the insistent seriousness of this view. The objectives of first importance are the realisation of an ideal for manhood which should be set before all mankind and is expressed in the traditional moral virtues, and together with this the exploitation of the highest goods. And we must exclude any practical philosophy which finds its chief principle in the free artistic creation of a beautiful individuality whether for oneself or for society. Yet there is a grace and a harmony of life which is not merely instrumental to other things, and within the scope left by the more serious demands a man's life is a poem which he makes, often no doubt a very bad poem; the same can be said of the social pattern. We might cover many pages with the problem, how far such grace can be a conscious objective; for on the one hand a man or a group can plainly suffer from inattention to it, while on the other, conscious cultivation seems insufferable and self-defeating.

What we call individuality in any man is very likely made up for the most part—anyhow the most serious part—of his interests, and the balance he holds between their several claims. But this is not an exhaustive account.

If we allow that the individual character of self and of society can be an end, however subordinate an end, then we must allow that a further formal principle is operative in rational behaviour. Whether we call it a further determination of essence or no is a matter of how we like to use our terms. *In actu secundo* the essence was not reckoned to receive formal development, but to be intensified by saturation with its proper objects; for it is the very principle, e.g. of the mind to grasp Being up to its capacity and the most extended exercise of this function does not develop that principle formally. But the *formalitas* we are speaking of does appear to enter into the teleological whole of the subjective pattern as such.[1] If then, we consider essence as the principle of teleological unitary pattern, this *formalitas* enters into the essence and indeed into the form. But if we consider essence as above all a principle of fact that is already determinate it will seem very odd to assign to the essence any formality which we voluntarily maintain but may in future modify or discard.

(v) *Essence as Limit and Goal*

We see then that this order of individuality raises the issue as between an essential pattern which is a limit, and one that is a goal. The distinction is made a little less sharp by our admission that even the limiting essential form is not all actual together but is a pattern binding on the future. The issue is not between the actual and the non-actual, but between the necessary rhythm and the chosen. If we are allowed for a moment to make a flight into Platonising metaphysics, the fully actual ground of both might be sought in God alone, the difference being in the manner of their communication to the creature; the limit being set to it as the law of its activity, by a divine fiat as it were, and the goal offered to its free rational appetition, whereby we (unconsciously) read our true calling out of the pages of the divine mind.

This metaphysical illustration is mythically expressed, and no more than an illustration; but it reminds us of a yet further distinction. For the essence appears to be determinate if not in fact as an imposed limit, at least ideally as the true calling of such a substance; and one that has imposed upon itself by perverse choice some other formality than the right, would therefore seem not to have realised its essence but to have missed it. And even though we put out

---

[1] For Aristotelianism this *formalitas* is no *formalitas* because it is an order of succession in acts. So we could not even discuss whether it enters into the essence.

of our heads all theology and regard this individual formality as the construction of a free creativity, it is still possible to make of one's life a bad poem and
miss the form that would have been the proper perfection of such a type. Yet
we can still say that the agent has modified his essence even if he has failed to
enrich it, and with this we must rest content for the present; declaring that the
essence is enhanced by right additions but modified by all.

But the issue 'Limit or goal?' is wider than the case of this individual
formalitas. How far is virtue itself the detailed exposition of the mere form of
rationality in its application to the life of a creature incarnate in human flesh?
Even though we grant that the serious part of any human ideal must be the
part which should be set before all humanity, we have still to ask whether the
human race is called to recognise only (*a*) its limiting essence, (*b*) the intrinsic
values of the several objects of which that essence makes it capable, or whether
it has not also to scale projected types of human life whose values are not
simply the values of the objects they make available. For when we have granted,
for example, that various objects are to be scaled in a certain order of worth, we
shall proceed to agree that, in spite of this, the lower are not to be utterly for-
saken. But having said this we find no sufficient criterion in either the values of
the objects or the exigencies of our limiting nature to tell us what is the true
balance to be held between the activities directed to those several types of
object. And so we do not escape the consideration of a formality of second act
which cannot be deduced but must be chosen as an end by some practical
wisdom. And this seems better expressed by the Platonic mythology than by
either of the Aristotelian mythologies. It is more like the appropriating of a
pattern laid up in heaven than it is like either 'tne imitation of deity as far as
our nature permits' or the untrammelling of our actual vital principle from
accidents that encumber its operation.

The importance of essence as a teleological conception is this. It seems that
the object of right appetition is always the creation, preservation or enhancement of being, whether one's own or another's. But being (as reality having
degree and therefore value) belongs only to substances. And reality in a substance can be actualised only as activity having relevance to its essential form,
which determines it to be this substance rather than that. Every valuable
activity, then, must either actualise an essential form or enrich it, or subserve
instrumentally one or other of these two aims. Enrichment may consist either
in the addition of further formal elements or in the satiation of the capacities
inherent in the existing form, e.g. by supplying contemplation with objects.

It follows that the teleological concept of essence—as the realisable being
of things—closely relates to the limiting concept. It covers the formal character
whose realisation is the positive enrichment and upbuilding of a substance
particularised by such and such a limiting form. And in that limiting form it is
clearly founded.

(vi) *Conclusion on Form, Essence and Substance*

To summarise, then, we have (*a*) the essential form which is the limiting pattern of a substance's future viewed from the inception of its existence;

(*b*) the essential form which is the limiting pattern of its future viewed from any given moment in its history;

(*c*) the essential form which together with (*b*) includes elements of structure or recurrent pattern voluntarily added as enrichments of the limiting pattern;

(*d*) the essential form which is the ideal of the limiting pattern as voluntarily enriched;

(*e*) any of these (*a-d*) taken as embracing in general the further elements required for its actualisation: i.e. the essence corresponding to each form;

(*f*) the essence not taken abstractedly, but as actually embodied in the required further elements, i.e. as substance.

Although some limiting pattern is inseparable from the activity of a finite will, it remains that we never know with certainty or exactness what in a given case that pattern is, for our opinion is based on induction. What changes can be introduced into the human pattern without the man ceasing to be a man? That involves yet another question—When is a man not a man? The vital activity of the form may be impoverished and diminished by inches. But all this is matter for observation, so far as we are concerned. We cannot conclude *a priori* 'Man is a social being; therefore Carthusian Monasticism won't do.' We can but observe. Still less can we say: 'Man is a creature of flesh and bone; therefore his vital pattern cannot be transferred into another medium after death.' We know nothing of the matter (because we cannot observe) but only that *as* a creature of flesh and bone he cannot function with his spinal cord severed, etc. What can or cannot happen to the human essence in the process of its development we do not know, because we cannot lay our finger on the characteristics which make up the citadel of its specific nature. And yet some limit there must undoubtedly be.

But within the conditions of our present existence—in the phases of human culture open to our observation—we can compile more and more evidence as to the variations of which the pattern is capable, both on the physical and on the voluntary level.

(vii) *How does Essence characterise Activity?*

Let us now ask, how form and essence, being such, specify or particularise activity? And the obvious answer is true as far as it goes. Activity is characterised by character, i.e. by its formal aspect; nothing else can characterise it, and it cannot be uncharacterised. When we are discussing the limits of form and essence, we are not adjusting them to activity; we are adjusting them (and the aspect of activity they characterise) to other elements of character (and the aspects of activity that these characterise); e.g. we distinguish that in the activity of a substance which is simply in accord with its essence, from that which in the activity of the same substance is 'accidental'. All that we have to assert of the relation between activity and essential form is that activity being, so far as we know, in substantial units, has necessary relation to an essential form which specifies it.

This assertion is formally correct, but it is liable to misinterpretation. We must guard against erroneous analogies. For example, if we say that activity is characterised by its form, and then think of that form as the rhythm or pattern of the activity's operation, imagination may supply the figure of wire twisted into one pattern here and another there, of water running here and there in different meanders. And so we find ourselves thinking of activity itself as constant in quality, like the water or the wire, and differing only as it traces several figures. This is false. Activity as developed in this and that structure, e.g. in the pattern of human and of bestial life, or in human life at different levels of explicit rationality, differs in quality and intensity; an act of choice is more an act than is an automatism. Intensities or qualities of act are intrinsically relative to certain structures, but they are not reducible to those structures; we can just as well say that the structures are dependent for their existence on the appropriate qualities or intensities in their acts, as *vice versa*.

There is nothing to prevent us, if we choose, from conceiving the two givens, activity-as-such, and formal schemes for activity to exemplify; and from then regarding the special quality of activity as the product of their union—if activity fulfils such a scheme it takes on such a quality. Such a way of conceiving would have affinities with the scholastic aphorism, that every creature participates 'existence' according to its capacity, for here there is presupposed a certain formality of each creature, and an intensity or degree of being proportionate thereto; and unless some such distinction is made, the 'capacity' and the 'filling' assigned to it will simply coincide in the tautology that every creature is what it is.

There is nothing to prevent us from talking thus, so long as we realise that our order is of thought and not of being; activity-as-such and formal patterns are not 'given' first, they are abstractions which cannot be given at all. It is even doubtful whether quality of activity does 'follow' wholly upon pattern—whether the pattern does more than prescribe the limits within which the degree of intensity will lie. It seems possible that an act of will formally the same might be flabbier or firmer in quality. Or perhaps not, if every element of form were known and reckoned. But the possibility of raising the question underlines the absurdity of the scheme we are considering. The concrete fact has always degree as well as pattern, and it is from this that we start.

Probably, indeed, we ought to make a further distinction. We have used 'quality' and 'intensity' as equivalents, and so they are, if we use 'quality' to mean simply degree, richness, positivity of existence. But it seems at least very plausible to maintain that activity possesses a quality of kind as well as a quality of degree, so that two acts between whose degree we should not distinguish would still differ in a sort of quality. This quality, again, would be correlative with a certain pattern, but it would not *be* that pattern.

This position really follows from our distinction between the apprehension of the *unum* and the analysis of its forms of unity. A piece of life, action, existence is more than its structural aspects, and the inclusive whole can be experienced as one. But this oneness must surely be or have a quality, or else what is it?

To return to the point from which we started. If we say that activity is characterised by character, or its formal aspect, we must understand 'character' and 'form' in a purely logical sense, i.e. as describing anything that can be the answer to the question: 'How, or of what sort, is it?' But 'character' in this sense includes qualities of degree and kind as well as aspects of structure. The 'it' which is not, but has, the character, is then mere activity-as-such, the being a real existence or operation. By another degree and sort of logical abstraction, this sheer it-ness, this activity-as-such, can be regarded as a 'character', and as an answer to the question 'what sort?' viz. when we take not real subjects for our field, but mental objects as such, and then proceed to ask whether they are entities, or elements in entities, etc.; but in the present context we are anyhow speaking of what things are in themselves, and then to be an instance of activity-as-such is not to have one character rather than another, but just to be something.

If then the essence is the character which makes activity-as-such to be of a particular species, it must include not only the structural aspects, but also the quality of degree and of kind which belong to the species. It may well be that the quality cannot be described, but only its structure; but that has reference not to reality but to our powers of speech. The essence, then, whether conceived as the limit or goal of the character of a certain continuous operation, determines the quality or qualities as well as the structure.

The theme of this whole section may be stated in a simple distinction. There is a relation of pattern (considered as such) to activity (as having quality). There is also a relation of activity-as-such to all that characterises it. These two relations are not the same. When we are talking of essence, we are thinking of the second distinction; essence is concerned with the more inclusive character. So too when we are talking of form, if we are speaking realistically; if nominalistically, meaning by 'form' the elements actually seized by a verbal definition, we shall presumably be employing the former distinction.

(viii) *Substantial Relations*

So much for the metaphysical analysis of the single substance. It is this that plays the principal part in the 'Cosmological Idea' and therefore in theological dialectic. But we have allowed a secondary and yet essential rôle in theological reasoning to the plurality and the interrelation of substances, and so it is proper to give a metaphysical description of substantial relations. This will be no more than a collection and classification of conclusions reached in previous chapters. We confine ourselves to relations that are real, i.e. which affect or express the activity of at least one substance. We have no need to treat of mere 'philosophical relations' which relate elements distinguished by our minds within what is really indivisible, or elements brought together by our minds from spheres that are actually unrelated in the relevant respect. We will proceed by the method of division.

A. *Effect, Ingredience.* This division results from our whole view of substance and the interrelation of substances. Real being is a whole of activity, concentrated in one focus, actual only in this concentration; and so the *effect* of an operation is immanent, and is found in its modification and prolongation of itself. But in determining itself thus and thus, it determines the field of other operations, and so constitutes an *ingredient* in them. This is an event not in the original operation, but in the others in which it becomes an ingredient. Every real event is a phase of activity, and passivity is an aspect of activity, and not an equal correlative. The activity of this operation has a passive aspect in so far as its form is limited and determined—often broken and spoilt—by the conditions set to it by its field of ingredients, i.e. its neighbours. But this field is a logical abstraction, it is nothing separate and actual, it is the form of the operation in so far as determined by the co-existence of other operations, and apart from this operation it would, *qua* such a field, have no existence, but would simply be the existence of the other operations each in itself.

The terminology 'Effect (immanent)—Ingredience (transitive)' well represents this state of affairs. If for ingredience we write 'affect' then we suggest that the passing over of some determination from the one operation to the other is itself an event, by which A affects B. This is absurd, for the relation by which an event conditions another event is not itself an event, or we should have an infinite regress. But we may usefully retain the word 'affect' to apply to cases where the conditioning of the other operation thus and thus is the intention of the operation from which the conditioning arises; and this may remain appropriate, even where for 'intention' some mysterious subconscious analogue, or animal purposiveness, is substituted. Thus we may speak of an act of affecting when one animal wounds another as an act of strategy in removing a rival, but not when the parasite, in nourishing itself, injures its carrier accidentally. In the former case there is a sort of intention to affect the operation of the rival, in order that, by his further operation, he may not be a tiresome ingredient in the aggressor's future field. In the latter case, nothing is intended about the victim but only about the aggressor's self-nourishment. The act of affecting, then, is not real as an event passing over from A to B, but it is real in A in so far as he intends the conditioning of B.

The relation of ingredience involves the uniformity of its working. Unless there was a rule according to which the conditioning of one activity was determined by the operation of another, so that such an operating in A involves such a conditioning of B, to say that operations condition one another would not even begin to mean anything. Ingredience without rule might be attributed to an omnipotent will, but hardly to anything else; for the will might simply say 'Let X be conditioned thus' and it would be so. But we have to describe ingredience divorced not only from omnipotence but even from all intention, as when the driver runs over the cat he never saw. Even where intention is present and we do will to affect, it is always by a choice between *given* alternatives, and these require a rule according to which they are given. Here, then, is one of the two bases for the axiom of uniformity; the other and equal basis being a principle intrinsic to each operation itself, viz. that it must be expressive of a certain nature or essence, as has been sufficiently enlarged upon. The axiom of uniformity is really twofold: it asserts (a) that the operation of any substance must accord with the recurrent rhythm of operation proper to that substance, (b) that the conditioning of one operation by another expresses a uniform rule—given X, then follows Y and not Z. We have already seen in detail that the (a) application of the axiom has no tendency to remove but only to condition free spontaneity; we have now to make the same observation about the (b) application.

For that which follows according to a rule upon the operation A is not the operation B but a conditioning of it, or modification of its field, in view of which B operates. That there are no alternatives left open to B by this conditioning, in no way follows. Perhaps we ought to say that A's operation leads to a direct and inescapable modification of B activities already enacted before B can recall or alter those activities, and again of B activities which are essentially unalterable in the relevant respect. For example, if I am looking in a certain direction, my sight is inescapably determined by what comes into the field of vision before I can decide to look elsewhere; and if a knife is stuck into my heart, my operation is permanently modified and time to reflect brings no power to evade.

It appears that the laws of physics are some sort of abstraction from the actual uniformity-rules of what we have called ingredience, and are concerned with the (b) application of the axiom of uniformity. Whereas such study as we have been making of the will, and perhaps some biological thinking, are principally concerned with the (a) application.

We will proceed now to divide ingredience, leaving effect alone, for we have dealt with it sufficiently in the description of finite substance. It is simply the operation of any activity as such, viewed as giving rise to its own new phase.

B. *Continuous, Discontinuous and Generative Ingredience. Continuous ingredience* is of a substance's own past phases in its present phase, in so far as past phases become the immediate and internal conditions of the present phase. In the case of a mind, the number and the pastness of phases which can be ingredients in the present are very considerable. *Discontinuous ingredience* is of the operations of other substances as ingredient in the field of a given substantial operation, and allows of no time-gap but seems to be rather associated with the form of space. The conditioning arises in field B at the time when the corresponding operation takes place in A. This statement is merely tautological; the correspondence of two fields is their mutual conditioning, and we have no room in which to think a time-lag between the event in the one and its ingredience in the other. But in so far as B reacts to the condition, this reacting takes time; time to develop, that is, not time to begin. If it took no time, we could not distinguish B's reaction from the passive modification of his field. All real time, like all real space, is within activity and its field, and not in the relation of one field to another. The discontinuous ingredients appear to me as placed in my spatial field, and so their getting placed in it cannot be seen to take time.

By contrast, continuous ingredience is bound up with the form of time; the past phase regarded as an event that *was*, was itself and its own world of time and space; but it relates itself to the present as an ingredient in the temporal field of the present, which it determines out of its pastness.

Generative ingredience is an ambiguous kind between the other two. When a substantial unit of activity arises or is created, it is not *ex nihilo*; something passes over from another unit or units; and yet in a manner inexplicable to us, continuity is broken. In so far as there is a budding-off or division, a side-by-side relation enters into the moment of generation together with the relation of succession; the ingredience of the 'parent' is into the spatial as well as temporal field of the offspring. Yet this relation cannot be thought to be the mere product of the other two relations; it has its own unique character in the arising of a new field, a new substance, or else the division of an old.

C. *Penetrable and Impenetrable Ingredience.* This division runs across that just given. All relations of ingredience except generation can constitute the ingredient an object to the recipient, supposing that the recipient is conscious. I remember my past, I am aware of present external objects. Yet sometimes consciousness penetrates the object and sees it from within and as it is for itself; sometimes consciousness merely knows *that* the object is for itself, but appreciates it only *as* it is ingredient in the field of consciousness. The qualifications that need to be made in this opposition have been detailed above (p. 243) and will here be taken for granted. It may here be remarked that when it was formerly said (p. 231) that our theory of perception was a causal one, it would have been more exact to describe it as a theory of ingredience. We perceive an object in so far as it is an ingredient in our existence; but this is not convertible: not everything, in so far as it is an ingredient, is perceived. The perception of an object, therefore, is not itself a metaphysical relation but is such a relation (ingredience) *qua* luminous in consciousness.

Of this luminosity there are two degrees, so that we say that the ingredience is either penetrable or impenetrable. Continuous ingredience may be penetrable or it may not. Some of the activity from which my conscious act arises is penetrable by strict memory, being near or above the conscious level itself. Other is impenetrable, being below it. Discontinuous ingredience seems to be all impenetrable; we do not have distinct inspection into other activities viewed as in themselves, though we may construct the diagram of their physical pattern and suppose their self-being from the analogy of our own. Yet this universal negative is not certain; if we appear to see into others' minds, this may indeed be by construction from obscure signs, or by physical affection of an unknown kind, as though, for example, telepathy had a basis analogous to wireless transmission. But it may be that there is an inspection which is indistinct but still direct, and merely *assisted* by the signs.

D. *Equal, Material-Formal and several nameless kinds of Discontinuous Ingredience.* It is *equal*, when the ingredience is reciprocal and in the same way: as when one Rugby football player charges another, or when a man moves a stone. In the former case, evidently. In the second case also, in so far as the last cause which displaces the stone is a group of physical constituents of the cells making up the man's skin, interacting with the constituents of the surface of the stone. But if we think of the man's mind as moving the cells, the relation is different: it is *material-formal*. For the man's soul operates as the form of his living body, i.e. of its general vital pattern, and not of the cells one by one, still less of the physical constituents in the cells. The operation of the body is the immediate operation of the soul, or self; the operations of the constituent cells are discontinuous ingredients for the operation of their form, and that of the form for those of the constituent cells.

Yet this ingredience is not equal, but of a singular kind, material-formal. The lowest physical operation, with no matter subject to it, has the universe, as it were, for its body; it is on the foundations of that shifting field that it has to maintain its own pattern. But the operation of the living organism has mastered and now controls an artificially stabilised immediate environment, in relation to whose operations its own is more securely actualised. The operations of the material units remain in themselves, but are bound in a very singular way by those of the superior form. This relation has impressed philosophers and been assigned enormous importance as an analogy for all sorts of metaphysical (and other) relations. Yet it is not the only type of discontinuous ingredience beside equal ingredience; we had to consider above the relation of the several parts of the ivy (p. 243f) and there is no *a priori* determination of the number of ways in which the forms of several operations may overlap and condition one another in nature; and so we have listed 'several nameless kinds' of discontinuous ingredience.

It would not serve our purpose to distinguish these, even if we had the requisite special knowledge; we have gone so far in subdivision merely in order to suggest how the several sorts of relation group themselves under our principal divisions, viz. Effect—Ingredience: Continuous Ingredience—Discontinuous Ingredience. It is with these that we shall operate in the theological dialectic.

PART III

DIALECTIC OF RATIONAL THEOLOGY

XXII

USIOLOGICAL ARGUMENTS (A): FROM ANALYSIS OF FINITE SUBSTANCE

Classification of Proofs

EVERY argument for God's existence must start from the world of finites, or from the nature of finite substances as such. And it must proceed from a distinction taken within the finite. 'If the world is, then God must be' may be true, but it is scarcely an argument. We must take some distinction within the finite and then claim to show that the co-existence of the elements distinguished, in the way in which they do co-exist, is intelligible only if God exists as the ground of such a co-existence.

The argument, therefore, has first to exhibit the finite co-existence which is its base, and then to convince us that this co-existence demands the divine existence. In thus proceeding, it is bound to make a violent jump in the middle. For it will exhibit a co-existence of elements which is revealed by the analysis of the finite order, upon the level of thought which has the finite for its object, and by the employment of finite principles alone. Such is the analysis of finite being which has been occupying the second part of this book. But when the argument proceeds to exhibit the co-existence revealed by such analysis as demanding the existence of God, it makes a jump from the finite to the infinite plane; for it is only because we in fact see the finite co-existence as the splintered image of God's existence, that we regard the finite elements as not merely co-existent (which would be a fact demanding no explanation) but composite (and therefore requiring in the simple a ground for their composition). We have argued this point in the first part of this work, and merely recall it here.

The argument therefore exhibits a distinction of elements within the creature in order to make us jump to the cosmological intuition, i.e. to the apprehension of God as the being in whom this distinction is, in its finite form, transcended—who is the 'coincidence' of these 'opposites'. But how does the argument lead us to make this intuitive jump? It may be sometimes enough to state the distinction and its transcendence in God, for the hearer or reader to see the conclusion. But the further removed he is from theistic ways of thought, the less likely is this to succeed; for he will not see what is meant by the notion of this transcendence, and so it will be necessary to help him out with analogies.

It is here that we come into the realm of dialectic proper. If, as is most naturally done, we treat the analogies as general principles from which the theological truth follows as an instance falling under the rule, we make a formal false syllogism or paralogism, as was shown at length in our first part—if, for example, we treat divine causality as an instance of a universal 'causality' and as logically required by the application of the universal causal rule to the case of the world as such. This is formal paralogism, for all analogical syllogisms have *quaternio terminorum* and are invalid. But we avoid the charge of paralogising, if we abandon the pretension of syllogising at all and allow that the 'syllogism' is not the simple application of a rule to an instance, but a challenge to us to recognise a genuine analogy and in doing so to arrive at the cosmological idea. Consequently there are two ways of presenting the theological dialectic. We may state the arguments as syllogisms and refute them—a procedure neither useful nor edifying. Or we may state the manner in which the given distinction in the finite acts as a splintered image of God and treat the quasi-syllogism as analogical illustration. And this is the method we shall use.

It follows that the arguments will differ essentially according to the finite distinction taken as the base of each, and this is the main principle of classification. But we note also a secondary classification which cuts right across this, and gives us two positions within each argument. For the finite distinction allows of two relations to the creative activity of God. Let the distinction be of the elements A and B. Then we may either

(1) take A for granted, and show the addition of B to it as necessarily the effect of divine action (or *vice versa*), or

(2) take neither for granted, but exhibit the combination AB as forming a nature so 'composite' that it must be regarded as derivative from that which is 'simple' in this respect.

Form (1) may be called *immanental* because it tries to exhibit God as effecting an operation within the finite system by modifying an existent A; form (2) *transcendental* because it tries to exhibit Him as the cause of the existence of that system as such. Now the human mind is inclined to proceed from the more particular to the more universal; men seem more readily aware of divine activity as expressed in some factor of their existence, than in the fact of that existence as a whole. And so the first form makes the easiest appeal and seems most natural. It is, however, philosophically absurd and must yield place to the second form, to which it acts simply as a bridge of approach.

In either form, but especially in the first, it is always possible to make an appeal to 'experience'. No longer content to exhibit the distinction in such a way as to evoke the cosmological idea which transcends it, we appeal to men to recognise that in particular instances of this distinction they have seen or habitually see the work of God. So, if we like, we may call this an *experiential* argument and reckon it as form (3). But it plainly is not on the same footing with the other two.

But, as we said above, the more important division of arguments is not this two- (or three-) fold formal division, but the material division according to the finite distinctions taken as the bases of the several arguments. And in this material division there is one principal division, between *usiological*[1] and *anthropological* arguments: those which find their basis in finite nature in general, and those which find it in the particular nature of man. The importance of this division follows from the conclusion of the first part of this book and from the tendency of the whole.

For (*a*) we have no direct knowledge of any particular mode of existence except our own. It would therefore be a waste of time to build theological arguments on the particular natures of frogs or electrons, and perhaps no sensible person has ever done so; if we pass outside human nature it is to argue from the higher generalisation of finite being as such.

(*b*) Our actual thought about God was seen to rest on these two bases. For logical clarity, we preferred the order which begins by considering God as the supreme existence, and proceeds to give content to this notion by borrowing from our own existence a modality of existence whereof God's existence must be the transcending archetype. But the opposite order is equally proper and closer to the order in which we come to know. Now we start from the other end; our own being presents us with the spectacle of a scale of degrees within itself, for freedom and knowledge 'aspire' to become more absolutely themselves and in so doing point to an archetype in which they are quit of their limitations. But, in so doing, they must utterly transcend our species of existence and become something other; and in the process of wrestling with this paradox, we cast our eyes on the world outside us and extend our 'interior scale' into the 'external scale'. As our several acts are all human acts but of various level, so the human form of substantial activity itself demands to stand in a scale of activity with the non-human forms; and so we rise to the thought of an activity which is the absolute form of activity as such. And this solves our paradox for us; it is as the absolute form of existence as such, that God is the archetype of humanity and yet not human.

Whichever way we proceed, therefore, whether from usiology to anthropology or from anthropology to usiology, both are really essential. Without anthropology we should not start, and without usiology we should not arrive. Though in exposition we start from one or other end, in our actual thought the two are implicitly present and complement one another throughout. Usiology by itself is too empty a scheme ever to be a real thought, while the principle of the anthropological ascent towards God is really usiological—it is that of ascent from finitude to the infinite. We shall take this distinction, then, as the grand division of our arguments, without supposing that the two classes can really do without one another. We will follow our previous order, and take the usiological first.

These are divided into two classes: (A) from the finitude of finite being, i.e. from the distinction of essence and existence or of activity and its modes,

---

[1] From οὐσία (being or essence). The hideous form 'ousiological' might be more easily recognised by some readers, but there are limits to what one is prepared to write.

(B) from substantial relations. Of these two classes (A) is far more important in itself, for from it we can conclude to a Supreme Being. But (B) makes an easier appeal to our minds, since its bases are more readily granted; and so it has some dialectical importance, even though its concealed principle throughout is the principle of (A) and even though it cannot reach the desired conclusion without calling in the aid of (A) to supplement its deficiencies. These points will become clear in the examples, so we will not dwell upon them further here.

A I. From the Distinction: Essence—existence

This is absolutely fundamental. All the theological arguments must ask in some form the question 'Why is it so?' of something in the world, in order to conclude it to have been made so by a being about whom the same question cannot be asked. Now the ultimate 'it', the subject which we can strip of no further predicates without abolishing it, is the existent (=activity) as such; and the first predicate, the first 'so' with which it is clothed, is the mode of its existence. To see the significance of the distinction is to see the possibility of the divine nature, i.e. of that in which existence is not limited by an essence but is its own essence. To admit the significance of the question 'Why is it so?' is to admit that existence limited by essence, when existence not so limited is possible, requires explanation; and the answer 'Because God has made it so' finds that explanation where alone it can be sought, in the activity of an unlimited existence. There is nothing dialectical so far; our actual implicit awareness of God's creative action in the finite is made explicit by a train of reasoning which analyses the finite by an implicit comparison with God, condemns it as composite by the same implicit comparison, and judges the composite to be dependent by the implicit awareness that this compositeness is the effect of divine creation, placing a qualified and finitised image of the divine being outside God.

True dialectic begins when we give reasons for the validity of the 'why?' question. This is what needs to be made clear to the ignorant. 'Why may not the composition of essence and existence be taken for granted? It looks all right.' We have, then, to try to make it look all wrong; and this can only be done by analogies. There is no *reason* why it is 'all wrong', i.e. non-self-explanatory; it just is so, and this must be appreciated. Our analogies can merely draw this out. Following the distinction stated above, we will take form (1) and form (2) of the argument in turn.

A I (1) *a. Taking essence for granted.* There is a multiplicity of actual essences. As essences they are simply different from one another, except in so far as they have generic or specific similarities; and some pairs lack these. And yet the actuality or existence of them all is in a manner identical; to all of them operation is common. Now this common characteristic is not an element which enters identically into the make-up of their otherwise different natures, so as to make them species of a common genus, for then they would all possess it in an equal degree and manner, which they do not. But neither can it belong to each essence *qua* that particular essence; for then it would be several in each, and its identity throughout the realm of essence would remain inexplicable.

But the puzzle is solved if we suppose that the identical character of actuality inflows upon the several essences, according to their several degrees of receptivity for it. From what source can it so inflow upon them? From a being in whom it exists in absolute degree, and who, therefore, need not by the same reasoning have himself received it from without.

A I (1) *b. Taking existence for granted:* for this seems equally reasonable; it is no easier to ask why disparate essences are variously filled with one existence, than to ask why existence is variously modified. We now argue thus. Existence is found limited by several degrees and modes, through its exemplification in various essences. It cannot be proper to existence as such to be limited so, or all existence would have one limit. Neither can the several measures arise by the addition of standard units of existence to one another; such a minimum unit is not thinkable, neither is it thinkable that any existent we like to take is an aggregate of standard existence-units. But it is not thinkable either that existence as such has no proper mode and degree; for divorced from any such, it is just nothing at all, for it is not a genus abstractible from its species. Its standard form, then, must be a maximum; and the finite existents must have their essential limit imposed upon them by a being himself not in need of such an imposition, i.e. himself the maximum existent.

These two arguments—the *a* and *b* of form (1)—refute one another and make recourse to form (2) necessary. For according to (*a*) it is not proper to presuppose existence, nor, according to (*b*), is it proper to presuppose essence; we require an argument in which neither is presupposed. But the absurdity does not lie simply in the contradiction of the two proofs, but in the procedure. Essence without existence *is not*, and therefore cannot be presupposed as the measure of it; and finite existence without essence *is not*, and cannot therefore receive the imposition of a measure.

This does not, however, destroy the whole value of the proofs, though it totally destroys the form of their conclusions. They still, by the arbitrary procedure of supposing first the one and then the other element, exhibit the curiosity of the relation between the two, and suggest that it is such as to require an external 'cause'.

The procedure of the proofs is really this. They assume the principle that 'relations of reason', in so far as valid, must be reducible to real relations. Now it is asserted that the reason, contemplating the world, finds itself under a genuine objective necessity to admit degrees of a common something, viz. existence, in many distinct essences. But this comparability of the many essences—or, to put it otherwise, this portioning out of the common existence—is a 'relation of reason' not a real relation. Comparability is not a manner of co-existing or interacting on the part of comparables; the occurrence of existence in divers portions is not yet known as an actual process of its portioning out. Each of the comparables, so far as we yet know, and each of the portions is a fact by itself, and the drawing of them into a single field is purely the act of the mind.

But now what are the real, existential or substantial relations from which the mind is making this abstract selection? What is the structure of actual process through which the mind takes this cross-section? The proofs pretend to proceed by the method of elimination: it is not this real relation, nor that—existence does not belong to all species generically nor to each specifically, therefore it does not belong to their forms or natures. It remains that the only possibility left should be admitted—that it enters them as a quasi-ingredient through the action of another substance itself outside the finite system. The method of proof (*b*) is similar.

Such a proof, to be valid, requires that we know *a priori* that we possess a complete set of possible real relations, one of which the case we are dealing with must perforce exemplify. A real relation which is not a case of the mutual complementariness of elements proper to the form of the substance (nor a case of interior effect, an alternative that does not need mentioning, since nothing makes its own existence or essence) must be a case of ingredience. But it is plainly absurd to take the scheme of known finite substantial relations as *a priori* exhaustive when we are in fact going to conclude to the operation of the infinite; it is absurd even when we are examining the case of a newly discovered inter-finite relation which bids fair to prove unique. The only valid conclusion, then, must be that of all the substantial relations we already know, one serves better than the rest as an analogic symbol by which we may in fact grasp the unique real relation that we seek. For this purpose it is not sufficient to state the most appropriate analogue; for if we do so, we may just as well conclude it to be inappropriate as appropriate. We see its appropriateness in contrasting it with the less appropriate alternatives. We have explained this at length in our discussion of analogical dialectic (*supra*, pp. 88ff). The essential point is that the inacceptable analogues are those which find the real relation within the finite, the acceptable that which goes outside it.

It was said earlier in this chapter that the characteristic argument for God's existence begins from a distinction which arises on the finite level of thought; from this, which we called its base, it makes a jump to the infinite level. The evidential weakness of the essence-existence argument is the non-obviousness of its finite base. Has it really any such base at all? Does the distinction 'essence-existence' arise at all, without the implicit application of the idea of the infinite? Do we not, then, start with crypto-theism and so argue to theism? Can it be said that we even provide a finite vehicle or *locus* in which crypto-theism naturally operates?

St. Thomas and Descartes both felt this need, and supplied it in various ways. According to the former, the essence-existence distinction does arise on the finite plane, when we consider the mutual comparability of substances in degree of value = reality = existence. On the simply finite plane, this means that they are measured by one another; if we take any as standard, the rest are above, below or level with it. We jump into crypto-theism when we take the step of recognising that our (arbitrarily chosen) standard itself, and any finite substance considered by itself, is a determinate measure of existence. For that involves an absolute standard.

Descartes, on the other hand, is restricted by his method to the consideration of the single substance, himself; he cannot use the comparison of substances for his basis. But he can use an internal comparison; there is the self he would be, but is not, and the self he is, but aspires to transcend. The self he would be is still, surely, a finite creature; and the jump into implicit theism occurs when he passes from the deficiency of myself from my ideal of myself, to the deficiency of myself from absolute existence.

Let this suffice for an examination of the first form of the essence-existence proof; we pass to the second and more satisfactory form.

A I (2). *From the interrelation of essence and existence.* Essence and existence are found together in substances without proper unity; that is to say that (*a*) as the two proofs have shewn, neither belongs to the other as constituent to essence or property to form, and (*b*) there is no form which embraces both as constituents, or from which both follow as properties; for while there may be said to be a form proper to substantial being which demands both existence and essence, both activity and a determinate mode of activity, this form fails to determine *what* mode or essence, and so fails to determine the composition of essence and existence in the particular substance. All modes or essences are substitutible for one another without removing existence as existence.

Therefore every particular union of the two is the work of a being in whom existence finds its own full possibility and so is its own essence; that is, all finites are creatures of the infinite.

This proof is simply the former two with removal of the absurdity that either essence or existence is presupposed and regarded as prior to their union. But it can no more be accepted as a true syllogism than they can. Its principles are in fact identical with theirs. It adds a fresh suggested analogy, (*b*), in the body of the argument; but on strictly logical ground the use made of it will not bear examination. The form of a substance is in its essence; when we are asking after form, we presuppose existence and ask what form it takes. And so to remark that essence and existence do not constitute a form is not really to make a point. The relation is plainly unique, and a relation in which all form stands as one term. But by the contrast we do draw out the singularity of this relation, in grasping which we are to grasp the cosmological truth.

The conclusion of the proof is still imperfect, though less so than those of the previous two. For it cannot get rid of the scheme of the determination of a determinable, if it is going to keep any hold whatever on the finite analogy. The determinable has simply been refined; it is no longer essence or existence, but the indeterminate essence-existence complex, the empty form of finitude. Still, the determination of this is not the determination of anything, but the causing of something to be where nothing was. Thus the scheme of the determination of a determinable, i.e. of causality in its widest sense, is simply an analogy, which points beyond itself to the inexpressible fact of creation. We have seen (p. 23f) that we assist our thought to this self-transcendence by the opposition of other finite analogies to this of determination (i.e. of ingredience).

A I (3). *From the experience of finitude.* The experiential form of this argument will be simply the appeal to any particular existence which puts itself upon us as the work of God, because we are then impressed with the fact of finitude elsewhere taken for granted. This may be through comparison, for instance of the speck of dust to the starry heavens; or when singular goodness, beauty or power appears to start from its finite setting and shew as the creative effect of infinite being.

A II. From the Actual and the Possible

An impoverished by-form of the essence-existence argument is that which substitutes the distinction 'possible-actual'. This distinction has no advantage but that of obviousness, and it has a number of drawbacks. It is not easy to exhibit it as a real distinction within the finite. For the question 'Why is this (existence) so (modified)?' it substitutes 'Why *is* this (essence) rather than that?' Since this question does not arise from a genuine analysis of the finite fact, it presumably arises from the contemplating mind's ability to think things otherwise. This ability cannot be admitted without question. Our concrete suppositions are but variations on the theme of actual existence arising out of the fanciful employment of our faculty for proposing alterations within the limits of that existence. We cannot suppose the general nature of the world or of ourselves otherwise without a pitiful abstractness which disqualifies our suggestions for the rôle of real possibilities; we cannot even suppose the detail of existence otherwise except by atomising it and leaving things without the real sequence they would need, to be actual in themselves. We can properly suppose otherwise only what we or the likes of us could make otherwise; and in that case finite causes (like ourselves) will sufficiently explain why it has in fact been made not otherwise but so. Any other supposed power to conceive it otherwise may be begotten by abstraction upon ignorance.

A II (1). *Presupposing the possible.* Since possible-actual is not a distinction between elements in the given, but between essence and its givenness, there is only one side to the first form of the argument. We must presuppose essence. Of the realm of essence, which is sometimes said not to exist but to subsist, only part is actualised in existence; or if all is actualised, it is actualised in an order that might have been otherwise (No, says Spinoza, and it is difficult to refute him; it is but one dogmatism against another). Then the sufficient cause for the actualisations must be found in a being whose actuality has not been thus arbitrarily selected.

What would such a being be? Here the ways divide. We may either say, a being who comprises all essences (i.e. all conceivables) in the only order in which they will coalesce into one being; or we may say, a being whose essence (whether it be all-inclusive or not) implies its own existence.

According to the former alternative, God need not be distinguished from the realm of essences itself; in Him all the possibilities (conceivabilities) co-exist in a perfectly tidy system, or, He is such a system existent. Since the possible essences are in fact abstractions, we must think of the divine being as a mind, for only in or as a mind can a system of abstractions form one being. The very differentia, then, of the divine mind is to be the kaleidoscope of infinite possibility. About such a being we need not ask why He is so, rather than otherwise; for He is all. Essence is what is, and He is all essence.

According to the latter alternative, the distinction between possibility and actuality is more rigidly adhered to. Why should all possibility, united in one being, be actual? It is not as with the Thomist doctrine, where existence and essence naturally belong together and it is only a matter of finding their position of rest or perfect mutual adjustment, and we have found God. No, we are beginning with essence as mere 'subsistent' possibility. How does anything, then, come to acquire actuality? Only if there is an essence whose own essential principles contain or imply its actual existence. This essence, then, *is*, and can become the cause of being to all the rest. But such an essence—it is claimed—is forthcoming; the ENS REALISSIMUM, or being which unites the maximum of positive predicates reconcilable in one subject, includes, by definition, the predicate of being actual and not possible only, for actuality is a form of positivity.

To criticise this theology would be a thankless task. Kant has said all that is necessary to say about it. He has taught us the flimsiness of 'mere possibility'; the absurdity of treating existence (=givenness) as a predicate; the utter unreality of the conception of the divine mind as an animated pool of all possible predicates. The fundamental difficulty is, that essence treated in this logical and abstract manner yields us a merely quantitative differentia for the divine infinity; God is the pool of all essence or the maximum addition of possible predicates in one subject. Such a conception is powerless to yield us any notion of God, unless it is covertly helped out by the *modus eminentior*—the fullness of essence is synthetised into one by a transcendent intensity of spiritual act, which can be called 'spiritual' and 'act' only by analogy. But the notion of the *modus eminentior* has no right to a place in this circle of ideas. It is borrowed from the degrees of *esse*, existence in St. Thomas's sense.

A II (2). *From the relation of actuality and possibility.* The special absurdity of the (1) form of the argument is that pure possibilities are presupposed as subsistent, and that God is made to operate upon them by actualising them; as though they were outline drawings, some of which a divine artist coloured in, while others He did not. The more chastened (2) form allows that essence and its actuality belong together *in general*, so that neither can be presupposed; but that one does not see why essence should be actual just in this scheme, order and extent. Things must have been *appointed* so (*gesetzt*); and so we look for their appointer in a being from whom such arbitrariness is eliminated and who determines his own content by an intelligible and apparently self-evident principle. Such a principle is, that his essence should be as rich as possible. But the notion of a 'maximum richness' either presupposes subsistent possibility from which to choose, and so recurs to the vice of argument (1); or else introduces the notion of a maximum intensity of *esse*, and so has recourse to the essence-existence idea.

If it is humble enough to adopt the latter course, this piece of dialectic is no longer wholly to be despised. The mere fact that things are as they are, and the conviction that they could be otherwise, makes an appeal to the unsophisticated mind;[1] and if it sets in train a pursuit which can only reach its goal by recurring to the essence-existence argument, it has performed a very valuable, if introductory, task. We shall see that the same can be said of most of the succeeding arguments.

[1] The child falls into a deep philosophical amazement over the question why, 'in spite of all temptations to belong to other nations', lands or times, he is born a twentieth-century Englishman.

XXIII

USIOLOGICAL ARGUMENTS (B): FROM SUBSTANTIAL
RELATIONS

B I. From Operation and Interior Effect

IN considering arguments from substantial relations we may as well follow our list, and start with interior effect. The centre of finite reality is the act, and the act is the actualisation of a form of operation. Yet the relation of the inchoate to the complete stage of the act is paradoxical. The form has to become enacted. When it is enacted, the act is over; until it is enacted, the form *is* not, or has a merely incipient and precarious hold on the activity which enacts it. We may try to stop the gap by employing the notion of 'potency'; but this is only a nominal solution, for all the difficulties inherent in the relation of the previous activity to the completed enactment remain within the notion of potency itself. It would seem intelligible, if either (*a*) the operation simply flowed through its course, and the form were the rhythm of its flow or (*b*) if the form were given in a state of actuality raised above process and from that eminence seized the process and conformed it to itself. A very ancient philosophical tradition complains that 'all things become, and nothing is'. It has often been thought that this scandal can be removed by the simple admission that the forms of the world are the rhythms of its flow, and that it is merely our thought that makes static diagrams of these. But this does not do justice to the nature of process as known from within. The form to be enacted does stand there as an objective to the process; the process is what it is in adopting and enacting this form; the paradox of 'coming to be' remains. The form is really the form of the effect, yet it informs the process which enacts the effect, and as soon as the enactment is complete, it ceases to be.

Such then, is the paradoxical distinction in the finite from which we start. We may try to ease it by calling in the field of 'ingredients', and regarding them as determining the process to the gradual attainment of the form. But this will not do; for the process is not subsequent to the field, it is only because a substantial activity is taking place that any field exists, or any ingredients enter it; the field is the external form of that activity. Nothing, then, is prior to the occurrence of some act, and the act, in so far as it occurs, has this paradoxical structure. In so far as it occurs, it must occur in view of, and shaped by, the ingredients in the field; none the less, for these to be given, it must be occurring.

But neither can we help ourselves out by appealing to the previous active phases of this substance. It is (once again) in view of them, and upon the basis of them, that it occurs, but none the less it occurs, having the principle of activity in itself (as each of the previous phases had in its own hour); and the activity still has this curious form.

On the base provided by these considerations it is easy to erect formal arguments of the first and second forms.

B I (1) *a. Taking the process of activity for granted.* Then it must be gradually informed with the form of the effect by the affective action of a being in whom this paradoxical distinction does not exist; who is an act simply and timelessly issuing in its own form, all temporality falling outside the act and within that which it affects.

B I (1) *b. Taking the form of the effect for granted* (for surely that which is something, the intelligible character, is rather to be presupposed than the unintelligible flow of activity). Then this is introduced into a certain field of particular circumstances by some power which accommodates it to them and them to it in a graduated process, such that the form becomes progressively dominant and the circumstances progressively modified. Such a power will be the activity of a form which acts simply, and not by gradual accommodation to any circumstances.

B I (2). *Taking neither the one element nor the other for granted*; for after all, these two previous proofs not only are in contradiction to one another, but (*a*) both presuppose abstractions which could not be by themselves, and (*b*) both destroy the reality of the finite act by making it the mere effect of another activity. Now, therefore, we presuppose neither, but seeing that the two factors are unable to coalesce simply into one self-dependent actuality, we suppose both to be held in existence, in their loose but mutually necessary connexion of activity, by a being from whom such looseness is absent.

The criticism of these arguments will follow the lines already laid down. It is, on the face of it, absurd to demand that the relation of form to act in real activity should be the same as that of form to filling in phenomena *qua* phenomena; and it is on this analogy that the proofs seem to build. As a formal refutation, it is enough to say that the enacted form plays the part it does play in real activity and that we cannot conceive that activity otherwise; that (as was demonstrated above at some length) the substantial UNUM is not to be looked for in any element of the operation nor in the perfect formal coherence of its elements into one form.

But the analogies perform a justifiable function if they reveal to us the incompleteness of finite substantial unity when judged, not by its own standard, but by that of infinite being which, through the veils of these analogies, we apprehend as the underlying ground of finite. And this particular argument is of importance because it introduces us to the idea of God as ACTUS PURUS. The finite act has an element of passivity in the very heart of it; it is drawn on by its own being and form, or conversely, that being and form are the subjects of actualisation. But in the infinite the form must simply act, and the act simply express itself. This does not indeed give us the whole sense of the traditional *actus purus*, for an act might be 'pure' within the terms of this argument and still have a limited form, which had been measured to it by a higher being. Such a being would still be 'passive' by the mere fact of having been created and assigned his limited rôle. So the argument only proves 'angels' as St. Thomas would say, and, if we wish to go further, we must invoke that from essence and existence, which exhibits the angels themselves as creatures.

B II. From Continuous Ingredience

The act appears to be the centre of substantial being, in such fashion that it is complete in itself and sufficient for existence: and yet it is continuous with previous acts in such fashion that it seems to make up one being with them. And yet each act, while it is, is itself, and all previous actual phases of the same substance are external to it. Here again we have a looseness of order which appears to demand external explanation. The interior principle of the act is sufficient to the act alone; if there are further phases, are they not added by the intervention of a creative power, himself exempt from such mutual externality of temporal order?

This might seem to be the basis of Descartes's argument, when he said that it was evident a temporal being (such as himself) had not in himself the power to continue his existence for a second moment. If we retorted upon the philosopher, 'No, nor the power to terminate it; it just depends whether you choose to demand a *causa tollens* for its ending, or a *causa ponens* for its continuing,' he would presumably reply: 'I take my stand upon what is contained within the clear idea of a temporal being. Such a being can be, and be itself, in any moment of its existence; it cannot require the past, which is no longer, nor the future, which is not yet. Therefore the addition of its present phase to its past phases, or of any future phase to its present phase, follows not from its nature. But neither does it seem to belong to it as an ability accidental to its nature. The only evidence for such an ability would be our seeming to possess it. But quite the contrary, my future becomes my present by no power of mine; my power is displayed only in what I do with it.'

If Descartes supposed that a being could be real in an indivisible atom of time alone, he was certainly talking nonsense, but if he meant, 'in the scope of a single act', then the position has some plausibility; though we must admit that the concession weakens a little the apparent force of the argument. For if we agree that being, in order to be itself, can and does seize and hold together a stretch of time, however small, the notion that it may cover a still longer stretch becomes more credible; and the beautiful clarity of 'the past is not now, the future is not yet' must be renounced. But we may still say that in fact the act appears existentially complete, and the continuity of it with past acts remains anomalous.

This argument from continuous ingredience is of very secondary importance. For first, it does not conclude to God, without support from the essence-existence argument, nor even to the Pure Act; but only to a temporal activity absolutely continuous and grasping its whole endless existence with the same grasp as our single act exercises upon its momentary duration. Secondly, it adds nothing to the far more radical argument from operation and effect, which excels it in its own kind. Thirdly, it is of no significance except in a certain context. It requires the suppositions (α) that the existence of the world requires the continuity of substances, (β) that generation is more evidently impossible as a finite operation without the support of the infinite, than is continuous ingredient. If we deny (α) then each act is itself and occurs upon a background supplied by previous acts, and there is nothing to worry about; if we deny (β), then each act can be generated from previous acts, and there is still nothing to worry about.

The formal refutation and material justification of this argument follow the previous models. For formal refutation it is enough to say that the continuity of a substance from act to act is what we experience it to be, and the making out that it is anomalous depends upon the demand that it should conform to an arbitrary standard of analogy. Time is what it is, and to object that that which was ought not to be ingredient in that which is, is to judge continuous (temporal) ingredience by the standard of discontinuous (spatial) ingredience. It is very true that another being cannot affect me from the past except mediately through the present, but my own past can so affect me, and is mine for that reason. But the argument can be materially justified if it leads us to appreciate the non-compositeness of God in respect of temporal succession, and if the anomaly we see in the finite arises not from the finite analogy as such, but from the implicit apprehension of God as the standard of unitary and self-sufficient existence.

It is evidently possible to construct formal arguments of the first and second forms here—Descartes's was of the first, since he concluded to a God who acts upon my (assumed) existence in order to continue it. But in so far as he said that it was evident this power was the same as that of creation, he implied an advance to the second; which sees that because continuous ingredience is necessary to substance as we know it, the inability of substance to perpetuate itself unaided is its inability to exist unaided—such a form of existence is dependent *as a whole.*

But perhaps what the argument lacks on the speculative side it makes up on the experiential. There is no doubt that the temporal condition of man's existence is frequently experienced by him most vividly as a form of finitude and of dependence. We cannot help thinking of ourselves as being something, and yet of all that we claim to be, nine hundred and ninety-nine thousandths are not actual now, but somehow projected in the past we once were, and the future we hope and intend to be hereafter; and it seems impossible to contemplate this without a strong movement of the mind to recognise ultimate reality in that Being alone who can say SUM QUI SUM, what I am I was not, nor shall be only, but am.

B III. From Discontinuous Ingredience: from Formality and Informality (Chaos)

Form is the form of an activity, or, taken in extent, of a substance. In discontinuous ingredience other activities, each with its own form, determine the field of a given activity. The detailed way in which they do so is accidental to the form of that activity. We say 'the detailed way', for doubtless it belongs to the form of the substance to act in a field of ingredients having such a *general* relation to it as the general forms of space and of physical interaction prescribe. But the occurrence of just these physical events rather than those is accidental to the form of the substance, and they may be more or less prejudicial to the functioning of that form. Certain substantial forms, to which ingredients are related as the matter of those forms, have a certain control over those ingredients which reduces the accidentality of the action of the ingredients relatively to the form; yet such control is never absolute and the element of accident remains, as when the cells of my body develop a cancerous growth and inhibit the function of the uniting vital form. It remains, then, that the world is a composition of form and chaos, each form struggling to dominate the irrelevance of an environment which is chaos relatively to its formal requirements. From this point we may develop the famous argument from design.

B III (1) *a. Presupposing chaos.* If the world were through and through perfectly coherent design or form, then that would be the nature of the world and no explanation would be required. The mystery is, that design should have got such a hold upon a material which seems 'naturally' to lack it. This cannot be the real home of form; it has plainly been imposed from above, by a supreme artificer ($\delta\eta\mu\iota o\hat{\nu}\rho\gamma o\varsigma$).

The great difficulty of this argument is the difficulty of presupposing chaos. Chaos is a chaos *of forms*; stripped of them it is nothing but the spatio-temporal scheme of the interaction of finite forms—the *materia prima* of an older philosophy: and we know it was ruled that prime matter could never have existed by itself nor have been created, but only co-created with some elements of form. It seems then that we must presuppose not naked chaos but a chaos of low-grade forms, in order to raise the question, how (since these do not need the higher forms for their existence) the higher were imposed on so recalcitrant a medium. Yet this way of stating the question has its own absurdity; for if the lowest forms, by themselves formal, can be taken for granted in their chaotic interaction, what fresh principle or fresh difficulty is raised by the interacting of higher forms with one another and with the lower in the same disorder? In spite of these absurdities, which will lead us to abandon form (1) of the argument for a (2) form, it is necessary to insist that the form we have given is the true form of the 'argument from design'. Many incorrect forms are in fact current; we will mention two.

(*a*) It is sometimes stated that the universe is a design or covered by a design; and as one system of action in me corresponds to the operation of one intelligence, so the far vaster and more complex system of the world to the operation of a proportionate intelligence. But there is no empirical evidence for the alleged fact. The stars are not a celestial ballet, nor even a celestial game of billiards. What those who say this probably mean is that the universe is governed by certain uniform laws of interaction. But these are not such a design as intelligence produces; they are the absolutely necessary conditions of any co-existence of substances and so are presupposed by all 'designs'. They are more like the criss-cross canvas on which the tapestry design is worked, than they are like that design. If you call the tapestry a design because, though the stitches of several colours are placed at random, they fall into square rows by virtue of the canvas's structure, then you may call the universe a 'design'. All grounds for asserting this in the other and proper sense went out with Ptolemy's system of astronomy.

(β) Or appeal is made to the fact of intelligent adaptation where we have no evidence for the presence of adequate intelligences; as in the evolution of the structure of insects, presumably not planned by themselves, nor plausibly assigned to chance variation. We then conclude not, as perhaps we should, to a number of little angels proportioned to the several effects, but to an all-wise and universal deviser. But the argument is absurd not only in the scope of the conclusion, but much more in the line of inference.

The quasi-purposive operation of vital force is a mystery to us, and we have no business to refer it to conscious choice, but rather to the working of a lower analogue of choice (*vide supra, passim*), which we partially experience in ourselves. Nature, unfortunately for this argument, commits shocking blunders also, and if anyone will object that our very partial knowledge does not allow us so to stigmatise them, we ought in fairness to reply that our congratulations upon nature's successes may be equally premature or ill-timed. No, nature appears to be a plurality of groping causes; and if groping causes do not satisfy us as a final explanation, because of their paradoxical mixture of blindness and quasi-intelligence, then neither will the human spirit, in which the same prin-ciple is found; and the proper development of this argument is quite different from that with which it began. We must not suggest that the intelligence of 'nature' (of which positively we know nothing and cannot establish any nega-tive) is inappropriate to its own effects; we must argue that finite activity is not the sufficient reason of anything, because it is largely controlled by instinctive and therefore blind, passively imposed, aims. But this is best conducted as an anthropological argument; since our talk about the blindness and yet pur-posiveness of 'nature' is talk about the impenetrable and unknown.

B III (1) *b. Presupposing form.* Surely it must have suffered violence from some external power in being thus chaotically interrelated or juxtaposed. This power must himself be supposed exempt from such juxtaposition. If the former argument, presupposing chaos, were absurd in its premise, this argument is as absurd in its conclusion. For why should a being, himself completely 'formal', i.e. harmonious, smash finite form against itself in chaotic destruction? The conflict between the argument of the proof and its conclusion is such that it is not usually known as a proof of God, but as the 'Problem of Evil'. Why should God cause the forms of human and animal existence to break against one another, and against inanimate nature, producing the most appalling deprivations and injuries in the physical, sensitive, and spiritual orders?

The problem is certainly formidable, on the level of form (1) arguments; for if we have to choose between (1) *a* and (1) *b*, the presupposition of chaos or of form, the latter is much more reasonable—the spoiling of form is secondary to form itself and evil parasitic upon good. But it is formidable only upon the form (1) level, whose absurdity it shares. If we advance to form (2) we are rid of it; and that is all that need be said about this venerable puzzle.

B III (2). *Taking neither form nor chaos for granted.* Admitting that the finite, as we know it, is a chaos of forms, we may argue as follows: In so far as there is an element of disorder in the universe, this implies some collocations of substance which cannot be derived from the formal principles of these substances nor from a form of their correlation. Accidental collocation is a mere fact, neither the form nor the expression of any finite operation, though several finite operations arise on the basis of it. It ought to be reduced to a real operation, on the part of a being not subject to accidental collocation with other things, nor to the accidental collocation of elements within itself. This noncomposite being, then, has placed or created composite being.

The formal fallacy of such an argument is its pretence that the interrelation between substances could be either a case of the interior order of a substance or the effect of a substance's action. It is in fact evidently unique; and the scandal of it as an order exterior to substance is reduced by the fact that this order is only actual in the sphere of each substance which focusses it (*vide supra*, p. 227). Equally fallacious is the treatment of divine causality as a case of (finite) substantial action.

The material justification of the argument is its evocation of our awareness of the dependent nature of the composite and the definition which it thus gives to our notion of God as non-composite in this regard. It leads us also to recognise an aspect of the creative act, and to consider it as the splintering of being by its reduction to the form of mutual externality. And thus it is that it can defy the 'Problem of Evil' attack. For granted that existence at our level must be splintered, collocated and accidently interrelated, it is not a matter of principle just what miseries arise; 'I could believe in God, were it not for cancer' is an absurd contention; for the nature of accident is to be irrational, nor can it be controlled by measure. It is a practical, not a speculative problem: of cancer research, not of theodicy. 'I believe in God because the world is so bad' is as sound an argument as 'I believe in God because the world is so good'. It could not be so bad if it were not so good, since evil is the disease of the good. But if it were purely good, it would be God. How God intervenes to save reasonable spirits out of the world-wreck is another matter, and not the business of rational theology at all.

B III (3). *From experience of good and evil.* This topic is rich in experiential argument of value: for though we have to set apart the (1) *a* form, it remains that the intention of the Creator is the reality and perfection of everything, so far as it can attain it; the accidental element pertaining rather to the baser medium which differentiates the creature from the Creator, and thereby provides the possibility of its distinct existence.[1] As we love our own distinct being, so must we endure the conditions of its possibility. Yet it is our reality that expresses the positive content of the divine purpose, and so it is no fancy but a natural intuition which apprehends the highest good as particularly an expression of the divine will and power.

B IV. From Discontinuous Ingredience: from Condition and Action

B IV (1). *Presupposing activity*. This topic arises in so far as we recognise that a finite agent can act only in view of ingredients arising in its field, and that these must be the result of operations taking place in other substances. But these operations were themselves conditioned by others, and so on. It is impossible to return in a circle, so that A should condition B, B C, C D, and D A; for time is not circular, and we are talking not of things but operations. We must then come back at last to a condition not itself conditioned, and this will be God. And this conclusion cannot be evaded by allowing an infinite regress in infinite (previous) time. There is no difficulty about infinite time, or an infinite series of events. But there is difficulty about an infinite regress of conditions. For these do not form a mere temporal series, such as Kant supposed, when he defined a cause as an event preceding another according to a certain law of uniform sequence. According to his definition the effect does not happen *because* of the 'cause'; its essential reason for occurring may effect it not through its 'cause' but as itself, as Berkeley supposed when he made every event the direct act of a God who merely chooses to place these immediate creations in due order of sequence. It is otherwise with true conditions: in view of them it is that the act essentially takes place. Unless, then, some condition had been simply given for some act, the act would not have occurred, and so no consequent act could have occurred. We can even, if we think it possible, intercalate an infinite number of links between this absolute beginning and any particular act; but the absolute beginning must be given.

Then God is proved as an agent, who acts with absolute freedom, from his own nature only, and in view of no conditions. Yet it would be irrational to think of his action as having constituted one far-off event in the remote past. For (*a*) the several series of conditions and conditioned seem to be indefinitely many; an act is conditioned not by one ingredient, but by a universe, and each constituent of this universe again in like manner; so that the creative act which is the original condition of finite action would be indefinitely multiple in its

---

[1] Of its existence distinct from the angels, if St. Thomas is right in supposing that immaterial spirits, finite but not passively conditioned in their existence by any field of other finites, are possible or indeed actual.

effect. And (β) the divine act cannot be thought to be like the many acts, temporal; for it has itself no temporal place, being unconditioned. Thus it is difficult to view it as standing in a temporal relation with its immediate effect.

It is here that the formal paralogism of this famous argument comes to light; for if God's action does not condition the first of the secondary causes by constituting its field of ingredients, then we have to grant that the principle demanding that such a field always be given, is false. What we are asserting is something different, viz. that first finite events could and did occur without a field, because they were *created*. But then we cannot conclude this from the principle it denies, but only from the tacit assumption that creation (whatever creation is—we shall not discover by the light of this argument alone) is the only possible alternative to a field. And if anyone would like to say that the first events just arose, and that the principle only holds good of subsequent events, what he says is not patently absurd.

The special weakness of this argument is that it places God's action in a series of finite actions of a clearly defined type; and in consequence the resultant analogy for the divine act is not in the least enlightening. What could be less like creativity than acting as a momentary field of conditioning ingredients for a particular finite act? Still, let us not abandon hope of better things; for this is a form (1) argument, and if we can advance it to a (2) form, it may yield more satisfactory results.

But what is the finite element which as a form (1) argument it presupposes? This does not seem at first sight quite clear: but until we have discovered it, we can hardly make the reform. At least it is presupposed that there is somehow given an act, waiting to actualise itself if only the condition is supplied. Such a potential act must be placed in an agent, i.e. in an already actual train of substantial activity specified by its own proper form. But such an agent must have been already in act in previous active phases, and if so, it was already conditioned, else how did it act? Moreover, if we presuppose one agent, why not many? Then the activity of one was already the condition of the other's. Thus by presupposing an act waiting upon a condition, one has presupposed an agent already conditioned. We are then at a loss how to conceive that first finite act waiting for nothing but a divine condition; the form of the act would have to be created as well as the condition of the act—yes, and the very occurrence of the act must be created, for the form can surely only come into being for the first time in the very operation of which it is the form. Thus to presuppose the act is absurd, whether naked or embodied potentially in an actual agent. Let us turn to a (2) form of argument which does not presuppose it.

B IV (2). *From condition and action.* Every agent, in order to be and to act, requires as prior to it a field of conditions in view of which it acts, and in which it exists. But this field is itself provided by other agents; of whom again each requires a field provided by agents already in act. Thus to every agent its field is prior; and yet that field has prior to it the agents whch give rise to it; to each of which again its field must be prior. Thus for anything to begin, we require an act and agent which conditions without being conditioned, or else a field of conditions based on no prior acts.

But if agent and field are understood in the sense of these terms as known to us, neither can pre-exist. Therefore both, i.e. a multiplicity of mutually conditioning agents, must be the effect of a being whose activity is not conditioned.

The proof thus phrased escapes some of the absurdities of form (1); and it has at least the value of making us sharply aware of the paradox of finite existence. For though we admit generation of substances, and even generation of species of substance through 'evolution' or 'emergence', it remains that the new being is generated from prior actualities and in some field; though we reduce the original cosmos to a few operations of simple type, each would be still presupposing its field, i.e. the others, and the difficulty remains.

But the only conclusion that is justified is that we have to suppose some original state of affairs in which there were not mutually conditioning agents of the sort we know. Such a pre-cosmic state might contain the principles of action in a confused, less differentiated form, from which the several interacting agents emerged by a specialisation and division, as in the system of Bergson. Such a state cannot be conceived by us—but neither can the being of God. The proof commands us to step outside our conceiving—but into what? Into God or into a less formed matrix of things? Either must be conceived by analogy from the known, and not as itself. And, if we are inclining to accept the Bergsonian hypothesis, we need not suppose a single actual beginning. It may be that such a matrix of existence is always inserting its developing product among the field of finites and is a principle of perpetual creation.

So far as the argument goes, and within the terms of it, this hypothesis makes a sufficient conclusion; it can be countered only by the support of other arguments. We may, for example, argue thus: If it is necessary, in the pursuit of intelligibility, to step outside the scheme of being that is conceivable by us in proper terms, surely we may as well have recourse to an hypothesis that provides sufficient reason all round, which this Bergsonian hypothesis fails to do; for how can this prime matrix of undifferentiated being account for the formal principles that arise in the process of its own differentiation? The supposed cases of evolution or emergence of species suggested by science we may be prepared to accept as they stand, without asking for sufficient reason; for at least they fall within the general categorial scheme of finite being. But if we are going to treat this scheme itself as an emergent, then the demand for a sufficient reason of the emergence is difficult to smother any longer. Our minds are naturally inclined to accept development when we can feel that what is essential is already given in what precedes, the development is a modification of it. But if the given contains so little of the result to follow as in the suggested hypothesis, it becomes for us not the essence which is modified but the mere material which is the condition for the revelation of the form. But then we demand a sufficient reason of the form. Now either the form is contained in the 'active virtue' of the less formed state from which it emerges, or it must be sought elsewhere. If it is in the less formed state, that state has occult properties of a quite unintelligible kind. And so we look for the sufficient reason in a being not himself subject to this kind of 'becoming'.

We see, then, that the argument from conditions succeeds only in so far as it raises the general question of sufficient reason, of which the essence-existence argument is the pure expression.

The argument is, of course, open to a far more fundamental criticism which cuts at the root of the whole dialectical development here displayed, and destroys all conclusions equally that can be drawn from it. Is it in fact necessary to accept the account of the condition-and-action relation which the argument presupposes? This account was, that it is in view of a pre-existent field that action develops; and this is anyhow part of the truth. But is it the whole truth? May it not be, that there is another side to action, which is not a response to the conditions in its field, but an expansion of activity over the field to reach and 'feel' the other activities which by their ingredience constitute that field? Let us have recourse to a diagram—

BCDEF constitute the field of A. If A's relation to this is of reaction simply to the conditions they provide, then their activity is prior to A's; but if A also radiates activity towards them, this is not so. For then the co-existence of substances may 'begin' with a radiation of activity from each towards the others, and these radiations mutually conditioning one another give rise to the field of each substance; as when several pebbles fall into a pool together, and the expanding rings find and shape one another. In the case of the pool, of course, there is a neutral medium, the water, in which the rings expand until they touch. In the case of our hypothetical substances, each must immediately impinge on the activities of its neighbours without any such intermediary.

Action then, we shall say, is no more responsive than affective; and so the problem of the regress in conditions never arises. All that remains is the problem of an infinite regress in temporal events, and that is not a problem. And so we must conclude that this famous argument is essentially vicious. It has a fault not shared by the other arguments we have considered. It seeks to show that a certain finite scheme of relation, while complete and intelligible in itself, is only so if God is made the first term in it. But the proper forms of argument exhibit the inherent paradox in some finite scheme of relation, so that we are led to view that whole scheme as not intelligible in itself, but only in so far as it has the support and supplement of divine activity throughout. This argument from conditions accepts without demur the real scandal of finitude, the mutual and incoherent externality of real operations, and chooses to argue from a small anomaly of detail falling within the sphere of finitude and admitting of solution in purely finite terms.

The very baseness of the argument gives it a spurious colour of demonstration; for it seems to be reasoning within the familiar scheme of finite categories instead of challenging their ultimate validity. But its popularity has another and a less disreputable ground. To think of God is to think of the Sufficient Reason; the commonest form of the search for reasons is through the regress of conditions; and so to look for God at the beginning of the series is the first act of the common-sense philosopher. So it comes to be felt that there must be a continuous passage from this common-sense argument to some philosophically tenable form. This is not really so: one has to learn that sufficient reason requires to be sought along other lines than this.

Attempts to put genuinely philosophical content into the argument are not likely, however, to cease. The favourite is that from potency and act. This is worked by slipping into the statement of the bases of the argument a highly questionable analysis of finite action. Every agent before he acts is a merely potential agent in this respect, for otherwise he would be acting thus already. Nothing that is potential can be raised to actuality without an efficient cause lying outside itself. But this efficient cause must come into action here and now if it is to begin to actualise the potential agent here and now; and so we begin a regress which must come back at last to something which actualises another without itself being actualised.

The argument in this form appears more genuinely metaphysical; for it exhibits finite action as that which, of its very nature, cannot act at all unless the activity of the infinite either directly or indirectly inflows upon it. But, as we have hoped to show in the body of this work, the analysis of temporal operation in terms of potency and act has no value on the finite level. Naturally the theist will admit that the scheme of the argument in this form is an acceptable shorthand expression of the theist *conclusions*; but it is hardly an argument from the finite, for it lacks a genuine finite base from which to start. If taken seriously, the potency-act scheme denies all spontaneity or originativeness to finite action whatsoever. For it acts just in so far as acted upon, and can be treated as a mere channel of activity. And this conclusion can really only be opposed by treating the efficient cause as not a total cause but a *conditio sine qua non*, in which case the argument falls back into the form which we gave it. It is very proper, no doubt, to object that no finite act is an act in the same sense as the infinite act, so that while we are thinking of God's creativity, all finite acts will seem to be mere effects. But this again is to assume what has to be demonstrated; it is to begin from the theology, and not from a paradox inherent in finite act. If indeed we analyse finite act on the finite level by the simple application of the potency-act division, we remove all knowledge of any really originative operation and with it any possibility of conceiving God's act by any analogy of the finite.

Here is the conclusion to the whole matter. The argument from conditions is no true argument. There is a proper form of the argument from discontinuous ingredience; this we have given already. It is that from order and chaos.

B V. From Generation

Philosophers have often wished to eliminate generation from their account of the finite and to resolve finite existence into the interactions of imperishable substance. Then what is normally regarded as generation will be reduced to variation of mode in substantial being. Even so, as former arguments have shown, the finitude and dependence of the interacting substances can be exhibited, without any notice taken of the fact that they are generated and decay. Yet this is a fact; the conservation of energy in the world (if such a principle is to be accepted as more than a tautology of physical method) does not mean the conservation of continuous operations, i.e. substances, but at most that none passes out of existence (on the physical level) without some other being either generated, or (if already existent) proportionately enhanced. Generation is a fact; the philosophers who have wished to get rid of it have done so on *a priori* grounds and in the face of apparent evidence.

Now if the mutual externality and real interaction of finite substances can be made an evidence of finitude and dependence even when they are supposed without beginning or end, surely the case must be strengthened by the admission of generation and decay; and even further strengthened, if we admit generation not only of individuals, but of species—or, as we commonly say, evolution. Yet, in one sense, we are embarrassed by the very strength of the case; for generation is so anomalous. We have really no notion of it, so that we cannot even begin our argument from non-analogical ground. This may be taken as just so much evidence that the relation cannot be self-explanatory but demands theology; the case, one might say, does not even need to be proved. But it is equally possible to derive the apparent anomaly from an accident of our ignorance; because we never, as conscious agents, become terms of the relation in question, we have no direct intuition of its nature. But this need not mean that it is paradoxical in itself.

After due warning thus given of the curious position of the proof we may as well state it. This, as has been suggested, is not at all difficult.

B V (1). *Presupposing the origination of the generated.* Generation is a real relation; yet it is not the action of any finite substance. The action of the generator is immanent like every other operation; but there is not, as in other cases, another real operation ready to take this action up into its field in the form of an ingredient; for the real operation which generation affects it also effects. But neither can the generated be regarded as numerically identical and substantially continuous with the generator. Therefore the relation of generation is neither the form of the act of the generator, nor of the generated, nor of a common substance which runs through them both. It is, then, the act of neither being; but must be attributed to another being, in whose notion is contained such a sort of agency as might give rise to a substance previously non-existent. But the God of the essence-existence argument is the only agent in our notion of whom any conception of such agency is contained. We therefore attribute the real agency of every generation to His act, the act of the generator providing the mere occasion of it.

B V (2). *From the relation of generator and generated.* The correction required to give us the second form of the proof is slight. We have only to realise that generation is, after all, a relation within the finite—a truth which the conclusion of the first proof in effect denies. We cannot allow—as there suggested —that God is the immediate and sole efficient cause of the new substance. We see, moreover, that generation and decay are not the mere sudden beginning and ending of substances; the only substances of which we have any clear knowledge are determined in their whole being by a life-cycle of gradual 'becoming' (growth) and declension. A substance, then, is not a simple form identical throughout its history, nor is its growth—still less its decline—the simple effect of its own effort; it itself waxes and wanes, and this is a datum for its operation. Therefore the world cannot be analysed into the simple operation of activities each specified by its form; we have everywhere the waxing and waning of the individual form. In this process the ingredient of other substantial activities plays a real part; yet not so that we can conceive the resultant system of operation as intelligible by itself, as the first form of the proof has shown. We conclude therefore to the active support of a being exempt from generation and decay. Such a being need not be God; but we have no positive idea of any being to whose nature it belongs to be unchangeable, except the God of the essence-existence argument.

The logical fault of this argument is the same as that of all the others, with the additional complication we first mentioned. Generation and the cycle of life belong to the only substance we know, and are inseparable from our conception of existence. As generation is the condition of substantial activity it could not be a case of substantial activity; it is evidently unique. Its peculiar obscurity to us is an accident of our position; for our conscious being is concerned always with the operation of the form that is, not with its becoming. Therefore from the uniqueness and obscurity of this relation no conclusion follows.

The material vindication of the argument is, again, that the analogies drawn from other relations both sharpen our sense for the uniqueness of this, and provide analogic material which we accept as a symbolism through which to think the actual apprehended relation of finite being, *qua* generated, to the infinite.

B VI. From Generation and Decay

Here is a by-form of the previous argument, having exactly the same nature and the same faults as the argument from conditions (B IV) and standing in the same relation as that to the true form of argument. As in B IV we supposed the sufficiency and intelligibility of the scheme of conditioned conditions, and used the existence of God merely to complete it, so here we suppose and accept the scheme of generation and decay, and introduce the existence of God simply as a guarantee of its permanent functioning.

The origins and focuses of operation are substances; but these, under the action of other substances, come into being and cease to be; yet so that there is no necessity of their being adequately replaced. There might, by accident, be a racial suicide of substance; of its higher species, very easily, e.g. of living things. But why not also of physical active units, since these can disintegrate, and the balancing out of force into inactivity can be conceived? In infinite time, this would be bound to have happened, unless there were a necessary being, i.e. an indestructible substance, capable not only of preserving its own existence but that also of other forms.

This argument is antique and presupposes the fixity of species. If new species can be generated, then the world can renew its youth and by a prodigality of innovation insure itself against the ravages of disastrous accident. No doubt Aristotle would have replied that the generation of species is unintelligible because the formal cause is nowhere prefigured in the efficient; we should have to have recourse to a being or group of beings which did contain it not formally but analogically and eminently. But in that case the generation of species can only be a continual running down of the world: the new must be inferior to the old, and so the world would have petered out in infinite time, unless there were at least some eminent being, exempt from accident and decay. But if we take the argument on to this ground, we change its nature; it becomes not a rounding off of the system of generation, but a critique of generation itself, in the instance of the generation of species.

The gist of the argument in any form is the dogmatic denial of spontaneity in Nature; Nature is just the mechanical operation of the principles already actual in her. Now no modern is going to accept this. Doubtless it is proper to say that the spontaneity of Nature is paradoxical because of its combination with deterministic passivity and because spontaneity is only penetrable to our intelligence in the form of explicit intention. This paradox inclines the mind to look beyond Nature for her sufficient reason, by the logic of the essence-existence argument. But it is quite another thing to regard Nature as the mere working out of her own principles in a sort of incarnate arithmetic and then to call in God to prevent her from some time finishing the sum and ruling a double line under the answer.

XXIV

ANTHROPOLOGICAL ARGUMENTS (C)

It follows from what has been already said in our analysis of rational theology that the place which the essence-existence argument holds among usiological proofs, will among the anthropological be held by an argument concerned with the 'interior scale', that is, with the 'ideas' and their relation to their human conditions or limitations. Now the 'ideas' express perfections of the intellect and the will, and therefore the argument from ideas has these obvious forms: from intellect, from will, and from the union of will with intellect. After reviewing these three, we will consider two others of minor importance.

C I. From the Distinction: Intellect as such, and its Human Impurities

Descartes, explaining his 'anthropological' proof of God, said that what it proved was the existence of 'a thinking being in general'. He meant by this, the existence of a pure case of the type 'thinking being'. Thinking beings in particular, he claimed to have shewn in the instance of himself, arose by the limitation of the pure thinking being. It was impossible to reflect upon the intellectual processes of a human mind, without regarding it as a diluted form of pure intelligence. The notion of pure intelligence remained prior, therefore; we must admit that we had an idea of it, and this could be derived from the simple apprehension of our own being. We do, then, apprehend our own mind not as something simple but as an effect of divine creativity.

Descartes's statement of this argument was very incautious, and so run into arguments of a different form as to obscure its proper nature; but we need not pretend to do more than to draw out his principles.

C I (1). *Presupposing either intellect or its limiting instruments.* Whenever we make a cognitive act, we implicitly suppose the notion of that which is in itself; for otherwise our act would not be cognitive, it would have no object. To suppose that which is in itself is to suppose (in general) a *manner* in which it is in itself; we cannot suppose self-being, without supposing that, as itself, it has some character rather than another, though we need not pretend here and now to know with any exactitude what that character is. Yet in so far as our act is cognitive, it is exercised by us as the apprehension of (at the least) a pheno-menon, or, it may be, an *ens rationis* founded in the nature of the thing. The more baffled we are by the sensuous or abstract manner of our apprehending, the more we contrast with it the ideal of an act of pure noesis which should see the thing as it is in itself. The inseparability of the notions 'thing in itself' and 'intuitive understanding' was epitomised by Kant in the use of noümenon (object of pure understanding) for 'thing in itself'.

But we do not merely contrast our sensuous and abstractive processes with the 'intuitive understanding'; for were that so, our cognitive acts would again not be cognitive: they would be mere enjoying of phenomena or playing with abstractions. Embedded in the phenomenon or the group of concepts is (however obscurely) the noümenon and therefore, in the act of sense or of thought, some act of noesis.

In so far, then, as we think of our acts as cognitive, we think of them as qualified and broken acts of noesis; in which sheer apprehension is filtered by the gross instruments of sense and thought that we are forced to use. Thus the notion of pure noesis is the simple conception from which we really start; we really begin with the notion of an apprehending intellect in general, which we particularise and narrow to our own case, but not as we narrow 'mammal' to 'horse' by adding the specific differentia. For mammal is essentially generic—it does not describe a complete being, but, in order to be, requires specific differentias. But the notion of the apprehending intellect in general is that of a complete act; our act is related to it not as the more determinate to the less, but as the impure and limited to the simple and absolute.

These conclusions can be disputed. It may be denied (a) that the notion of sheer noesis is simpler than that of my own 'impure' noesis, (β) that the notion of sheer noesis is fully determinate and free from generic abstraction.

(a) It is not simple, for I can only think about it by means of fairly complicated analogies. If I think of the 'intuitive understanding' I apply the comparison both of self-knowledge and of the knowledge of phenomena *qua* phenomena. I think first of an apprehension of the real act of all being, which should be as penetrating as my apprehension of my own most conscious and explicitly rational acts; but then I think of the clarity of the apprehension as raised to the degree realised in the perception of phenomena *qua* phenomena (in my awareness, for example, that I am enjoying the simple visual experience which I am enjoying). And again, since neither the perception of my own acts nor the perception of phenomena *qua* phenomena contains the moment of intellectual penetration, I may throw in the analogy of mathematical knowledge—the intuitive understanding, while it sees its objects in the round, sees all the principles of their structure alive and operating in them. So far from being simple, then, and presupposed by all types of cognitive act, the notion is complex, and draws its material from every kind of cognitive act.

(β) It is not determinate—is not the notion of a complete act, but is an abstraction from a complete act. For we cannot conceive such an act in concrete fullness; if we attempt to do so, we have to make it an absurd amalgam of all our acts, as has just been shown. This amalgam itself cannot be conceived; if we wish to conceive, we must return in all humility to some simple type of human act, in which (as we have declared) some measure of noesis is embedded.

The reader who has followed the argument of this book hitherto will be at no loss to answer these objections. (a) The idea of noesis, just because it is simple and because it is unique, cannot be thought *about* except by analogy; but that will not prevent its playing an original part in our thought. It, and the notions of the several human cognitive acts, are presupposed to one another in different ways. In so far as we think of them as cognitive, we presuppose this notion; in so far as we try to qualify or determine the nature of this notion, we presuppose them. Even though we never think *of* it, without in some rudimentary way thinking *about* it, and therefore supplying some element of analogic commentary, no absurdity or vicious circle arises. We become aware of intellect as such, and our particular acts of intellect, together; and so we can understand each through the other, so long as the word 'through' does not describe the same logical relation in the two cases.

(β) The notion, indeed, is not properly determinate, in the sense that we have not a complete conception of it formally; but dynamically it plays the part of a determinate, for it is the conception of an act in which noesis, freed from the limitation from which in us it is never freed, properly apprehends its object. How such a paradoxical indeterminate-determinate is possible, we have explained in our analysis (pp. 49ff), where we saw it to be bound up with the 'interior scale'. It is because we experience intellect progressively overcoming, though never escaping, the limitations of its human condition, that we are able to distinguish it from the several types of acts in which it is found.

Now if we *see* our cognitive acts to participate in pure noesis in several degrees and several modes, then there is no reason to doubt that this is true. We cannot, of course, immediately conclude that there is an absolute noesis, and that our acts are broken reflections of its light. All we can conclude is that noesis appears in us as degrees of a simple and absolute apprehension. But whether any mind has that apprehension pure, has still to be discovered.

We may argue thus. By sliding up the scale through various modes and degrees within our own conscious operation, noesis reveals itself as independent of its embodiments and capable of aspiration beyond them. And the notion of it in pure absoluteness is natural to us, and presupposed in all our thinking about our cognitive acts. Therefore its determination to a particular mode and degree or to a particular range of modes and degrees is arbitrary; it does not follow from the notion of noesis. Whereas if we start from the form of a determinate cognitive act, then we cannot see how noesis, if it essentially belongs to such a form, can proceed to transcend it or sink below it. We ought to suppose then either (1) that our states of sense, imagination, or terminological discourse, in themselves blind, act as recipients upon which the pure light of noesis inflows according to the capacity of each, from a source itself free from such composition, or (2) that pure noesis is modified, limited, and diminished to these several degrees by shackles of various finitude at the hands of a being not himself subject to such composition.

Both these suggestions have the absurdity of all form (1) arguments; one seems no better than the other, yet they are contraries; and both destroy the real unity of the finite being. My act of intellect is mine; nothing is more mine. It cannot be an infusion from above, or a certain limitation imposed from time to time upon an impersonal force of pure understanding. And the modification of noesis is not external to it in this sense. It belongs to it to have some mode and degree; even if its 'proper' mode and degree be an absolute one. Nor can the 'recipients' of the first conclusion be presupposed to the noesis which they 'receive'. It and they mutually require one another. We turn, then, to a form (2) argument.

C I (2). *From the relation of intellect to its limitations.* The self is unitary— it is more really one than any other existence which falls within the scope of our knowledge. Yet in its cognitive aspect it shows a paradoxical qualification of this unity. For it would not be cognitive, unless it implicitly believed that its imperfect act of apprehension is a substitute for an act of perfect apprehension, which it cannot achieve and yet strives to approach. This approach it makes by increasing its mastery over the necessary tools of sense and ratiocination. Thus, in a manner, it identifies itself with the element of sheer apprehension within its own act; this constitutes the self of the self, its spirituality, a spirituality which can never, in fact or in conception, exist but in one or other of its imperfect expressions, yet which transcends them in the paradoxical manner described.

We cannot, however, say that cognitive spirit requires of its nature just such and such a level of expression; or the occurrence of the several levels, and the tendency to rise above them all, would be unintelligible. Nor, for an identical reason, can we suppose a fixed form of the human spirit which has as necessary constituents acts of just such and such a level; on the contrary, the 'human essence', or my individual essence, must be regarded as a limit of considerable elasticity, within which cognitive activity stretches its bodily leash indefinitely far in many directions without ever breaking it. Nor can we begin from the limiting conditions of the spiritual act—from physiological and psychological mechanism—and suppose that a certain physiological or psychological event simply carries with it a cognitive act of a certain level. For that is plainly to deny the one spiritual activity which to a large extent determines its own level and rises from one to another.

The human spirit, then, is revealed as a substance in which cognitive activity has been apportioned to a certain limiting condition, and the grounds of the apportionment cannot be found in any formal element within the self. We recur, then, to the act of a being in whom spirituality is not thus arbitrarily limited, the 'thinking being in general' of Descartes. Such a being must have apportioned cognition to its limitation and the limitation to cognition—i.e. have created the sort of mind we are.

This argument, which so much resembles that from essence and existence, has an apparent flaw in its conclusion which that had not. It is supposed to justify us in recurring to a being in whom the *cognitive* act exists free from such composition. In the case of essence and existence, we could be sure that the removal of 'composition' from the supreme being would leave him still *existent*, since nothing which is can fail to be such. We cannot with the same immediacy affirm that the non-composite cause of our mixed spirituality is spiritual. He need only be such a form of existence as to transcend the type of 'composition' with which we are concerned. It is not strictly evident that such existence can properly be described as spiritual. It might be something else unimaginable, the cause of spiritual being. We can proceed to the spirituality of this being only by recurrence to the essence-existence argument. God is the supreme existent. To the supreme existent all the riches of existence belong; spirituality therefore among the rest, *modo eminentiori*. And in fact spirit is the only being of which we have interior knowledge; in terms of it we must and do think of God. But we have dealt with this topic in the Analysis.

The other flaws of the argument are those which we have learnt to recognise as common form. The argument only in fact demonstrates that the unity of the self is not any one of several types we arbitrarily suggest. But if anyone wishes to draw, not a theistic, but a left-wing Hegelian conclusion, no logical error arises. If it be said that the unity of the self just does lie in this paradox of aspiration and of internal conflict of the spirit with its conditions, and that the elevation of the spirit to completeness and acquiescence would be equivalent to its extinction, then the man who says so cannot be confuted in words. We can reply only that this is very true of spirit as we are it; but that we for our part have a crepuscular yet convincing apprehension of transcendent spirit complete and yet alive; and that the Hegelian position does not do justice to the mind's natural belief as that belief arises in the existential situation. For the idea of the perfect knower presents itself as just what it claims to be; a sophisticated and a by no means inevitable analysis is required to effect the immanentist reduction, and persuade us that our idea can only be realised in our own imperfect acts. Rational theology can provide an alternative analysis and so set our thought free to return to its natural channel.

The true argument against this Hegelian position must then be that there is a stateable alternative to it, and an alternative which does less violence to the natural form of human aspiration after cognitive objectivity. Hegelianism of this sort will appear to the theist as a half-way retreat towards the denial and betrayal of reason. Reason is bound up with the idea of perfect apprehension; and now this is reduced to the equivocal position of an immanent idea, always actual indeed, but actual only in effort after ever varying expression in a medium which is proper and necessary to it, yet which frustrates its perfect realisation. For knowledge must be defined as the intellectual vision of what is, as it is; and since our acts do not achieve this, they are knowledge by their approximation to, or more exactly their participation in, knowledge. But this involves at least the belief that perfect apprehension is thinkable, and intrinsically possible, though not for us. Otherwise the ideal of the goal of knowledge, to know things as they are, is a mirage; and it is no more true that cognition depends on striving after it, than that an aeroplane designer's efforts draw their value from his striving after a model which should travel with no friction at the speed of light.

F.F.J.

Our case, then, rests on an appeal to faith in objective reason. But even if it be granted, we have not proved the existence of the perfect knower; we have merely shewn that the human cognitive acts are cognitive by 'participation in the form' of perfect knowledge. To shew that the form is not only the possible, but the actual, shape of a complete instance, requires a further step, viz. the demand after sufficient reason for the participated intellect that we are, with the accompanying intuition that the perfect intellect is self-explanatory, the participated not so.

C II. From the Distinction: Will as such, and its Human Limitations

We have now to state a parallel argument from the will. The central aim of the will is not so evident as that of the intellect; there is no doubt that the business of the intellect is to know that which is. The will's aim might seem to be moral sincerity, or subjection to the guidance of intellect. Yet these appear to be instrumental; the primary aim of will is to realise being, in proportion to the value of the (possible) being to be realised. Since being is act, and will effects act, will is in itself by its effect the creation of being. And by its affect it can foster other being. All will, then, produces being of a sort; but if we recognise a scale of being, then we shall make it the true direction of will to create and foster the highest being; to make itself and other substances good after the kind proper to each, and to foster the better kinds in preference to the inferior.

Now it seems that we must define true will in this way, if we are to understand what it is; as we had to define intellect as the apprehension of being, so must we define will as the creation of being. And yet (as with the other definition) this definition fits none but God. Only God can be supposed freely to will His own being and other being for the worth of it. Our will—as we previously explained at excessive length—is tied to a determinate finite pattern which it cannot but will, and which provides the basis upon which it weaves its 'super-pattern' of more truly voluntary activity. Yet the principle upon which the willing of the super-pattern must be judged and justified is the principle of pure, absolute, or divine will; our voluntary behaviour is right, if it creates or fosters being (in the sense of our definition of will), so far as the tied operation of its nature allows. And even this tied operation has in the end to be judged by the same standard; for if I am considering the support of another man's physical being or the sacrifice of my own, I have to value it as a form of being, and to view the tied and biologically necessitated will as a form of blind creativity, productive of that being.

My will, then, 'participates' in creativity as does my intellect in apprehension. The intention to 'imitate God, as far as in me lies' is as integral a part of will as it is of cognition, and here as there is the very form of objectivity. My will is bound by its physical basis and limited in its scope to those beings which interact with my physical being; and even these it cannot make objectives to its activity simply in proportion to their worth, but always also in proportion to their relevance; for my life has after all got to be mine, tied to my body, and my acts must fit into this pattern. If then I let go the idea of a will whose determination is purely objective, if this idea is active in my mind neither explicitly nor implicitly, I shall fall into a misunderstanding of the will and its aim; I shall make some principle of my human finitude the principle of will, whether it be a set of rules or of 'values' or the principle of coherence or some other.

From this point we may follow the previous argument step by step. As there, so here, we must recognise that to have shown the 'participated' nature of the human will is not to have proved the existence of any will that is 'unparticipated' and absolute. The distinction between the pure voluntariness of our will and its limitations is on the face of it a 'distinction of reason founded in reality', and we have still to make the further step of discovering the real order, that is, the concrete process of act, in which it is founded; which (to put it otherwise) constrains our minds to make this particular abstraction from itself. Here we must have recourse to the principle of 'sufficient reason' and ask with Descartes, 'How is it that I, who have, and am in willing essentially relative to, the idea of perfection, am myself none the less finite?' 'Sufficient reason'—must we repeat it?—is not an *a priori* universal principle, applied as a syllogistic major premise; it is simply the principle of asking the question concerning 'grounds' where that question is seen to be significant; and the question cannot be significant unless we know the *kind* of answer that is required. It is only because we see, in a confused and implicit manner, the divine will effecting the existence of the human will, that, at a more explicit level of thought, we recognise the demand for a 'sufficient reason' of the participatedness of the human will; and so proceed to an explicit recognition of the divine cause.

We will not weary the reader by drawing out the dialectic of the argument in detail, since the previous argument provides so exact a model.

C III. From the Distinction: Intellectual and Voluntary Activity

Understanding and creation are rather distinct aspects of every fully human act, than different acts. Human activity, taken as a whole, is a response to what is believed to be the case; and contains the moments both of cognition and of enactment. In a previous chapter we shewed the naturalness of regarding the principal types of human act as specialisations of an original type. In that original type the cognitive and creative aspects would be already present; specialised types have developed the one or the other. But it remains that the cognitive act is still an act; it is the creation of something, viz. of a formalised piece of 'behaviour', a manipulation of signs or images. Its purpose is wholly to act as a vehicle for the accompanying noesis, because without some behaviour-reaction no noesis can take place. But it remains an act, none the less, and not merely an 'act of understanding'. It is a piece of behaviour also. And we have seen that it has a necessary alliance with other pieces of behaviour which are not formalised and symbolical, but real; we cannot think about anything about which we can do nothing but think.

Understanding, to be real and a part of me, must be an act, for I am activity. An understanding which was thought of as a passive mirroring of that which is, could form no part of any real being; it would be itself a phenomenon requiring an active subject to contemplate it. The required act cannot take place in the object, or in a supposed sensuous or mental double, a *species impressa*, projected by the object. It must take place in the subject; the subject, as such, exists in this act. Then in making my act of sign-manipulation I become aware of the object, (or if you like, of the impressed species,) with such abstraction as this act prescribes. And so my act of understanding becomes indeed an act of understanding as well as of sign-manipulation; but this act of understanding is not a state of mirroring, but an act of grasping, and the centre of its temporal enactment is in the manipulation, not in the noesis; although the noesis is made thereby a process, and itself temporalised.

We see, then, that the imperfection of the act of understanding is a function of its relation to the act of will, to the mental behaviour. For that which the will makes is a set arrangement of signs, and therefore the matter of apprehension is limited to certain abstract aspects in the object which are marked by the signs. A perfect understanding would be possible only if what the will made were the object of understanding itself. Then a complete noesis would take place; for complete noesis is the absolute possession of the whole character of the thing by the mind, when the mind 'is, in a manner, all' its objects. But this cannot happen through the conformity of the mind to pre-existent things. It cannot enact their perfect image, for then it would have to know them first, and would have therefore no need of any such act; it can only enact a symbolic scheme and see what, thereby, it is enabled to grasp. Neither is the notion intelligible of a mind whose activity should be the simple mirroring of all the plurality of things; for such a mind would have no principle of unity in its act, it would fall apart into the plurality which it contemplates and become a moving waxwork of the confused pageant of finite existence. It remains, then, that perfect understanding is possible only to a creative mind, which enacts or makes that which it understands, and understands it in the making of it. Thus alone can the form of the object be possessed by the subject, for it becomes the form of the subject's acts.

Conversely it may be shown that the perfect act of will, or of creativity, is possible only when the relation of will and understanding has been elevated to that of an identity between the two. For we can only be said truly to make, when we both know what we are making and make it not under dictation but spontaneously. But the act of will in us is (either an act giving rise to apprehension by providing it with a vehicle, or) a response to apprehension, by which we express our faith in it and make a judgment upon it. Such an act either is simply dictated by the previous apprehension and thus is not spontaneous, or else adds an element of spontaneity beyond what apprehension simply dictated, and then is in so far blind. There is in every judgment or decision an element of blindness—of a choice in which we throw the reins on the neck of the horse. The horse is not 'instinct' or 'desire', where 'desire' is a brute force fully outside will, but is a simplified, implicit level of will, to which, for the moment, we have to let ourselves sink. The agony of this process, when serious decisions have to be made, is familiar to all reflective minds; the dilemma between keeping a firm hold on the intelligible grounds of choice, and being able to contribute the element of spontaneity, of what is simply our own, and so turn the scale one way or the other, when the intelligible grounds do not suffice of themselves to turn it. We have discussed the blindness of creativity, and the lack of spontaneity in action from sufficient knowledge, when we were dealing with the several kinds of freedom.

Now this dilemma, which prevents will from ever being perfectly itself, arises from the mutual externality of will and understanding. Will could only be both spontaneous and intelligent, if the two coincided, so that what I enact were what I apprehended. But this would be possible only for an absolute will, which should act not in response to a pre-existent given universe, nor to a pre-existent given nature in himself, but should apprehend what he enacts and enact what he apprehends.

From this double basis the third anthropological argument can proceed after the pattern of the other two. We cannot here, any more than there, proceed directly from the idea of this unitary perfection of a spiritual being to conclude that such a being exists. We have arrived, so far, at the threefold scheme:

(α) Unity of will and intellect at a level of implicit act below consciousness.

(β) Distinction of will and intellect at the level of rational consciousness.

(γ) Identity of will and intellect at an ideal level.

The third of this series is at present no more than an idea. Yet it represents a form in which the human spirit 'participates'. Not only do we aspire after freedom and knowledge, and therefore after their interpenetration; we actually possess them in some degree. The mysterious act of judgment in which both noesis of real being and choice of right action take place, is not after all a mere throwing of the reins on the horse's neck, not a mere relapse to level (α) among those just named, for then there would be none of that intellectual agony of decision of which we spoke above, nor would the previous intellectual acts have any influence on the process; we should have relapsed into the merely animal. This does not happen; in a way unintelligible to us the spark leaps from intellect to will, and the judgment, though dark, is not blind. But this mutual penetration of the acts, unintelligible in itself, is naturally and inevitably conceived as a 'participation' in a complete and luminous unity of them. To be a unity of intellect and will is to be spirit and person; spirituality and personality, therefore, we see as 'participated'.

From this position we can proceed to form (1) and form (2) arguments.

C III (1). *Presupposing intellect, presupposing will, or presupposing unitary spirit.* In form (1) there are three possible bases. We may argue: (*a*) That the intellect in us, intrinsically infinite, is limited by a finite activity of will. For it seems plausible to conceive of an actual total noesis of all things as prior to the mind, actualised however in the mind only fragmentarily in proportion as we develop the will-acts which provide it with vehicles. And this would resemble the position of those Arabian Aristotelians, who posited one universal intellect in us all, particularised as yours and mine by the acts of imagination by which we appropriate some element of the universal apprehension in particular consciousness.

(*b*) That the will in us, intrinsically infinite, is limited by our finite understanding. For the will may be conceived capable of affirming anything intellect presents, and enacting anything intellect lets it see to be possible. All then depends upon the scope of the intellect. And this is one of the positions of Descartes.

(*c*) That the pure and unitary form of intellectual will and creative intellect is mixed in us with finite conditions, called for convenience 'the body', which conditions break it up and qualify it. This position might be called Platonic.

According to (*a*), we should conclude that intellect has been limited in us through the addition of finite will, by a being in whom it is not so limited: according to (*b*), that will has been limited in us through the addition of intellect, by a being in whom it is not so limited: according to (*c*), that will-intellect has been limited in us through the addition of 'the body' by a being in whom it exists pure.

Of these three (*c*) is preferable, since there is nothing to be said for identifying the infinite element in us with will rather than intellect, or intellect rather than will. Yet (*c*) retains the absurdity of all form (1) arguments. The 'participated' form, in being participated, becomes formally other than its pure self, and appropriate to the conditions of finitude imposed upon it; apart from these it is unthinkable, and in being made thinkable apart from them must be raised to a 'more eminent' mode; in which mode it is not thinkable by us, except in the curiously diminished sense in which the notion of God is by us thinkable. We must, then, have recourse to a form (2) argument and a form (2) conclusion.

C III (2). *From the interrelation of intellect and will.* The unity of intellect and will in us is incomplete. Yet there is nothing in the nature of intellect or will as such which demands just such a looseness of unity, nor yet in the form of their interrelation; as is shewn by the fact that we aspire after and actually achieve within ourselves several degrees of such unity. And yet the will and intellect, as they exist at any given level, require the looseness of unity proper to that level. Our existence is an organism of acts at such finite levels. Thus we conclude, not that a pure intellectual will (= creative intellect) has been diluted in us, but that a diluted intellectual will has been created in us.

This argument must avail itself of the essence-existence argument to establish its conclusion, just as the other two anthropological arguments must do; and is open to the same Hegelianising criticism and the same form of defence. We will not weary the reader by the repetition.

C IV. From Moral Obligation

The remaining forms of anthropological argument are concerned not with the relation of elements within the human act, but with the relation of its formal object to existent reality. In the case of intellect, this yields no argument, since the formal object of intellect is anything existent in so far as it exists. If we admitted an argument here, we should fall into the absurdities of the epistemological argument, which finds a problem in the fact that the formal object of intellect (the intelligible) coincides with actual existence. We have already seen that this is not a problem, because there is no character of intelligibility distinct from the character of existence when considered in relation to an intellect. But the formal object of the *will* appears to be not what is, but what should be, and the relation of this to existence is a venerable puzzle. Of the resultant dialectic there are two obvious forms; from duty or morality in the narrower sense, and from the pursuit of perfection.

C IV (1). *Presupposing the will.* The claims of morality upon us are reducible to the claims of being, actual or projected (*vide supra*, p. 153f); we must either support or enhance the best, both in our own pattern of existence, and in that of others. To do so is to be rational or moral, i.e. to realise our own nature *qua* rational. But now, setting error aside, since it limits what becomes an object for our will but is not intrinsic to our will—we may act rationally or not, by our mere use or abuse or non-use of will. So that our own essence (in its rational aspect) becomes a kind of object to us, it transcends us; to realise it is our task.

But if so, our essence in so far as we do not exemplify it appears not to be inherent in us, nor existent as the rule of our being. It is presumably inherent, then, in some being for whom this paradoxical division does not exist; viz. inherent as an intention in the will of God, who wills it steadily.

This argument is a very fair rejoinder to any optimist-rationalist theory like that of Kant, which declares the 'real self' to be the pure, inviolable, rational self. No, we say, nothing is more our self than our voluntary behaviour, and if there is a pure rationality which somehow transcends our behaviour, it is other than we, and may be God.

This is a respectable argument, and proposes in a striking case the looseness of existence from essence. But it has the absurdity of all (1) forms. We cannot presuppose rational activity, and then bring in God to dangle its essence in front of its nose. The activity is relative to the essence. Such essence is for rational choice, and rational choice is of such essence. We pass therefore to the (2) form.

C IV (2). *From the relation between will and the obligatory.* The human subject, being such as we have described, is a composite being and presumably founded in the incomposite. We see the possibility of the following hierarchy: (a) Activity which is determined by its essence simply, and to which its essence is not an object; (β) Activity on which its essence is incumbent as an object of choice; (γ) Activity which simply chooses its own essence. Then it seems inevitable to conclude that the third has created the second. Yes; but only because we claim to understand the third and condemn the second as composite by that standard. The third cannot be demonstrated from the second; in contemplating the second we see the third.

C IV (3). *From the experience of duty*. Duty makes upon us an absolute claim, which is experienced as something other than the claim either of our own rationality, or of other finite entities. Non-theist statements either reduce our sense of duty or do not appear to be accounts of that which we have. Our sense of duty finds itself at home only in a world where existence is the expression of the divine will.

Such arguments as these cannot be developed without a great deal of space and a subtle power of expressing *nuances*. One thinks of Professor A. E. Taylor's *The Faith of a Moralist*.

C V. From the Pursuit of Perfection

Not only does our (fixed) essence *qua* rational appear to transcend us in the manner just described; our essence appears also to transcend its own fixed form. Rationality, indeed, is a formal scheme which remains constant; yet it is a very thin abstraction, little more than a formula, as we have seen (p. 146ff). Within this frame we are called to realise an ever higher and finer perfection, of which we do not see more than a few steps ahead. So our essence is our task in a second sense; not only to live up to, but to modify. Yet the modifications are neither arbitrary nor derivable from rationality as such (which is merely the principle bidding us choose them when seen) nor determined by particular circumstance. Where is the ideal? We are not free to make it as we will, nor is it what we are. It must be proposed to us by God.

This argument is as good as the last, but no better. Its (1), (2) and (3) follow the same lines. The refutation of it will lie in the declaration that moral creativity is *sui generis*, and the dilemma: 'Is the ideal given, or arbitrarily chosen?' a false dilemma arising from the ignoring of the very nature of rational freedom. And the nerve of the argument really lies in the indemonstrable implicit knowledge that there is a Being in whom the ideal and actual essences are identical.

These are all the theistic arguments that we will consider. Our choice and management of them has been a compromise between two aims—that of systematic development from the principles of the philosophy expounded in this book, and that of the classification and evaluation of traditional or current arguments. From the former point of view, we should in any case be content to draw the line here. From the latter, we must confess our task incompletely performed, though without much shame or regret. Only the poet's 'hundred tongues and throat of brass' could do complete justice to it; and then it is likely that the formidable battery of noise might have been employed to better purpose.

CONCLUSION

The true conclusion of this book is found in the dialectical proofs themselves, but a few words may be of use in limiting the scope of that conclusion. The knowledge of God to which rational theology leads us—the knowledge of Him which is bound up with an apprehension of the universal aspects of finite existence or of human existence—is the knowledge of existent perfection conceived through the analogy of spirit, and the knowledge that this Being is the creator of all finite existence. But that is all. We learn from it that all finites, in being themselves and expressing their natures in their acts, are expressing also the creativity of God who creates through them. But no sound reason for a belief in Providence is deducible from these premises.

Finite events are derivative from the efficacy of finite principles; these principles are in substance and substances are found, in virtue of their very finitude, to express the act of infinite deity. But they express it in their finite act. The man expresses it in being a man, and the microbe in being a microbe and killing the man, and the God of rational theology, we may conclude if we like, is equally but no more than equally concerned on both sides. It may well be that the chaotic interrelation of forms in space and time is the simple condition of finitude or of our level of finitude, that it does not and cannot positively express the mind of God, nor be overruled by His direction for the benefit of the higher finite beings, such as we flatter ourselves to be.

As with providence, so it is with grace. In so far as our own natural act expresses spirituality it is expressing its creator to the degree that our nature allows. And this act is itself, because finite, the effect of that infinite on which the finite depends. But we cannot conclude that there is possible a divine activity other than that of natural creation which supernaturally enhances or corrects our act.

On the other hand, neither providence nor grace is excluded by the scheme of rational theology, as they would be excluded by a consistent pantheism, for instance. For to be God and Creator is to be one absolutely complete in His being, who has freely brought the finite world into existence for its sake, not His. That no further activities can issue from such a Being for the good of His creatures, and no new relation other than that of creation be established by Him with us, is a negative which rational theology has no power to establish. One can, indeed, if one chooses and as has traditionally been done, draw *probable* arguments from rational theology in favour of providence and grace—'Surely such a God would . . .' But it is equally possible to state counter-arguments; and even the traditional arguments presuppose that we know (which from rational theology alone we never could know) what providence and grace are, and that they are not contradictory terms.

For this knowledge, as well as for any convincing proof that God acts by providence or grace either within this world or by calling into being a new to redress the balance of the old, we must turn to the field of particular 'contingent' events, and see whether He habitually so acts, or whether in one or more revealing events He has given the promise of so acting. Rational theology deals with God and Freedom, but not with Immortality, Providence or Grace, except in considering their mere possibility when the idea of them has come from another quarter.

As I wrote this, the German armies were occupying Paris, after a campaign prodigal of blood and human distress. Rational theology will not tell us whether this has or has not been an unqualified and irretrievable disaster to mankind and especially to the men who died. It is another matter, if we believe that God Incarnate also died, and rose from the dead. But rational theology knows only that whether Paris stands or falls, whether men die or live, God is God, and so long as any spiritual creature survives, God is to be adored.

Date Due

CPSIA information can be obtained
at www.ICGtesting.com
Printed in the USA
BVHW050126080223
658057BV00003B/78